Usage and Style

The
Everyday
Writer

The
Everyday
Writer

ANDREA A. LUNSFORD
STANFORD UNIVERSITY

Coverage for multilingual writers with

Paul Kei Matsuda
ARIZONA STATE UNIVERSITY

Christine M. Tardy
UNIVERSITY OF ARIZONA

7TH EDITION

bedford/st.martin's
Macmillan Learning

Boston | New York

For Bedford/St. Martin's

Vice President, Editorial, Macmillan Learning Humanities: Edwin Hill
Executive Program Director for English: Leasa Burton
Executive Program Manager: Stacey Purviance
Senior Executive Editor: Michelle M. Clark
Senior Media Editor: Barbara G. Flanagan
Associate Editor: Melissa Rostek
Assistant Editor: Aislyn Fredsall
Director of Content Development, Humanities: Jane Knetzger
Marketing Manager: Vivian Garcia
Senior Digital Content Project Manager: Ryan Sullivan
Senior Workflow Project Manager: Lisa McDowell
Production Supervisor: Robin Besofsky
Senior Media Project Manager: Allison Hart
Editorial Services: Lumina Datamatics, Inc.
Composition: Lumina Datamatics, Inc.
Text Permissions Manager: Kalina Ingham
Photo Permissions Editor: Angela Boehler
Photo Researcher: Richard Fox, Lumina Datamatics, Inc.
Director of Design, Content Management: Diana Blume
Text Design: Claire Seng-Niemoeller
Cover Design: William Boardman
Illustrator: GB Tran
Printing and Binding: King Printing Co., Inc.

Printed in the United States of America.

1   2   3   4   5   6   24   23   22   21   20

For information, write: Bedford/St. Martin's, 75 Arlington Street, Boston, MA 02116

ISBN 978-1-319-36111-2 (Spiral-bound)
ISBN 978-1-319-36115-0 (Paper-bound)
ISBN 978-1-319-36117-4 (Loose-leaf Edition)

Acknowledgments

Text acknowledgments and copyrights appear at the back of the book on page 575, which constitutes an extension of the copyright page. Art acknowledgments and copyrights appear on the same page as the art selections they cover.

How to Find Help in This Book

The Everyday Writer provides a writing reference you can use easily on your own — at work, in class, even on the run. Its many menus and features will help you find the information you need.

Quick Access Menu   On the inside front cover you'll find a brief overview of the book's contents, divided into twelve color-coded sections that correspond to the book's tabs.

Contents   The inside back cover has a table of contents that includes chapter titles, most major headings, and sample writing. It gives a closer look inside each chapter.

Tab Contents   On the back of each tabbed divider, you'll find the contents of that tab listed in depth, with page numbers.

The Top Twenty   The Top Twenty tab section provides guidelines for recognizing, understanding, and editing the most commonly identified issues in student writing today.

Lists of Examples for Citing Your Sources   Each documentation section has its own color-coded tab — gold for MLA style, green for APA style, and purple for *Chicago* style. Look for Lists of Examples within each section to find models for citing sources. Source maps illustrate the process of citing common types of sources.

Glossaries and Index   The index lists everything covered in the book. You can look up a topic either by its formal name (*ellipses*, for example) or, if you're not sure what the formal name is, by a familiar word you use to describe it (such as *dots*). The index also includes definitions of important terms. A glossary of usage, which helps with commonly confused words, appears in the glossary/index tab at the back of the book as well.

Revision Symbols   The list of symbols at the back of the book can help you learn more about marks or comments that an instructor or reviewer may make on your draft.

Page navigation help

① **Guides at the top of every page.** Headings on left-hand pages tell you what chapter you're in, while headings on the right identify the section. Tabs identify the chapter number and section letter.

② **"Multilingual" icons.** Help for speakers of all kinds of English is integrated throughout the book. Content that may be of particular interest to international students and other English language learners is identified with a "Multilingual" icon. Boxed tips called **"Language, Culture, and Context"** set off additional help. A directory to all content for multilingual writers appears at the back of the book.

③ **Hand-edited examples.** Many examples are hand-edited, allowing you to see an error or unconventional usage and its revision at a glance. Pointers make examples easy to spot on the page.

④ **Boxed tips.** Many chapters include **"Quick Help"** boxes that provide an overview of important information. These are listed in the Index. **"Talking the Talk"** boxes offer help with academic language and concepts. **"Considering Disabilities"** boxes offer tips on making your work accessible to audiences with different abilities.

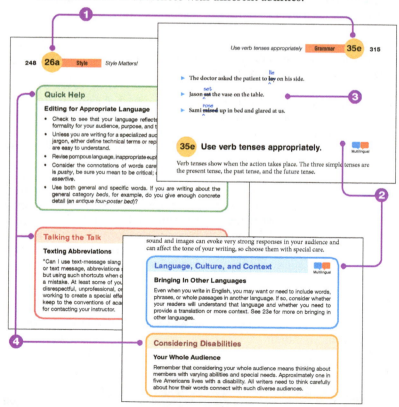

Preface

More than ever before, students today are *writers* — every day, every night, all the time; writing is all around them, like the air they breathe, so much so that they may not even notice. From blogging to texting to tweeting to telling a Snap story and posting to YouTube, Instagram, and other sites, student writers are participating widely in what philosopher Kenneth Burke calls "the conversation of humankind," an open conversation that can include engaging people from all across the globe, respectfully and fairly, even those with whom they may not agree.

Yet even as student writers have more opportunities to reach other people around the world, so do others have the ability to reach them, and not always with good intent. When hackers steal personal information, when trolls and bots masquerading as citizens unleash waves of misinformation, and when it's increasingly possible to carry out mind control projects on the Internet — then writers have a special need for *defensive* reading and writing. They need to be able to become fact-checkers, to be able to spot dubious messages and images, and to make sure they aren't adding to the problem by re-tweeting and forwarding mindlessly.

> This edition includes a new focus on "opening your mind" by listening carefully and fairly to the views of others and discovering ways to build common ground.

These ever-expanding opportunities for writers, as well as the challenges that inevitably come with them, have inspired this edition of *The Everyday Writer,* which includes a new focus on "opening your mind" by listening carefully and fairly to the views of others and discovering ways to build common ground: stronger emphasis on critical, defensive reading and thinking that help identify false information; new advice on how to engage in and encourage civil rather than rancorous or divisive discourse; and more attention to the ways in which writers can experiment with language and language varieties. As in past editions, I have placed great emphasis on multimodal composing, design, writing that inspires and makes something happen in the world, writing that works across disciplines, and the citation and documentation challenges that come with sources in new genres. What remains constant is the focus on the "everydayness" of writing and on friendly, down-to-earth, practical advice for how to write well in a multitude of situations and across a range of genres and media.

> What remains constant is the focus on the "everydayness" of writing and on friendly, down-to-earth, practical advice.

What also remains constant is the focus on rhetorical concerns. In a time of so many challenges and possibilities, taking a rhetorical perspective is particularly important. Why? Because a rhetorical perspective rejects either/or, right/wrong, black/white approaches to writing in favor of asking what choices will be most appropriate, effective, and ethical in a given writing situation. A rhetorical perspective also means considering alternative points of view openly and fairly while also attending to the purposes you want to achieve and the audiences you want to reach. Writers today need to maintain such a rhetorical perspective every day, and *The Everyday Writer*, Seventh Edition—a friendly, accessible companion— gives every writer the tools to make good decisions.

What's different about this edition?

The Everyday Writer, Seventh Edition, is a friendly, easy-to-use tool for civil discourse and for promoting open-minded inquiry and rhetorical experimentation among new academic writers. It includes:

An emphasis on openness as a key habit of mind   The seventh edition encourages new academic writers to adopt an open-mindedness that allows them to see disagreement as opportunity and to communicate ethically, responsibly, and respectfully with those who have other perspectives and positions. A *revised opening chapter* (p. 3) provides a frame for the handbook as a tool for developing the habits of open-minded readers, listeners, writers, and speakers.

1   Expectations for College Writing

Open your book, open your mind

What does it mean to be in college? It means becoming the self and the thinker and the writer you most want to be. It means engaging with challenging new ideas and with people who are different from you in many ways. It means opening your books (including this one!) but also opening your mind. Indeed, openness is a theme that many groups across the country are pursuing as one way to bridge the divisions that keep people apart, isolated in their own echo chambers. The Listen First Project is one such group, dedicated to understanding and to healing "our frayed national fabric." With its nationwide National Conversation Project, Listen First aims to open minds across the country. The group's approach models the kind of civil discourse you can practice as a college writer and thinker.

1a   Choose openness.

You may find yourself in classes or living in a dorm with people who hold diametrically opposed views on a range of topics, and you might have work together to solve academic, social, and even professional challenges. While it's easy to diss—or dismiss—others in online settings, it's much harder to do so when you know the person is sitting right there with you. That's one reason your classes and other campus spaces are so important for learning: they put you face-to-face with others you may not agree with or understand, and allow you to open your mind and your world.

New strategies for defensive reading, critical thinking, and fact-checking   Students are entering our colleges and universities familiar with reading online sources but perhaps inexperienced when it comes to questioning those sources or approaching them with skepticism. Revised advice for critical reading and thinking (pp. 63–73) and new tips for fact-checking (p. 140) help students to identify and respond to information and misinformation in news sources and in social media.

Quick Help

Guidelines for Checking Facts

Begin to practice what media analyst Howard Rheingold calls "crap detection," which means reading defensively and identifying information that is false or deceptive. The following tips can help you to become a good fact-checker:

- Identify the information that is presented as *fact* in a source. Ask questions: does this seem accurate? complete? trustworthy? Check to see if the source presents a bibliography or list of works cited.
- Search for other credible sources (Rheingold suggests three) that corroborate the facts you are checking. If you can't find sources that verify the fact, be suspicious.
- Use non-partisan fact-checkers like PolitiFact, FactCheck.org, and the Sunlight Foundation. Snopes.com is also useful for fact-checking general rumors and memes.
- Be on the lookout for clickbait headlines and titles — that is, those that say "click me, click me" — and for nonstandard URLs.
- Pay attention to the tone with which facts are presented. If the tone is sensational or highly exaggerated, take care that the facts are not also exaggerated.

A broader presentation of language use Grounded in the argument that language is power, *The Everyday Writer* coaches students in following — and in experimenting with — conventions. A *new chapter on language and identity* (p. 229) helps students think more openly and carefully about the language we claim as our own and language used to label us and others. And a *revised*

chapter on language varieties (p. 231) fosters a new openness to translingual composition — with excerpts from student writing. Attention to *gender-neutral pronoun use* (pp. 242, 340) raises awareness about writing to include rather than exclude. Finally, the popular *Top Twenty* editing guide is now in its own tabbed section (p. 273).

A stronger emphasis on narrative as an approach to academic writing Some students come to college imagining academic writing as a formulaic, boring, or difficult enterprise. The seventh edition reimagines the role of narrative — of *story* — in argumentative and analytical writing, making these common academic genres more personal and approachable (see pp. 97–98). The new edition also includes a *powerful new primary text by Andrea Lunsford* that will help students see narrative as a possible subject for academic writing. "The Challenge of (Re)Inventing Stories" (p. 67) helps students examine narratives in our culture and teaches rhetorical responsibility.

New and powerful student writing in common genres With more student writing than other handbooks of its kind, *The Everyday Writer* introduces new academic examples that model research writing in MLA style (p. 447), rhetorical analysis (p. 91), and critical reading (p. 75). We are honored to include a *new speech* as part of the revised "Writing to Make Something Happen in the World"

chapter; Naomi Wadler's address at the 2018 March for Our Lives rally (pp. 221–22) offers a compelling look at gun violence from the perspective of an empowered and inspiring young writer.

What hasn't changed?

Rhetorical grounding *The Everyday Writer* is built on the idea that empowering writers and strengthening their skills starts with creating awareness of the choices they have and encouraging reflection on the choices they make.

Highly visual; friendly and easy to use The handbook's friendly design and plentiful illustrations encourage students to open the book and use it. We've worked hard to make sure that information in the book is easy to find and inviting to read. Former users tell us they have found the checklists and boxes ("Quick Help," "Talking the Talk") clear and helpful.

Comprehensive coverage of critical thinking, critical reading, and argument *The Everyday Writer* supports students with practical advice to help them complete the most common types of college reading and writing assignments.

Awareness that academic writing is multimodal Throughout the book, rhetorical considerations assume that students are producing a variety of print and digital compositions — websites, wikis, annotated playlists, illustrated essays, PechaKucha presentations, and more.

Integrated advice about U.S. academic English Information for multilingual writers is integrated throughout the book and accessible to students from all language, cultural, and educational backgrounds. We acknowledge that international students and Generation 1.5 English speakers aren't the only students puzzled by English structures and academic genres. Look for the "Multilingual" icon ▇▇ and boxes called "Language, Culture, and Context."

Up-to-date advice on research and documentation As best practices for research continue to evolve, so does *The Everyday Writer*. Students can count on illustrated help for writing with, citing from, and integrating sources in MLA, APA, and *Chicago* style.

True Tales of *The Everyday Writer* A comic-style insert tells seven real students' stories about using *The Everyday Writer* to find help in various writing situations. Award-winning comics artist GB Tran (author and illustrator of *Vietnamerica*) brings students' experiences with the book to life.

Tips based on the writing moves of experts Informed by corpus linguistics research and the good advice of Laura Aull, the handbook includes tips for using transitions, treating opposing points of view, restating evidence, and communicating certainty.

What *else* hasn't changed? Bedford/St. Martin's puts you first.

From day one, our goal has been simple: to provide inspiring resources that are grounded in best practices for teaching reading and writing. For more than thirty-five years, Bedford/St. Martin's has partnered with the field, listening to teachers, scholars, and students about the support writers need. We are committed to helping every writing instructor make the most of our resources.

How can we help you?

- Our editors can align our resources to your outcomes through correlation and transition guides for your syllabus. Just ask us.
- Our sales representatives specialize in helping you find the right materials to support your course goals.
- Our *Bits* blog on the Bedford/St. Martin's English Community (**community.macmillan.com**) publishes fresh teaching ideas weekly, such as Andrea Lunsford's "Teacher to Teacher" blog — which features hundreds of posts, including her popular Multimodal Mondays posts. You'll also find easily downloadable professional resources like *Teaching with Lunsford Handbooks*.
- Contact your Bedford/St. Martin's sales representative or visit **macmillanlearning.com** to learn more.

Print and digital options for *The Everyday Writer*

Choose the format that works best for your course, and ask about our packaging options that offer savings for students.

PRINT

- To order *The Everyday Writer*, Seventh Edition (APA Update), spiral-bound with tabs, use ISBN 978-1-319-36111-2. For paperback, use ISBN 978-1-319-36115-0.
- To order *The Everyday Writer with Exercises*, Seventh Edition (APA Update), spiral-bound with tabs, use ISBN 978-1-319-36113-6.
- To order *The Everyday Writer*, Seventh Edition (APA Update), loose-leaf, use ISBN 978-1-319-36117-4 (Classic) or 978-1-319-36118-1 (with exercises). This format does not have a traditional binding; its pages are loose and hole-punched to provide flexibility and a lower price to students. It can be packaged with our digital platform for additional savings.

DIGITAL

- *Innovative digital learning space.* Bedford/St. Martin's suite of digital tools makes it easy to get everyone on the same page by putting student writers at the center. For details, visit **macmillanlearning.com/college/us/englishdigital**.

- *Popular e-book formats.* For details about our e-book partners, visit **macmillanlearning.com/ebooks**.

- *Inclusive Access.* Enable every student to receive their course materials through your LMS on the first day of class. Macmillan Learning's Inclusive Access program is the easiest, most affordable way to ensure all students have access to quality educational resources. Find out more at **macmillanlearning.com/inclusiveaccess**.

Your Course, Your Way

No two writing programs or classrooms are exactly alike. Our Curriculum Solutions team works with you to design custom options that provide the resources your students need. (Options below require enrollment minimums.)

- *ForeWords for English.* Customize any print resource to fit the focus of your course or program by choosing from a range of prepared topics, such as Sentence Guides for Academic Writers.

- *Macmillan Author Program (MAP).* Add excerpts or package acclaimed works from Macmillan's trade imprints to connect students with prominent authors and public conversations. A list of popular examples or academic themes is available upon request.

- *Bedford Select.* Build your own print handbook or anthology from a database of more than 900 selections, and add your own materials to create your ideal text. Package with any Bedford/St. Martin's text for additional savings. Visit **macmillanlearning.com/bedfordselect**.

Acknowledgments

I am deeply grateful to Michelle Clark, editor extraordinaire, whose wisdom, clear-eyed judgment, efficiency, and great good humor sparkle on every page of this book: I am one very fortunate author to have had her guidance and her inspiration. I am also especially grateful to Leah Rang for continuing skillful management of my "Teacher to Teacher" blog on *Bits*; to Aislyn Fredsall, whose editorial help on print and digital products—especially *Teaching with Lunsford Handbooks*, my weekly blog posts, and a new series of writing videos—repeatedly saved the day; to Melissa Rostek, who stepped in to cowrite engaging video scripts; to Barbara Flanagan and

Adam Whitehurst for their heroic work on handbook media; to Allison Hart for managing the endlessly multiplying media production tasks; to Claire Seng-Niemoeller and Diana Blume for their brilliant contributions to art and design; to William Boardman for another beautiful cover; to Julie Dock for her meticulous copyediting; and to Ryan Sullivan, the best content project manager ever.

Many thanks, also, to the unfailingly generous and supportive members of the Bedford/St. Martin's team: Edwin Hill, Leasa Burton, Stacey Purviance, Vivian Garcia, Tracey Kuehn, Elise Kaiser, Angie Boehler, and Lisa McDowell. I will also always be grateful for the advice and counsel of Carolyn Lengel and Jimmy Fleming, who have added in so many ways to the effectiveness of my textbooks.

I am once again tremendously grateful to comics artist GB Tran, whose simple, elegant, yet "everyday" drawings add so much to the visual appeal of *The Everyday Writer* and who worked with us to develop the student comic. I am also indebted to Paul Kei Matsuda and Christine Tardy for their helpful additions to the multilingual writer coverage of this book; to Laura Aull for her fascinating research with corpus linguistics and her useful advice on using these tools with students; and to Jeanne Bohannon (Kennesaw State University) for her fine work on *Teaching with Lunsford Handbooks*. I have also benefited greatly from the excellent advice of some very special colleagues: Tarez Samra Graban (Florida State University), who made time for conversations about translingual composition, about language and identity, and about making the handbook even more rhetorically focused; Kristin van Eyk and Ryan McCarthy (University of Michigan), who helped me think about language use and student writing; and Rex Lee Jim.

I owe special thanks to the group of student writers whose work and voices appear in and enrich this book and the digital content: Michelle Abbott, Carina Abernathy, Martha Bell, Brett Bittiger, Alec Braun, Jamie Bridgewater, Tony Chan, Yishi Chen, Cyana Chilton, Samyuktha Comandur, Matteo Cuervels, Justin Dart, Ayadhiri Diaz, Brittany Dirks, Halle Edwards, Caroline Fairey, Paola Garcia-Muniz, John Garry, Allyson Goldberg, Ashley Harris, Cameron Hauer, Joanna Hays, Kiara James, Jackson Kim, James Kung, Megan Lange, Emily Lesk, Isaias Lima, Brandon Ly, Keith Mackler, Luisa Matalucci, Liz McElligott, Benjy Mercer-Golden, William Murray, Thanh Nguyen, Stephanie Parker, Rachel Quarta, Rachel Ramirez, Tawnya Redding, Amanda Rinder, Julia Sakowitz, David Sherman, Bonnie Sillay, Shuqiao Song, Nandita Sriram, Apeksha Vanjani, He Wanhua, Caroline Warner, and Shravan Yandra.

Once again, I have been guided by a group of hardworking and meticulous reviewers, including Stefan Britt, Mid Michigan College; Laurie Buchanan, Clark State Community College; William Carney, Cameron University; Cathy Clements, State Fair Community College; Theresa Conefrey, Santa Clara University; Gabriel Cutrufello, York College of

Pennsylvania; Josie Decatur, Texas Southern University; Darren DeFrain, Wichita State University; Jason DePolo, North Carolina A&T State University; Matt Dietsche, Wisconsin Indianhead Technical College; Violet Dutcher, Eastern Mennonite University; James Farrelly, University of Dayton; Zachary Garrett, Shawnee Community College; Kristina Gray, University of Minnesota–Crookston; Benjamin Harley, University of South Carolina; Christopher Harris, California State University–Los Angeles; Rebecca Kouider, Gaston College; Amanda Livanos, Southern Adventist University; Hilda Ma, St. Mary's College of California; Loren Marquez, Salisbury University; Kellie Matherly, Grayson County College; Debra Matier, College of Southern Idaho; Kathleen McConnell, San Jose State University; Shelley McEuen, College of Southern Idaho; Sylvia Newman, Weber State University; Jared Odd, Lindsey Wilson College; Lisa Ruch, Bay Path University; Jessica Saxon, Craven Community College; Kay Siebler, Missouri Western State College; Daniel Stanford, Pitt Community College; Drew Stowe, Anderson University; Ryan Thornsberry, Shawnee Community College; Christopher Thurley, Gaston College; Alan Trusky, Florence-Darlington Technical College; Kristen Weinzapfel, North Central Texas College; Anne Wheeler, Springfield College; Erin Whitford, Howard College; and Concetta Williams, Chicago State University.

Finally, and always, I continue to learn from students everywhere, who serve as the major inspiration for just about everything I do; from the very best sisters, nieces, and nephews anyone has ever had; and from my beloved grandnieces, Audrey and Lila: this book is for all of you.

Andrea A. Lunsford

Our writing center promotes learning through doing, so the explanations and examples in *The Everyday Writer* are really helpful.

The Top Twenty* is always a great starting place.

*See Ch. 32.

One student wanted to cite a presentation by a Disney executive to a campus club. The transcript and slides weren't available.

We tried Purdue OWL, but we didn't know what search terms to use. The APA handbook is incredibly hard to use—there was no way to decipher it in time.

So I opened *The Everyday Writer*, flipped to the APA tab, and skimmed through the List of Examples.* It was specific and helpful.

The format makes everything so easy!

*See Ch. 60.

I have tutored so much with the help of this handbook that I know any issues I might encounter are covered.

I'm Fernando Sanchez.

I'm a sophomore at San José State studying graphic design.

SAN JOSÉ STATE UNIVERSITY

I'm from a small country town called Arbuckle, near Sacramento.

When I grew up, it was normal for me to see people walking lambs down the street.

It's a different world here in Silicon Valley. I'm surrounded by companies that need design, that need new ideas.

Once I had to write an essay pointing out fallacies in an advertisement. There was so much I could say.

I go beyond the question. I have TOO MANY ideas.

So I ended up on clustering in *The Everyday Writer,* * for generating ideas.

*See 3a.

It took me a while to try clustering. But when I actually tried it, I could see how useful it is.

It kept me from dragging in information that didn't belong.

I could SEE when I was getting to something that wasn't related to my topic.

The *Everyday Writer* saved my grade for that class.

It's a friendly book. It's like sitting down with a teacher who's actually showing you: "Try this out!"

One of my early tutoring experiences was with a student who had a lot of trouble with the order of her words,* in making the transition from Spanish to English.

She had a very strong voice as a writer.

*See 34a.

I told her, "If you follow the advice in *The Everyday Writer* and get more comfortable with English word order...

...you can meet the conventions of US academic writing so you don't lose the meaning."

I think that session made a lightbulb come on for both of us.

SMACK

Writing is a way we define ourselves and make meaning out of the world.

Whether they're spoken or written, I'm a firm believer in the power of words.

My name is Jackson Kim, and I'm from Winchester, Virginia.

VIRGINIA MILITARY INSTITUTE

I really hated writing in elementary and middle school—I didn't think I was any good at it. But in high school I had a really good teacher who got me into English.

Now I'm a junior working on a degree in English at Virginia Military Institute.

I've spent a lot of time in the grammar section of *The Everyday Writer*. I needed to learn some basic grammar again when I came to college. Sentence-level issues can shape the way your argument is perceived, so I really love working with this section of the book.

I'm taking a legal writing class, and we're supposed to be really direct. The information on passive and active voice* in the book was really helpful.

*See 35g.

I have one instructor who is very strict with first drafts...

...but he allows us to keep revising until we get the grades we want. I got an essay back from him covered in comments, with a grade I was not happy with yet.

I brought it to a workshop in class. Looking through the feedback from other students was very intimidating.

I had no clue where to start. Some people liked a certain part of the essay, and other people said it was irrelevant.

The chapter "Reviewing, Revising, and Editing"* in *The Everyday Writer* helped me a ton.

I made a list of where the reviewers agreed and where they disagreed...

*See Ch. 5.

...so I was able to rank the comments in order of what I thought was most important.

Then I revised my essay, focusing on advancing and supporting the thesis.

It ended up being one of the essays that I'm most proud of writing.

Someday I want to be an inspector for the USDA, and I know I'll have to write reports about what I see and whether animals are being treated correctly.

When I got my first research assignment, I had never written a research paper before.

I didn't know what I should do and how I should set it up. So I used the research tab in *The Everyday Writer* to help me.

A lot of things were going in my mind— should I write about this subject? Should I write about that?

But then I read you should write about something you know something about, that you want to explore more fully.* That's what helped me the most.

*See 10a.

*See Ch. 32.

When I have questions, I go to this book, and it helps me figure out the answers.

Once I was creating a poem to put in a card for this girl, and my friends were making fun of me because my poem was so wrong.

We argued about what to capitalize and how to put the poem together. If I switched to a new line, should I capitalize the first word?

So I looked it up.*

*See 50a.

The card went over well!

Thanks, *Everyday Writer*!

Look around in *The Everyday Writer* and see how it can help you.

The
Everyday
Writer

▲ **For visual analysis** This image shows people writing with a variety of tools. Writing processes differ from writer to writer and from situation to situation. What are your writing processes?

Writing Rhetorically

There may be people who like various aspects of the writing process. For some, it may be the excitement of facing a blank page. (Hate them!) For others, it could be a sense of getting a sentence just right. (Jerks!) There may be those who like the revision process, who can go over what they've produced with a cold eye and a keen ear and feel a satisfaction in making it better. (Liars!)

— RACHEL TOOR

1 Expectations for College Writing

Open your book, open your mind

What does it mean to be in college? It means becoming the self and the thinker and the writer you most want to be. It means engaging with challenging new ideas and with people who are different from you in many ways. It means opening your books (including this one!) but also opening your mind. Indeed, openness is a theme that many groups across the country are pursuing as one way to bridge the divisions that keep people apart, isolated in their own echo chambers. The Listen First Project is one such group, dedicated to understanding and to healing "our frayed national fabric." With its nationwide National Conversation Project, Listen First aims to open minds across the country. The group's approach models the kind of civil discourse you can practice as a college writer and thinker.

1a Choose openness.

You may find yourself in classes or living in a dorm with people who hold diametrically opposed views on a range of topics, and you might have to work together to solve academic, social, and even professional challenges. While it's easy to diss — or dismiss — others in online settings, it's much harder to do so when you know the person is sitting right there with you. That's one reason your classes and other campus spaces are so important for learning: they put you face-to-face with others you may not agree with or understand, and allow you to open your mind and your world.

Openness is one way to get the most out of college and learn from others who are different from you. The authors of *The Framework for Success in Postsecondary Writing* identify eight key abilities — which they call "habits of mind" — that support success in college, and openness is one of them:

curiosity	persistence
openness	responsibility
engagement	flexibility
creativity	metacognition

It's worth noting that cultivating these habits of mind will help you to think *rhetorically* — that is, with careful attention to the full context in any communication situation. And doing so is a major key to success in college — and beyond.

Considering the full context of your college work also means considering what your instructors will most likely expect of you. Certainly they will expect you not only to be open to learning from and with people of widely different backgrounds and perspectives but also to think critically and rhetorically, to reflect on and assess your own learning, to consider ethical issues, to identify and solve problems, to do meaningful research, and to present the knowledge you construct in a variety of genres and media. Your success will depend on communicating clearly, respectfully, and openly — and on making appropriate choices for your context and your audience.

1b   Use social media wisely.

Social connections today involve so much writing that you probably write more out of class than in class. Writing on social media allows writers to reach large audiences and to get instant response.

On Twitter, for example, you can compose short bursts of 140 or 280 characters, tagging content, tweeting at groups and individuals, and pointing toward links to start discussions, participate in ongoing conversations, and invite others to join you. But you can also encounter bots and trolls, mean-spirited "haters," and even stalkers. As Steve Kerr, head coach of the Golden State Warriors, points out, social media writing "can come back and haunt you quickly." He suggests paying careful attention to what you write and to whom and always remembering that there's a person on the other side of that message. Further, you need to think twice about information you get from social media: spreading rumors and false information is as easy as a retweet. Keep in mind that being an effective writer and reader and a rhetorical thinker calls for both being responsible (one of those habits of mind!) for what you post and being skeptical of what you read on social media.

1c   Position yourself as an academic writer.

You may have less familiarity with academic writing contexts than you do with informal social media writing. You may not have written anything very lengthy or done much research. The full contexts for your college writing will require you to face new challenges and even new definitions of *writing*; you may be asked, for example, to create a persuasive website or infographic, or to research, write, and deliver a multimedia presentation. And if you grew up speaking and writing in other languages, the transition to producing effective college work in English can pose both opportunities and challenges.

Expectations for U.S. academic writing

Instructors sometimes assume that students are already familiar with expectations for college writing. To complicate the matter, there is no single "correct" style of communication in any country, including the United States. Further, what is considered good writing in one field of study is not necessarily "good" in another. Within a field, different rhetorical situations and genres may call for different ways of writing. In business, for example, memos are usually short and simple, while a market analysis report may require complex paragraphs with tables, graphs, and diagrams. Even the variety of English often referred to as "standard" covers a wide range of styles (see Chapter 23). In spite of this wide variation, several features are often associated with U.S. academic English in general:

- conventional grammar, spelling, punctuation, and mechanics
- organization that links ideas explicitly (see 3e)
- an easy-to-read type size and typeface, conventional margins, and double spacing
- explicitly stated claims supported by evidence (see Chapter 9)
- careful documentation of all sources (see Chapters 54–64)
- consistent use of an appropriate level of formality (see 23c)
- conventional use of idioms (see Chapter 41)
- use of conventional academic genres, such as literature reviews, research essays, lab reports, and research proposals (see 2e)

Remember, though, that such conventions can and will change and that new contexts always require new conventions. As new genres appear, writers are experimenting in exciting ways and questioning old conventions, especially in terms of style. So academic writing itself is changing, opening up to new ways of approaching topics and new ways of getting points across (see 9f for a discussion of narrative elements in argument writing). Keep this in mind as you approach your college writing assignments, and talk with instructors and fellow students about how you can make your academic writing fresh and exciting and sound like *you*.

Authority

In the United States, most college instructors expect student writers to begin to establish their own authority—to become constructive critics who can analyze and interpret the work of others. But what does establishing authority mean in practice? Try the following:

- Assume that your informed opinions count and that your audience expects you to present them in a well-reasoned manner.
- Show your familiarity with the ideas and works of others, both from the assigned course reading and from points your instructor and classmates have made.

Directness and clarity

Your instructors will often expect you to get to the point quickly and to be direct throughout an essay. Research for this book confirms that readers depend on writers to organize and present their material — using sections, paragraphs, sentences, arguments, details, and source citations — in ways that aid understanding. Good academic writing prepares readers for what is coming next, provides definitions, and includes topic sentences. (See 24c for a description of the organization that instructors often prefer in student essays.) To achieve directness in your writing, try the following strategies:

- State your main point early and clearly.
- Avoid hedging your statements. Instead of writing *I think the facts reveal*, come right out and say *The facts reveal* (see Chapter 9).
- Use appropriate evidence, such as examples and concrete details, to support each point.
- Make transitions from point to point obvious and clear. The first sentence of a new paragraph should reach back to the paragraph before and then look forward to what is to come (see 4d).
- Guide readers by using sentences that link together smoothly (see 4d).
- Follow logical organizational patterns (see 4c).
- Format the project appropriately for the audience and purpose you have in mind (see Chapter 18).

Talking the Talk

Conventions

"Aren't conventions just rules with another name?" Not entirely. Conventions — agreed-on practices of grammar, punctuation, and style — convey shorthand information from writer to reader. But unlike hard-and-fast rules, conventions are flexible; a convention appropriate for one time or situation may be inappropriate for another. You may also choose to ignore conventions at times to achieve a particular effect. (Notice the sentence fragment *Not entirely* at the beginning of this box, for example.) As you become more experienced and confident in your writing, you will develop a sense of which conventions to apply in different writing situations.

1d   Read and listen respectfully and actively.

Your instructors expect you to be an active reader, one who brings an inquiring mind and talks back to texts and topics. You also need to be an active and attentive listener who respects the perspectives of others and is open to new and challenging ideas. And remember that stating your own informed opinions needn't be combative; just as you listen respectfully to others' opinions, so they should listen to yours.

Respectful reading and listening

One of the benefits of college is learning new things and encountering people and ideas that at first may seem completely foreign to you. While you may seek out only like-minded people on social media, in your college classes you will encounter a great diversity of perspectives. Psychologists find that engaging with such differences is actually good for us, helping us broaden our viewpoints and open our minds. Your instructors will expect you to bring such openness to class discussions and to the texts you encounter. Here are some tips for doing so.

BEING AN OPEN-MINDED LEARNER

- Understand what others are saying before drawing conclusions about what they have said. This requires careful and respectful listening and reading.
- Practice empathy by looking at the issue from the other person's or author's point of view, trying to understand where they are coming from and why they are making certain points.
- Try to be invitational rather than confrontational.

Then, when you feel you have a good understanding of the message or text, you can bring your full critical abilities to bear, making counterpoints or offering your own point of view, though always with fairness and respect.

Active reading and listening

The following strategies (and the detailed advice in Chapter 7) will help you read and listen *actively*. And remember that online, you may often need to read *defensively*. The following tips can help you do both.

BEING AN ACTIVE READER AND LISTENER

- Note the name of the author and the date and place of publication or presentation; these offer clues to the writer's or speaker's purpose and audience.
- Understand the overall content of a text or presentation well enough to summarize it (12a).
- Formulate critical questions, and bring these questions up in class.

- Understand each sentence, and make connections between sentences and paragraphs. Keep track of repeated themes or images and how they contribute to the entire piece.
- Note the author's attitude toward and assumptions about the topic. Then think about how the attitude and assumptions might affect the author's thinking.
- Be defensive as you note the author's sources: what evidence does the writer or speaker rely on, and why? Are the sources accurate and reliable? How can you tell?
- Distinguish between the author's stance, or position, and the author's reporting on the stances of others. Watch for phrases that signal an opposing argument: *While some have argued that . . . , In the past . . . ,* and so on.
- Engage. If online readings allow you to post a comment, take advantage of the opportunity to get your voice into the conversation.

Class participation

Some cultures view speaking up in class as inappropriate or even rude. In U.S. colleges, however, doing so is expected and encouraged. Some instructors even assign credit for class participation. The challenge is to contribute without losing track of the overall aims of the class and without monopolizing discussion. These guidelines can help:

- Be prepared by having completed the reading or writing homework.
- Follow the conversation closely and write notes that can help you join in.
- Make sure your comments are relevant. Ask a question, take the conversation in a new direction, or summarize or analyze what others have said.

1e Plan research.

One of the most exciting aspects of college is engaging in research that is important to you. You might start out just being curious about how many students on your campus are vegetarians, for example, and end up with a research project for a sociology class that then becomes part of a multimedia presentation about eating healthy foods that you present to your kid sister's third-grade class. Many of your writing assignments will require extensive formal research with a wide range of sources from various media as well as information drawn from observations, interviews, or surveys.

Research can help you access important information that you didn't know, even if you know a topic very well. And no matter what you discover, college research is an important tool for establishing credibility with your audience members and thus gaining their confidence. Often, what you write will be only as good as the research on which it is based. (For more on research, see Chapters 10–12.)

1f   Use digital tools effectively.

Your instructors will often expect you to communicate both in and out of class using a variety of media. You may be asked to post to course management systems, lists, blogs, and wikis, and you may respond to the work of others on such sites. In addition, you will probably contact your instructor and classmates using email and text messages. Because digital communication is so common, it's easy to fall into the habit of writing informally. If you forget to adjust style and voice for different occasions and readers, you may undermine your own intentions.

Best practices for formal messages and posts

Email was once seen as highly informal, but you probably use it today mainly for more formal purposes, particularly to communicate for work and for school. When writing most academic and professional messages, then, or when posting to a public list that may be read by people you don't know well, follow the conventions of academic English, and be careful not to offend or irritate your audience — remember that jokes may be read as insults and that ALL CAPS may look like shouting. Finally, proofread to make sure your message is clear and free of errors, and that it is addressed to your intended audience, before you hit SEND.

Best practices for informal situations

Sometimes audiences expect informality. When you write in certain situations — Twitter posts, for example, and most text messages — you can play with (or ignore) the conventions you would follow in formal writing. Most people receiving text messages expect shorthand such as *u* for "you," but be cautious about using such shortcuts with an employer or instructor. You may want to stick to a more formal method of contact if your employer or instructor has not explicitly invited you to send text messages — or texted you first.

Even when you think a situation calls for an informal tone, be attuned to your audience's needs and your purpose for writing. And when writing for any online writing space that allows users to say almost anything about themselves or to comment freely on the postings of others, bear in mind that anonymity sometimes makes online writers feel bolder than they would be in a face-to-face discussion. Don't say anything you would want to remain private, and even if you disagree with another writer, avoid personal attacks.

2   Rhetorical Situations

What do a documented essay on environmental justice, a Facebook message objecting to the site's privacy breaches, a tweet to other students in your psychology class, a letter to the editor of your local newspaper, and a website devoted to women's health all have in common? To communicate effectively, the writers of these texts must analyze their particular situation and then respond to it in appropriate ways.

Make good choices for your rhetorical situation.

If it is true that "no man [or woman] is an island," then it is equally true that no piece of writing is an island, isolated and alone. Instead, writing is connected to a web of other writings as a writer extends, responds to, or challenges what others have said. All writing exists within a rich and broad context, and all writers listen and respond to others, even as they shape messages about particular topics and for their particular purposes and audiences.

A *rhetorical situation* is the full set of circumstances or the context surrounding any communication. When you communicate, whether you're posting on social media, creating a video, or writing an essay for a class, you need to consider and make careful choices about all the elements of your situation.

Elements of the rhetorical situation

The rhetorical situation is often depicted as a triangle to present the idea that three important elements are closely connected — your *text*, including your topic and the message you want to convey (2b); your role as *communicator*, including your purpose and your stance, or attitude, toward the text and topic (2c); and your *audience* (2d). If all the pieces making up the

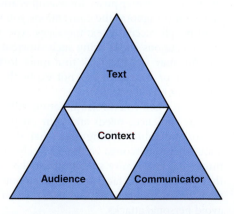

larger triangle don't work together, the communication will not be effective. But important as these elements are, they are connected to a *context* that shapes all the angles of the triangle. Considering context fully requires you to consider other questions about the rhetorical situation, such as what kind of text you should create (2e) and what conventions you should follow to meet audience expectations about appearance and delivery (2f).

Informal and formal rhetorical situations

Most people write in some rhetorical situations without analyzing them closely. When you post something on a friend's social media page, for example, you probably spend little time pondering what your friend values, how to phrase your message, which links or photos would best emphasize your point, or why you're taking the time to post. However, academic and other formal rhetorical situations may seem less familiar than the social writing you share with friends. Until you understand clearly what such situations call for, allow extra time to analyze the overall context, the topic and message, the purpose and stance, the audience, and other elements carefully.

The opportune moment (kairos)

In ancient Greece, Kairos, the god of opportunity, was depicted as running, with a prominent lock of hair on his forehead but a bald head in back. Seizing the opportune moment meant grabbing the hair as Kairos approached; once he passed, the moment was gone. Considering rhetorical situations means thinking seriously about *kairos*, the appropriate time and the most opportune ways to get your point across. Take advantage of *kairos* to choose appropriate timing and current examples and evidence for your rhetorical situation. For example, students in 2017 and 2018 who chose to write about the power of protest could draw on timely stories about the national anthem protests in the NFL or the gun safety movement following school shootings in Florida and Texas.

2b Plan your text's topic and message.

An instructor or employer may tell you what topic to write about, but sometimes the choice will be yours. When the topic is left open, you may procrastinate because you can't decide what to do. Experienced writers say that the best way to choose a topic is literally to let it choose you. Look to the topics that compel, confuse, or pose a problem for you: these are more likely to engage your interest and produce your best writing.

Deciding on a broad topic is an essential step before beginning to write, but you need to go further than that to decide what you want to say about one aspect of your topic and how you will shape what you want to say into a clear, powerful message.

2c Consider your purpose and stance as a communicator.

Whether you choose to communicate for purposes of your own or have a purpose set for you by an instructor or employer, you should consider carefully the purpose, or reason, for any communication. For the writing you do that is not connected to a class or work assignment, your reason for writing may be very clear to you: you may want to convince neighbors to support a community garden or tell blog readers what you like about your new phone. Even so, analyzing exactly what you want to accomplish and why can make you a more effective communicator.

Purposes for academic assignments

An academic assignment may clearly explain why, for whom, and about what you are supposed to write. But some college assignments seem to come out of the blue, with no specific purpose, audience, or topic. Because comprehending the assignment is crucial to your success in responding to it, make an effort to understand what your instructor expects. Discuss any questions you have with your instructor or your classmates.

- What is the primary purpose of the piece of writing — to explain? to persuade? to entertain? to achieve some other purpose?
- What purpose did the instructor want to achieve — to make sure you have understood something? to evaluate your thinking and writing abilities?
- What are your own purposes in this piece of writing — to learn about a topic? to share your ideas? to express feelings? How can you achieve these goals?
- What, exactly, does the assignment ask you to do? Look for words such as *analyze, compare, describe, explain,* and *prove.* Remember that these words may differ in meaning from discipline to discipline.

Stances for academic assignments

Thinking about your position as a communicator and your rhetorical stance, or your attitude toward your text and topic, will help you to communicate effectively.

- Where are you coming from on this topic? What is your overall attitude toward your topic? How strong are your opinions?

RHETORICAL SITUATIONS: CONSIDER YOUR PURPOSE AND STANCE

Always keep your purpose in mind.

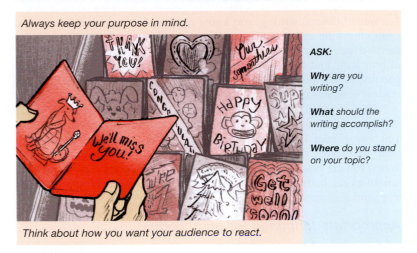

ASK:

Why are you writing?

What should the writing accomplish?

Where do you stand on your topic?

Think about how you want your audience to react.

- What social, political, religious, personal, or other influences account for your attitude? Will you need to explain any of these influences?
- What is most interesting to you about the topic? Why do you care about it?
- What conclusions do you think you might reach as you complete your text?
- How will you establish your credibility? How will you show you are knowledgeable and trustworthy?
- How will you convey your stance? Should you use words alone, combine words and images, include sound, or include something else?

2d   Analyze your audience.

Every communicator can benefit from thinking carefully about who the audience is, what the audience already knows or thinks, and what the audience needs and expects to find out. Effective communicators develop the ability to write for a variety of audiences, using language, style, and evidence appropriate to particular readers, listeners, or viewers. Even if your text can theoretically reach people all over the world, focus your analysis on those you most want or need to reach and those who are most likely to take an interest.

Informal and formal audiences

For some informal writing, you know exactly who your audience is, and communicating appropriately may be a simple matter. It's still worth remembering that when you post in a public space, you may not be aware of how large and varied your online audience can be. Can your friend's parents or your prospective employer see your social media posts. Who's reading your impassioned blog comments?

Even if you write with ease in tweets and texts to friends, you may struggle when asked to write for an instructor or for a "general audience." You may wonder, for example, what a general audience might know about your topic, what they value, or what evidence they will find persuasive. When you are new to academic writing, making assumptions about such questions can be tricky. If you can identify samples of writing that appeal to a similar audience, look for clues about what that audience expects.

Appropriate language for an audience

If your readers can't understand what you mean, they're not likely to accept your points. Ask yourself whether the language of your text is as clear as it needs to be for your audience. For academic writing, consider whether to use any specialized varieties of English along with academic English. How will these choices help you connect to your audience?

As you think about your audience, consider how you want them to respond to both the words and the images you use. And remember that sound and images can evoke very strong responses in your audience and can affect the tone of your writing, so choose them with special care.

Language, Culture, and Context

Multilingual

Bringing In Other Languages

Even when you write in English, you may want or need to include words, phrases, or whole passages in another language. If so, consider whether your readers will understand that language and whether you need to provide a translation or more context. See 23e for more on bringing in other languages.

Considering Disabilities

Your Whole Audience

Remember that considering your whole audience means thinking about members with varying abilities and special needs. Approximately one in five Americans lives with a disability. All writers need to think carefully about how their words connect with such diverse audiences.

2e   Think about genres and media.

You may be familiar with the word *genre* as it applies to movies (comedy, action) or music (hip-hop, punk). But *genre* is also used to describe forms of writing, such as research essays and lab reports. Over time, genres develop conventions — such as the types of content, rhetorical strategies, and kinds of language used. Most audiences begin to expect those conventional features in the genre. But genres are flexible, not cookie-cutter templates. Genres can be produced in different *media*, such as digital or print forms. *Media* refers to how the text is delivered to its audience.

Features of genres

If you are not sure what kind of text you are supposed to write, ask your instructor, classmates, or a writing center tutor for clarification and examples. Look carefully at the samples to make sure you understand the conventional expectations, and ask questions about the genre's typical features.

- What does the genre look like? How is the text laid out? How are headings, sidebars, and other elements incorporated into the main text? Are its sections long or short? If visuals or media elements are included, how and why are they used? (See Chapter 18.)
- What topics are usually found in this genre? What type of content is rare?
- How does the text introduce the topic? Is the main point stated explicitly or implicitly?
- How are the key terms defined? What background information is provided?
- Are sentences short, long, simple, complicated? Is passive voice common?
- What is the level of formality? Does the text use contractions such as *he's* and *can't*? Does the text use technical jargon or slang?

Talking the Talk

Genre Names

"What does my instructor mean by *essay*?" Writing assignments often mention a specific genre, such as *essay* or *report*, but genre names can be confusing. The same genre may work differently in different contexts, or people may use the same term in various ways. Depending on the field, an essay might be a personal narrative, a critical analysis, or even a journal article. Even when the name of the genre sounds familiar to you, look for specific instructions for each assignment or analyze examples provided by the instructor.

- Does the text take a personal stance (*I*, *we*), address the audience directly (*you*), or talk about the subject without explicitly referring to the writer or the reader?
- Are sources used? How are they introduced and cited in the text?
- Who reads this genre, and why? Does the genre usually aim to inform, to persuade, to entertain, or to serve some other purpose?
- What medium is typically used for this genre? Are visual images or audio commonly used? If so, for what purposes?
- How much flexibility do you have in ignoring or stretching the boundaries of the genre?

Multimodal genres for academic work

Much college writing is still done in traditional print-based genres, but this is changing. You may have the option to create multimodal writing using audio, video, images, and words in combination. Make sure that your choices are appropriate for your topic, purpose, audience, and genre. You may start off planning to write a traditional academic essay and then discover as you proceed that a different genre or medium may offer more effective ways to communicate your point (see 20b). One student, Will Rogers, who had been assigned to write an essay about something that most people take for granted, focused on a giant construction crane. After he interviewed the crane's operator, who had left college after his first year to take the job, the student decided that his project would work better and be more powerful as a video. That way, viewers could actually see the crane operator and hear his voice as he described the decisions he had made.

You may be asked to create a work in one genre or medium, such as a print-based research project, and translate it to another type of composition, such as a multimedia presentation or podcast. Such translations may not be as straightforward as they seem. Just as filmmakers may streamline plot and conflate characters when they create a movie version of a book, developing a thesis and supporting it effectively may require different strategies if you are turning a paper-based work into a digital form. You may need extra planning time.

 ## 2f   Consider language and style.

Although most instructors will expect standard academic English for academic assignments, you may also need to use specialized occupational or professional varieties of English — those characteristic of medicine, say, or music. Be open minded: you may wish to use regional, communal, or other varieties of English to connect with certain audiences or to catch the sound of someone's spoken words. You may even need to use words from a language other than English — in quoting someone, perhaps, or capturing a cultural phenomenon. Think about what language varieties will be most appropriate for reaching your audience and accomplishing your purposes (see Chapter 23).

You will also want to think carefully about style: should you be casual and breezy, somewhat informal, formal, or extremely formal? Your style will be important in creating the tone you want, one that is appropriate to your assignment, audience, topic, purpose, and genre.

Remember that visual and audio elements can influence the tone of your writing. Such elements create associations in viewers' minds: one audience may react more positively than another to an element such as a rap or heavy metal soundtrack, for example. You can influence the way your work is perceived by analyzing your audience and choosing audio and visual elements that set a mood appropriate to your goals.

A sample rhetorical situation

Let's see how one writer analyzes a rhetorical situation. Emily Lesk, a student in a first-year English course, gets an assignment that asks her to "explore the ways in which one or more media have affected an aspect of American identity." (More examples of Emily's work appear in 5b.) Because Emily is interested in advertising, she plans first to investigate how advertising might help shape American identity. Deciding that such a broad topic is not manageable in the time she has available, however, she shifts her focus to advertising for one company that seems particularly "American," Coca-Cola.

Since Emily's primary audience includes her instructor and her classmates, she needs to find ways to connect with them on an emotional as well as a logical level. She will do so, she decides, first by telling a story about being drawn into buying Coca-Cola products (even though she didn't really like the soft drink) because of the power of the advertising. She thinks that others in her audience may have had similar experiences. If we were to use the rhetorical triangle from 2a to map out **Emily's writing situation**, it might look like this:

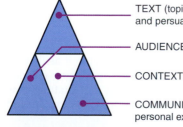

TEXT (topic/message): Advertising is powerful and persuasive

AUDIENCE: Instructor and peers

CONTEXT: Brief academic essay for a writing class

COMMUNICATOR (purpose/stance): Reflect on a personal experience, draw audience in with story

Here is a portion of Emily's first draft and the visual she chose to illustrate her story:

Even before setting foot in the Promised Land three years ago, I knew exactly where I could find the Coke T-shirt. The shop in the central block of Jerusalem's Ben Yehuda Street did offer other shirt designs, but the one with the bright white "Drink Coca-Cola Classic" written in Hebrew cursive across the chest was what drew in most of the dollar-carrying tourists. While waiting almost twenty minutes for my shirt (depicted in fig. 1), I watched nearly everyone ahead of me say "the Coke shirt, *todah rabah* [thank you very much]."

Fig. 1. Hebrew Coca-Cola T-shirt. Personal photograph by author.

At the time, I never thought it strange that I wanted one, too. Yet, I *had* absorbed sixteen years of Coca-Cola propaganda.

Thinking about how she relates to her audience brings Emily to reflect more deeply on herself as the writer: Why has she chosen this topic? What does it say about her beliefs and values? What is her attitude toward her topic and toward her audience? What does she need to do to establish her credentials to write on this topic and to this audience?

Finally, Emily knows she will need to pay careful attention to the context in which she is writing: the assignment is due in two weeks, so she needs to work fast; the assignment calls for an essay written in academic English, though she plans to include some dialogue and a number of visuals to keep it lively; and since she knows she tends to sound like a know-it-all, she determines to work carefully on her tone and style.

3 Exploring, Planning, and Drafting

Some writers just plunge right into their work and develop it as they go along. Others find that they work more effectively by making detailed blueprints before they begin drafting. Your planning and drafting may fall anywhere along this spectrum. As you plan and draft, you explore and narrow your topic, decide on your thesis, organize materials to support that central idea, and sketch out a plan for your writing. As one student said, this important beginning work is the time in the writing process "when the rubber meets the road."

3a Explore your topic.

The point is so simple that we often forget it: we write best about topics we know well or are curious about. So among the most important parts of the entire writing process are choosing a topic that will engage your interest, exploring that topic by surveying what you know about it or determining how you might extend your thinking on the topic. You can explore a topic in many ways; the goal is to find strategies that work well for you.

STRATEGIES FOR EXPLORING A TOPIC

- Brainstorm. Try out ideas, alone or with another person. Jot down key words and phrases about the topic, and see what they prompt you to think about.

- Freewrite — write without stopping — for ten minutes or so to see what insights or ideas you come up with. You can also "freespeak" by recording your thoughts on a phone or other device.

- Draw or make word pictures of your topic.

- Play around with metaphors and similes: if your topic were a food, what would it be; what is your topic most like in the animal world? Get creative!

- Try clustering — writing your topic on a sheet of paper or screen, then writing related thoughts near the topic idea. Circle each idea or phrase and then draw lines to show how the ideas are connected. (See p. 20.)

- Ask questions. What is it? What caused it? What are its consequences? Who does it appeal to and why? What is it like or unlike? What larger system is it a part of? What do other people say about it?

- Browse sources to find out what others say about the topic.

- Check out images or videos related to your topic to see if they spark ideas.

- Collaborate! Talking with friends and classmates about your ideas almost always leads to new — and sometimes better — ideas. Talking with others will also help you to articulate your major points more clearly.

EMILY LESK'S CLUSTERING

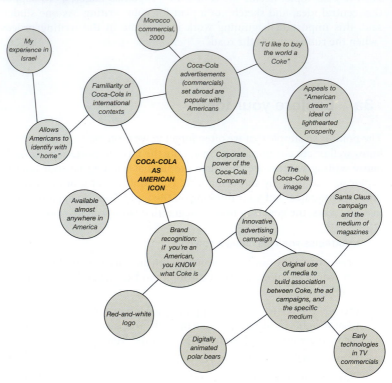

Language, Culture, and Context

Using Your Best Language to Explore Ideas

For generating and exploring ideas, you may be most successful at coming up with good ideas quickly and spontaneously if you work with your most familiar and comfortable language or language variety. Later in the process of writing, you can choose the best of these ideas and begin working with them in academic English.

WORKING THESIS: PLAN YOUR APPROACH

Survey what you know about the topic.

ASK:

What is your **connection** *to the topic?*

What does your audience need to **know**?

How can you make your topic **manageable**?

Remember that there are many possible paths to approaching a topic.

3b   Narrow your topic.

After exploring ideas, you may have found a topic that interests you and that you think would also be interesting to your readers. The topic, however, may still be too large to be manageable. If that is the case, narrow your topic by focusing on a single aspect or part of it.

Student writer Emily Lesk planned to discuss how advertising affects American identity, but she knew that such a topic was far too broad. After thinking about products that are pitched as particularly "American" in their advertising, she posted a Facebook message asking friends to "name products that seem super-American." She quickly got responses ranging from Hummers and Winchester rifles to "soft toilet paper," Spam, Wheaties, and apple pie. One friend identified Coca-Cola, a product Emily associated with many memorable advertising campaigns.

3c   Craft a working thesis statement.

Academic and professional writing in the United States often contains an explicit thesis statement. The thesis functions as a promise to readers, letting them know what main idea the writer will discuss. Your readers may (or may not) expect you to craft the thesis as a single sentence near the beginning of the text. If you want to suggest a thesis implicitly rather than stating one explicitly, if you plan to convey your main argument somewhere other than in your introduction, or if you prefer to make your thesis longer than a single sentence, consider whether the rhetorical situation

WORKING THESIS: REFINE YOUR TOPIC

Match your approach to the requirements of the topic.

ASK:

How will your audience **connect** to your topic?

How can you help them see your **perspective**?

What is the most **persuasive message** for this context?

Remember that you are creating a working *thesis that you can change as you go.*

allows such flexibility. For an academic project, also consult with your instructor about how to meet expectations.

It's often useful to establish a working thesis statement early in your writing process. The word *working* is important here because your thesis may well change as you write — your final thesis may be very different from the working thesis you begin with. Even so, a working thesis focuses your thinking and research, and it helps keep you on track.

A working thesis should have two parts: a *topic*, which indicates the subject matter the writing is about, and a *comment*, which makes an important point about the topic.

▶   In the **graphic novel** *Fun Home*, **illustrations and words combine to make meanings that are more subtle than either words alone or images alone could convey**.

A successful working thesis statement has three characteristics:

1. It is potentially *interesting* to the intended audience.
2. It is as *specific* as possible.
3. It limits the topic enough to make it *manageable*.

You can evaluate a working thesis by checking it against each of these characteristics, as in the following examples:

▶   **Graphic novels combine words and images.**

INTERESTING?   The topic of graphic novels could be interesting, but this draft of a working thesis has no real comment attached to it — instead, it states a bare fact, and the only place to go from here is to more bare facts.

▶ In graphic novels, words and images convey interesting meanings.

SPECIFIC?   This thesis is not specific. What are "interesting meanings," exactly? How are they conveyed?

▶ Graphic novels have evolved in recent decades to become an important literary genre.

MANAGEABLE?   This thesis would not be manageable for a short-term project because it would require research on several decades of history and on hundreds of texts from all over the world.

WORKING THESIS: CRAFT YOUR MESSAGE

Draft a working thesis.

Consider this a starting point for organizing and planning your draft.

ASK:

*Should your thesis be **implicit** or **explicit** for this context and audience?*

*Are you conveying your **own** message — not just facts?*

Does your working thesis help you understand where to go next?

Language, Culture, and Context

Multilingual

Stating a Thesis Directly

In some cultures, stating the main point directly may be considered rude or inelegant. In U.S. academic and business practices, however, readers often expect the writer to make key points and positions explicit. Unless your main point is highly controversial or hard for the reader to accept (such as a rejection letter), state your main point early — before presenting supporting details.

3d   Gather information.

Writing often calls for research. Your curiosity may be triggered by a found object or image that you want to learn more about. An assignment may specify that you conduct research on your topic and cite your sources. Even if you're writing about a topic on which you're an expert, you may still find that you don't know enough about some aspect of the topic to write about it effectively without doing research.

You may need to do research at various stages of the writing process — early on, to help you understand or define your topic, and later, to find additional examples and illustrations to support your thesis. Once you have developed a working thesis statement, consider what additional information, opinions, visuals, and media you might need. For more on conducting research, see Chapter 10.

3e   Organize information.

While you're finding information on your topic, think about how you will group or organize that information to make it accessible and convincing to readers. At the simplest level, writers most often group information in their writing projects according to four main principles — space, time, logic, and association.

Spatial organization

Spatial organization of texts allows the reader to "walk through" your material, beginning at one point and moving around in an organized manner — say, from near to far, left to right, or top to bottom. It can be especially useful when you want the audience to understand the layout of a structure or the placement of elements and people in a scene: texts such as a museum visitors' audio guide, a written-word description of a historic battlefield, or a video tour of a new apartment might all call for spatial organization. Remember that maps, diagrams, and other graphics may help readers visualize your descriptions more effectively.

Chronological organization

Organization can also indicate *when* events occur, usually chronologically from first to last. Chronological organization is the basic method used in cookbooks, lab reports, instruction manuals, and many stories and narrative films. You may find it useful to organize information by describing or showing the sequence of events or the steps in a process.

Logical organization

Organizing according to logical patterns means relating pieces of information in ways that make sense. Following is an overview of some of the most commonly used logical patterns: illustration, definition, division and classification, comparison and contrast, cause and effect, problem and solution, analogy, and narration. For examples of paragraphs organized according to these logical patterns, see 4c.

Associational organization

Some writers organize information through a series of associations that grow directly out of their own experiences and memories. In doing so, they may rely on a sensory memory, such as an aroma, a sound, or a scene. Associational organization can work well in essays or projects of many kinds, but it is particularly useful in personal narrative, where the writer follows a chain of associations to render an experience vividly for readers, as in this description:

> Flying from San Francisco to Atlanta, I looked down to see the gentle roll of the Smoky Mountains begin to appear. Almost at once, I was transported back to my granny's porch, sitting next to her drinking iced tea and eating peaches. Those fresh-picked peaches were delicious — ripened on the tree, skinned, and eaten with no regard for the sticky juice trickling everywhere. And on special occasions, we'd make ice cream, and Granny would empty a bowl brimming with chopped peaches into the creamy dish. Now — that was the life!

Combined organizational patterns

In much of your writing, you will want to use two or more principles of organization. You might, for example, combine several passages of narration with vivid examples to make a striking comparison, as one student did in an essay about the dramatic differences between her life in her Zuñi community and her life as a teacher in Seattle. In addition, you may want to include not only visuals but sound and other multimedia effects as well.

 3f   Make a plan.

At this point, you will find it helpful to write out an organizational plan, outline, or storyboard. To do so, begin with your thesis; review your exploratory notes, research materials, and visual or multimedia sources; and then list all the examples and other good reasons you have to support the thesis. (For more on paragraph-level organization, see Chapter 4.)

Quick Help

Organizing Visuals and Media in Academic Writing

- Use video and still images to capture your readers' attention and interest in a vivid way, to emphasize a point you make in words, to present information that is difficult to convey in words, or to communicate with audiences with different language skills.

- For presentations, consider what your audience should look at as they listen to you.

- If you are using visuals and words together, consider both the way each image or video works on its own and the way it works in combination with the words you use.

- If you are using visuals to illustrate a written-word text, place each visual as near as possible to the words it illustrates. Introduce each visual clearly (*As the map to the right depicts . . .*). Comment on the significance or effect of the visual (*Figure 1 corroborates the firefighters' statements . . .*). Label each visual appropriately, and cite the source. See 54e (MLA), 58e (APA), or 62c (*Chicago*).

An informal plan

One informal way to organize your ideas is to figure out what belongs in your introduction, body paragraphs, and conclusion. A student who was writing about solutions to a problem used the following plan:

SAMPLE INFORMAL PLAN

WORKING THESIS

▶ Increased motorcycle use demands the reorganization of campus parking lots.

INTRODUCTION

give background and overview (motorcycle use up dramatically), and include photograph of overcrowded lot

state purpose — to fulfill promise of thesis by proposing solutions

BODY

describe current situation (share my research at area parking lots)

describe problem in detail (report on statistics; cars vs. cycles), and graph my findings

present two possible solutions (enlarge lots or reallocate space)

CONCLUSION

recommend against first solution because of cost and space

recommend second solution, and summarize advantages

A formal outline

Even if you have created an informal written plan before drafting, you may wish (or be required) to prepare a more formal outline, which can help you see exactly how the parts of your writing will fit together — how your ideas relate, where you need examples, and what the overall structure of your work will be. Even if your instructor doesn't ask you to make an outline or you prefer to use some other method of sketching out your plans, you may want to come back to an outline later: doing a retrospective outline — one you do after you've already drafted your project — is a great way to see whether you have any big logical gaps or whether parts of the essay are in the wrong place.

Most formal outlines follow a conventional format of numbered and lettered headings and subheadings, using roman numerals, capital letters, arabic numerals, and lowercase letters to show the levels of importance of the various ideas and their relationships. Here is a partial formal outline of student Julia Sakowitz's essay; you can read the entire essay in Chapter 57.

SAMPLE FORMAL OUTLINE (PARTIAL)

Thesis: Although there is no simple solution for tourism in Harlem, small minority- and resident-owned businesses have the potential to benefit the community more directly and widely while causing fewer social and economic problems.

Student Writing

I. Economic development policy, particularly the Upper Manhattan Empowerment Zone (UMEZ), has played a major role in shaping tourism's growth in Harlem.

   A. The UMEZ specifically focuses on black and Latino cultural initiatives as a means of drawing tourism.

   B. Recent scholarship on tourism in Harlem suggests that marketing black and Latino culture is Harlem's golden ticket to escape economic marginalization.

   C. Benefits of cultural tourism include revenue, cultural flourishing, community pride, tolerance, and de-stigmatization.

II. Cultural tourism comes with significant complications for residents.

    A. The power dynamic between tourists and residents is skewed in favor of the tourists, who can treat residents as "something to be consumed like a Broadway show."

    B. Commercial gentrification stems from increased tourism.

    C. Residential gentrification often follows commercial gentrification, leading to increased displacement of original Harlem residents.

III. Small tour companies advertise authenticity as part of their appeal to tourists.

    A. *Welcome to Harlem* (Johnson) features six different tours and workshops given by Harlem residents.

    B. Many Harlem-based tour companies suffer from lack of visibility when hotels and tour companies recommend larger, outside tour companies that can afford to pay commission.

    C. Authenticity and self-representation are extremely important to the success of Harlem-based tour companies.

A storyboard

The technique of storyboarding — working out a narrative or argument in visual form — can be a good way to come up with an organizational plan, especially if you are developing a video essay, website, or other media project. You can find storyboard templates online to help you get started, or you can create your own storyboard by using note cards or sticky notes. Even if you're writing a more traditional word-based college essay, however, you may find storyboarding helpful; take advantage of different colors to keep track of threads of argument, subtopics, and so on. Flexibility is a strong feature of storyboarding: you can move the cards and notes around, trying out different arrangements, until you find an organization that works well for your writing situation.

Use linear organization when you want readers to move in a particular order through your material. An online report might use the following linear organization:

LINEAR ORGANIZATION

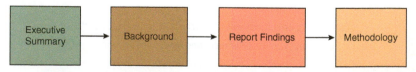

Executive Summary → Background → Report Findings → Methodology

A hierarchy puts the most important material first, with subtopics branching out from the main idea. A website on dog bite prevention might be arranged like this:

HIERARCHICAL ORGANIZATION

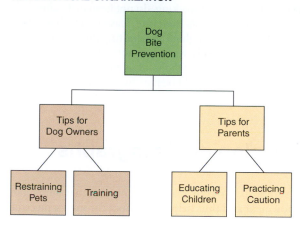

A spoke-and-hub organization allows readers to move from place to place in no particular order. Many portfolio websites are arranged this way:

SPOKE-AND-HUB ORGANIZATION

Whatever form your plan takes, you may want or need to change it along the way. Writing has a way of stimulating thought, and the process of drafting may generate new ideas. Or you may find that you need to reexamine some data or information or gather more material.

3g   Create a draft.

No matter how good your planning, investigating, and organizing have been, chances are you will need to return to these activities as you draft. This fact of life leads to the first principle of successful drafting: be flexible. If you see that your organizational plan is not working, do not hesitate to alter it. If some information or medium now seems irrelevant, leave it out, even if you went to great lengths to obtain it. Throughout the drafting process, you may need to refer to points you have already written about. You may learn that you need to do more research, that your whole thesis must be reshaped, or that your topic is still too broad and should be narrowed further.

4   Developing Paragraphs

Paragraphs serve as signposts for your readers — pointers that anticipate what they need to know next and thus help guide them through a piece of writing. A look through a popular magazine will show paragraphs working this way: the first paragraph of an article almost always aims to get our attention and to persuade us to read on, and subsequent ones often indicate a new point or a shift in focus or tone.

Put most simply, a paragraph is a group of sentences or a single sentence set off as a unit. All the sentences in a paragraph usually revolve around one main idea.

Quick Help

Guidelines for Drafting

- **Have all your information close at hand** and arranged according to your organizational plan. Stopping to search for a piece of information can break your concentration or distract you.

- **Write in stretches of at least thirty minutes.** Writing can provide momentum, and once you get going, the task becomes easier.

- **Don't let small questions bog you down.** Just make a note of them in brackets — or in all caps — or make a tentative decision and move on.

- **Remember that first drafts aren't perfect.** Concentrate on getting all your ideas written down, and don't worry about anything else.

- **Stop writing at a place where you know exactly what will come next.** Doing so will help you start easily when you return to the draft.

Quick Help

Editing Paragraphs

- What is the topic sentence of each paragraph? Is the main idea clear? (4a)
- Does the last sentence of each paragraph in some way conclude that paragraph's discussion? If not, does it need to?
- Within each paragraph, how does each sentence relate to the main idea? Revise or eliminate any that do not. (4a)
- How completely does each paragraph develop its main idea? What details and images are included? Are they effective? Do any paragraphs need more detail? (4b)
- What other methods of development might make the paragraph more effective? (4c)
- Within each paragraph, how well do transitions carry readers from one idea to the next? (4d)
- Are the paragraphs clearly linked? Do any links need to be added? Are any of the transitions from one paragraph to another artificial? (4d)
- How does the introductory paragraph catch readers' interest? How does the last paragraph draw the piece to a conclusion? (4e)

4a Focus on a main idea.

An effective paragraph often focuses on one main idea. A good way to achieve such unity is to state the main idea clearly in one sentence (the topic sentence) and then relate all other sentences in the paragraph to that idea.

Topic sentence

The following paragraph opens with a clear topic sentence, and the rest of the paragraph builds on the idea stated in that sentence:

> Our friendship was the source of much happiness and many memories. We grooved on every new recording from Jay-Z. We sweated together in the sweltering summer sun, trying to win the championship for our softball team. I recall the taste of pepperoni pizza as we discussed the highlights of our team's victory. Once we even became attracted to the same person, but luckily we were able to share his friendship.

Other related sentences

Whether the main idea of a paragraph is stated in a topic sentence or is implied, make sure that all other sentences in the paragraph contribute to the main idea. In the preceding example about friendship, all of the sentences clearly relate to the point that is made in the first sentence. The result is a unified paragraph.

4b Provide details.

An effective paragraph develops its main idea by providing enough details — including visual details — to hold the reader's interest. Without such development, a paragraph may seem lifeless and abstract.

A POORLY DEVELOPED PARAGRAPH

No such thing as human nature compels people to behave, think, or react in certain ways. Rather, from our infancy to our death, we are constantly being taught, by the society that surrounds us, the customs, norms, and mores of a distinct culture. Everything in culture is learned, not genetically transmitted.

THE SAME PARAGRAPH, REVISED

A child in Los Angeles decorates a Christmas tree with shiny red ornaments and sparkling tinsel. A few weeks later, a child in Beijing celebrates the Chinese New Year with feasting, firecrackers, and gift money in lucky red envelopes. It is not by instinct that one child knows how to decorate the tree while the other knows how to celebrate the New Year. No such thing as human nature compels people to behave, think, or react in certain ways. Rather, from the time of our infancy to our death, we are constantly being taught, by the society that surrounds us, the customs, norms, and mores of one or more distinct cultures. Everything in culture is learned, not genetically transmitted.

Though both paragraphs present the same point, only the second one comes to life. It does so by bringing in specific details *from* life, including images that show readers what the paragraph describes. We want to read this paragraph because it appeals to our senses and our curiosity (why are red envelopes considered lucky?).

Details in visual texts

Details are important in both written and visual texts. If you decide to use an image because of a particular detail, make sure your readers will notice what you want them to see. Crop out any unnecessary information — making sure, however, not to distort the message by doing so — and clarify what's important about the image in your text or with a caption. If you are taking a photo to illustrate a blog post on street food, for example, you will need to decide whether you should crop the image to focus on the food or whether your discussion calls for the photo to include more of the surroundings.

4c Use effective methods of development.

Writers can choose from among several patterns for developing paragraphs. Often in an essay, you will combine patterns as needed to achieve your purpose.

Narrative

A narrative paragraph uses the chronological elements of a story to develop a main idea. The following is one student's narrative paragraph that tells a personal story to support a point about the dangers of racing bicycles with flimsy alloy frames:

> People who have been exposed to the risk of dangerously designed bicycle frames have paid too high a price. I saw this danger myself in last year's Putney Race. An expensive graphite frame failed, and the rider was catapulted onto Vermont pavement at fifty miles per hour. The pack of riders behind him was so dense that other racers crashed into a tangled, sliding heap. The aftermath: four hospitalizations. I got off with some stitches, a bad road rash, and severely pulled tendons. My Italian racing bike was pretzeled, and my racing was over for that summer. Others were not so lucky. An Olympic hopeful, Brian Stone of the Northstar team, woke up in a hospital bed to find that his cycling was over — and not just for that summer. His kneecap had been surgically removed. He couldn't even walk.

Description

A descriptive paragraph uses specific details to create a clear impression. Notice how the following paragraph includes details to describe the appearance of the skyscraper and its effect on those who see it.

> The Chrysler Building, completed in 1930, still attracts the eyes of tourists and New Yorkers alike with its shiny steel exterior. The Chrysler cars of the era are incorporated into the design: the eagle-head gargoyles on the upper vertices of the building are shaped like the automobiles' hood ornaments, and winged details imitate Chrysler radiator caps. At night, an elaborate lighting scheme spotlights the sleek, powerful eagles from below — turning them into striking silhouettes — and picks out each of the upper stories' famed triangular windows, arching up into the darkness like the rays of a stylized sun.

Definition

Often you may need to write an entire paragraph in order to define a word or concept, as in the following example:

> Economics is the study of how people choose among the alternatives available to them. It's the study of little choices ("Should I take the

chocolate or the strawberry?") and big choices ("Should we require a reduction in energy consumption in order to protect the environment?"). It's the study of individual choices, choices by firms, and choices by governments. Life presents each of us with a wide range of alternative uses of our time and other resources; economists examine how we choose among those alternatives.   – TIMOTHY TREGARTHEN, *Economics*

Example

One of the most common ways of developing a paragraph is by illustrating a point with one or more examples.

> The Indians made names for us children in their teasing way. Because our very busy mother kept my hair cut short, like my brothers', they called me Short Furred One, pointing to their hair and making the sign for short, the right hand with fingers pressed close together, held upward, back out, at the height intended. With me this was about two feet tall, the Indians laughing gently at my abashed face. I am told that I was given a pair of small moccasins that first time, to clear up my unhappiness at being picked out from the dusk behind the fire and my two unhappy shortcomings made conspicuous.   – MARI SANDOZ, "The Go-Along Ones"

Division and classification

Division breaks a single item into parts. Classification groups many separate items according to their similarities. A paragraph evaluating a history course might divide the course into several segments — textbooks, lectures, assignments — and examine each one in turn. A paragraph giving an overview of many history courses might classify the courses in a number of ways — by time periods, by geographic areas, by the kinds of assignments, or by some other principle.

DIVISION

> We all listen to music according to our separate capacities. But, for the sake of analysis, the whole listening process may become clearer if we break it up into its component parts, so to speak. In a certain sense, we all listen to music on three separate planes. For lack of a better terminology, one might name these: (1) the sensuous plane, (2) the expressive plane, (3) the sheerly musical plane. The only advantage to be gained from mechanically splitting up the listening process into these hypothetical planes is the clearer view to be had of the way in which we listen.
> – AARON COPLAND, *What to Listen for in Music*

CLASSIFICATION

> Two types of people are seduced by fad diets. Those who have always been overweight turn to them out of despair; they have tried everything, and yet nothing seems to work. A second group of people to succumb

appear perfectly healthy but are baited by slogans such as "look good, feel good." These slogans prompt self-questioning and insecurity — do I really look good and feel good? — and as a direct result, many healthy people fall prey to fad diets. With both types of people, however, the problems surrounding such diets are numerous and dangerous. In fact, these diets provide neither intelligent nor effective answers to weight control.

Comparison and contrast

When you compare two things, you look at their similarities; when you contrast two things, you focus on their differences. You can structure paragraphs that compare or contrast in two basic ways. One way is to present all the information about one item and then all the information about the other item, as in the following paragraph:

> You could tell the veterans from the rookies by the way they were dressed. The knowledgeable ones had their heads covered by kerchiefs, so that if they were hired, tobacco dust wouldn't get in their hair; they had on clean dresses that by now were faded and shapeless, so that if they were hired they wouldn't get tobacco dust and grime on their best clothes. Those who were trying for the first time had their hair freshly done and wore attractive dresses; they wanted to make a good impression. But the dresses couldn't be seen at the distance that many were standing from the employment office, and they were crumpled in the crush.
>
> – MARY MEBANE, "Summer Job"

Or you can switch back and forth between the two items, focusing on particular characteristics of each in turn.

> Malcolm X emphasized the use of violence in his movement and employed the biblical principle of "an eye for an eye and a tooth for a tooth." Martin Luther King Jr., on the other hand, felt that blacks should use nonviolent civil disobedience and employed the theme "turning the other cheek," which Malcolm X rejected as "beggarly" and "feeble." The philosophy of Malcolm X was one of revenge, and often it broke the unity of black Americans. More radical blacks supported him, while more conservative ones supported King. King thought that blacks should transcend their humanity. In contrast, Malcolm X thought they should embrace it and reserve their love for one another, regarding whites as "devils" and the "enemy." The distance between King's thinking and Malcolm X's was the distance between growing up in the seminary and growing up on the streets, between the American dream and the American reality.

Analogy

Analogies — comparisons that explain an unfamiliar thing in terms of a familiar one — can also help develop paragraphs.

Since the advent of Hollywood editing, back in the earliest days of cinema, the goal of filmmakers has been for us to feel the movement of the camera but not to be aware of it, to look past the construction of the media, to ignore the seams in the material. Just as an Olympic diver smiles and hides the effort as she catapults skyward and manages to pull off multiple flips while seemingly twisting in both directions, good storytelling — whether oral, in print, or visual — typically hides the construction and the hard work that go into making it. Both the medal-winning dives and the best stories are more intricate than they appear.

– STEPHEN APKON, *The Age of the Image: Redefining Literacy in a World of Screens*

Cause and effect

You can often develop paragraphs by explaining the causes of something or the effects that something brings about. The following paragraph discusses the causes that led pediatrician Phil Offit to study science and become a physician:

To understand exactly why Offit became a scientist, you must go back more than half a century, to 1956. That was when doctors in Offit's hometown of Baltimore operated on one of his legs to correct a club foot, requiring him to spend three weeks recovering in a chronic care facility with 20 other children, all of whom had polio. Parents were allowed to visit just one hour a week, on Sundays. His father, a shirt salesman, came when he could. His mother, who was pregnant with his brother and hospitalized with appendicitis, was unable to visit at all. He was five years old. "It was a pretty lonely, isolating experience," Offit says. "But what was even worse was looking at these other children who were just horribly crippled and disfigured by polio." That memory, he says, was the first thing that drove him toward a career in pediatric infectious diseases.

– AMY WALLACE, "An Epidemic of Fear"

Process

Paragraphs that explain a process often use the principle of time or chronology to order the stages in the process.

In July of 1877, Eadweard Muybridge photographed a horse in motion with a camera fast enough to capture clearly the split second when the horse's hooves were all off the ground — a moment never before caught on film. His next goal was to photograph a sequence of such rapid images. In June of 1878, he set up twelve cameras along a track, each connected to a tripwire. Then, as a crowd watched, a trotting horse raced down the track pulling a two-wheeled carriage. The carriage wheels tripped each camera in quick succession, snapping a dozen photographs. Muybridge developed the negatives and displayed them to an admiring public that same morning. His technical achievement helped to pave the way for the first motion pictures a decade later.

Problem and solution

Another way to develop a paragraph is to open with a topic sentence that states a problem or asks a question about a problem and then to offer a solution or answers in the sentences that follow — a technique used in this paragraph from a review of Ted Nordhaus and Michael Shellenberger's book *Break Through: From the Death of Environmentalism to the Politics of Possibility*:

> Unfortunately, at the moment growth means burning more fossil fuel. . . . How can that fact be faced? How to have growth that Americans want, but without limits that they instinctively oppose, and still reduce carbon emissions? [Nordhaus and Shellenberger's] answer is: investments in new technology. Acknowledge that America "is great at imagining, experimenting, and inventing the future," and then start spending. They cite examples ranging from the nuclear weapons program to the invention of the Internet to show what government money can do, and argue that too many clean-energy advocates focus on caps instead.
>
> – Bill McKibben, "Can Anyone Stop It?"

Reiteration

Reiteration is a method of development you may recognize from political speeches or some styles of preaching. In this pattern, the writer states the main point of a paragraph and then restates it, hammering home the point and often building in intensity as well. In the following passage from her speech at the 2019 World Economic Forum, environmental activist Greta Thunberg, a teen, reiterates her ideas about the size of the climate change crisis and her desire for adults to act:

> We are at a time in history where everyone with any insight of the climate crisis that threatens our civilisation — and the entire biosphere — must speak out in clear language, no matter how uncomfortable and unprofitable that may be. We must change almost everything in our current societies. The bigger your carbon footprint, the bigger your moral duty. The bigger your platform, the bigger your responsibility. Adults keep saying: "We owe it to the young people to give them hope." But I don't want your hope. I don't want you to be hopeful. I want you to panic. I want you to feel the fear I feel every day. And then I want you to act. I want you to act as you would in a crisis. I want you to act as if our house is on fire. Because it is.   – Greta Thunberg

4d   Make paragraphs flow.

A paragraph has coherence — or flows — if its details all fit together clearly in a way that readers can easily follow. When you arrange information in a particular order (as described in 3e), you help readers move from one point to another. Regardless of your organization, however, be aware of several other ways to achieve paragraph coherence.

Repetition of key words and phrases

Weaving in repeated key words and phrases — or pronouns pointing to them — not only links sentences but also alerts readers to the importance of those words or phrases in the larger piece of writing. Notice in the following example how the repetition of key words helps hold the paragraph together:

> Over the centuries, shopping has changed in function as well as in style. Before the Industrial Revolution, most consumer goods were sold in open-air markets, customers who went into a shop were expected to buy something, and shoppers were expected to bargain for the best possible price. In the nineteenth century, however, the department store changed the relationship between buyers and sellers. Instead of visiting several market stalls or small shops, customers could now buy a variety of merchandise under the same roof; instead of feeling expected to buy, they were welcome to browse; and instead of bargaining with merchants, they paid a fixed price for each item. All of these changes helped transform shopping from serious requirement to psychological recreation.

Parallelism

Parallel structures can help connect the sentences within a paragraph. As readers, we feel pulled along by the force of the parallel structures in the following example:

> William Faulkner's "Barn Burning" tells the story of a young boy trapped in a no-win situation. If he betrays his father, he loses his family. If he betrays justice, he becomes a fugitive. In trying to free himself from his trap, he does both.

Transitions

Transitions are words such as *so, however*, and *thus* that signal relationships between sentences and paragraphs. Transitions help guide the reader from one idea to another. To understand how important transitions are in directing readers, try reading the following paragraph, from which all transitions have been removed.

A PARAGRAPH WITH NO TRANSITIONS

In "The Fly," Katherine Mansfield tries to show us the real personality of the boss beneath his exterior. The fly helps her to portray this real self. The boss goes through a range of emotions and feelings. He expresses these feelings to a small but determined fly, whom the reader realizes he unconsciously relates to his son. The author basically splits up the story into three parts, with the boss's emotions and actions changing quite measurably. With old Woodifield, with himself, and with the fly, we see the boss's manipulativeness. Our understanding of him as a hard and cruel man grows.

If we work at it, we can figure out the relationship of these sentences to one another, for this paragraph is essentially unified by one major idea. But the lack of transitions results in an abrupt, choppy rhythm; the paragraph lurches from one detail to the next, dragging the confused reader behind. See how much easier the passage is to read and understand with transitions added.

THE SAME PARAGRAPH WITH TRANSITIONS

In "The Fly," Katherine Mansfield tries to show us the real personality of the boss beneath his exterior. The fly in the story's title helps her to portray this real self. In the course of the story, the boss goes through a range of emotions. At the end, he finally expresses these feelings to a small but determined fly, whom the reader realizes he unconsciously relates to his son. To accomplish her goal, the author basically splits up the story into three parts, with the boss's emotions and actions changing measurably throughout. First with old Woodifield, then with himself, and finally with the fly, we see the boss's manipulativeness. With each part, our understanding of him as a hard and cruel man grows.

Quick Help

Making Connections with Transitions

Writers use transitions to show a variety of relationships between ideas: to show contrast (*on the other hand*); to put ideas in sequence (*first*, *next*, *finally*); to counter an idea (*however*, *nevertheless*); to show a causal relationship (*due to*, *as a result*); to compare (*in the same way*, *likewise*, *similarly*); to add an idea (*also*, *in addition*); or to illustrate a point (*for example*). Professor Laura Aull's research shows that expert academic writers use a wider range and variety of transitions than student writers do and that the transitions are closely tied to their purpose. Experts are most likely to use transitional markers to show contrast, sequence, addition, comparison, and illustration. Look closely at the transitional words and phrases in your writing. Is their purpose clear and appropriate? Overusing causal transitions can make your writing seem to jump to conclusions too quickly, while overusing countering transitions can make your writing seem more aggressive than you intend. Take a tip from expert writers and take particular care with transitions that show cause and effect and countering.

Commonly used transitions

TO SIGNAL SEQUENCE AND TIME

after a while, afterward, again, and then, as long as, as soon as, at last, at that time, before, besides, earlier, finally, first . . . second . . . third, immediately, in the meantime, in the past, last, lately, later, meanwhile, next, now, presently, simultaneously, since, so far, soon, still, then, thereafter, until, when

TO ADD IDEAS

again, also, furthermore, in the same way, likewise, moreover, similarly, too

TO SHOW CONTRAST OR COUNTERARGUMENT

although, but, despite, even though, however, in contrast, indeed, in spite of, instead, nevertheless, nonetheless, on one hand . . . on the other hand, on the contrary, regardless, still, though, while, yet

TO SIGNAL EXAMPLES AND ILLUSTRATIONS

for example, for instance, in fact, of course, specifically, such as, the following example, to illustrate

TO SIGNAL CAUSE AND EFFECT

accordingly, as a result, because, consequently, due to, hence, so, then, therefore, thereupon, thus, to this end

TO SIGNAL PLACE

above, adjacent to, below, beyond, closer to, elsewhere, far, farther on, here, near, nearby, opposite to, there, to the left, to the right

TO SIGNAL SUMMARY, REPETITION, OR CONCLUSION

as a result, as has been noted, as I have said, as mentioned earlier, as we have seen, in any event, in conclusion, in other words, in short, on the whole, therefore, to summarize

4e Work on opening and closing paragraphs.

Opening paragraphs

Even a good piece of writing may remain unread if it has a weak opening paragraph. In addition to announcing your topic, an introductory paragraph must engage readers' interest and focus their attention on what is to follow. One common kind of opening paragraph follows a general-to-specific sequence, in which a writer opens with a general statement and then gets more and more specific, concluding with the thesis. The following paragraph illustrates such an opening:

The human organism is adapted to function in face-to-face encounters. We know that face-to-face is the most effective way to pitch woo. And face-to-face is obviously the best way to transact an intimate relationship long term. But while we know this, there's much more to face-to-face interaction than meets the naked eye. And it is of grave importance. We risk losing a great deal in any heavy shift of social traffic onto exclusively electronic media.   – MARIAM THALOS, "Why I Am Not a Friend"

In the Thalos paragraph, the opening sentence introduces a general subject, and the last sentence presents the thesis, which the rest of the essay will develop.

OTHER EFFECTIVE WAYS OF OPENING

- with a quotation: *There is a bumper sticker that reads, "Too bad ignorance isn't painful."* – NIKKI GIOVANNI, "Racism 101"
- with an anecdote: *Social networking pioneer Howard Rheingold begins his digital journalism course each year with a participatory experiment. Shut off your cell phones, he tells his students. Shut your laptop. Now, shut your eyes.* – CATHY DAVIDSON, *Now You See It*
- with a question: *Why are Americans terrified of using nuclear power as a source of energy?*
- with a strong opinion: *Men need a men's movement about as much as women need chest hair.* – JOHN RUSZKIEWICZ, *The Presence of Others*

Concluding paragraphs

A good conclusion wraps up a piece of writing in a satisfying and memorable way. A common and effective strategy for concluding is to restate the central idea (but not word for word), perhaps specifying it in several sentences, and then ending with a much more general statement.

Lastly, and perhaps greatest of all, there was the ability, at the end, to turn quickly from war to peace once the fighting was over. Out of the way these two men [Generals Grant and Lee] behaved at Appomattox came the possibility of a peace of reconciliation. It was a possibility not wholly realized, in the years to come, but which did, in the end, help the two sections to become one nation again . . . after a war whose bitterness might have seemed to make such a reunion wholly impossible. No part of either man's life became him more than the part he played in this brief meeting in the McLean house at Appomattox. Their behavior there put all succeeding generations of Americans in their debt. Two great Americans, Grant and Lee — very different, yet under everything very much alike. Their encounter at Appomattox was one of the great moments of American history.   – BRUCE CATTON, "Grant and Lee: A Study in Contrasts"

OTHER EFFECTIVE WAYS OF CONCLUDING

- with a quotation
- with a question
- with a vivid image
- with a call for action
- with a warning

5   Reviewing, Revising, and Editing

The Roman poet Horace once advised aspiring writers to get distance from their work by putting it away for *nine years*. Although impractical for college writers, Horace's advice holds some truth: putting your draft aside even for a short time can give you more objectivity about your writing.

Make time to review your work (by yourself or with others) and to revise, edit, and proofread. Reviewing calls for reading your draft with a critical eye and asking others to look over your work. Revising involves reworking your draft on the basis of the review, making sure the draft is clear, effective, complete, and well organized. Editing involves attending to sentence-level details.

5a   Review your writing.

After giving yourself and your draft a rest, review the draft by rereading it carefully for meaning, recalling your purpose and audience, reconsidering your stance, and evaluating your organization and use of visuals.

Meaning

When you pick up the draft again, don't sweat the small stuff. Instead, concentrate on your message and on whether you have expressed it clearly. Note any places where the meaning seems unclear.

Purpose

If you responded to an assignment, make sure that you have produced what was asked for. If you set out to prove something, have you succeeded? If you intended to propose a solution to a problem, have you set forth a well-supported solution rather than just an analysis of the problem?

Audience

How appropriately do you address your audience members, given their experiences and expectations? Will you catch their interest, and will they be able to follow your discussion?

Stance

Ask yourself one central question: where are you coming from in this draft? Consider whether your stance appropriately matches the stance you started out with, or whether your stance has legitimately evolved.

Organization

One way to check the organization of your draft is to outline it. After numbering the paragraphs, read through each one, jotting down its main idea. Do the main ideas clearly relate to the thesis and to one another? Can you identify any confusing leaps from point to point? Have you left out any important points?

Genre and media

You decided to write in a particular genre, so think again about why you made that choice. Is writing in this genre the best way to achieve your purpose and reach your audience? Does the draft fulfill the requirements of the genre? Would any content in your draft be more effective presented in another genre — for example, as a print handout instead of a presentation slide? Should you consider "translating" your work into another medium (see Chapters 3 and 20)?

Look closely at any images, audio, and video you have chosen to use. How do they contribute to your draft? Make sure that all visuals and media files are labeled with captions and sources, and remember to refer to visuals and media and to comment on their significance to the rest of your text.

Language, Culture, and Context

Multilingual

Asking an Experienced Writer to Review Your Draft

One good way to make sure that your writing is easy to follow is to have someone else read it. You might ask someone who is experienced in the kind of writing you are working on to read over your draft and to point out language or patterns that are unclear or ineffective.

5b   Get the most from peer review.

In addition to your own critical appraisal and that of your instructor (5c), you will probably want to get responses to your draft from friends, classmates, or colleagues. In a writing course, you may be asked to respond to the work of your peers as well as to seek responses from them.

The role of peer reviewers

One of the main goals of a peer reviewer is to help a writer see a draft differently. When you review a draft, you want to *show* the writer what does and doesn't work about particular aspects of the draft — and where you are still curious or confused. Visually marking the draft can help the writer absorb at a glance the revisions you suggest.

Different stages in the writing process call for a peer reviewer to have different strategies and focus areas.

Early-stage drafts	Intermediate-stage drafts	Late-stage or final drafts
○ Offer direction, options	○ Say which parts of the draft are clear	○ Help with first and last impressions
○ Help the writer think of ways to expand ideas	○ Say which parts of the draft confuse readers	○ Help with sentence construction
○ Ask questions	○ Identify which claims lack sufficient evidence	○ Suggest stronger word choice or a different tone
○ Offer examples	○ Tell the writer if their approach reaches or misses the target audience	○ Say how the format can be improved
○ Help the writer imagine the final draft		
○ Don't focus on grammar	○ Praise and offer constructive criticism	

Language, Culture, and Context

Multilingual

Understanding Peer Review

If you are not used to giving or receiving criticisms directly, you may be uneasy with a classmate's challenges to your work. However, constructive criticism (saying how you might improve a draft) is appropriate to peer review. Your peers will expect you to offer your questions, suggestions, and insights.

PEER REVIEW: WORK WITH A WRITER

Give your full attention to offering as much help as you can.

ASK:

*What does the writer want you to **focus** on for this stage of the draft?*

*Can you restate the **main points** as you see them?*

*What **specific** suggestions do you think will improve the draft?*

Make sure that the writer can move forward when you're finished.

Quick Help

Guidelines for Peer Response

- **Initial thoughts.** What are the main strengths and weaknesses of the draft? What might confuse readers? What is the most important thing the writer says in the draft?
- **Assignment.** Does the draft carry out the assignment?
- **Title and introduction.** Do the title and introduction tell what the draft is about and create interest? How else might the draft begin?
- **Thesis and purpose.** Paraphrase the thesis: *In this paper, the writer will . . .* Does the draft fulfill that promise?
- **Audience.** How does the draft interest and appeal to its audience?
- **Rhetorical stance.** Where does the writer stand? What words indicate the stance?
- **Supporting points.** List the main points, and review them one by one. How well does each point support the thesis? Do any need more explanation? Do any seem confusing or boring?
- **Visuals, media, and design.** Do visuals, if any, add to the key points? Do media files play properly and serve their intended purpose? Is the design clear and effective?
- **Organization and flow.** Is the writing easy to follow? How effective are transitions between sentences and between paragraphs?
- **Conclusion.** Does the draft conclude memorably? Is there another way it might end?

Reviews of Emily Lesk's draft

On the following pages are the first paragraphs of Emily Lesk's draft, as reviewed by two students, Beatrice Kim and Nastassia Lopez. Beatrice and Nastassia reviewed the draft separately and combined their comments on the draft they returned to Emily. As this review shows, Nastassia and Bea agreed on some of the major problems—and good points—in Emily's draft. Their comments on the draft, however, revealed some different responses. You, too, will find that different readers do not always agree on what is effective or ineffective. In addition, you may find that you simply do not agree with their advice. In examining responses to your writing, you can often proceed efficiently by looking first for areas of agreement (*everyone was confused by this sentence—I'd better revise it*) or strong disagreement (*one person said my conclusion was "perfect," and someone else said it "didn't conclude"—better look carefully at that paragraph again*).

Student Writing

All-Powerful Coke

I don't drink Coke. Call me picky for disliking the soda's saccharine aftertaste. Call me cheap for choosing a water fountain over a twelve-ounce aluminum can that costs a dollar from a vending machine but only pennies to produce. Even call me unpatriotic for rejecting the potable god that over the last century has come to represent all the enjoyment and ease to be found in our American way of life. But don't call me a hypocrite when I admit that I still identify with Coke and the Coca-Cola culture.

I have a favorite T-shirt that says "Drink Coca-Cola Classic" in Hebrew. It's Israel's standard tourist fare, like little nested dolls in Russia or painted horses in Scandinavia, and before setting foot in the Promised Land three years ago, I knew where I could find one. The T-shirt shop in the central block of a Jerusalem shopping center did offer other shirt designs ("Maccabee Beer" was a favorite), but that Coca-Cola shirt was what drew in most of the dollar-carrying tourists. I waited almost twenty minutes for mine, and I watched nearly everyone ahead of me say "the Coke shirt" (and "thanks" in Hebrew).

Comment (NL): I'm not sure the title says enough about your argument.

Comment (NL): The first sentence is a good attention-getter.

Comment (BK): The beginning seems kind of abrupt.

Comment (BK): What does this mean? Will other members of your audience know?

Comment (NL): The style of repeating "call me" is good, but I'm not sure the first three have much to do with the rest of the essay.

Comment (NL): Do you need these details? Will any of this be important later?

Comment (NL): One of what? A doll or a horse?

Comment (BK): Saying it in Hebrew would be cool here.

At the time, I never asked why I wanted the shirt. I do know, though, that the reason I wear it often, despite a hole in the right sleeve, has to do with its power as a conversation piece. Few people notice it without asking something like, "Does that say Coke?" I usually smile and nod. They mumble a compliment and we go our separate ways. But rarely does anyone want to know what language the world's most famous logo is written in. And why should they? Perhaps because Coca-Cola is a cultural icon that shapes American identity.

Throughout the company's history, marketing strategies have centered on putting Coca-Cola in scenes of the happy, carefree American life we never stop striving for. What 1950s teenage girl wouldn't long to see herself in the soda shop pictured in a Coca-Cola ad appearing in a 1958 issue of *Seventeen* magazine? A clean-cut, handsome man flirts with a pair of smiling girls as they laugh and drink Coca-Colas. And any girls who couldn't put themselves in that perfect, happy scene could at least buy a Coke for consolation. The malt shop — complete with a soda jerk in a white jacket and paper hat — is a theme that, even today, remains a symbol of Americana.

> **Comment (NL):** This transition works really well. I wasn't sure where this was going, but here you are starting to clue the reader in.

> **Comment (NL):** Good detail! Lots of people can relate to a "conversation piece" shirt.

> **Comment (NL):** Good question! But I don't think the next sentence really answers it.

> **Comment (BK):** Is this the thesis? It kind of comes out of nowhere.

> **Comment (BK):** OK, here I am beginning to understand where your argument is going.

> **Comment (NL):** Maybe this is a little too broad?

> **Comment (BK):** *Any* girls? Really?

The writer's role in peer review

Remember that your reviewers should be acting as coaches, not judges, and that their job is to help you improve your essay as much as possible. Listen to and read their comments carefully. If you don't understand a particular suggestion, ask for clarification, examples, and so on. Remember, too, that reviewers are commenting on your writing, not on *you*, so be open and responsive to what they recommend. But you are the final authority on your essay; you will decide which suggestions to follow and which to disregard.

5c   Consult instructor comments.

Instructor comments on your writing can help you identify mistakes, particularly ones that you make repeatedly, and can point you toward issues that prevent your writing from being as effective as it could be. Whether or not you have a chance to revise a piece of writing, you should look closely at the comments from your instructor.

In responding to student writing, however, instructors sometimes use phrases or comments that are a kind of shorthand — comments that are perfectly clear to the instructor but may not be clear to the students reading them. The instructor comments in the following chart, culled from over a thousand first-year student essays, are among those that you may find puzzling. Beside each comment you'll find tips intended to allow you to revise as your instructor recommends. If your paper includes a puzzling comment that is not listed here, be sure to ask your instructor what the comment means and how you can fix the problem.

Instructor Comment	Actions to Take in Response
thesis not clear	Make sure that you have a main point, and state it directly. The rest of the paper will need to support the main point, too — this problem cannot be corrected by adding a sentence or two. (3c)
trying to do too much *covers too much ground*	Focus your main point more narrowly (4a) so that you can explain your topic fully in a project of the assigned length. You may need to cut back on some material and then provide evidence and details to expand what remains.
hard to follow *not logical* *incoherent* *jumps around* *parts not connected* *transition*	If overall organization is unclear, try mapping or outlining and rearranging your work. (3e) See if transitions and signals or additional explanation will solve the problem.
too general *vague*	Use concrete language and details, and make sure that you have something specific and interesting to say. (Chapter 26) If not, reconsider your topic.
underdeveloped *thin* *sparse*	Add examples and details, and be as specific as possible. (Chapter 26) You may need to do more research. (Chapters 10–12)
what about the *opposition?* *one-sided*	Add information on why some people disagree with you, and represent their views fairly and completely before you refute them. Recognize that reasonable people may hold views that differ from yours. (9g)

Instructor Comment	Actions to Take in Response
repetitive *you've already said this*	Revise any parts of your writing that repeat an argument or point; avoid using the same evidence over and over.
awk *awkward*	Ask a peer or your instructor for suggestions about revising awkward sentences. (Chapters 26–31)
syntax *awkward syntax* *convoluted*	Read the sentence aloud to identify the problem; revise or replace the sentence. (Chapters 26–31)
unclear	Find another way to explain what you mean; add any background information or examples that your audience may need to follow your reasoning.
tone too conversational *not an academic voice* *too informal*	Consider your audience and genre, and revise material that may suggest that you are not serious about the topic, audience, or assignment. (Chapter 26)
pompous *stilted* *stiff*	Make sure you understand the connotations of the words that you use. Revise material that adds nothing to your meaning, no matter how impressive it sounds. (26a)
set up quotation *integrate quotation*	Read the sentence containing the quotation aloud; revise it if it does not make sense as a sentence. Introduce every quotation with information about the source. Explain each quotation's importance to your work. (12b)
your words? *source?* *cite*	Mark all quotations clearly. Cite paraphrases and summaries of others' ideas. Give credit for help from others, and remember that you are responsible for your own work. (Chapter 12)

5d Revise.

Approach comments from peer reviewers or from your instructor in several stages. First, read straight through the comments. Take a few minutes to digest the feedback and get some distance from your work. Then make a revision plan — as elaborate or as simple as you want — that prioritizes the changes needed in your next draft.

If you have comments from more than one reviewer, you may want to begin by making two lists: (1) areas in which reviewers agree on needed changes, and (2) areas in which they disagree. You will then have to make choices about which advice to take and which to ignore from both lists. Next, rank the suggestions you've chosen to address.

Focus on comments about your purpose, audience, stance, thesis, and support. Leave any changes to sentences, words, punctuation, and format for later in the process; your revision of bigger-picture issues comes first.

Be prepared to revise heavily, if necessary; if comments suggest that your thesis isn't working, for example, you may need to change the topic or the entire direction of your text. Heavy revision is not a sign that there's something wrong with your writing; on the contrary, major revision is a common feature of serious, goal-oriented writing.

Once you are satisfied that the revisions adequately address your major concerns, make corrections to sentences, words, and punctuation.

Thesis statement

Make sure that your thesis states the topic clearly and comments on what is particularly significant about the topic (3c). In addition, ask yourself whether the thesis statement is narrowed and focused enough to be thoroughly supported. If not, take time now to refine or limit your thesis further.

When you revise your thesis, remember also to revise the rest of the draft accordingly.

REVISING AND EDITING: READ ALL COMMENTS CAREFULLY

Analyze feedback from your instructor and other readers.

ASK:

What **additional questions** do you have about the feedback?

Which comments are most important and **useful**?

Which comments will point you toward the most improved **next** draft?

Remember: how you respond to suggestions is up to you.

Support

Make sure that each paragraph relates to or supports the thesis statement and that each paragraph has sufficient detail to support the point it is making. Eliminate unnecessary material, and identify sections that need further details or examples.

Organization

Should any sections or paragraphs be moved to clarify your point or support your thesis statement more logically? Are there any paragraphs or parts of paragraphs that don't fit with the essay now or that are unnecessary? Look for confusing leaps or gaps, and identify places where transitions would make the writing easier to follow.

Title, introduction, and conclusion

Does the title give information and draw readers in? Does the introduction attract their interest and present the topic in a way that makes them want to keep reading? Does the conclusion leave readers satisfied or fired up and ready to take action? Because readers notice beginnings and endings more than other parts of a piece of writing, pay special attention to how you introduce and conclude your work.

Visuals, media, and design

As you check what you've written about your topic, you also need to take a close look at the way your text looks and works. Do your visuals, audio, and video (if any) help you make your points? How can you make this content more effective? Do you use design effectively for your genre and medium? Is your text readable and inviting?

Talking the Talk

Revision

"I thought I had revised my assignment, but my instructor said I'd just corrected the typos." It's always a good idea to clarify what *revision* means with a particular instructor. Generally, though, when a writing instructor asks for a revision, minor corrections will not be enough. Plan to review your entire draft, and be prepared to make major changes if necessary. Look for sentence-level errors and typos later, during the editing stage, since these may disappear or change as you revise.

5e Edit.

Once you have revised a draft for content and organization, look closely at your sentences and words. Turning a "blah" sentence into a memorable one—or finding exactly the right word to express a thought—can result in writing that is really worth reading. As with life, variety is the spice of sentences. You can add variety to your sentences by looking closely at their length, structure, and opening patterns.

Sentence length

Too many short sentences, especially one following another, can sound like a series of blasts on a car horn, whereas a steady stream of long sentences may tire or confuse readers. Most writers aim for some variety in the length of their sentences (26d).

Sentence structure

Using only simple sentences can make your writing sound choppy, but overusing compound sentences can result in a singsong rhythm, and strings of long complex sentences may sound—well, overly complex. Try to vary your sentence structure. (See 26d.)

Sentence openings

Most sentences in English follow subject-predicate order and hence open with the subject of an independent clause, as does the sentence you are now reading. But opening sentence after sentence this way results in a jerky, abrupt, or choppy rhythm. You can vary sentence openings by beginning with a dependent clause, a phrase, an adverb, a conjunctive adverb, or a coordinating conjunction (26d).

Emily Lesk's second paragraph tells the story of how she got her Coke T-shirt in Israel. Before she revised her draft, every sentence in this paragraph opened with the subject: *I have a favorite T-shirt, It's Israel's standard tourist fare, I waited.* . . . In her revision, Emily deleted some examples and <u>varied her sentence openings</u> for a dramatic and easy-to-read paragraph:

> <u>Even before</u> setting foot in Israel three years ago, I knew exactly where I could find the Coke T-shirt. The tiny shop in the central block of Jerusalem's Ben Yehuda Street did offer other designs, but the one with a bright white "Drink Coca-Cola Classic" written in Hebrew cursive across the chest was what drew in most of the dollar-carrying tourists. <u>While waiting</u> almost twenty minutes for my shirt, I watched nearly every customer ahead of me ask for "the Coke shirt, *todah rabah* [thank you very much]."

Sentences beginning with it and there

As you go over the opening sentences of your draft, look especially at those beginning with *it* or *there*. Sometimes these words can create a special emphasis, as in *It was a dark and stormy night*. But they can also appear too often. Another, more subtle problem with these openings is that they may be used to avoid taking responsibility for a statement. The following sentence can be improved by editing:

> ► ~~It is necessary to~~ raise student fees.
>
> The university must raise student fees.

Tone

Tone refers to the attitude a writer's language conveys toward the topic and the audience. In examining the tone of your draft, think about the topic, your own attitude toward it, and that of your intended audience. Does your language create the tone you want to achieve (humorous, serious, impassioned, and so on), and is that tone appropriate, given your audience and topic?

Word choice

Word choice — or diction — offers writers an opportunity to put their personal stamp on a piece of writing. Becoming aware of the kinds of words you use should help you get the most mileage out of each word. Check for connotations, or associations, of words and make sure you consider how any use of slang, jargon, or emotional language may affect your audience (see Chapter 26).

Spell checkers

While these software tools won't catch every spelling error or identify all problems of style, they can be useful. Most professional writers use their spell checkers religiously. Remember, however, that spell checkers are limited; they don't recognize most proper names, foreign words, or specialized language, and they do not recognize homonym errors (*there* vs. *their*, for example).

Document design

Before you produce a copy for final proofreading, reconsider one last time the format and the "look" you want your text to have. This is one last opportunity to think carefully about the visual appearance of your final draft.

For more on document design, see Chapter 18. For more on the design conventions of different disciplines, see 54e (MLA), 58e (APA), or 62c (*Chicago*).

Proofreading the final draft

Take time for one last, careful proofreading, which means reading to correct any errors or other inconsistencies in spelling and punctuation. To proofread most effectively, read through the copy aloud, making sure that you've

Quick Help

Word Choice

- Are the nouns primarily abstract and general or *concrete* and *specific*? Too many abstract and general nouns can result in boring prose.

- Are there too many nouns in relation to the number of verbs? This sentence is heavy and boring: *The effect of the overuse of nouns in writing is the placement of strain on the verbs.* Instead, say this: *Overusing nouns places a strain on the verbs.*

- How many verbs are forms of *be* — *be*, *am*, *is*, *are*, *was*, *were*, *being*, *been*? If *be* verbs account for more than about a third of your total verbs, you are probably overusing them.

- Are verbs *active* wherever possible? Passive verbs are harder to read and remember than active ones. Although the passive voice has many uses, your writing will gain strength and energy if you use active verbs.

- Are your words *appropriate*? Check to be sure they are not too fancy — or too casual.

used punctuation marks correctly, that all sentences are complete (unless you've used intentional fragments or run-ons for special effects) — and that no words are missing. Then go through the copy again, this time reading backward so that you can focus on each individual word and its spelling.

A student's revised draft

Student Writer

Emily Lesk

Following are the first three paragraphs from Emily Lesk's edited and proofread draft that she submitted to her instructor. Compare these paragraphs with those from her reviewed draft in 5b.

Emily Lesk

Professor Arraéz

Electric Rhetoric

November 15, 2018

Red, White, and Everywhere

America, I have a confession to make: I don't drink Coke. But don't call me a hypocrite just because I am still the proud owner of a bright red shirt that advertises it. Just call me an American.

Even before setting foot in Israel three years ago, I knew exactly where I could find the Coke T-shirt. The tiny shop in the central block of Jerusalem's Ben Yehuda Street did offer other designs, but the one with a bright white "Drink Coca-Cola Classic" written in Hebrew cursive across the chest was what drew in most of the dollar-carrying tourists. While waiting almost twenty minutes for my shirt (depicted in fig. 1), I watched nearly every customer ahead of me ask for "the Coke shirt, *todah rabah* [thank you very much]."

At the time, I never thought it strange that I wanted one, too. After having absorbed sixteen years of Coca-Cola propaganda through everything from NBC's Saturday morning cartoon lineup to the concession stand at Camden Yards (the Baltimore Orioles' ballpark), I associated the shirt with singing along to the "Just for the Taste of It" jingle and with America's favorite pastime, not with a brown fizzy beverage I refused to consume. When I later realized the immensity of Coke's corporate power, I felt

Fig. 1. Hebrew Coca-Cola T-shirt. Personal photograph by author.

somewhat manipulated, but that didn't stop me from wearing the shirt. I still don it often, despite the growing hole in the right sleeve, because of its power as a conversation piece. Few Americans notice it without asking something like "Does that say Coke?" I usually smile and nod. Then they mumble a one-word compliment, and we go our separate ways. But rarely do they want to know what language the internationally recognized logo is written in. And why should they? They are interested in what they can relate to as Americans: a familiar red-and-white logo, not a foreign language. Through nearly a century of brilliant advertising strategies, the Coca-Cola Company has given Americans not only a thirst-quenching beverage but a cultural icon that we have come to claim as our own.

6 Reflecting

Research demonstrates a connection between careful reflection and learning: thinking back on what you've learned and assessing it help make that learning stick and help you use the knowledge gained in other courses and other assignments. As a result, first-year college writing courses are increasingly encouraging students to take time for such reflection. Whether or not your instructor asks you to write a formal reflection, whenever you finish a major piece of writing or a writing course, you should make time to think back over the experience and see what lessons you can learn from it.

6a Reflect to present your work effectively.

You may find it useful (or you may be required) to reflect on the work you have done for a course as part of your preparation for submitting a portfolio of your best work.

Portfolio guidelines

In preparing a portfolio, use these tips:

- *Consider your purpose and audience.* Do you want to fulfill course requirements, show work to a prospective employer, keep a record of what you've done for personal reasons, or something else? Answering these questions will help you make decisions about the portfolio's contents and delivery.

- *Based on the portfolio's purpose, decide on the number of entries.* You may decide to include a wide range of materials — from essays, problem sets, and photos to web texts, multimedia presentations, a résumé, or anything else that is relevant — if readers can select only the pieces that interest them. For a portfolio that will be read from beginning to end, however, you should limit yourself to five to seven examples of your writing — work that shows your strengths as a writer.

- *Consider organization.* What arrangement will make most sense to readers — chronological order, by genre, or by topic?

- *Think carefully about layout and design.* Will you include a menu, a table of contents, or appendices? How will you use color, font and type size, and other elements of design to enhance your portfolio (see Chapter 18)? Remember to label and date each piece of writing in the portfolio to help readers follow along easily. For print portfolios, number pages in consecutive order.

- **Edit and proofread** each piece in your portfolio and the reflective statement. Ask for responses from peers or an instructor.

Reflective statements

One of the most common writing assignments today is a reflective statement — often in the form of a letter, memo, or home page — that explains and analyzes a student's work in a writing course.

To create a reflective statement, think carefully about the impression it should give, and make sure your tone and style set the stage appropriately. Reflect on the strengths and weaknesses of your writing, using specific examples to provide evidence for each point you make. What are the most important things you have learned about writing — and about yourself as a writer — during the course?

If the reflective statement introduces your portfolio, follow your instructor's guidelines carefully. Unless asked to do otherwise, describe the portfolio's contents and explain why you have chosen each piece.

6b A student's reflective statement

Here is a shortened version of the cover letter that James Kung wrote to accompany his first-year writing portfolio.

Student Writer

James Kung

December 6, 2018

Dear Professor Ashdown:

"Writing is difficult and takes a long time." This simple yet powerful statement has been uttered so many times in our class that it has essentially become our motto. During this class, my persuasive writing skills have improved dramatically, thanks to many hours spent writing, revising, polishing, and thinking about my topic. The various drafts, revisions, and other materials in my portfolio show this improvement.

I entered this first-quarter Writing and Rhetoric class with both strengths and weaknesses. I have always written fairly well-organized essays. However, despite this strength, I struggled throughout the term to narrow and define the various aspects of my research-based argument.

The first aspect of my essay that I had trouble narrowing and defining was my major claim, or my thesis statement. In my "Proposal for Research-Based Argument," I proposed to argue about the case of Wen Ho Lee, the Los Alamos scientist accused of copying restricted government documents. I stated, "The Wen Ho Lee incident deals with the persecution of not only one man, but a whole ethnic group." You commented that the statement was a "sweeping claim" that would be "hard to support."

I spent weeks trying to rework that claim. Finally, as seen in my "Writer's Notebook 10/16/18," I realized that I had chosen the Lee case because of my belief that the political inactivity of Asian Americans contributed to the case against Lee. Therefore, I decided to focus on this issue in my thesis. Later I once again revised my claim, stating that the political inactivity did not cause but rather contributed to racial profiling in the Wen Ho Lee case.

I also had trouble defining my audience. I briefly alluded to the fact that my audience was a "typical American reader." However, I later decided to address my paper to an Asian American audience for two reasons. First, it would establish a greater ethos for myself as a Chinese American. Second, it would enable me to target the people the Wen Ho Lee case most directly affects: Asian Americans. As a result, in my final research-based argument, I was much more sensitive to the needs and concerns of my audience, and my audience trusted me more.

I hope to continue to improve my writing of research-based arguments. Sincerely,

James Kung

James Kung

6c   Reflect to learn.

Careful reflection turns out to be a key element in the move from writing for social reasons to writing for a wider public to accomplish bigger goals. When you reflect on your writing, you help ensure that what you have learned *transfers* — that is, that you will be able to use what you've learned in other disciplines and situations. Without time for reflection, you may feel that you are plunging from one assignment to the next, trying desperately to keep ahead of the syllabus, without being able to assimilate what you are learning. Try to make time to think about questions like these after every important piece of writing you do, either for school or for other purposes.

- What lessons have you learned from writing — from an individual piece of writing or an entire course?
- From what you have learned, what can you apply to the work you will do for other classes and to the writing you do for personal reasons?
- What aspect of your writing do you feel most confident about — and why do you feel this way?
- What aspect of your writing needs additional work, and what plans do you have for improving?
- How has writing helped you clarify your thinking, extend your knowledge, or deepen your understanding?
- Identify a favorite passage in your writing; try to articulate what you like about it.
- How would you describe your development as a writer?
- What goals do you have for yourself as a writer?

6d   A student's reflective blog post

Student Thanh Nguyen created a political poster for a course on immigration. On his personal blog, he posted the image that he created with a few reflective notes about what he had learned. Here is the image, along with a portion of his post:

It's not too obvious what I was trying to get at in the poster, which is my own fault in the design process. I replaced the cherubs/angels from Michelangelo's *Creation of Adam* with ICE agents and politicians to comment on their anti-immigrant practices. I guess I just wanted to address popular rhetoric dehumanizing undocumented folks in this country. They're people, too, you know? With families, lives, hopes, dreams, fears, and beating hearts. Yet so many families are fractured because some children are forbidden to join their parents when deported, so many people are denied due process and proper trials because apparently you don't get them if you don't have a sheet of paper to legitimize your existence, and a lot of other messed-up stuff. As an artistic response to that, I just threw in a decapitated Statue of Liberty (lol stole/appropriated it from Cloverfield) and what I think she should say. . . .

▲ **For visual analysis** This image shows a person noticing a variety of transportation options. Which option would you choose in this situation, and why? Critical thinking requires you to analyze and make choices, and effective argument provides good reasons for making a particular choice.

Critical Thinking and Argument

To repeat what others have said requires education; to challenge it requires brains.

— MARY PETTIBONE POOLE

7 Critical Reading

If you list all the reading you do in a day, you will no doubt find that you are reading a lot — and that you are reading in different ways for different reasons, and using different tools and media. Reading critically has always meant questioning, commenting, analyzing, and reflecting thoughtfully on a text — whether it's a white paper for a psychology class, a graphic novel, a Super Bowl ad, a business email, or a YouTube video. But in a time of 24/7 newsfeeds, misinformation, and fake news, critical reading demands *defensive* reading strategies that will help protect you from being manipulated by the texts you read. In addition, critical reading today calls on readers to engage with and understand messages from people and groups who may be very different from them. So while it's important to remain skeptical until you're sure a text is accurate, it's also important to remember that there are often real people on the other side of the screen, people you want to engage with respectfully and responsibly (see 8b and 9g). In any case, most important to critical reading is *attention*: focusing intently and purposefully on any text you approach. And remember that reading and writing are closely intertwined: if you want to become a better writer, you need to become a better reader.

7a Consider reading collaboratively.

Especially for difficult or high-stakes reading, there's nothing better than tackling the task with others. Research shows, in fact, that if you read and take notes on an assigned reading in small groups, understanding of the text improves, as do test scores based on the material.

TIPS FOR EFFECTIVE COLLABORATIVE READING

- Join two or three classmates to form a reading group; make sure you all know what the specific reading assignment is and when it is due. Trade contact information.
- Decide whether you will proceed in person or online. If in person, find a convenient time to meet; if online, set a deadline by which each member will have participated.
- Professor of history Aiala Levy asks her students to set up a shared folder on Google Drive and then use a Google Doc to share their

notes as they read, annotate, and respond to assigned texts. Exchanging views on a text in this way helps you see perspectives or points of view you might not have considered and gives you a chance to test out your own ideas about what you are reading.

- Use differences of opinion on the text's ideas and meanings to sharpen your thinking.

7b Preview the text; consider the source.

Find out all you can about a text before beginning to look closely at it, considering its context, author or sponsor, subject, genre, and design.

PREVIEWING THE CONTEXT

- Where have you encountered the work? Are you encountering the work in its original context? For example, an essay in a collection of readings may have been previously published in a magazine; a speech you watch on YouTube may have been delivered originally to a live or televised audience.
- Is there reason to suspect the work is fake? For example, a retweet you receive from someone you don't know may have been taken out of context or be false, or a photo you find in a blog post may have been altered from its original.
- What can you infer from the original or current context of the work about its intended audience and purpose?

LEARNING ABOUT THE AUTHOR OR SPONSOR

- What information can you find about the author or sponsor of the text?
- What purpose, expertise, values, and possible agenda might you expect this person or sponsor to have? What assumptions do you think the author or sponsor holds? How trustworthy is this person or persons and how do you know?

PREVIEWING THE SUBJECT

- What do you know about the subject of the text?
- What do you expect the main point to be? Why?
- What opinions may you already have about the subject?

- What unspoken assumptions underlie your opinions: that is, where do your opinions come from and how informed and reasonable are they?
- What would you like to learn about the subject?

CONSIDERING THE TITLE, MEDIUM, GENRE, AND DESIGN

- What does the title (or caption or other heading) indicate?
- In what medium (or media) does the work appear? Is it a video on YouTube? a printed advertising brochure? a speech stored in iTunes? an animated cartoon on television? or some combination of media? What role does the medium play in achieving the purpose and connecting to the audience?
- What is the genre of the text — and what can it help illuminate about the intended audience or purpose? Why might the authors or creators have chosen this genre?
- How is the text presented? What do you notice about its formatting, use of color, visuals or illustrations, overall design, general appearance, and other design features?

Student preview of an assigned text

Samyuktha Comandur and Caroline Fairey, students in a first-year writing class, read and analyzed "The Challenge of (Re)Inventing Stories," by Andrea A. Lunsford. Some of the preview notes they made before reading the text appear below. (See 7c–e for both the text and the additional steps in the critical reading process from these students.)

Student Writer
Samyuktha Comandur

Student Writer
Caroline Fairey

PREVIEW OF ANDREA LUNSFORD'S TEXT, "THE CHALLENGE OF (RE)INVENTING STORIES"

- The text is a speech delivered on July 1, 2018, to members of the Bread Loaf Teacher Network, a community of teachers of writing. Andrea Lunsford has been a part of the BLTN for many years—she is speaking to an audience of her peers.

Information on context

- This version of the speech is a transcript—a reader might interpret certain phrases differently than someone who listened to the live speech. Look out for rhetorical devices that work best orally!

- Searched Google for Lunsford's credentials. She's a professor of writing and rhetoric at Stanford, and has over 9,000 books, chapters, essays, studies, and articles credited to her on Google Scholar. She is also author of the textbook that our school uses in its first-year writing program.

  About the author

- The genre is a persuasive speech. Lunsford wants her audience to be inspired to take action after hearing her evidence.

  Note about the genre

- Includes lots of references to current social media movements and even some hashtags. Even a reader who wasn't sure about the date of this speech could easily identify it as contemporary.

- The word "reinventing" in the title is formatted unusually. I wonder if Lunsford will talk about "inventing," "reinventing," or both?

  Note about the formatting of the title

- The main topic will probably be something about seeing stories differently. Since the speech is persuasive, Lunsford also includes a call-to-action at the end, which suggests a specific course of action for her audience to take.

  A prediction

7c   Where reading meets writing: Annotate and respond.

After you've carefully previewed a text, you're ready to read it — with pen or mouse in hand. So while you are reading, you will also be writing: making notes in margins or on sticky notes, raising questions, marking confusing passages, and so on. As you do so, you'll be paying very close attention to the content of the text and to the points the author is making, as well as to the intended audience, the genre and design of the piece, the context in which it was written, and the author's stance and tone. Pay attention to the key terms and ideas and the author's use of evidence. After your first reading, does the text leave questions unanswered?

CRITICAL READING: READ CAREFULLY

What do you find out by going through the text from start to finish?

ASK:

*How does the text **fit** with your expectations?*

*What are the **major points** in the text? How are they supported?*

*How well do you **understand** the content?*

Get everything you can from your first reading.

Student annotation of an assigned text

Following is an excerpt from "The Challenge of (Re)Inventing Stories," a presentation delivered by Andrea A. Lunsford at a teachers' workshop, with annotations made by students Samyuktha Comandur and Caroline Fairey.

The Challenge of (Re)Inventing Stories

ANDREA A. LUNSFORD

Bread Loaf / BLTN / 2018

Why is it important to me to think of rhetorical traditions, and of the work we do as teachers of writing and rhetoric, in terms of narrative, of story? In the most simple terms, because story is the universal genre, because stories lie at the base of all cultures, because our lives are attempts to tell particular stories that can guide us, and because, in Anne Haas Dyson and Celia Genishi's telling book title, we have a *Need for Story.*

> **Caroline Fairey:** The speaker uses repetition ("because . . . because . . . because . . .") as a device for emphasis and to respond to her own opening question.

I want to argue not only that it is important to understand, challenge, explore, and remake the stories we tell about rhetoric, its origins, principles, and practices—but also because it is important to take on the *responsibility* for story, for narrative, and for the way stories shape our experience of the world. Along with Lyotard and

> **Samyu Comandur:** This example is aimed at people who keep up with the scholarly community, but it may be unfamiliar to students like me who are not aware of Lyotard's work as a 20th-century philosopher. References to other scholars and thinkers help us see Lunsford's credibility.

scholars in many other disciplines, we have interrogated and rejected the master narratives that have held enormous power over our lives. We know in our bones what Nigerian writer Chimamanda Ngozi Adichie calls "The Danger of a Single Story," what happens when whole groups of richly complex people are reduced to a single narrative. In her remarkable 2009 TED talk of that title, Adichie tells about her life as a child in

> **Caroline Fairey:** Lunsford uses "we" here to remind the audience that she is a part of their peer group, not a distant authority.

Nigeria, growing up reading British and American stories and writing her own stories with characters that all had "fair hair and blue eyes." That was a single story that shaped her way of reading and writing. In her talk, she says it's fairly simple to create a single story: just "show people as one thing and one thing only, over and over again, and that is what they will become." Adichie notes that stories are enmeshed in structures of power, that how they are told, when they are told, how many are told are all dependent on power, and the ultimate power is to tell the story of another person—but to make it THE definitive story of that person. Or that people. Or that culture.

Perhaps all times have been defined by struggles over stories—who gets to tell them and who has the power to create and reify them. But certainly our own time is rife with the struggle over stories, over narratives. In early 2018, even military officials in this country were talking about a "war of narratives." And we have witnessed attempts to create a "single story" of past American greatness and the steps some see as "necessary" to recapture it.

On a more hopeful note, of course, we have only to think of #OccupyWallSt, #BlackLivesMatter, #MeToo, #TimesUp, #indigenouswomenrise, #lagenteunida, and many others, to see efforts to create narratives that can displace a single story about groups of people and cultures. In a recent issue of *Anthropology News*, Anna Babel traces the forces at work in the discourse of #MeToo and shows how they create a story that has had effects internationally. As she says in "The Invisible Walls of the Whisper Network,"

> **Samyu Comandur:** To make her message more relatable, the speaker uses a variety of social media movements that a younger audience might be familiar with.

> #MeToo does not *create* a community; it opens an existing community to public discussion. The #MeToo hashtag asks people to open their eyes and ears to stories they may have once been able to ignore. It might be easy to ignore or dismiss one woman, but can you discount the stories of nearly every woman you know?

I want all of us to take on the project not only of examining and challenging stories that crush dreams and choke freedoms, but also to work hard at creating and maintaining stories that are worthy of our best vision of ourselves. What I want is for us to pursue what I am calling

> **Caroline Fairey:** These verbs, "crush" and "choke," conjure images of violence, even though the nouns are abstract. It definitely helps the audience feel the weight of these words and think about what's at stake.

narrative justice. Because I don't see how we can ever achieve social justice, for example, when the narratives in which people are trapped and silenced simply will not allow for it. Hence the need for *just narratives,* which can then lay the groundwork for social justice.

I believe our work can stand as testimony to a future in which scholars and teachers and practitioners of rhetoric will continue to broaden and deepen the scope of rhetoric, that we will link hands, and stories, with rhetors around the globe, to listen carefully and respectfully to those who argue for single narratives, but then to resist the dangerous narratives we hear daily: "only guns can keep us safe," "immigrants are criminals," "climate change is a hoax." We ignore or dismiss such stories at our peril. Instead, we need to listen to them, to understand them, to trace the roots of their power, and then work to check them. Against them, we are already at work creating inclusive and respectful stories that reflect our best selves, our best values.

> **Samyu Comandur:** The speaker uses these examples because she seems confident that her audience will agree that these narratives are dangerous.

> **Caroline Fairey:** Or was this list written to make them examine their own "single-narrative" beliefs?

7d Summarize the main ideas.

When you feel that you have read and thoroughly understood a text, try to summarize the content in your own words. A summary *briefly* captures the main ideas of a text and omits information that is less important. Try to identify the key points in the text, find the essential evidence supporting those points, and explain the contents concisely and fairly, so that a reader unfamiliar with the original can make sense of it all. Deciding what to leave out can make summarizing a tricky task — but mastering this skill can serve you well in all the reading you do in your academic, professional, and civic life. To test your understanding — and to avoid unintentional plagiarism — it's wise to put the text aside while you write your summary. (For more information on writing a summary, see 11b.)

Talking the Talk

Critical Thinking

"Are criticizing and thinking critically the same thing?" *Criticize* can sometimes mean "find fault with," but you don't have to be negative to think critically. Instead, critical thinking means asking good questions — and not simply accepting what you see at first glance. By asking not only what words and images mean, but also how meaning gets across, critical thinkers consider why a text makes a particular claim, what writers may be leaving out, and how to tell whether evidence is accurate and believable. If you're considering questions like these, then you're thinking critically.

Student summary of an assigned text

Students Samyuktha Comandur and Caroline Fairey, whose critical reading notes appear in this chapter, summarized the "Challenge" speech that is printed in 7c. Here is Samyu's summary:

Student Writing

In "The Challenge of (Re)Inventing Stories," a speech given at a teacher's conference, Andrea Lunsford argues for the examination and rejection of the single, simplistic stories that describe human experience. Lunsford uses the occasion of speaking to a group of educators as a powerful call to action, and she references philosophers, literary figures, and linguists to help her do so. The social consequences of falling prey to simplistic narratives are made clear; Lunsford suggests that if we do not pursue "narrative justice" and give individuals and groups the opportunity to voice their experiences, they will not be heard and will be unlikely to grow beyond the circumstances and stories that now trap them. According to Lunsford, all immigrants, for example, might continue to be labeled as "criminals." This speech highlights the responsibility of the educators, scholars, and speakers to create more inclusive environments for stories to be told and to question power structures that allow single narratives to define whole groups of people.

7e   Analyze and reflect on the text.

When you feel that you understand the meaning of a text, move on to your analysis — your overall interpretation of the text or some aspect of it — by asking additional questions about the text.

ANALYZING IDEAS AND EXAMPLES

- What are the main points in this text? Are they implied or explicitly stated?
- Which points do you agree with? Which do you disagree with? Why?
- Does anything in the text surprise you? Why, or why not?
- What kinds of examples does the text use? What other kinds of evidence does the text offer to back up the main points? Can you think of other examples or evidence that should have been included?
- How does the text get its meaning across?
- Are viewpoints other than those of the author or creator included and treated fairly?
- How trustworthy and valid are the sources the text cites or refers to?
- What assumptions does the text make? Are those assumptions valid?

CRITICAL READING: ANALYZE

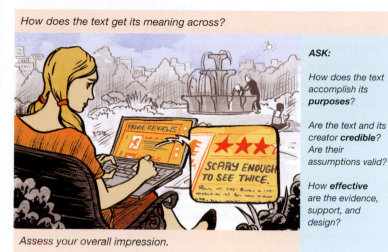

How does the text get its meaning across?

ASK:

How does the text accomplish its **purposes**?

Are the text and its creator **credible**? Are their assumptions valid?

How **effective** are the evidence, support, and design?

Assess your overall impression.

ANALYZING FOR OVERALL IMPRESSION

- Do the authors achieve their purpose? Why, or why not?
- What intrigues, puzzles, or irritates you about the text? Why?
- What else would you like to know?

Student analysis of an assigned text

After previewing, reading, annotating, and summarizing the text, students Samyuktha Comandur and Caroline Fairey analyzed the text. Here is Caroline's analysis:

In "The Challenge of (Re)Inventing Stories," Andrea Lunsford, Stanford University professor and long-time member and teacher with the Bread Loaf Teacher Network, turns a scholarly topic into a compelling call-to-action. She pairs powerful word choice and inclusive rhetoric with established, well-known sources, and engages in a long-standing tradition of storytelling practices. Ultimately, she is able to lead her audience to an effective and surprising conclusion.

As a presenter at a conference for teachers of writing and rhetoric, Lunsford already possesses authority, but she builds her credibility through referencing the authority of others.

Student Writing

Captures the presenter's purpose

Student writer's thesis

The audience of this speech—teachers of writing and rhetoric from around the country—would no doubt be familiar with the content of Adichie's famous TED talk. Both the TED stage and popular magazines like *Anthropology Now*, which Lunsford references later, toe the line between scholarly and popular. The speaker's references to current popular social media movements show the audience that she is also tuned in to popular interpretations of storytelling and rhetoric as well as academic ones.

Notes how the presenter is in tune with her audience

Lunsford uses several other rhetorical techniques to win the favor of her audience. The repeated use of the first-person plural pronoun, "we," emphasizes both the connection among teachers of writing and rhetoric from all backgrounds and the speaker's own inclusion in the peer group that she is addressing. She also repeatedly uses parallelism and repetition to drive her strongest points home. Repetition and parallel structures can make any piece of writing more powerful, but they are particularly effective with speeches because they remind the audience of the important points and slow down the delivery for emphasis.

Notes effect of specific strategies the presenter uses

In a sense, Lunsford supports her main argument through what she is doing even more than what she is saying. She uses more than one story (Adichie, Babel) to inform the audience of the importance of multiple points of view. She also adapts some of the elements of a good story—the very narrative elements that inform every aspect of our lives, according to this speech—to create the speech itself. The third and fourth paragraphs, specifically, feature the appearance of conflict, escalation, and hope in the face of a great danger. The first-person plural and word choice also play a role in creating a sense of story throughout the speech; the "we" becomes a united front not just in understanding, but in joining forces to combat the "single story." Choosing phrases like "crush dreams," "choke freedoms," and "resist dangerous narratives" gives a sense of urgency, of the real threat that single stories pose.

References to specific passages strengthen the analysis

Lunsford's speech ends with a surprising call to action. Instead of calling for the eradication of the single story, she asks her audience to consider where such stories come from and to work with empathy, not force, to dismantle them. If she had started out with this idea of "listening carefully and respectfully to those who argue for single narratives," the argument might have been ineffective with an audience of her peers. But since the speaker prefaced her final point with both credible sources and compelling, familiar narrative structures, the point is likely received by the audience as both a well-thought-out scholarly reaction and a viable way of inspiring her audience to seek narrative justice.

7f   Think critically about visual texts.

You can use the steps given in 7b–e to read any kind of text, from a scholarly article for a research project to an Instagram image. You may be at least as accustomed to reading visual texts as you are to reading words, whether or not you take time to make a formal analysis of what you see. But pausing to look closely and reflect on how a visual text works can make you more aware of how visuals convey information and provoke thought or action.

On p. 74, a Pulitzer Prize–winning photograph (by Craig F. Walker of the *Denver Post*) appears with its caption. This image appeared as part of a series documenting the experiences of a Colorado teenager, Ian Fisher, who joined the U.S. Army to fight in Iraq.

Talking the Talk

Visual Texts

"How can an image be a text?" In its traditional sense, a *text* involves words on paper. But now we spend at least as much time reading and analyzing images — including moving images — as we spend on printed words. So it makes sense to broaden the definition of *text* to include anything that sends a message. That's why images, ads, videos, films, and the like are often called *visual texts*.

CRAIG F. WALKER/DENVER POST/GETTY IMAGES

During a weekend home from his first assignment at Fort Carson, Colorado, Ian walked through a Denver-area mall with his new girlfriend, Kayla Spitzlberger, on December 15, 2007, and asked whether she wanted to go ring shopping. She was excited, but working out the financing made him nervous. They picked out the engagement ring in about five minutes, but Ian wouldn't officially propose until Christmas Day in front of her family. The couple had met in freshman math class but never really dated until now. The engagement would end before Valentine's Day.

An analysis of this photograph made the following points:

Student Writing

The couple are in the center of the photo—and at the center of our attention. But at this moment of choosing an engagement ring, they do not look "engaged" with each other. Kayla looks excited but uncertain, as if she knows that Ian feels doubts, but she hopes he will change his mind. She is looking right at him, with her body leaning toward him but her head leaning away: she looks very tentative. Ian is looking away from Kayla, and the expression on his face suggests that he's already having second thoughts about the expense of the ring (we see his wallet on the counter by his elbow) and perhaps even about asking Kayla to marry him. The accompanying caption helps us interpret the image, telling us about the couple's brief history together and

Notes what is foregrounded in image and relates it to "main point" of visual

Analyzes why they "do not look 'engaged' with each other"

noting that the engagement will last less than two months after this moment. But the message comes through pretty clearly without words.

Ian and Kayla look as if they're trying on roles in this photograph. She looks ready to take the plunge, and he is resisting. These attitudes conform to stereotypical gender roles for a man and woman considering marriage (or going shopping, for that matter). The woman is expected to want the marriage and the ring; the man knows that he shouldn't show too much enthusiasm about weddings and shopping. It's hard for the reader to tell whether Ian and Kayla really feel that they are making good or careful choices for their situation at this moment or whether they're just doing what they think they're supposed to do under the circumstances.

The reader also can't tell how the presence of the photographer, Craig F. Walker, affected the couple's actions. The photo is part of a series of images documenting Ian Fisher's life after joining the military, so Walker had probably spent a lot of time with Ian before this photo was taken. Did Ian want to give a particular impression of himself on this day? Were he and Kayla trying on "adult" roles in this situation? Were they feeling pressure to produce a memorable moment for the camera? And what was Walker thinking when he accompanied them to the mall and took this photograph? Did he foresee the end of their engagement when he captured this revealing moment? What was his agenda?

7g   A student's critical reading of a text

Following is an excerpt of a student essay written by Shuq-iao Song, based on her critical reading of Alison Bechdel's graphic novel *Fun Home: A Family Tragicomic*. Shuqiao's critical reading involved looking closely at the words, at the images, and at how the words and images together create a very complex story. For more on Shuqiao Song's slide presentation of this essay, see pp. 206–12.

Student Writer

Shuqiao Song

Song 1

Shuqiao Song

Dr. Andrea Lunsford

English 87N

13 March 2014

Residents of a DysFUNctional *HOME*

Introduces author of the work she is discussing, along with her major topic

In a 2008 online interview, comic artist Alison Bechdel remarked, "I love words, and I love pictures. But especially, I love them together—in a mystical way that I can't even explain" ("Stuck"). Indeed, in her graphic novel memoir, *Fun Home: A Family Tragicomic,* text and image work together in a mystical way: text *and* image. But using both image and text results not in a simple summation but in a strange relationship—as strange as the relationship between Alison Bechdel and her father. These strange pairings have an alluring quality that makes Bechdel's *Fun Home* compelling; for her, both text and image are necessary. As Bechdel tells and shows us, alone, words can fail; alone, images deceive. Yet

Student writer's thesis statement

her life story ties both concepts inextricably to her memories and revelations such that only the interplay of text and image offers the reader the rich complexity, honesty, and possibilities in Bechdel's quest to understand and find closure for the past.

The idea that words are insufficient is not new—certainly we have all felt moments when language simply fails us and we are at a loss for words, moments like being "left . . . wordless" by "the infinite gradations of color in a fine sunset" (Bechdel, *Fun* 150). In those wordless moments, we strain to express just what we mean. Writers are especially aware of what is lost between word and meaning; Bechdel's comment on the translation of Proust's *À la Recherche du Temps Perdu* is a telling example of the troubling gap:

> After Dad died, an updated translation of Proust came out.
> *Remembrance of Things Past* was retitled *In Search of Lost*
> *Time.* The new title is a more literal translation

Song 3

The Bechdels' elaborately restored house is the gilded, but tense, context of young Alison's familial relationships and a metaphor for her father's deceptions. "He used his skillful artifice not to make things, but to make things appear to be what they were not," Bechdel notes alongside an image of her father taking a photo of their family, shown in fig. 1 (*Fun* 16). The scene represents the nature of her father's artifice; her father is *posing* a photo, an image of their family.

First example in support of thesis

Fig. 1. Alison's father posing a family photo (Bechdel, *Fun* 16).

In that same scene, Bechdel also shows her own sleight of hand; she manipulates the scene and reverses her father's role and her own to show young Alison taking the photograph of the family and her father posing in Alison's place (fig. 2). In the image, young Alison symbolizes Bechdel in the present—looking back through the camera lens to create a portrait of her family. But unlike her father, she isn't using false images to deceive. Bechdel overcomes the treason of images by confessing herself as an "artificer" to her audience (*Fun* 16). Bechdel doesn't . . .

Second example in support of thesis

Fig. 2. Alison and her father trade places (Bechdel, *Fun* 17).

Song 8

Works Cited

Uses
MLA style
appropriately

Bechdel, Alison. *Fun Home: A Family Tragicomic*. Houghton Mifflin,
2006.

---. "An Interview with Alison Bechdel." Interview by Hillary
Chute. *MFS Modern Fiction Studies,* vol. 52, no. 4, Winter 2006,
pp. 1004-13. *Project Muse,* doi:10.1353/mfs.2007.0003.

---. "Stuck in Vermont 109: Alison Bechdel." Interview by Eva
Sollberger. *YouTube,* 13 Dec. 2008, www.youtube.com/
watch?v=nWBFYTmpC54.

Chabani, Karim. "Double Trajectories: Crossing Lines in *Fun Home.*"
GRAAT, no. 1, Mar. 2007, pp. 1-14.

Gardner, Jared. "Autography's Biography, 1972-2007." *Biography,*
vol. 31, no. 1, Winter 2008, pp. 1-26. *Project Muse,*
doi:10.1353/bio.0.0003.

Magritte, René. *The Treachery of Images*. 1929, Los Angeles County
Museum of Art, collections.lacma.org/node/239578.

8   Analyzing Arguments

In one sense, all language has an argumentative edge. When you greet
friends, you are indirectly convincing them that you're glad to see them.
When you tell a bedtime story to a child, you're subtly arguing that it's time
to sleep. Even news reporting that strives for objectivity and evenhanded-
ness has clear argumentative overtones: when a news outlet highlights a
particular story, for example, the editors are arguing that this subject is
more important than others that it did not highlight. Since argument is so
pervasive, you need to be able to recognize and use it effectively — and to
question your own arguments as well as those of others.

But just what do we mean by "argument"? "Argument" does not only mean trying to win out over someone else. Of course, getting others to accept our point of view and in that sense "winning" is one reason for argument, but by no means is it the only one or even the most important. Today writers argue for other important reasons: to join in exploration of an important issue; to explain something to ourselves and others, often using storytelling to add to understanding; to help make important decisions; even to meditate. Keep this in mind as you read and analyze arguments: they may have goals that go far beyond simply "winning."

8a Think critically about argument.

Critical thinking is a crucial component of argument, for it guides you in both examining and forming arguments. Here are some ways to think critically about argument:

- *Check understanding.* First, understand what is being argued and why. If you need to find out more about an unfamiliar subject to grasp the argument, do the research. And remember that reading and note-taking with others can help you with understanding.

- *Play the believing — and the doubting — game.* Begin by playing the *believing game*: put yourself in the position of the person creating the argument to see the topic from that person's point of view as much as possible. Once you have given the argument sympathetic attention, play the *doubting game*: look skeptically at each claim, and examine each piece of evidence to see how well (or poorly) it supports the claim.

- *Ask pertinent questions.* Whether you are thinking about others' ideas or your own, you should question unstated purposes and assumptions, the writer's qualifications, the context, the goal of the argument, and the evidence. What objections might be made to the argument?

- *Interpret and assess information.* All information that comes to you has a perspective — a spin. Your job is to identify the perspective and assess it, examining its sources and finding out what you can about its context.

- *Assess your own arguments.* The ultimate goal of all critical thinking is to reach your own conclusions. These, too, you must question and assess.

Quick Help

Analyzing an Argument

Here are some questions that can help you judge the effectiveness of an argument:

- What is the overall purpose of the argument? How do you know?
- What conclusions about the argument can you reach by playing both the believing and the doubting game, by saying "yes" or "maybe" before saying "no"? (8a)
- What cultural contexts inform the argument, and what do they tell you about where the writer is coming from? (8b)
- What emotional, ethical, and logical appeals is the writer making in support of the argument? (8c)
- How has the writer established credibility to write about the topic? (8c)
- What is the claim (or arguable statement)? Is the claim qualified in any way? (8e)
- What reasons and assumptions support and underlie the claim? (8e)
- What evidence backs up the assumptions and claim? How current and trustworthy or accurate are the sources? (8e)
- How and why does the writer use visuals or other media to support the argument? (8c)
- What fallacies can you identify, and what effect do they have on the argument's persuasiveness? (8f)
- What is the overall impression you get from analyzing the argument? Are you convinced?

8b Recognize cultural contexts.

To understand as fully as possible the arguments of others, pay attention to clues about cultural context and to how that context may affect the writer or creator's ideas and beliefs. Put yourself in that person's position and read openly and respectfully before looking skeptically at every claim and examining the evidence. Above all, watch out for your own assumptions as you analyze what you read or see: just because you assume that statistics count more than, say, precedent drawn from religious belief, don't assume that all writers agree with you. Take a writer's cultural beliefs into account before you analyze an argument.

8c Identify an argument's basic appeals.

Aristotle categorized argumentative appeals into three types: emotional appeals that speak to readers' hearts and values (*pathos*), ethical appeals that support the writer's character (*ethos*), and logical appeals that use facts and evidence (*logos*).

Emotional appeals

Emotional appeals stir your feelings and remind you of deeply held values. When politicians argue that the country needs more tax relief, they almost always use examples of one or more families they have met, stressing the concrete ways in which a tax cut would improve the quality of their lives. Doing so creates a strong emotional appeal. Some have criticized the use of emotional appeals in argument, claiming that they manipulate the audience. Emotional appeals can certainly do that, but nonetheless they are an important part of almost every argument. Critical readers are perfectly capable of "talking back" to such appeals by analyzing them, deciding which are acceptable and which are not.

Ethical appeals

Ethical appeals support the credibility, moral character, and goodwill of the argument's creator. We may admire an athlete, for example, but should we hire the insurance company the athlete promotes? To identify ethical appeals in arguments, ask yourself these questions: How does the creator of the argument demonstrate knowledge and credibility on the subject? What sort of character does he or she build, and how? More important, is that character trustworthy? How can you tell whether the creator of the argument has the best interests of the audience in mind? Do those interests match your own, and, if not, how does that alter the effectiveness of the argument?

Logical appeals

Logical appeals are often viewed as especially trustworthy: "The facts don't lie," some say. Of course, facts are not the only type of logical appeals, which also include firsthand evidence drawn from observations, interviews, surveys, experiments, and personal experience; and secondhand evidence drawn from authorities, the testimony of others, and reported data. Critical readers need to examine logical appeals just as carefully as emotional and ethical ones. What is the source of the appeal — and is that source trustworthy, or might the "facts" have been made up? Are all terms clearly defined? Has the logical evidence presented been taken out of context, and, if so, does that change its meaning?

Appeals in a visual argument

This poster, from TurnAround, a group that helps victims of domestic violence, is intended to strike a chord with abusers as well as their victims. The dramatic combination of words and image builds on an analogy between a child and a target and makes strong emotional and ethical appeals.

The bull's-eye that draws your attention to the center of the poster is probably the first thing you notice. Then you may note that the "target" is a child's body with arms, legs, and a head. The caption "A child is not a target" reinforces the connection.

This poster's stark image and headline appeal to viewers' emotions, offering the uncomfortable reminder that children can be victims of domestic violence. The design causes viewers to see a target first and only afterward recognize that the target represents a child—an unsettling experience. But the poster also offers ethical appeals ("TurnAround can help") to show that the organization is credible and that it supports the worthwhile goal of ending "the cycle of domestic violence" by offering counseling and other support services. Finally, it uses the logical appeal of a statistic, noting that TurnAround has served "more than 10,000 women, children and men each year" and giving specific information about where to get help.

8d Recognize the use of stories in argument.

The TurnAround poster makes an argument, but it also tells a story about a child who is being set up like a target for assault. In fact, narrative—someone's story—is often a major part of the arguments you will view and read and analyze, and with good reason: in every culture, stories play a key role in communicating and creating knowledge.

You can see narrative arguments at work in most movies today: think of *Coco* or *Black Panther*, for instance, both movies that use stories to make an overall argument about the crucial importance of family remembrance or the revisioning of African American history.

You will also see stories or narratives featured in written arguments. Rachel Carson's book *Silent Spring,* which argued successfully that the use of pesticides was destroying our environment, opens with a story. Here's an excerpt of the first paragraph:

> There was once a town in the heart of America where all life seemed to be in harmony with its surroundings. The town lay in the midst of a checkerboard of prosperous farms, with fields of grain and hillsides of orchards. . . . The countryside was, in fact, famous for the abundance and variety of its bird life, and when the flood of migrants was pouring through in spring and fall, people came from great distances to observe them. Other people came to fish streams, which flowed clear and cold out of the hills and contained shady pools where trout lay. So it had been from the days, many years ago, when the first settlers raised their houses, sank their wells, and built their barns.

Carson continues the story, noting that now the trees and grasses are withered, the fish and birds are dead—and the cause of this devastation has been human activity. This story introduces and frames her entire argument against the use of pesticides.

You can also see stories at work in student essays in this book: Julia Sakowitz's argument about tourism in Harlem (see Chapter 57) opens with a narrative about her own experiences of and interest in Harlem, a story that gets readers' attention and leads them to the heart of her argument. And Cameron Hauer's argument about threats to public lands in the U.S. (see 8g) begins with a story about his skiing and hiking as a teen in the Pacific Northwest. Be sure to watch out for how writers use stories in their essays and arguments, and take some tips on how you might use them in your own work.

8e Understand Toulmin's elements of argument.

In philosopher Stephen Toulmin's framework for analyzing arguments, most arguments contain common features: a *claim* or *claims*; *reasons* for the claim; *assumptions*, whether stated or unstated, that underlie the argument (Toulmin calls these *warrants*); *evidence* or *backing*, such as facts, authoritative opinions, examples, and statistics; and *qualifiers* that limit the claim in some way.

Claims

Claims, or arguable statements, are statements that a writer wants to convince a reader to accept or consider. Longer essays may include a series of linked claims or several separate claims that you need to analyze before

ELEMENTS OF TOULMIN ARGUMENT

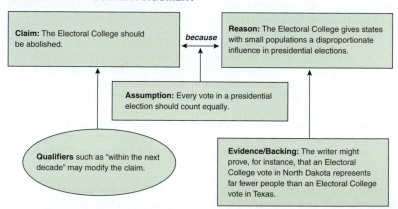

you agree to accept them. Claims worthy of arguing are those that are debatable: to say "Ten degrees Fahrenheit is cold" is a claim, but it is probably not debatable—unless you are describing northern Alaska, where ten degrees might seem balmy. In the example on the previous page, the claim that the Electoral College should be abolished is certainly arguable; a web search will turn up numerous arguments for and against this claim.

Reasons

A claim is only as good as the reasons attached to it. If a student claims that course portfolios should be graded pass or fail because so many students in the class work full-time jobs, critical readers may question whether that reason is sufficient to support the claim. In the preceding example, the writer gives a reason—that states with small populations have too much influence over the Electoral College—to support the claim of abolishing the institution. As you analyze claims, test each reason by asking how directly it supports the claim, how timely it is, and what counter-reasons you could offer to question it.

Assumptions

Putting a claim and reasons together often results in what Aristotle called an *enthymeme,* an argument that rests on an assumption the writer expects the audience to hold. These assumptions (which Toulmin calls *warrants*) that connect claim and reasons are often the hardest to detect in an argument, partly because they are often unstated, sometimes masking a weak link. As a result, it's especially important to identify the assumptions in arguments you are analyzing. Once the assumption is identified, you can test it against evidence and your own experience before accepting it. If a writer argues that the Electoral College should be abolished because states with small populations have undue influence on the outcome of presidential elections, what is the assumption underlying this claim and reason? It is that *presidential elections should give each voter the same amount of influence.* As a critical reader, remember that such assumptions are deeply affected by culture and belief: ask yourself, then, what cultural differences may be at work in your response to any argument.

Evidence or backing

Evidence, which Toulmin calls *backing,* also calls for careful analysis. In an argument about abolishing the Electoral College, the writer may offer as evidence a statistical analysis of the number of voters represented by an Electoral College vote in the least populous states and in the most populous states, a historical discussion of why the Founders developed the

Electoral College system, or studies showing that voters in states where one political party dominates feel disengaged from presidential elections. As a critical reader, you must evaluate all evidence the writer offers, asking how it relates to the claim, whether it is appropriate and timely, and whether it comes from a credible source.

Qualifiers

Qualifiers offer a way of limiting or narrowing a claim so that it is as precise as possible. Words or phrases that signal a qualification include *many*, *sometimes*, *in these circumstances*, and so on. Claims having no qualifiers can sometimes lead to overgeneralizations. For example, the statement *The Electoral College should be abolished* is less precise than *The Electoral College should be abolished by 2028*. Look carefully for qualifiers in the arguments you analyze, since they will affect the strength and reach of the claim.

Elements of a visual argument

Visual arguments can also be analyzed using these Toulmin methods. Look closely at the advertisement on this page. If you decide that this advertisement is claiming that people should adopt shelter pets, you might word a reason like this: *Dogs and cats need people, not just shelter.* You might note that the campaign assumes that people make pets happier (and that all pets deserve happiness)—and that the image backs up the overall message that this inquisitive, well-cared-for dog is happier living in a home with a human than in a shelter. Considering unstated qualifiers (should *every* person consider adopting a shelter pet?) and thinking about potential evidence for the claim would help you complete an analysis of this visual argument.

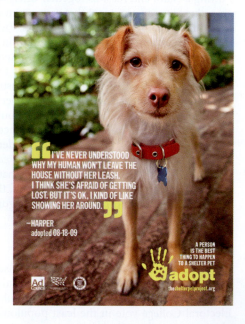

8f Think critically about fallacies.

Fallacies, instances of false logic, have traditionally been viewed as serious flaws that damage the effectiveness of an argument. But arguments are often complex in that they always occur in some specific rhetorical situation and in some particular place and time; thus what looks like a fallacy in one situation may appear quite different in another. The best advice is to learn to identify fallacies but to be cautious in jumping to conclusions about them. Rather than thinking of them as errors you can use to discredit an arguer, you might think of them as barriers to common ground and understanding, since they often shut off rather than facilitate debate.

Verbal fallacies

AD HOMINEM

Ad hominem charges make a personal attack rather than focusing on the issue at hand.

▶ **Who cares what that fat loudmouth says about the health care system?**

GUILT BY ASSOCIATION

Guilt by association attacks someone's credibility by linking that person with a person or activity the audience considers suspicious or untrustworthy.

▶ **She does not deserve reelection; her husband had extramarital affairs.**

FALSE AUTHORITY

False authority is often used by advertisers who show famous actors or athletes testifying to the greatness of a product about which they may know very little.

▶ **He's today's greatest NASCAR driver — and he banks at National Mutual!**

BANDWAGON APPEAL

Bandwagon appeal suggests that a great movement is underway and the reader will be a fool or a traitor not to join it.

▶ **This new phone is everyone's must-have item. Where's yours?**

FLATTERY

Flattery tries to persuade readers by suggesting they are thoughtful, intelligent, or perceptive enough to agree with the writer.

▶ You have the taste to recognize the superlative artistry of Bling diamond jewelry.

PARALIPSIS—SAYING WHAT YOU SAY YOU WON'T

Paralipsis occurs when speakers or writers say they will NOT talk about something, thus doing the very thing they say they're not going to do, as does Robert Downey Jr.'s character in *Iron Man 2*.

▶ I'm not saying I'm responsible for this country's longest run of uninterrupted peace in 35 years! . . . It's not about me!

VEILED THREAT

Veiled threats try to frighten readers into agreement by hinting that they will suffer adverse consequences if they don't agree.

▶ If Public Service Electric Company does not get an immediate 15 percent rate increase, its services to you may be seriously affected.

FALSE ANALOGY

False analogies make comparisons between two situations that are not alike in important respects.

▶ The volleyball team's sudden descent in the rankings resembled the sinking of the *Titanic*.

BEGGING THE QUESTION

Begging the question is a kind of circular argument that treats a debatable statement as if it had been proved true.

▶ Television news covered that story well; I learned all I know about it by watching TV.

POST HOC FALLACY

The post hoc fallacy (from the Latin *post hoc, ergo propter hoc*, which means "after this, therefore caused by this") assumes that just because B happened *after* A, it must have been *caused* by A.

▶ We should not rebuild the town docks because every time we do, a hurricane comes along and damages them.

NON SEQUITUR

A non sequitur (Latin for "it does not follow") attempts to tie together two or more logically unrelated ideas as if they were related.

▶ **If we can send a spaceship to Mars, then we can discover a cure for cancer.**

EITHER-OR FALLACY

The either-or fallacy insists that a complex situation can have only two possible outcomes.

▶ **If we do not build the new highway, businesses downtown will be forced to close.**

HASTY GENERALIZATION

A hasty generalization bases a conclusion on too little evidence or on misunderstood evidence.

▶ **I couldn't understand the lecture today, so I'm sure this course will be impossible.**

OVERSIMPLIFICATION

Oversimplification claims an overly direct relationship between a cause and an effect.

▶ **If we prohibit the sale of alcohol, we will get rid of binge drinking.**

STRAW MAN

A straw-man argument misrepresents the opposition by pretending that opponents agree with something that few reasonable people would support.

▶ **My opponent believes that we should offer therapy to the terrorists. I disagree.**

Visual fallacies

Fallacies can also take the form of misleading images. The sheer power of images can make them especially difficult to analyze — people tend to believe what they see. Nevertheless, photographs and other visuals can be manipulated to present a false impression.

MISLEADING PHOTOGRAPHS

Faked or altered photos are, unfortunately, fairly common. In 2018, *Teen Vogue* ran a story that featured Emma González, Parkland shooting survivor and gun control activist, tearing a target shooting poster in half. A quick internet search will show you an altered image of González tearing the US constitution in half — an image that was posted on Gab, a social media platform with a conservative audience.

Original photo.   Altered photo.

Today's technology makes such photo alterations easier than ever, if also easier to detect with a reverse image search using Google or Tin Eye. But photographs need not be altered to try to fool viewers. Think of all the photos that make a politician look misleadingly bad or good. In these cases, you should closely examine the motives of those responsible for publishing the images.

MISLEADING CHARTS AND GRAPHS

Facts and statistics, too, can be presented in ways that mislead readers. On page 91, the bar graph on the left purports to deliver an argument about how differently Democrats, on the one hand, and Republicans, on the other, felt about a particular issue. Look closely and you'll see a visual fallacy: the vertical axis starts not at zero but at 53 percent, so the visually large difference between the groups is misleading. In fact, a majority of all respondents agree about the issue, and only eight percentage points separate Democrats from Republicans (in a poll with a margin of error of +/− seven percentage points). Look at the bar graph on the right; the vertical axis begins at zero and the data is presented more accurately.

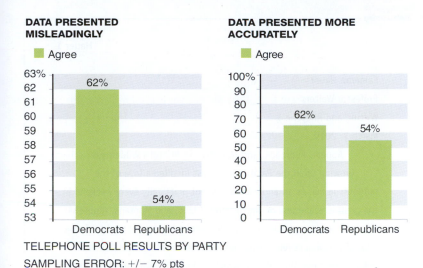

DATA PRESENTED MISLEADINGLY

■ Agree

TELEPHONE POLL RESULTS BY PARTY
SAMPLING ERROR: +/− 7% pts

DATA PRESENTED MORE ACCURATELY

■ Agree

8g A student's rhetorical analysis

For a class assignment, Cameron Hauer was asked to analyze the emotional, ethical, and logical appeals in a *New York Times* op-ed article in which Nicholas Kristof argues that America's public lands are being threatened.

Student Writer

Cameron Hauer

Hauer 1

Cameron Hauer

Professor Walters

Writing and Rhetoric 1

March 7, 2019

Appeal, Audience, and Narrative in Kristof's Wilderness

Growing up in the Pacific Northwest instilled a love of the

outdoors in me. As an adolescent, I spent practically every weekend in

the pristine wilderness of Washington, Idaho, and Montana. Alpine ski

trips and weeklong backpacking treks were a big part of my life. I owe

a lot of personal development and fond memories to America's vast

public wilderness, the value of which Nicholas Kristof captures stirringly

in his *New York Times* op-ed column, "Fleeing to the Mountains." He

warns, however, that America's wilderness is under attack.

To strengthen his case for the specialness of America's

wildlands, Kristof relies on ethical and emotional appeals: a lively

account of his family's backpacking trips and the ways they free

people from the buzz and hum of modern life. Kristof's style here

ranges from breezy and playful (the wilderness is "heaven with

blisters") to awestruck and reverent (it is "our inheritance and shared

playground"). He also offers personal testimony; having spent time

in wild places, Kristof is well positioned to describe their virtues. He

invites readers to share this ethic, to see the joy of open spaces, and

to regard them as a sacred inheritance.

Halfway through the column, Kristof shifts his focus to address

threats facing our wilderness. He lays blame on those in power, like

members of the current administration, who, Kristof alleges, "see this

heritage as an opportunity for development" and are "systematically

handing over America's public lands for private exploitation in ways

that will scar the land forever." He moves to using logos rather than

the ethos and pathos of the earlier sections. Whereas earlier he tries

to evoke a particular feeling and ethic, his present goal is to marshal

facts—including the administration's lifting of a moratorium on new

mining leases and the opening up of new lands to fossil fuel

extraction—to convince readers that public lands in the U.S. are

Side annotations:

Uses personal experience to help establish ethos

Provides succinct overview of Kristof's argument

States Kristof's claims

Transition to Kristof's discussion of threats to wilderness

Focuses on Kristof's use of ethical and emotional appeals

Shows how Kristof engages his audience

Hauer 2

under threat. Kristof lessens the abruptness of this shift in appeal by maintaining his narrative of wilderness as an inheritance.

Several elements of Kristof's argument give insight into his context and audience. The place of Trump in Kristof's narrative is significant. The policies Kristof describes are simply the implementation of long-standing Republican priorities and have little to do with Trump himself. But in Kristof's rhetorical context—a left-of-center newspaper in 2017—choosing Trump as an anti-environmental symbol is a strong, if obvious, rhetorical move. The mention of the sitting president invites Kristof's liberal readership to adopt a pro-wilderness platform as one plank of a broader anti-Trump agenda.

Analyzes Kristof's intended audience

There are some notable omissions in Kristof's argument. In his framing, wildlands are either public and devoted to use by the people or privatized for resource extraction and for "ranches for the rich." To a liberal already inclined to value publicly owned resources, this framework may be convincing, but conservatives often view public ownership of natural resources with suspicion. Kristof portrays public ownership as a means of providing equal access for all Americans, but rural conservatives may view it as a way that valuable resources are turned into playgrounds for yuppies. They may also resist Kristof's portrayal of private ownership as promoting degradation and waste, viewing it instead as a way for hardworking people to make a living off the land.

Practices critical reading to point out Kristof's omissions

Considers opposing viewpoints

Another evasion in Kristof's argument, one that may stand out sharply to left and right, is his characterization of public lands as "a bastion of equality." This is true in a sense—most public lands are open to everyone, free of charge; but in practical terms, access to wilderness requires a salary and paid time off, among other things. In a country where millions struggle to make ends meet, frequent recreational use of America's wildlands remains out of reach.

Questions Kristof's assumption that wilderness is accessible to all

These evasions and omissions may indicate Kristof's biases and his own rhetorical stance, but they are not damning. An op-ed article is, after all, crafted for a particular audience. To address the concerns of staunch conservatives would require Kristof to adopt different rhetorical strategies. Kristof's readers are likely a self-selected group

Hauer 3

Underscores
Kristof's
major
purpose

of liberal-minded people already sympathetic to his views. His rhetorical goal is not to convince a group of adversaries of his position but to persuade a group of amenable readers that this particular issue—and this particular ethic—is one that they should adopt as their own.

Hauer 4

Work Cited

Follows MLA
style

Kristof, Nicholas. "Fleeing to the Mountains." *New York Times,*

12 Aug. 2017, www.nytimes.com/2017/08/12/opinion/sunday/

hiking-pacific-crest-trail.html.

9   Constructing Arguments

Writing you do in college and beyond will often require you to develop convincing arguments, a task that calls for careful planning and reasoning and attention to both the context of the argument and its intended audience. Sometimes instructors will assign an argument on a specific topic; other times, you may have a choice. In either case, remember that these assignments belong to you and that they offer opportunities to explore new ideas, to test the limits of your thinking, to do research that will allow you to gain expertise, and to make your voice heard on issues that are important to you. If the topic is assigned, look for ways to shape it to your own interests; if it is an open inquiry, think about what you want to make happen as a result of your argument. What you discover may be of lasting importance to you and, perhaps, to others.

9a   Understand purposes for argument.

While winning is an important purpose of argument, it is by no means the only one.

TO WIN The most traditional purpose of academic argument, arguing to win, is common in campus debating societies, in political debates, in trials,

> ## Quick Help
>
> ### Reviewing Your Argument
>
> - What is the purpose of your argument—to win? to convince others? to explore an issue? (9a)
> - Is the point you want to make arguable? (9b)
> - Have you formed a strong working thesis with a clear claim and good reasons? (9c)
> - Have you considered your audience sufficiently in shaping your appeals? (9e)
> - How have you fully established your own credibility in the argument? (9f)
> - How have you used logical and emotional appeals in your argument? (9h and i)
> - If you use sources, how effectively are they integrated into your argument? (9j)
> - How is your argument organized? (9k)

and often in business. The writer or speaker aims to present a position that will prevail over some other position.

TO CONVINCE Often, out-and-out defeat of another's position is not only unrealistic but undesirable. Instead, the goal might be to convince another person to change his or her mind. Doing so calls on a writer to provide *compelling reasons* for an audience to accept some or all of the writer's conclusions.

TO UNDERSTAND A writer often enters into a conversation with others to seek the best understanding of a problem, explore all approaches, and choose the best options. Argument to understand does not seek to conquer others or even to convince them. A writer's purpose in many situations — from trying to decide which job to pursue to exploring the best way to care for an elderly relative — will be to share information and perspectives in order to make informed political, professional, and personal choices.

9b Determine whether a statement can be argued.

At school, at home, or on the job, you will often need to convince someone or decide something. To do so, start with an arguable statement, which should meet three criteria:

1. It attempts to convince readers of something, change their minds about something, or urge them to do something — or it explores a topic in order to make a wise decision.

2. It addresses a problem for which no easily acceptable solution exists or asks a question to which no absolute answer exists.
3. It presents a position that readers might realistically have varying perspectives on.

> **UNARGUABLE STATEMENT** Women's magazines earn millions of dollars every year from advertising.

This statement does not present a position; it states a fact that can easily be verified and thus offers a poor basis for argument.

> **ARGUABLE STATEMENT** Advertisements in women's magazines contribute to the poor self-image that afflicts many young women.

This statement seeks to convince, addresses a problem — poor self-image among young women — that has no clear-cut solution, and takes a position many could disagree with.

9c Make a claim and draft a working thesis.

Once you have an arguable statement, you need to develop it into a working thesis (3c). One way to do so is to identify the elements of an argument (8e): the claim or arguable statement; one or more reasons for the claim; and assumptions, sometimes unstated, that underlie the claim and reasons.

To turn a claim into a working thesis for an argument, include at least one good reason to support the arguable statement.

> **REASON** Pesticides endanger the lives of farm workers.
>
> **WORKING THESIS (CLAIM WITH REASON ATTACHED)** Because they endanger the lives of farm workers, pesticides should be banned.

9d Examine your assumptions.

Once you have a working thesis, examine your assumptions to help test your reasoning and strengthen your argument. Begin by identifying underlying assumptions that support the working thesis.

> **WORKING THESIS** Because they endanger the lives of farm workers, pesticides should be banned.
>
> **ASSUMPTION 1** Workers have a right to a safe working environment.
>
> **ASSUMPTION 2** Substances that endanger the lives of workers deserve to be banned.

It's worth considering your unspoken assumptions carefully: what evidence do you have to support them? What values do they reflect and where did those values come from? Learning to think critically about your own assumptions can help you identify biases that may color your thinking. Once you have a working thesis, you may want to use qualifiers to make it more precise and thus less susceptible to criticism. The preceding thesis might be qualified in this way:

▶ Because they *often* endanger the lives of farm workers, *most* pesticides should be banned.

9e Shape your appeal to your audience.

Arguments and the claims they make are effective only if they appeal to the appropriate audience. For example, let's say you want to argue for increased lighting in parking garages on campus. You might appeal to an audience of fellow students with one kind of evidence; however, if your audience is school administrators, you may find you need to change your approach.

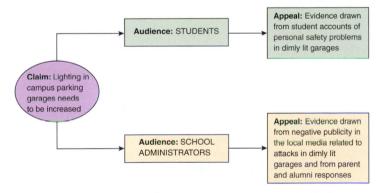

9f Consider the use of narratives or stories.

Because storytelling is such a common way of communicating, *narratives* can be very persuasive in helping readers understand and possibly accept an argument. You might decide to open an argument with a vivid story that embodies the major point you want to make: opening an argument essay on the devastating effects of global climate change, for example, might begin with the story of an Alaskan village that is now under so much water that it must be abandoned. In fact, it may be helpful to think of your entire argument as following a *narrative arc*, from a dramatic and vivid opening story through other stories that provide evidence for the points you are making, to a conclusion that says "the end." Narratives that use video and audio to capture the faces and voices of the people involved are often particularly compelling.

Stories drawn from your own experience can also be very effective, for they help make your point in true-to-life terms and help readers relate to you and your experiences. Note that in such cases the use of first-person (*I*) is appropriate.

When you include stories in an argument, ask the following questions:

- Does the narrative support your thesis or major point?
- Does the narrative reflect the values you truly hold?
- Will the story's significance to the argument be clear to readers?
- Is the story one of several good reasons or pieces of evidence — or does it have to carry the main burden of the argument?

For examples of academic arguments that begin with narratives, see Cameron Hauer's rhetorical analysis (8g) and Julia Sakowitz's research essay (Chapter 57).

Quick Help

Showing Certainty in an Argument

How much certainty should you show when you're making an arguable claim? You may know that it's safer to say "*most* students believe" than "*all* students believe," but think carefully about when you should qualify or downplay a claim and when you can show greater confidence. Research conducted by Professor Laura Aull shows that expert academic writers in all disciplines tend to qualify their claims by using "hedges" — words such as *seems*, *might*, *generally*, *relatively*, *some*, or *likely* — and that expert writers are less likely to use intensifiers or "boosters" that show a high level of certainty — words such as *clearly*, *always*, *never*, and *must*. In contrast, student writers use many more "boosters" than "hedges." Learn from the experts: guard against overconfidence and aggressive critique of others' perspectives. Overstating the truth of your claim can make you seem unfair or less credible to readers. Academic claims usually make room for alternative points of view, and they are more often qualified and cautious than absolutely certain.

9g Establish credibility through ethical appeals.

To make your argument convincing, you must first gain the respect and trust of your readers, or establish credibility with them. In general, writers can establish credibility by making ethical appeals (8c) in four ways.

Knowledge

Writers and speakers can establish credibility first by showing that they know what they're talking about. To decide whether you know enough to argue an issue credibly, consider the following questions:

- Can you provide information about your topic from sources other than your own knowledge?
- How reliable are your sources? (See 11d on spotting misinformation and fake news.)
- If sources contradict one another, can you account for or resolve the contradictions?
- Would a personal experience relating to the issue help support your claim?

These questions may well show that you must do more research, check sources, resolve contradictions, refocus your working thesis, or even change your topic.

Common ground

Some arguments are doomed before they even begin because the two sides never even listen to one another. One way to get beyond such an impasse is to listen openly and respectfully to the perspectives of others and, if possible, to find some common ground. The following questions can help you find common ground in presenting an argument.

- What are all the differing perspectives on this issue (including those that differ from your own)? Where might they overlap?
- What common ground can all sides agree on?
- How can you show that standing on this common ground will be of benefit to everyone involved?
- How can you use language — word choice, analogies or other figures of speech, varieties of English, or languages other than English (see Chapter 23) — to establish common ground with your audience?

Quick Help

Building *Ethos* through Careful Restatement

Expert writers, says linguist Laura Aull, use "reformulation" or restatement to help build credibility and signal their own take on the evidence they're presenting. Phrases like *in other words*, *that is to say*, and *to be precise* show that a writer is interpreting information for the reader; *especially* or *in particular* emphasize what the writer finds particularly important; *in fact* or *indeed* show that a writer is contrasting an existing view. Expert writers use such phrases to restate and underscore their interpretation and introduce their own voices into their writing far more often than student writers do. Like transitions, these restatements help showcase the writer's reason for organizing the text in a particular way or emphasize the relation between ideas or parts of a text. How can you use restatement to build your *ethos*, or credibility? Look for — and ask peer reviewers to point out — opportunities to restate others' ideas.

Fairness

In arguing a position, the most effective writers deal fairly with opposing arguments (also called counterarguments). After all, people are more inclined to listen to writers who seem to consider other views fairly than to those who ignore or distort such views. The following questions can help you make sure you are being open-minded:

- How can you show that you are considering and respecting all significant points of view?
- How can you demonstrate that you understand and empathize with points of view other than your own?
- What can you do to show that you have considered evidence carefully, even when it does not support your position?

Some writers, instead of demonstrating fairness, may make unjustified attacks on an opponent's credibility. Avoid such attacks in your writing.

Visuals that make ethical appeals

In arguments and other kinds of writing, visuals can combine with text to present a writer or an organization as trustworthy and credible. Like businesses, many

SUSTAINABLE FOOD LABORATORY

Language, Culture, and Context

Multilingual

Counting Your Own Experience

You may have been told that personal experience doesn't count in making academic arguments. If so, reconsider this advice. Showing an audience that you have relevant experience with a topic can carry strong persuasive appeal with English-speaking readers.

institutions and individuals are using logos and other images to brand themselves as they wish the public to see them. The Sustainable Food Laboratory logo, seen here, suggests that the organization is concerned about both food production and the environment.

Visuals that make ethical appeals add to your credibility as a writer. Just as you consider the impression your social media profile photo makes on your audience, you should think about what kind of case you're making for yourself when you choose images and design elements for your argument.

9h Use effective logical appeals.

Credibility alone cannot and should not carry the full burden of convincing readers. The logic of the argument, the reasoning behind it, is as important as its ethos.

Examples and precedents

Just as an authentic picture can sometimes be worth a thousand words, so can a well-conceived example be valuable in arguing a point. Examples are used most often to support generalizations or to bring abstractions to life. In making the general statement that popular media send the message that a woman must be thin to be attractive, you might include these examples:

> At the supermarket checkout, a tabloid publishes unflattering photographs of a young singer and comments on her apparent weight gain in shocked captions that ask "What happened?!?" Another praises a star for quickly shedding "ugly pounds" after the recent birth of a child. The cover of *Cosmopolitan* features a glamorously made-up and airbrushed actress in an outfit that reveals her tiny waist and flat stomach. Every woman featured in the magazine's ads is thin — and the context makes it clear that readers are supposed to think that these women are beautiful.

Precedents are examples taken from the past. If, as part of a proposal for making the engineering library more accessible by adding an additional wheelchair ramp, you point out that the university has added such ramps to three other libraries on campus, you are arguing on the basis of precedent.

The following questions can help you check any use of example or precedent:

- How representative are the examples?
- Are the examples sufficient in strength or number to lead to a generalization?
- In what ways do they support your point?
- How closely does a precedent relate to your point? Are the situations really similar?
- How timely is the precedent? (An example from 1985 may not apply today.)

In research writing, remember to identify your sources for any examples or precedents not based on your own knowledge or research.

Authority and testimony

Another way to support an argument logically is to cite an authority. The use of authority figured prominently in the controversy over smoking. Following the U.S. surgeon general's 1964 announcement that smoking is hazardous to health, millions of Americans quit smoking, largely persuaded by the authority of the scientists offering the evidence. Today authorities are making similar arguments about vaping.

Ask the following questions to be sure you are using authorities effectively:

- Is the authority a "real" authority — or are credentials false or overstated?
- Is the authority *timely*?
- Is the authority *qualified* to judge the topic at hand?
- Is the authority likely to be *known and respected* by readers?
- Are the authority's *credentials* clearly stated and verifiable?

Testimony — the evidence that an authority presents in support of a claim — is a feature of much contemporary argument. If testimony is timely, accurate, representative, and provided by a respected authority, then it, like authority itself, can add powerful support.

In research writing, you should cite your sources for authority and for testimony not based on your own knowledge.

Causes and effects

Showing that one event is the cause or the effect of another can help support an argument. Suppose you are trying to explain, in a petition to change your grade in a course, why you were unable to take the final exam. You might trace the causes of your failure to appear — your illness or the theft of your car, perhaps — so that the committee reading the petition would reconsider the effect — your not taking the exam.

Tracing causes often lays the groundwork for an argument, particularly if the effect of the causes is one we would like to change. In an environmental science class, for example, a student may argue that a law regulating smokestack emissions from utility plants is needed because (1) acid rain on the East Coast originates from emissions at utility plants in the Midwest, (2) acid rain kills trees and other vegetation, (3) utility lobbyists have prevented Midwestern states from passing laws controlling emissions, and (4) if such laws are not passed, acid rain will soon destroy most eastern forests. In this case, the fourth point ties all of the previous points together to provide an overall argument from effect: if X, then Y.

Inductive and deductive reasoning

Traditionally, logical arguments are classified as using either inductive or deductive reasoning; in practice, the two often work together. Inductive reasoning is the process of making a generalization based on a number of specific instances. If you are ill on ten occasions after eating seafood, for example, you might draw the inductive generalization that seafood makes you ill. You may not be certain that seafood is to blame, but the probability lies in that direction.

Deductive reasoning, on the other hand, reaches a conclusion by assuming a general principle (the major premise) and then applying that principle to a specific case (the minor premise). In practice, this general principle is usually derived from induction. The inductive generalization *Seafood makes me ill,* for instance, could serve as the major premise for the deductive argument *Since all seafood makes me ill, the shrimp on this buffet is certain to make me ill.*

Deductive arguments have traditionally been analyzed as syllogisms: reasoning that contains a major premise, a minor premise, and a conclusion.

MAJOR PREMISE	All people die.
MINOR PREMISE	I am a person.
CONCLUSION	I will die.

Syllogisms, however, are too rigid to serve in arguments about questions that have no absolute answers, and they often lack any appeal to an audience. Aristotle's more flexible alternative, the enthymeme, asks the audience to supply the implied major premise. Consider the following example:

> Because they harm other children, bullies should be disciplined by schools.

You can analyze this enthymeme by restating it in the form of two premises and a conclusion.

MAJOR PREMISE	Students who harm other children should be disciplined by schools.
MINOR PREMISE	Bullies harm other children.
CONCLUSION	Bullies should be disciplined by schools.

Note that the major premise is one the writer can count on an audience agreeing with or supplying: safety and common sense demand that schools should discipline children who harm other students. By implicitly asking the audience to supply this premise to the argument, the writer engages the audience's participation.

Toulmin's system (8e) looks for claims, reasons, and assumptions instead of major and minor premises.

CLAIM	Bullies should be disciplined by schools.
REASON(S)	Bullies harm other children.
ASSUMPTION	Students who harm other children should be disciplined by schools.

Note that in this system the assumption — which may be unstated — serves the same function as the assumed major premise in an enthymeme.

Whether it is expressed as a syllogism, an enthymeme, or a claim, a deductive conclusion is only as strong as the premise or reasons on which it is based.

Visuals that make logical appeals

Visuals that make logical appeals can be especially useful in arguments, since they present factual information that can be taken in at a glance. The U.S. Census Bureau used this simple chart to make a statement about disaster preparedness. Consider how long it would take to explain all the information in the following chart with words alone.

MEASURING AMERICA

October 2018

How Ready Are We?
Natural Disaster or Emergency Preparedness

To better understand the needs of first responders and other emergency workers, the 2017 American Housing Survey asks U.S. residents how prepared they are for disasters.

100 80 60 40 20 0 20 40 60 80 100

No **Yes**

Emergency Water Supply
At least three gallons or 24 bottles of water for each person in the household. — Not Reported* — 58.6%

Nonperishable Emergency Food
Household has enough nonperishable food to sustain everyone in the household for three days. — 81.3%

Prepared Emergency Evacuation Kit — 52.9%

Emergency Meeting Location — 36.5%

Communication Plan
The communication plan must include a contingency for the disruption of cell phone service. — 26.4%

Evacuation Vehicle(s)
Vehicle(s) must be reliable and able to carry all household members, pets, and supplies up to 50 miles away. — 91.0%

Evacuation Funds
If you had to evacuate your home for a safe place at least 50 miles away, do you have financial resources to meet expenses of up to $2,000? — 75.6%

Generator Present
Asked of 1-unit buildings and multiunit buildings with 2 to 4 units. — 18.7%

Access to Financial Information — 80.8%

* Not reported: Households did not provide a response to this question.
Source: U.S. Census Bureau and U.S. Department of Housing and Urban Development, 2017 American Housing Survey.

United States Census Bureau

U.S. Department of Commerce
Economics and Statistics Administration
U.S. CENSUS BUREAU
census.gov

U.S. DEPARTMENT OF HOUSING AND URBAN DEVELOPMENT

9i Use appropriate emotional appeals.

Most successful arguments appeal to our hearts as well as to our minds — as is vividly demonstrated by the debate over whether aid to Puerto Rico was sufficient after Hurricane Maria devastated the island in 2017. Facts and figures (logical appeals) convince us that the problem is real and serious. What elicits an outpouring of support, however, is the arresting emotional power of stories and images of people affected by the disaster. But credible writers take care when they use emotional appeals; audiences can easily begin to feel manipulated when an argument tries too hard to appeal to their pity, anger, or fear.

Concrete descriptive details

Like photographs, vivid words can bring a moving immediacy to any argument. A student may amass facts and figures, including diagrams and maps, to illustrate the problem of wheelchair access to the library. But only when the student asks a friend who uses a wheelchair to accompany her to the library does the student writer discover the concrete details necessary to move readers. The student can then write, "Manisha inched her heavy wheelchair up the entrance ramp, her arms straining, her face pinched with effort."

Figurative language

Figures of speech are the special effects of language: they can paint a detailed and vivid picture by making striking comparisons between something you are writing about and something else that helps a reader visualize, identify with, or understand it (26a). As such they are not "decoration" but crucial elements in human communication.

Figures of speech include metaphors, similes, and analogies. Most simply, metaphors compare two things directly:

> Serena Williams, the trailblazer
>
> old age, the evening of life

Similes make comparisons using *like* or *as*:

> Serena Williams is like a trailblazer.
>
> Old age is like the evening of life.

Analogies are extended metaphors or similes that compare an unfamiliar concept or process to a more familiar one. For more about these special effects of language, see Chapter 26.

Visuals that make emotional appeals

Visuals that make emotional appeals can also add substance to your argument. To make sure that such visual appeals will enhance your argument, test them out with several potential readers to see how they interpret the appeal. Consider, for example, this photograph depicting a Boston rally of gun-rights advocates. The image includes a group of protesters, one of whom is holding a sign saying "More gun laws will not stop mad men from killing," with a large yellow "Don't Tread on Me" flag in the foreground. Readers who generally oppose laws regulating gun ownership in the United States may feel very differently about this image than readers who tend to support restrictions.

RICK FRIEDMAN/CORBIS/GETTY IMAGES

9j   Consult sources.

Academic arguments almost always call for using sources. The key to persuading people to accept your argument is providing good reasons; even if your assignment doesn't specify it, consulting reliable sources is often the most effective way of finding and establishing these reasons. Accurate, reliable, and truthful sources can help you to do the following:

- provide background information on your topic
- demonstrate your knowledge of the topic to readers
- cite authority and testimony in support of your thesis
- discover and consider opinions that differ from yours and thus sharpen your thinking, qualify your thesis if necessary, and demonstrate fairness to opposing arguments

For a more thorough discussion of finding and evaluating sources, see Chapters 10–11.

9k   Organize your argument.

Once you have assembled good reasons and evidence in support of an argumentative thesis, you must organize your material to present the argument convincingly. Although there is no universally favored, one-size-fits-all organizational framework, you may want to use one of the following patterns.

The classical system

The system of argument often followed by ancient Greek and Roman orators is now referred to as *classical*. You can adapt the ancient format to written arguments as follows:

1. Introduction
   - Gain readers' attention and interest.
   - Establish your qualifications to write about your topic.
   - Establish common ground with readers.
   - Demonstrate fairness.
   - State or imply your thesis.

2. Background: Present any necessary background information, including relevant personal narrative.

3. Lines of argument
   - Present good reasons (including logical and emotional appeals) in support of your thesis.
   - Present reasons in order of importance, with the most important ones generally saved for last.
   - Demonstrate ways your argument may be in readers' best interest.

4. Alternative arguments
   - Examine alternative points of view.
   - Note advantages and disadvantages of alternative views.
   - Explain why one view is better than other(s).

5. Conclusion
   - Summarize the argument if you choose.
   - Elaborate on the implication of your thesis.
   - Make clear what you want readers to think or do.
   - Reinforce your credibility.

The Toulmin system

This simplified form of the Toulmin system (8e and 9h) can help you organize an argumentative essay:

1. Make your claim (arguable statement).
   - ▶ The federal government should ban smoking.

2. Qualify your claim if necessary.
   - ▶ The ban would be limited to public places.

3. Present good reasons to support your claim.
   - ▶ Smoking causes serious diseases in smokers.
   - ▶ Nonsmokers are endangered by others' smoke.

4. Explain the assumptions that underlie your claim and your reasons. Provide additional explanations for any controversial assumptions.

ASSUMPTION	The Constitution was established to "promote the general welfare."
ASSUMPTION	Citizens are entitled to protection from harmful actions by others.
ADDITIONAL EXPLANATION	The United States is based on a political system that is supposed to serve the basic needs of its people, including their health.

5. Provide additional evidence to support your claim (such as facts, statistics, testimony, and other logical, ethical, or emotional appeals).

STATISTICS	Cite the incidence of deaths attributed to secondhand smoke.
FACTS	Cite lawsuits won against large tobacco companies, including one that awarded billions of dollars to states in reparation for smoking-related health care costs.
FACTS	Cite bans on smoking already imposed on indoor public spaces in many cities.
AUTHORITY	Cite the surgeon general.

6. Acknowledge and respond to possible counterarguments.

COUNTER-ARGUMENT	Smokers have rights, too.
RESPONSE	The suggested ban applies only to public places; smokers are free to smoke in private.

7. Finally, state your conclusion in the strongest way possible.

Rogerian or invitational argument

The psychologist Carl Rogers argued that people should not enter into disputes until they can thoroughly and fairly understand the other person's (or persons') perspectives. From Rogers's theory, rhetoricians Richard Young, Alton Becker, and Kenneth Pike adapted a four-part structure that is now known as Rogerian argument:

- The introduction describes the issue, problem, or conflict in enough detail to demonstrate that the writer fully grasps and respects alternative points of view.
- The writer then fairly describes the contexts in which such alternative positions might be valid.

- The writer offers his or her position on the issue and explains in what circumstances and why that position would be valid.
- Finally, the writer explains how those who hold alternative positions can benefit from adopting the writer's position.

Like Rogerian argument, invitational rhetoric, first proposed by Sonja Foss and Cindy Griffin, has as its goal getting people to work together effectively, to listen respectfully, and to identify with each other; it aims for connection and collaboration. Such arguments call for structures that are closer to good two-way conversations or freewheeling dialogues than a linear march from thesis to conclusion. If you use such an organizational plan, you might

- begin with an introduction that recognizes varying positions and perspectives on the topic and makes it clear that the major goal is understanding
- describe each perspective fairly and respectfully, if possible using the words of those who advocate the perspectives
- conclude by identifying and exploring common ground and what it might lead to

If you try developing such a conversational structure, you may find that it opens up a space in your argument for new perceptions and fresh ideas.

9I   Consider design and delivery.

Asked to name the three most important parts of rhetoric, the ancient orator Demosthenes said: *delivery, delivery, delivery*. In short, while what speakers said was important, the way they said it was of even greater importance. Today, we live in a time of information overload, when many powerful messages are vying for our attention. Getting and keeping an audience's attention is all about delivery. Figuring out the medium of delivery (print? digital? in-person?) and the appropriate genre is also important, as is designing the argument to appeal to your audience.

- What medium will best get and hold your audience's attention? print? video? in-person presentation? social media post? Choosing just the right one is important to your success.
- What genre is most appropriate for your message? a report? a narrative? an essay? a brochure?
- What word choice, style, and tone will be most successful in delivering your message?

- What visual style will appeal to your intended readers, set a clear tone for your argument, and guide readers through your text?
- Are visual and media elements clearly integrated into your argument? Place images close to the text they illustrate, and label each one clearly. Make sure that audio and video files appear in appropriate places and are identified for users.

9m A student's argument essay

In this argument essay, Benjy Mercer-Golden argues that socially conscious businesses and traditional for-profit businesses can learn from each other in ways that benefit businesses, consumers, and the environment. His essay has been annotated to point out the various parts of his argument as well as his use of good reasons, evidence, and appeals to logic and emotion.

Student Writer

Benjy Mercer-Golden

Mercer-Golden 1

Benjy Mercer-Golden

Professor Sood

English 102

28 November 2012

Provocative word choice for title

Lessons from Tree-Huggers and Corporate Mercenaries:
A New Model of Sustainable Capitalism

Emotional appeals through use of vivid imagery

Televised images of environmental degradation—seagulls with oil coating their feathers, smokestacks belching gray fumes—often seem designed to shock, but these images also represent very real issues: climate change, dwindling energy resources like coal and oil, a scarcity of clean drinking water. In response, businesspeople around the world are thinking about how they can make their companies greener or more socially beneficial to ensure a brighter future for humanity. But progress in the private sector has been slow and inconsistent.

Thesis establishing purpose

To accelerate the move to sustainability, for-profit businesses need to learn from the hybrid model of social entrepreneurship to ensure that the company is efficient and profitable while still working for social change, and more investors need to support companies with long-term, revolutionary visions for improving the world.

Claim related to thesis

In fact, both for-profit corporations and "social good" businesses could take steps to reshape their strategies. First, for-profit corporations need to operate sustainably and be evaluated for their performance with long-term measurements and incentives.

Opposing viewpoint to establish writer's credibility

The conventional argument against for-profit companies deeply embedding environmental and social goals into their corporate strategies is that caring about the world does not go hand in hand with lining pockets. This morally toxic case is also problematic from

Rebuttal

a business standpoint. A 2012 study of 180 high-profile companies by Harvard Business School professors Robert G. Eccles and George Serafeim and London Business School professor Ioannis Ioannou

Mercer-Golden 2

shows that "high sustainability companies," as defined by
environmental and social variables, "significantly outperform
their counterparts over the long term, both in terms of stock
market and accounting performance." The study argues that the
better financial returns of these companies are especially evident
in sectors where "companies' products significantly depend upon
extracting large amounts of natural resources" (Eccles et al.).

Such empirical financial evidence to support a shift toward
using energy from renewable sources to run manufacturing
plants argues that executives should think more sustainably,
but other underlying incentives need to evolve in order to
bring about tangible change. David Blood and Al Gore of
Generation Investment Management, an investment firm
focused on "sustainable investing for the long term" ("About"),
wrote a groundbreaking white paper that outlined the perverse
incentives company managers face. For public companies, the
default practice is to issue earnings guidances—announcements
of projected future earnings—every quarter. This practice
encourages executives to manage for the short term instead of
adding long-term value to their company and the earth (Gore
and Blood). Only the most uncompromisingly green CEOs would
still advocate for stricter carbon emissions standards at the
company's factories if a few mediocre quarters left investors
demanding that they be fired. Gore and Blood make a powerful
case against requiring companies to be subjected to this
"What have you done for me lately?" philosophy, arguing that
quarterly earnings guidances should be abolished in favor of
companies releasing information when they consider it
appropriate. And to further persuade managers to think
sustainably, companies need to change the way the managers get

Annotations (right margin):

Transition referring to ideas in previous paragraph

Details of claim

Logical appeals using information and evidence in white paper

Ethical appeal to companies

Partial solution proposed

Mercer-Golden 3

paid. Currently, the CEO of ExxonMobil is rewarded for a highly profitable year but is not held accountable for depleting nonrenewable oil reserves. A new model should incentivize thinking for the long run. Multiyear milestones for performance evaluation, as Gore and Blood suggest, are essential to pushing executives to manage sustainably.

Claim extended to socially responsible businesses

Logical appeals

But it's not just for-profit companies that need to rethink strategies. Social good–oriented leaders also stand to learn from the people often vilified in environmental circles: corporate CEOs. To survive in today's economy, companies building sustainable products must operate under the same strict business standards as profit-driven companies. Two social enterprises, Nika Water and Belu, provide perfect examples. Both sell bottled water in the developed world with the mission of providing clean water to impoverished communities through their profits. Both have visionary leaders who define the lesson that all environmental and social entrepreneurs need to understand: financial pragmatism will add far more value to the world than idealistic dreams. Nika Water founder Jeff Church explained this in a speech at Stanford University:

> Social entrepreneurs look at their businesses as nine parts cause, one part business. In the beginning, it needs to be nine parts business, one part cause, because if the business doesn't stay around long enough because it can't make it, you can't do anything about the cause.

Additional logical appeals

When U.K.-based Belu lost £600,000 ($940,000) in 2007, it could only give around £30,000 ($47,000) to charity. Karen Lynch took over as CEO, cutting costs, outsourcing significant parts of the company's operations, and redesigning the entire business model; the company now donates four times as much to charity

Mercer-Golden 4

(Hurley). The conventional portrayal of do-gooders is that they tend to be terrible businesspeople, an argument often grounded in reality. It is easy to criticize the Walmarts of the world for caring little about sustainability or social good, but the idealists with big visions who do not follow through on their promises because their businesses cannot survive are no more praiseworthy. Walmart should learn from nonprofits and social enterprises on advancing a positive environmental and social agenda, but idealist entrepreneurs should also learn from corporations about building successful businesses.

Return to thesis: businesses should learn from one another

The final piece of the sustainable business ecosystem is the investors who help get potentially world-changing companies off the ground. Industries that require a large amount of money to build complex products with expensive materials, such as solar power companies, rely heavily on investors—often venture capitalists based in California's Silicon Valley (Knight). The problem is that venture capitalists are not doing enough to fund truly groundbreaking companies. In an oft-cited blog post titled "Why Facebook Is Killing Silicon Valley," entrepreneur Steve Blank argues that the financial returns on social media companies have been so quick and so outsized that the companies with the really big ideas—like providing efficient, cheap, scalable solar power—are not being backed: "In the past, if you were a great [venture capitalist], you could make $100 million on an investment in 5–7 years. Today, social media startups can return hundreds of millions or even billions in less than 3 years." The point Blank makes is that what is earning investors lots of money right now is not what is best for the United States or the world.

Transition to second part of thesis signaled

Problem explained

Reasons in support of claim

There are, however, signs of hope. PayPal founder Peter Thiel runs his venture capital firm, the Founders Fund, on the

Transition signaling reason for optimism

Mercer-Golden 5

philosophy that investors should support "flying cars" instead of new social media ventures (Packer). While the next company with the mission of making photo-sharing cooler or communicating with friends easier might be both profitable and valuable, Thiel and a select few others fund technology that has the potential to solve the **Reason presented** huge problems essential to human survival.

The world's need for sustainable companies that can build products from renewable energy or make nonpolluting cars will inevitably create opportunities for smart companies to make money. In fact, significant opportunities already exist for venture capitalists willing to step away from what is easy today and shift their investment strategies toward what will help us continue to live on this planet tomorrow—even if seeing strong returns may take a few more years. Visionaries like Blank and Thiel need more allies (and dollars) in their fight to help produce more pioneering, sustainable companies. And global warming **Emotional appeal** won't abate before investors wise up. It is vital that this shift happen now.

Logical appeal

When we think about organizations today, we think about nonprofits, which have long-term social missions, and corporations, which we judge by their immediate financial returns like quarterly **Thesis revisited** earnings. That is a treacherous dichotomy. Instead, we need to see the three major players in the business ecosystem—corporations, social enterprises, and investors—moving toward a *single* model of long-term, sustainable capitalism. We need visionary companies that not only set out to solve humankind's biggest problems but also have the business intelligence to accomplish these goals, and we need investors willing to fund these companies. Gore and Blood argue that "the

Mercer-Golden 6

imperative for change has never been greater." We will see this change when the world realizes that sustainable capitalism shares the same goals as creating a sustainable environment. Let us hope that this realization comes soon.

Quotation, restatement of thesis, and emotional appeal close argument

Mercer-Golden 7

Works Cited

"About Us." *Generation*, 2012, www.generationim.com/about/.

Blank, Steve. "Why Facebook Is Killing Silicon Valley." *Steveblank
.com*, 21 May 2012, steveblank.com/2012/05/21/why
-facebook-is-killing-silicon-valley/.

Church, Jeff. "The Wave of Social Entrepreneurship." Entrepreneurial
Thought Leaders Seminar, NVIDIA Auditorium, Stanford, 11 Apr.
2012. Lecture.

Eccles, Robert G., et al. "The Impact of a Corporate Culture of
Sustainability on Organizational Process and Performance."
Working Knowledge, Harvard Business School, 14 Nov. 2011,
hbswk.hbs.edu/item/the-impact-of-corporate-sustainability-on
-organizational-process-and-performance.

Gore, Al, and David Blood. "Sustainable Capitalism." *Generation*, 15
Feb. 2012, www.generationim.com/media/pdf-generation
-sustainable-capitalism-v1.pdf.

Hurley, James. "Belu Boss Shows Bottle for a Turnaround." *Daily
Telegraph*, 28 Feb. 2012, www.telegraph.co.uk/finance/
businessclub/9109449/Belu-boss-shows-bottle-for-a
-turnaround.html.

Knight, Eric R. W. "The Economic Geography of Clean Tech Venture
Capital." Oxford University Working Paper Series in Employment,
Work, and Finance, 13 Apr. 2010. *Social Science Research
Network*, doi:10.2139/ssrn.1588806.

Packer, George. "No Death, No Taxes: The Libertarian Futurism of a
Silicon Valley Billionaire." *The New Yorker*, 28 Nov. 2011, www
.newyorker.com/magazine/2011/11/28/no-death-no-taxes.

▲ **For visual analysis** This illustration shows a research project in progress, with the researcher about to evaluate source information on the "perfect pie." What questions have you answered with the help of credible sources?

Research

Research is formalized curiosity. It is poking and prying with a purpose.

— ZORA NEALE HURSTON

10   Doing Research

If you haven't thought of yourself as a "researcher," think again! Whether you are figuring out the best software to use for a project or investigating ways to earn money while going to school, you are doing research. And in college, you are part of a research *community* — one that values the work of researchers and knows that the results of that research can lead to breakthroughs or to ways to improve lives. Of course, instructors will sometimes assign a research project for you to carry out, but even in these instances, you might have a chance to shape the project to your interests and make it your own. In other classes, you will have an opportunity to create your own assignment, choosing a topic or issue you want to explore and finding ways to do so, perhaps doing field research (interviews, surveys, observations) alongside or instead of research with traditional print and online sources.

Keep in mind that while research can help you produce a project and earn a grade, it can also be the way that you make your mark — make something good happen in the world around you. What starts out as a school obligation (researching a youth community garden, for example, and initiating a letter-writing campaign) may very well turn into a meaningful life change (healthier eating habits in a community).

10a   Prepare for a research project.

Whether you are assigned a research topic or select one of your own, preparing to begin that research means taking a long look at what you already know, the best ways to proceed, and the amount of time you have to find out what you need to know.

Analyze your assignment

In an introductory writing course, you might receive an assignment like this one:

> Choose a topic of special interest to you, and use it as the basis for a research essay of approximately two thousand words that makes and substantiates a claim. You should use a minimum of five to eight credible, authoritative sources.

TOPIC

If the assignment allows you to choose your own topic, consider the following questions:

- What topics do you know something about? Which would you like to explore?
- What topics do you care most about? What might you like to become an expert on?
- What topics evoke a strong reaction from you, whether positive or negative?

Be sure to get responses about your possible topic from your instructor, classmates, and friends. Ask them whether they would be interested in reading about the topic, whether it seems manageable, and whether they know of any good sources for information.

SITUATION

Be sure to consider the rhetorical situation (see Chapter 2) of any research project:

AUDIENCE

- Who will be the audience for your research project (2d)?
- Why will they be interested in the topic? What will they want to know? What will they already know?
- What do you know about their backgrounds and assumptions about the topic?
- What response do you want from them?
- What kinds of evidence will you need to convince them?
- What will your instructor expect?

PURPOSE

- If you can choose the purpose, what would you like to accomplish (2c)?
- The key words in an assignment can give clues about the purpose. Does the assignment ask that you *describe, survey, analyze, persuade, explain, classify, compare,* or *contrast*?

YOUR ATTITUDE TOWARD THE TOPIC (STANCE)

- What is your attitude toward your topic? Are you curious about it? an advocate for it? critical of it? Do you like it? dislike it? find it confusing — and if so, why?
- What influences have shaped your thinking on the topic (2c)?

SCOPE

- How long is the project supposed to be? Base your research and writing schedule on the scale of the finished project (brief vs. long paper or presentation, a simple vs. complex website) and the amount of time you have to complete it.

- How many and what kind(s) of sources should you use (10e)? What kind(s) of visuals — charts, maps, photographs, and so on — will you need? Will you use sound or video files? What field research might you do — interviewing, surveying, or observing (10h)?

Here is a sample schedule for a research project.

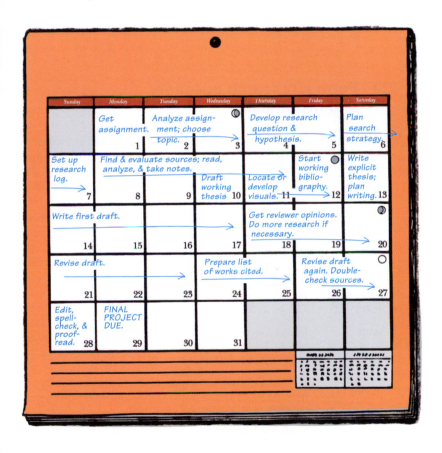

10b Form a research question and hypothesis.

Once you have analyzed your task, chosen your topic, and narrowed it (see 3b), formulate a research question that you can tentatively answer with a hypothesis. The hypothesis, a statement of what you anticipate your research will show, needs to be manageable, interesting (see 3c), and debatable.

Julia Sakowitz, the student whose research paper appears in Chapter 57, made the following move from general topic to a narrowed topic and then to a research question and hypothesis:

TOPIC	How tourism affects residents/neighborhoods
NARROWED TOPIC	How tourism in Harlem affects its residents
ISSUE	Many types of tourism business are operating in the historic Harlem neighborhood, not all of which bring benefits for residents.
RESEARCH QUESTION	Which type of tourism business is more beneficial to the residents of Harlem, a small local and minority-owned business or an outside tour company?
HYPOTHESIS	Small, local, minority-owned tour businesses seem to benefit the residents of Harlem more than those businesses that come in from outside of Harlem.

10c   Plan your research.

Once you have formed a hypothesis, determine what you already know about your topic. Tap your memory for sources by listing everything you can remember about *where* you learned about your topic. What you know comes from somewhere (social media, articles, courses, conversations), and that somewhere can serve as a starting point for your research. (See 3a for more strategies for exploring ideas.)

Next, develop a research plan by answering the following questions:

- What kinds of sources (books, journal articles, databases, websites, government documents, reference works) and how many sources will you need to consult (10e)?
- How current do your sources need to be?
- How can you determine the location and availability of the kinds of sources you need?

One goal of your research plan is to build a strong working bibliography (11b). Carrying out systematic research and keeping careful notes on your sources will make developing your works-cited list or bibliography easier.

Finally, setting up a *research log* — a physical notebook, digital file, or Google doc in which you record ideas about sources and keep track of what you find and read — will make writing and documenting your sources efficient and accurate.

10d   Move from hypothesis to working thesis.

As you gather and evaluate the information you find in print and online sources and through field research, you will probably refine your research question and change your hypothesis significantly. Only after you have explored your hypothesis, tested it, and sharpened it by reading, writing, and talking with others does it become a working thesis.

Student writer Julia Sakowitz, a native New Yorker, did quite a bit of research on tourism in Harlem, focusing first on the policies that led to change in Harlem over the past three decades, which she learned about through traditional library and online sources. When she started to interview Harlem residents and local business owners, she shifted her attention to the effects of tourism on members of the local community and developed a new working thesis. For Julia Sakowitz's research essay, see Chapter 57.

In doing your own research, you may find that your interest shifts, that a whole line of inquiry is unproductive, or that your hypothesis is simply wrong. The process of research, of consulting a number of credible sources, pushes you to learn more about your hypothesis and to make it more precise.

10e   Understand different kinds of sources.

Consulting sources is something you'll do throughout your research project. With so much information coming at you 24/7, this can be a daunting task, one that may be made more manageable by thinking of the different kinds of sources available to you. Sources can include data from interviews and surveys, books and articles in print and online, websites, film, podcasts, video, images, and more. Consider these important differences among sources.

Scholarly and popular sources

While nonacademic sources can help you get started on a research project, you will usually want to depend on authorities in a field, whose work generally appears in scholarly journals. The following list will help you distinguish scholarly and popular sources:

SCHOLARLY	POPULAR

Title often contains the word *Journal*	*Journal* usually does not appear in title
Available mainly through libraries and library databases	Available outside of libraries (at newsstands or from a home Internet connection)
Few commercial advertisements	Many advertisements
Authors identified with academic credentials	Authors are usually journalists or reporters hired by the publication, not academics or experts
Summary or abstract appears on first page of article; articles are fairly long	No summary or abstract; articles are fairly short
Articles cite sources and provide bibliographies	Articles include quotations but omit citations and bibliographies

Primary and secondary sources

Primary sources provide firsthand knowledge, and secondary sources report on or analyze the research of others. Primary sources are basic sources of raw information, including your own field research; films, works of art, or other objects you examine; literary works you read; and eyewitness accounts, photographs, news reports, and historical documents (such as letters and speeches).

Secondary sources are descriptions or interpretations of primary sources, such as researchers' reports, reviews, biographies, and encyclopedia articles. Often what constitutes a primary or secondary source depends on the purpose of your research. A critic's evaluation of a film, for instance, serves as a secondary source if you are writing about the film but as a primary source if you are studying the critic's writing.

 ## Use web and library resources.

To find scholarly, popular, primary, secondary, traditional, and multimedia sources, you will most often turn to the web or to your college library.

Starting with online searches

Many writers begin doing research by turning to Google. The number of results, however, can be overwhelming, giving you much more than you could possibly evaluate or, eventually, use. Nevertheless, doing a quick Google search can give you an overview of what's out there. Wikipedia also offers a good place to begin research, though most instructors warn against citing an article from Wikipedia because its author is often unknown and its information may not be entirely credible. But the entries are relatively short, clearly written, and well organized; they can point to themes or issues you can then pursue on trusted sites such as Google Scholar.

Unlike Google, which captures (nearly) everything related to your topic, Google Scholar filters a search, pulling up only articles from scholarly sources. And with Google Scholar, you can pull up a full text rather than simply an abstract or an excerpt from an article.

Finding authoritative sources on the open web

You can find many sources online that are authoritative and reliable. For example, the Internet enables you to enter virtual libraries that allow access to some collections in libraries other than your own. Online collections housed in government sites can also be reliable and useful sources. The following have useful online collections of articles:

The Library of Congress (www.loc.gov)

National Institutes of Health (www.nih.gov)

U.S. Census Bureau (www.census.gov)

For current national news, consult online versions of reputable newspapers such as the *Washington Post* or the *Chicago Tribune* or sites like C-SPAN.org for news.

Some scholarly journals (such as those from Berkeley Electronic Press) and general-interest magazines (including *Slate* and *Salon*) are published only on the web, and many other publications, like *Newsweek*, the *New Yorker*, and the *New Republic*, make at least some of their contents available online for free.

10g Consult your library's staff, databases, and other resources.

You may have gotten a good start by using Google, Wikipedia, and filtered searches like those from Google Scholar, but you can capitalize on that good start by turning now to the sources available to you for free through your college library.

Reference librarians

The staff of your library, especially reference librarians, will willingly help you access and use the many databases the library subscribes to. If your writing instructor does not schedule a library orientation, it's worth making an appointment to talk with a librarian about your research project and get specific recommendations about databases and other helpful places to continue your research. To get the most helpful advice, whether online or in person, pose *specific* questions — not "Where can I find information about computers?" but "Where can I find information on the history of messaging technologies?"

Catalogs and databases

Your library's computers hold many resources not available on the web or not accessible to students except through the library's system. One of these resources is the library's own catalog, but most libraries also subscribe to a large number of databases — digital collections of information, such as indexes to journal and magazine articles, texts of news stories and legal cases, lists of sources on particular topics, and compilations of statistics — that have been vetted by scholars and that students can access for free. Your library may also have software that allows you to search several databases at once.

Many library search engines offer a variety of search options to help you combine keywords (*sleep deprivation* AND *college*), search for an exact phrase (*sleep habits of college students*), or exclude items containing particular keywords (*sleep deprivation* NOT *new parents*). Often they can limit your search in other ways as well, such as by date or language. Look for a "refine your search" box or consider checking "full text" and "scholarly peer review" to make sure you will get the most relevant, complete, and authoritative texts for your project.

General and specialized indexes

Different indexes cover different groups of periodicals; articles written before 1990 may be indexed only in a print volume. General indexes of periodicals list articles from general-interest magazines (such as *Time*), newspapers, and perhaps some scholarly journals. General indexes are useful for finding current sources on a topic. Specialized indexes, which tend to include mainly scholarly periodicals, may focus on one discipline (as the education index ERIC does) or on a group of related disciplines (as Social Sciences Abstracts does).

Full text and abstracts

Be sure not to confuse an abstract with a complete article. Full-text databases can be extremely convenient — you can read and print out articles directly from the computer, without the extra step of tracking down the periodical in question. However, if you limit yourself to full-text databases you may miss out on graphics and images that appeared in the print version of the periodical. You can also take advantage of abstracts, which give you a very brief overview of the article's contents so you can decide whether you need to spend time finding and reading the full text.

To locate a promising article that is not available in a full-text digital version, check to see whether a print version is available in your library's periodicals room.

Books

Libraries categorize books by the *author's name*, by the *title*, and by one or more *subjects*. If you can't find a particular source under any of these headings, you can search by using a combination of subject headings and keywords. Such searches may turn up other useful titles as well. Catalog entries for print books may indicate whether a book has been checked out and, if so, when it is due.

Bibliographies

Look at any bibliographies (lists of sources) in books or articles you are using for your research; they can lead you to other valuable resources. In addition, check with a reference librarian to find out whether your library has more extensive bibliographies devoted to the area of your research.

Other library resources

In addition to books and periodicals, libraries give you access to many other useful materials that might be appropriate for your research.

- *Special collections and archives.* Your library may house archives and other special materials that are often available to student researchers. One student, for example, learned that her university owned a vast collection of twentieth-century posters. With help from a librarian, she was able to use some of these posters as primary sources for her research project on German culture after World War II.

- *Audio, video, multimedia, and art collections.* Many libraries have areas devoted to media and art, where they collect films, videos, paintings, and sound recordings.

- *Government documents.* Many libraries have collections of historical documents produced by local or state government offices. Check with a librarian if government publications would be useful sources for your topic. You can also look at the online version of the U.S. Government Printing Office at www.govinfo.gov for electronic versions of government publications.

- *Interlibrary loans.* To borrow books, videos, or audio materials from another library, use an interlibrary loan. You can also request copies of journal articles from other libraries. Some loans can take time, so plan ahead.

10h   Conduct field research.

Many research topics that interest you may call for you to collect field data. The "field" may be many things — a classroom, a church, a laboratory, or a social media site. As a field researcher, you will need to discover *where* you can find relevant information, *how* to gather it, and *who* might be your best providers of information. Also remember that carrying out research on people ("human subjects") may require permission from your college Institutional Review Board, the group that ensures research will not result in harm to people. Observing whether and when motorcycle riders are able to find parking space in the campus lots will probably not require permission, but observing kindergarten students in a local classroom probably will. Talk with your instructor about whether or not you may need such permission.

Interviews

Some information is best obtained by interviewing—asking direct questions of other people, as Julia Sakowitz did. If you can talk with an expert in person, on the phone, or online, you might get information you could not have obtained through any other kind of research.

Your first step is to find interview subjects. Has your research generated the names of people you might contact directly? Brainstorm for additional names, looking for authorities on your topic and people in your community, and then write, call, or email them to try to arrange an interview.

When you have identified someone to interview, prepare your questions. You will probably want to ask several kinds of questions. Questions about facts and figures (*How many employees do you have?*) elicit specific answers and don't invite expansion or opinion. You can lead the interviewee to think out loud and to give additional details by asking open-ended questions: *How do you feel now about deciding to enlist in the military after 9/11?*

Avoid any questions that would encourage vague answers (*What do you think of youth today?*) or yes/no answers (*Should laws governing student loans be changed?*). Instead, ask questions that must be answered with supporting details (*Why should laws governing student loans be changed?*).

Student writer Julia Sakowitz wrote seven questions in preparation for her interview with a small business owner in her native Harlem.

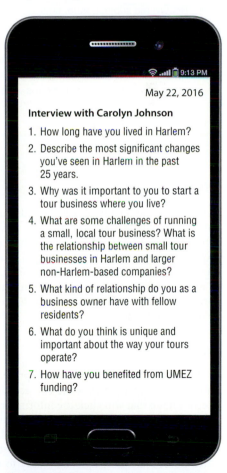

9:13 PM

May 22, 2016

Interview with Carolyn Johnson

1. How long have you lived in Harlem?
2. Describe the most significant changes you've seen in Harlem in the past 25 years.
3. Why was it important to you to start a tour business where you live?
4. What are some challenges of running a small, local tour business? What is the relationship between small tour businesses in Harlem and larger non-Harlem-based companies?
5. What kind of relationship do you as a business owner have with fellow residents?
6. What do you think is unique and important about the way your tours operate?
7. How have you benefited from UMEZ funding?

Sample questions for a personal interview

Quick Help

Conducting an Interview

- Determine your exact purpose, and be sure it relates to your research question and hypothesis. Make sure you know enough about your topic to ask intelligent and useful questions.

- Set up the interview early in your research process. Specify how long it will take, and if you wish to record the session, ask permission to do so.

- Prepare a written list of factual and open-ended questions. If the interview proceeds in a direction that seems fruitful, do not feel that you have to ask all of your prepared questions.

- Record the subject, date, time, and place of the interview.

- Even if you are recording, take notes. Ask your interviewee for permission to use video, audio, or quotations in your project.

- Always thank those you interview, both in person and in a letter or email.

- After the interview, check facts and other information you gained, especially anything that seems questionable. You may want to interview other people who can vouch for — or discredit — such information.

Observations

Before you conduct any observation, decide exactly what you want to find out, and anticipate what you are likely to see. Are you going to observe an action repeated by many people (such as pedestrians crossing a street), a sequence of actions (such as a medical procedure), or the interactions of a group (such as a church congregation)? Also decide exactly what you want to record and how. And keep in mind that just as a photographer has a particular angle on a subject, so an observer always has an angle on what he or she is looking at.

Surveys

To do survey research, you need a representative sample of people (a subset of a group that matches the characteristics of the whole group) and a questionnaire that will elicit the information you need.

On any questionnaire, the questions should be clear and easy to understand and designed so that you will be able to analyze the answers easily. Questions that ask respondents to say yes or no or to rank items on a five-point scale are particularly easy to tabulate. And leaving room for

> ## Quick Help
>
> ### Conducting an Observation
>
> - Determine the purpose and method of the observation, and be sure it relates to your research question and hypothesis.
> - Determine whether you will need permission to conduct the observation, record the observation, and take photos. If necessary, make appointments to conduct the observations.
> - Brainstorm about what you are looking for, but don't be rigidly bound to your expectations.
> - Decide what materials or equipment you may need and make sure it works.
> - Develop a system for recording data. Consider using a "split" notebook or screen: on one side, record your observations directly; on the other, record your thoughts and interpretations either during or after the observation.
> - Record the date, time, and place of the observation.
> - Trust your instincts: you may observe something you weren't looking for but strikes you as interesting and important. Make a note of it.
> - Go back over your notes, looking for recurring actions and other patterns, and make a note to come back to them when you begin to analyze your data.

"other" or "additional information" may help you get information that a simple yes/no misses.

Because tabulating the responses takes time and because people sometimes resent answering long questionnaires, limit the number of questions to no more than twenty.

Analyzing and interpreting data

To make sense of the information you have gathered, first try to find a focus, since you can't pay equal attention to everything. This step is especially important in analyzing results from observations or survey questionnaires.

Go back over your notes and results, looking for patterns or trends. In an observation of motorcycle riders looking for parking, you may note a pattern related to the time of day that is busiest, or a certain part of the parking lot that seems to be favored. In your survey results, you may note that women tend to answer one way, men another. You're looking for all such patterns that will help you interpret your findings. Remember to

Quick Help

Designing a Survey Questionnaire

- Write out your purpose, and review your research question and hypothesis to determine the kinds of questions to ask.
- Figure out how to get a representative sample of the group you want to survey and decide how to reach them — by written survey through email or on SurveyMonkey? By phone or face to face?
- Decide what kind of survey questions to use:

MULTIPLE CHOICE

Please choose your favorite site for studying:

_____ dorm

_____ library

_____ writing center

_____ campus café

_____ outdoor spot

LEVEL OF AGREEMENT

Please indicate how much you agree with this statement:
I have a favorite place to study.

_____ strongly agree

_____ agree

_____ strongly disagree

_____ disagree

OPEN-ENDED

Where on campus do you most like to study?

_____

_____

- Draft questions that call for short, specific answers.
- Test the questions on several people, and then revise any questions that seem unfair, ambiguous, too hard to answer, or too time consuming.
- Draft a cover letter or invitation email that introduces the survey. Be sure to state your deadline.
- If you are using a print questionnaire, make sure to leave adequate space for answers.
- Proofread the questionnaire carefully.
- Record the responses you receive, using a blank survey to tally responses or creating a spreadsheet to track findings.

identify quotations you may want to use later; these can help illustrate the points you make.

Next, synthesize the data by looking for recurring words or ideas that fall into patterns. Establish a system for coding your information, labeling each pattern you identify—a plus sign for every positive response on a questionnaire, for example. If you ask classmates to review your notes or data, they may notice other patterns.

Finally, interpret your data by summing up the meaning of what you have found and articulating insights. Why are the patterns you've identified important? What is the significance of your findings? Be careful not to make large generalizations.

11 Evaluating Sources and Taking Notes

Judging whether a source is useful depends to a great extent on your topic, purpose, and audience. On almost any topic you can imagine (How can food be produced more sustainably? Why have a "death café" movement? Who reads fan fiction?), you will need research to answer the question, which means reading sources, gathering data, and thinking critically about these sources. With most topics, in fact, the challenge will not be finding sources so much as figuring out *which* sources to consult in the limited time you have available. Learning to identify reliable, credible, and useful sources allows you to use your time wisely, and taking effective notes allows you to put the sources to work for you.

11a Understand why writers use sources.

Writers use sources for many reasons:

- to provide background information or context an audience will need
- to help explain or define concepts clearly
- to provide evidence and support for points the writer is making
- to add to the writer's authority and credibility
- to add special emphasis to a point
- to provide other perspectives on a topic, including counter-evidence

As you begin to work with your sources, make notes in your research log about why you plan to use a particular source. You should also begin your working bibliography.

11b Create a working bibliography or an annotated bibliography.

A working bibliography is a list of sources that you may use for your project. As you find and begin to evaluate research sources — articles, books, websites, and so on — you should record information that will allow you to find the source again and cite it correctly. The emphasis here is on *working* because the list may include materials that end up not being useful. For this reason, you don't absolutely need to put all entries into the documentation style you will use. See Chapter 56 (MLA), Chapter 60 (APA), and Chapter 63 (*Chicago*). If you do follow the required documentation style, however, that work will be done when you prepare the final draft.

The following chart will help you keep track of the information you should try to find:

Type of Source	Information to Collect (if applicable)
Online/digital source	Author(s), title of document, title of site, editor(s) of site, sponsor of site, publication information for print version of source, name of database or online service, date of publication or last update, date you accessed the source, URL (or DOI or other stable locator)
Part of a book	Call number, author(s) of part, title of part, author(s) or editor(s) of book, title of book, place of publication, publisher, year of publication, inclusive page numbers for part
Print article	Call number of publication, author(s) of article, title of article, name of publication, volume number, issue number, date of issue, inclusive page numbers for article

For other kinds of sources (films, recordings, visuals), you should also list the information required by the documentation style you are using and note where you found the information.

Annotated bibliography

You might want (or be assigned) to annotate your working bibliography to include a summary of the sources' contents as well as publishing information because annotating can help you understand and remember the main ideas in each source you read. Your instructor might also ask you to evaluate the source by noting its strengths or weaknesses (11c) or by commenting on the usefulness of the source to your project.

The following single entry shows a student's annotation for one source.

SAMPLE ANNOTATED BIBLIOGRAPHY ENTRY (MLA STYLE)

Dávila, Arlene. "Empowered Culture? New York City's Empowerment Zone
and the Selling of El Barrio." *The Annals of the American Academy of
Political and Social Science,* vol. 594, no. 1, July 2004, pp. 49-64. *JSTOR,*
www.jstor.org/stable/4127693.

> NYU sociology professor Arlene Dávila explains that programs
designed to stimulate tourism in Harlem have largely ignored Latino/a
residents of East Harlem, known as *El Barrio.* Rather than blaming
leaders of Harlem's black neighborhoods, which she suggests are seen
as more marketable to tourists, she questions the anti-Latino bias of
the economic policies of the Upper Manhattan Empowerment Zone.
Dávila calls for debate about the problems that come with treating
culture as a commodity. Although the article is older, Dávila's argument
is a valuable one. She provides a counterpoint to the idea that
economic initiatives adopted since the 1990s have benefited all
Harlemites. I can also use her analysis of culture as a product to set
up my conclusion.

In this annotated bibliography entry for an article Julia Sakowitz used in
her essay on tourism in Harlem (see Chapter 57), she opens by summarizing Dávila's argument in the first three sentences and then explains why
the source is useful to her in the last three sentences, thus combining description and evaluation in her bibliographical note.

Talking the Talk

Research with an Open Mind

"What's wrong with looking for sources that back up what I want to
say?" When you start researching a topic, keep an open mind: investigate every important source, even if you think you won't agree with it.
If all your sources take the same position you take, you may be doing
some pretty selective searching — and you may be missing part of the
picture. Who knows? You may change your position after learning more
about the topic. Even if you don't, ignoring counterarguments and other
points of view harms your credibility, suggesting that you haven't done
your homework.

11c   Evaluate a source's usefulness and credibility.

Of course you will want the information and ideas you glean from sources to be not just persuasive but also reliable and credible, so you must evaluate each potential source carefully. Doing so is especially important because false information can circulate widely, especially online. (See 7b for more on identifying false and misleading sources.) In addition, the following guidelines can help you assess the usefulness and credibility of sources:

- *Your purpose.* What will this source add to your research project? Does it support a major point, demonstrate that you have done thorough research, or help establish your own credibility?

- *Relevance.* How closely related is the source to the narrowed topic you are pursuing? You may need to read beyond the title and opening paragraph to check for relevance.

- *Audience and level of specialization.* General sources can be helpful as you begin your research, but you may then need the authority or currency of more specialized sources. On the other hand, specialized works may be hard to understand. Who is the intended audience for the source — the general public? experts in the field? advocates or opponents? How does this fit with your concept of your own audience?

- *Credentials of the author and publisher or sponsor.* What are the author's credentials and expertise? Can you tell if the author is cited by others? What can you learn about the publisher or sponsor of the source? For example, is it a newspaper known for integrity, or is it an amateur's blog? Is it sponsored by a professional or government organization or academic institution or by a questionable group you've never heard of?

- *Date of publication.* Recent sources are often more useful than older ones, particularly in the sciences or other fields that change rapidly. However, in some fields — such as the humanities — the most authoritative works may be older ones.

- *Accuracy of the source.* How accurate and complete is the information in the source? How thorough is the list of works cited that accompanies the source? Can you find other sources that corroborate what your source is saying? If not, be skeptical.

- *Stance of the source.* Identify the source's point of view or rhetorical stance, and scrutinize it carefully. Does the source present facts, or does it interpret or evaluate them? If it presents facts, what is included and what is omitted, and why? If it interprets or evaluates information that is not disputed, the source's stance may be obvious, but at other times, you will need to think carefully about the source's goals (11d). What does the author or sponsoring group want? to convince you of an idea? sell you something? call you to action in some way?

- **Cross-references to the source.** Is the source cited in other works? If you see your source cited by others, notice how they cite it and what they say about it to find additional clues to its credibility.

11d Read sources critically.

For those sources that you want to analyze more closely, reading with a critical eye can make your research process more efficient. Use the following tips to guide your reading.

Keep your research question in mind

With your research question in mind, determine how the source material supports or refutes your hypothesis and whether any quotations or data from the source help you answer your research question.

Preview a source before you commit

Looking quickly at the various parts of a source can provide useful information and help you decide whether to explore that particular source more thoroughly.

- *Basic elements* such as title and subtitle, copyright page, home page, table of contents, index, footnotes, and bibliography provide critical information.
- *Abstracts* routinely precede journal articles and offer a summary of the discussion.
- A *preface* or *foreword* generally discusses both the writer's purpose and thesis.
- *Subheadings* can alert you to how much detail is given on a topic.
- A *conclusion* or *afterword* may summarize or draw the strands of an argument together.
- For a digital source, click on some of the *links* to see if they're useful, and see if the overall *design* of the site is easy to navigate.

Check the author's stance and tone

Read with an eye for the author's perhaps unstated overall rhetorical stance, or perspective, as well as for facts or explicit opinions. Also pay attention to the author's tone, the way his or her attitude toward the topic and audience is conveyed. The following questions can help:

- Is the author a strong advocate or opponent of something? a skeptical critic? a specialist in the field? Are there any clues to why the author takes this stance?

- How does this stance affect the author's presentation and your reaction to it?

- What facts does the author include? Can you think of any important information that is left out — and why the author may have done so?

- What is the author's tone? Is it cautious, angry, flippant, serious, impassioned? What words indicate this tone?

Quick Help

Guidelines for Checking Facts

Begin to practice what media analyst Howard Rheingold calls "crap detection," which means reading defensively and identifying information that is false or deceptive. The following tips can help you to become a good fact-checker:

- Identify the information that is presented as *fact* in a source. Ask questions: does this information seem accurate? complete? trustworthy? Check to see if the source presents a bibliography or list of works cited.

- Search for other credible sources (Rheingold suggests three) that corroborate the facts you are checking. If you can't find sources that verify a fact, be suspicious.

- Use nonpartisan fact-checkers like PolitiFact, FactCheck.org, and the Sunlight Foundation. Snopes.com is also useful for fact-checking general rumors and memes.

- Be on the lookout for clickbait headlines and titles — that is, those that say "click me, click me" — and for nonstandard URLs.

- Pay attention to the tone with which facts are presented. If the tone is sensational or highly exaggerated, take care that the facts are not also exaggerated.

Check the author's argument and evidence

Every piece of writing takes a position. Even a scientific report implicitly "argues" that we should accept it and its data as reliable. As you read, look for the main point or the main argument the author is making. Identify the reasons the author gives to support his or her position. Then try to determine *why* the author takes this position.

- How persuasive is the evidence? Can you think of a way to refute it?
- Can you detect any questionable logic or fallacious thinking in the argument (8f)?
- Does this author disagree with arguments you have read elsewhere? If so, what causes the disagreements — differences about facts or about how to interpret facts?

11e   Synthesize sources.

When you read and evaluate a source — for example, when you consider its purpose and relevance, its author's credentials, its accuracy, and the kind of argument it is making — you are *analyzing* the source. Analysis requires you to take apart something complex (such as an article in a scholarly journal) and look closely at the parts to understand the whole better. For academic writing, you also need to *synthesize*; in other words, you need to group similar pieces of information together and look for patterns. Synthesis helps you put your sources and your own knowledge and experience together in an original argument. Synthesis is the flip side of analysis: you already understand the parts, so your job is to assemble them into a new whole.

To synthesize sources for a research project, try the following tips:

- *Read the material carefully.* For tips on reading with a critical eye, see Chapter 7.
- *Determine the most important ideas in each source.* Take notes on each source. Identify and summarize the key ideas of each piece.
- *Form a position.* Review the key ideas of each source and figure out how they fit together. Look for patterns: discussions of causes and effects, specific parts of a larger issue, background information, and so on. Be sure to consider the complexity of the issue, and demonstrate that you have considered more than one perspective.
- *Summon evidence to support your position.* You might use paraphrases, summaries, or direct quotations from your sources as evidence, or your personal experience or prior knowledge. Integrate

SYNTHESIS: FINDING PATTERNS

Look through your sources carefully.

ASK:

What are the **key** ideas in each source?

What **patterns** can you identify?

How do the sources' **perspectives** relate to your own perspective?

Acknowledge that the related ideas you find may not fit smoothly together.

SYNTHESIS: COMBINING IDEAS

Weave your sources into your text.

ASK:

Why are you using each source?

How do your sources **fit** with what you want to say?

How can you **arrange** your ideas and others' ideas for the best effect?

Make sure your sources support your own voice and message.

quotations properly (see Chapter 12), and keep your ideas central to the piece of writing.

- ***Deal with counterarguments.*** You don't have to use every idea or source available — some will be more useful than others. However, ignoring evidence that opposes your position makes your argument weaker. You should fairly consider the valid opinions that differ from yours, and try to explain why they may be misguided or incomplete.

- *Combine your source materials effectively.* Be careful to avoid simply summarizing or listing information from your sources. You also need to comment on the sources, showing how they support and fit into the points you are making. If possible, weave the various sources together rather than discussing your sources one by one.

12 Integrating Sources and Avoiding Plagiarism

The process of absorbing your sources and integrating them gracefully into your own writing is one of the challenges but also one of the pleasures of research. When you integrate sources appropriately into your work, they don't take over your writing or drown out your voice. Instead, they work in support of your own good ideas.

Your writing is always influenced in some way by what you have read and experienced. As a writer, you need to understand current definitions of plagiarism, which have changed over time and vary from culture to culture, as well as the concept of intellectual property — works protected by copyright or by alternatives such as a Creative Commons license — so you can give credit where credit is due. An age of instant copying and linking may someday lead to revised understandings about who can "own" a text. But in college today, you should cite your sources carefully and systematically to avoid plagiarism, the use of someone else's words and ideas as if they were your own.

12a   Decide whether to quote, paraphrase, or summarize.

When you write, decisions about when and where to use exact language from a source or whether to paraphrase or summarize ideas from a source are yours to make. The following guidelines can help you decide whether to quote, paraphrase, or summarize.

QUOTE

- wording that is so memorable or powerful, or expresses a point so perfectly, that you cannot change it without weakening its meaning
- authors' opinions you wish to emphasize

- authors' words that make clear you are considering varying perspectives
- respected authorities whose opinions support your ideas
- authors whose opinions challenge or vary greatly from those of others in the field

PARAPHRASE

- passages you do not wish to quote but that use details important to your point

SUMMARIZE

- long passages in which the main point is important to your point but the details are not

12b   Integrate quotations, paraphrases, and summaries effectively.

Following are some general guidelines for integrating source materials into your writing.

Quotations

Quotations give the *exact words* of a source. Quotations from respected authorities can help establish your credibility and show that you are considering various perspectives. However, because your essay is primarily your own work, limit your use of quotations.

BRIEF QUOTATIONS

Short quotations should run in with your text and be enclosed by quotation marks (48a).

> In Miss Eckhart, Welty recognizes a character who shares with her "the love of her art and the love of giving it, the desire to give it until there is no more left" (10).

LONG QUOTATIONS

If you are following the style of the Modern Language Association (MLA), set off a prose quotation longer than four lines. For APA guidelines, see 58e. For *Chicago* guidelines, see 62c.

The following long quotation follows MLA style:

A good seating arrangement can prevent problems; however, *withitness*, as defined by Woolfolk, works even better:

> Withitness is the ability to communicate to students that you are aware of what is happening in the classroom, that you "don't miss anything." With-it teachers seem to have "eyes in the back of their heads." They avoid becoming too absorbed with a few students, since this allows the rest of the class to wander. (359)

This technique works, however, only if students actually believe that their teacher will know everything that goes on.

INTEGRATING QUOTATIONS SMOOTHLY INTO YOUR TEXT

Carefully integrate quotations into your text so that they will flow smoothly and clearly into the surrounding sentences. Use a signal phrase or verb, such as those identified in the following examples and list.

> As writer Eudora Welty notes, "learning stamps you with its moments. Childhood's learning," she continues, "is made up of moments. It isn't steady. It's a pulse" (9).

> In her essay, Haraway strongly opposes those who condemn technology outright, arguing that we must not indulge in a "demonology of technology" (181).

Notice that the examples alert readers to the quotations by using signal phrases that include the author's name. When you cite a quotation in this way, you need put only the page number in parentheses.

SIGNAL VERBS

acknowledges	concludes	emphasizes	replies
advises	concurs	expresses	reports
agrees	confirms	interprets	responds
allows	criticizes	lists	reveals
answers	declares	objects	says
asserts	describes	observes	states
believes	disagrees	offers	suggests
charges	discusses	opposes	thinks
claims	disputes	remarks	writes

Quick Help

Guidelines for Quoting

- Copy quotations carefully, with punctuation, capitalization, and spelling *exactly* as in the original. Enclose the quotation in quotation marks.
- Use square brackets if you introduce words of your own into a quotation or make changes in it, and use ellipses if you omit material.
- Use a signal verb or phrase as a boundary between your own ideas and the quotation.

BRACKETS AND ELLIPSES

In direct quotations, enclose in brackets any words you change or add, and indicate any deletions with ellipsis points (49f).

> "There is something wrong in the [Three Mile Island] area," one farmer told the Nuclear Regulatory Commission soon after the plant accident ("Legacy" 33).

> Economist John Kenneth Galbraith has pointed out that "large corporations cannot afford to compete with one another. . . . In a truly competitive market someone loses" (qtd. in Key 17).

Quick Help

Commenting on or Evaluating Your Source Material

Your choice of signal verbs often reveals your attitude toward or relationship to your sources. Signal verbs like *proves*, *demonstrates*, *shows*, or *establishes* suggest that you take a positive view of the information in the source, while signal verbs like *fails*, *lacks*, *refuses*, *overlooks*, or *ignores* suggest that you take a critical view. In between are more neutral verbs (*argues*, *indicates*, *suggests*, *notes*) indicating an objective relationship to the source material. Professor Laura Aull's research shows that advanced academic writers favor neutral signal verbs, which build the writer's ethos as fair and evenhanded. She also finds that these expert writers rarely use verbs associated with opinions or feelings (*feels*, *believes*, *thinks*), while student writers use them a great deal. You can learn from the experts to look very closely at the verbs you choose when you are reporting what your sources say.

Paraphrases

A paraphrase accurately states all the relevant information from a passage *in your own words and sentence structures*, without any additional comments or elaborations. A paraphrase is useful when the main points of a passage, their order, and at least some details are important but the exact wording is not. Unlike a summary, a paraphrase always restates *all* the main points of a passage in the same order and often in about the same number of words.

ORIGINAL

Language play, the arguments suggest, will help the development of pronunciation ability through its focus on the properties of sounds and sound contrasts, such as rhyming. Playing with word endings and decoding the syntax of riddles will help the acquisition of grammar. Readiness to play with words and names, to exchange puns and to engage in nonsense talk, promotes links with semantic development. The kinds of dialogue interaction illustrated above are likely to have consequences for the development of conversational skills. And language play, by its nature, also contributes greatly to what in recent years has been called *metalinguistic awareness*, which is turning out to be of critical importance in the development of language skills in general and of literacy skills in particular.

– DAVID CRYSTAL, *Language Play* (180)

The following paraphrase starts off well enough, but it moves away from paraphrasing the original to inserting the writer's ideas; Crystal says nothing about learning new languages or pursuing education.

UNACCEPTABLE PARAPHRASE: STRAYING FROM THE AUTHOR'S IDEAS

Crystal argues that playing with language — creating rhymes, figuring out how riddles work, making puns, playing with names, using invented words, and so on — helps children figure out a great deal about language, from the basics of pronunciation and grammar to how to carry on a conversation. Increasing their understanding of how language works in turn helps them become more interested in learning new languages and in pursuing education (180).

Because the underlined phrases below are either borrowed from the original without quotation marks or changed only superficially in language and structure, these paraphrases plagiarize the original.

UNACCEPTABLE PARAPHRASE: USING THE AUTHOR'S WORDS

Crystal suggests that language play, including rhyme, helps children improve pronunciation ability, that looking at word endings and decoding the syntax of riddles allows them to understand grammar, and that other kinds of dialogue interaction teach conversation. Overall, language play may be of critical importance in the development of language and literacy skills (180).

UNACCEPTABLE PARAPHRASE: USING THE AUTHOR'S SENTENCE STRUCTURES

Language play, Crystal suggests, will improve pronunciation by zeroing in on sounds such as rhymes. Having fun with word endings and analyzing riddle structure will help a person acquire grammar. Being prepared to play with language, to use puns and talk nonsense, improves the ability to use semantics. These playful methods of communication are likely to influence a person's ability to talk to others. And language play inherently adds enormously to what has recently been known as *metalinguistic awareness*, a concept of great magnitude in developing speech abilities generally and literacy abilities particularly (180).

Here is a paraphrase of the original passage that expresses the author's ideas accurately and acceptably:

ACCEPTABLE PARAPHRASE: IN THE STUDENT WRITER'S OWN WORDS

Crystal argues that playing with language — creating rhymes, figuring out riddles, making puns, playing with names, using invented words, and so on — helps children figure out a great deal, from the basics of pronunciation and grammar to how to carry on a conversation. This kind of play allows children to understand the overall concept of how language works, a concept that is key to learning to use — and read — language effectively (180).

Notice that the writer uses a signal phrase — "Crystal argues" — to introduce the source's ideas smoothly into her own text. The verb *argues* shows the writer communicating a neutral relationship to the source material.

Quick Help

Guidelines for Paraphrasing

- Include all main points and any important details from the original source, in the same order in which the author presents them.
- State the meaning in your own words and sentence structures. If you want to include especially memorable language from the original, enclose it in quotation marks.
- Represent the author's ideas in a way that shows you understand the ideas.
- Cite the source even if you have paraphrased it and have not used any exact language.

Quick Help

Guidelines for Summarizing

- Include just enough information to recount the main points you want to cite. A summary is usually far shorter than the original.
- Use your own words. If you include any language from the original, enclose it in quotation marks.
- Represent the author's ideas in a way that shows you understand the ideas.
- Cite the source even if you have summarized it and have not used any exact language.

Language, Culture, and Context

Multilingual

Identifying Sources

While some language communities and cultures expect audiences to recognize the sources of important documents and texts, thereby eliminating the need to cite them directly, conventions for writing in North America call for careful attribution of any quoted, paraphrased, or summarized material in your work. When in doubt, explicitly identify your sources.

Summaries

A summary is a significantly shortened version of a passage or even of a whole chapter or work that captures main ideas *in your own words*. Unlike a paraphrase, a summary uses just enough information to record the main points you wish to emphasize. Introduce summaries clearly, usually with a signal phrase that includes the author of the source, as the underlined words preceding the summary in this example indicate.

> Professor of linguistics Deborah Tannen says that she offers her book *That's Not What I Meant!* to those wanting to strengthen communication between women and men. Tannen goes on to illustrate how communication breaks down and then to suggest that a full awareness of what she calls "genderlects" can improve relationships (297).

12c Integrate visuals and media effectively and ethically.

Choose visuals and media wisely, whether you use video, audio, photographs, illustrations, charts and graphs, or other kinds of images. Integrate all visuals and media smoothly into your text.

- *Does each visual or media file make a strong contribution to the written message?* Tangential or purely decorative visuals and media may weaken the power of your writing.

- *Are you sure that the work is accurate and credible?* Could the visual have been altered in some way? (See Chapter 11 for more on evaluating images and visuals.)

- *Is each visual or media file appropriate and fair to your subject?* An obviously biased perspective may seem unfair or manipulative to your audience.

- *Is the work appropriate for and fair to your audience?* Visuals and media should appeal to various members of your likely audience.

Whenever you post documents containing visuals or media to the web, make sure you check for copyright information. While it is considered "fair use" to use such materials in an essay or other project for a college class, once that project is published on the web, you might infringe on copyright protections if you do not ask the copyright holder for permission to use the visual or media file. If you have questions about whether your work might infringe on copyright, ask your instructor for help.

Talking the Talk

Saying Something New

"What can I say about my topic that experts haven't already said?" All writers — no matter how experienced — face this problem. As you read more about your topic, you will soon see areas of disagreement among experts, who may not be as expert as they first appear. Notice what your sources say and, especially, what they don't say. Consider how your own interests and experiences give you a unique perspective on the topic. Slowly but surely you will identify a claim that you can make about the topic, one related to what others say but taking a new angle or adding something different to the discussion.

Like quotations, paraphrases, and summaries, visuals and media need to be introduced and commented on in some way. They also need to be cited properly according to the guidelines for the style you are using. See 54e (MLA), 58e (APA), or 62c (*Chicago*) for details.

12d Understand why acknowledging sources matters.

Acknowledging, or citing, sources says to your reader that you have done your homework, that you have gained expertise on your topic, and that you are credible. Acknowledging your sources can also demonstrate fairness and open-mindedness when you have considered several points of view. In addition, recognizing your sources can help provide background for your research by placing it in the context of other thinking. Most of all, you should acknowledge sources to help your readers follow your thoughts and know where to go to find more information on your topic.

12e Know which sources to acknowledge.

As you carry out research, it is important to understand the distinction between materials that require acknowledgment (in in-text citations, footnotes, or endnotes; and in the works-cited list or bibliography) and those that do not.

Materials that do not require acknowledgment

- *Common knowledge.* If most readers already know a fact, you probably do not need to cite a source for it. You do not need to credit a source for the statement that Barack Obama was reelected president in 2012, for example.
- *Facts available in a wide variety of sources.* If a number of encyclopedias, almanacs, or textbooks include a certain piece of information, you usually need not cite a specific source for it.
- *Your own findings from field research.* If you conduct observations or surveys, simply announce your findings as your own. Acknowledge people you interview as individuals rather than as part of a survey.

Materials that require acknowledgment

- *Quotations, paraphrases, and summaries.* Whenever you use another person's words, ideas, or opinions, credit the source. Even though the wording of a paraphrase or summary is your own, you should still acknowledge the source.

- *Facts not widely known or claims that are arguable.* If your readers would be unlikely to know a fact, or if an author presents as fact a claim that may or may not be true, cite the source. If you are not sure whether a fact will be familiar to your readers or whether a statement is arguable, cite the source.

- *Visuals from any source.* Credit all visual and statistical material not derived from your own field research, even if you yourself create a graph or table from the data provided in a source.

- *Help provided by others.* If an instructor gave you a good idea or if friends responded to your draft or helped you conduct surveys, give credit.

12f Recognize patchwriting.

Integrating sources into your writing can be a significant challenge. In fact, as a beginning researcher, you might do what Professor Rebecca Howard calls "patchwriting"; that is, rather than integrate sources smoothly and accurately, you patch together words, phrases, and even structures from sources into your own writing, sometimes without citation. The author of this book remembers doing such "patchwriting" for a middle school report on her hero, Dr. Albert Schweitzer. Luckily, she had a teacher who sat patiently with her, showing her how to paraphrase, summarize, and quote from sources correctly and effectively. So it takes time, effort, and good instruction to learn to integrate sources appropriately. Patchwriting is sometimes considered plagiarism even if you didn't mean to plagiarize.

Language, Culture, and Context

Multilingual

Adapting Structures from the Writing of Experts

If you are not accustomed to writing in a particular academic genre, you may find it useful to borrow and adapt transitional devices and pieces of sentence structure from other people's writing in the genre or discipline you are working in. Be careful to borrow only structures that are generic and not ideas or sentences that come from a particular, identifiable writer. You should not copy any whole sentences or sentence structures verbatim, or your borrowing may seem like plagiarism.

ORIGINAL ABSTRACT FROM A SOCIAL SCIENCE PAPER	EFFECTIVE BORROWING OF STRUCTURES FROM A GENRE
Using the interpersonal communications research of J. K. Brilhart and G. J. Galanes, and W. Wilmot and J. Hocker, along with T. Hartman's personality assessment, I observed and analyzed the leadership roles and group dynamics of my project collaborators in a communications course. Based on results of the Hartman personality assessment, I predicted that a single leader would emerge. However, complementary individual strengths and gender differences encouraged a distributed leadership style, in which the group experienced little confrontation and conflict. Conflict, because it was handled positively, was crucial to the group's progress.	Drawing on the research of Deborah Tannen on men's and women's conversational styles, I analyzed the conversational styles of six first-year students at DePaul University. Based on Tannen's research, I expected that the three men I observed would use features typical of male conversational style and the three women would use features typical of female conversational style. In general, these predictions were accurate; however, some exceptions were also apparent.

This example illustrates effective borrowing. The student writer borrows phrases (such as "drawing on" and "based on") that are commonly used in academic writing in the social sciences to perform particular functions. Notice how the student also modifies these phrases to suit her needs.

12g Build trust by upholding your integrity and avoiding plagiarism.

Effective writing always involves trust between writers and their audiences: in putting your name on something, you are saying to your readers, "you can trust that what I say here is accurate and that I am responsible for its contents." Plagiarism destroys that trust. While there are many ways to destroy trust and damage academic integrity, two that are especially important are inaccurate or incomplete acknowledgment of sources in citations — sometimes called unintentional plagiarism — and plagiarism that is deliberately intended to pass off one writer's work as another's.

Whether intentional or not, plagiarism can result in serious consequences. At some colleges, students who plagiarize fail the course automatically; at others, they are expelled. Instructors who plagiarize, even inadvertently, have had their degrees revoked and their books withdrawn from publication. Outside academic life, eminent political, business, and scientific leaders have been stripped of positions and awards because of plagiarism.

Inaccurate or incomplete citation of sources

If your paraphrase is too close to the wording or sentence structure of a source (even if you identify the source), if you do not identify the source of a quotation (even if you include the quotation marks), or if you fail to indicate clearly the source of an idea that is not your own, you may be accused of plagiarism even if your intent was not to plagiarize. Inaccurate or incomplete acknowledgment of sources often results either from carelessness or from not learning how to borrow material properly in the first place (12e and f).

Deliberate plagiarism

Deliberate plagiarism is what most people think of when they hear the word *plagiarism*: handing in an essay written by a friend or downloaded from an essay-writing company; copying and pasting passages directly from source materials without acknowledgment; failing to credit the source of an idea or concept in your text. This form of plagiarism is troubling because it represents dishonesty and deception. Those who intentionally plagiarize present the hard thinking and hard work of someone else as their own, and they claim knowledge they don't have, thus deceiving their readers.

Language, Culture, and Context

Multilingual

Plagiarism as a Cultural Concept

Many cultures do not recognize Western ideas about plagiarism, which rest on a belief that language and ideas can be owned by writers. Indeed, in many countries other than the United States, and even within some communities in the United States, using the words and ideas of others without attribution is considered a sign of deep respect as well as an indication of knowledge. In academic writing in the United States, however, you should credit all materials except those that are common knowledge, that are available in a wide variety of sources, or that are your own creations (photographs, drawings, and so on) or your own findings from field research.

Quick Help

Guarding against Plagiarism

- Maintain an accurate and thorough working bibliography. (11b)
- Establish a consistent note-taking system, listing sources and page numbers and clearly identifying all quotations, paraphrases, summaries, statistics, and visuals.
- Identify all quotations with quotation marks — both in your notes and in your essay. Be sure your summaries and paraphrases use your own words and sentence structures. (12b)
- Give a citation or note for each quotation, paraphrase, summary, arguable assertion or opinion, statistic, and visual that is from a source. Prepare an accurate and complete list of sources cited according to the required documentation style. (See the MLA, APA, or *Chicago* sections of this book.)
- Plan ahead on writing assignments so that you can avoid the temptation to take shortcuts.

Deliberate plagiarism is also fairly simple to spot: your instructor will be acquainted with your writing and likely to notice any shifts in the style or quality of your work. In addition, by typing a few words from an essay into a search engine, your instructor can identify "matches" very easily.

12h Write and revise a research project.

Everyday decisions often call for research and writing. In trying to choose between colleges in different towns, for example, one student made a long list of questions to answer: Which location had the lower cost of living? Which school offered more financial aid? Which program would be more likely to help graduates find a job? After conducting careful research, he was able to write a letter of acceptance to one place and a letter of regret to the other. In much the same way, when you are working on an academic project, there comes a time to draw the strands of your research together and articulate your conclusions in writing.

Quick Help

Guidelines for Writing a Research Project

- **Review the key elements of your writing situation.** What is your central purpose? What other purposes, if any, do you have? What's your stance toward your topic? Are you an advocate, a critic, a reporter, an observer? What audience(s) are you addressing? How much background information will they need?

- **Write out an explicit thesis statement.** Doing so allows you to articulate your major points and see how well they carry out your purpose and appeal to your audience.

- **Test your thesis.** Could the wording of your thesis be more specific? Is there anything you can do to increase your audience's interest in and engagement with your thesis? What evidence from your research supports each aspect of your thesis? What additional evidence might you need?

- **Experiment with ways to organize your writing.** Will an outline help you to visualize the sections of your project? If not, try note cards, sticky notes, a list, or some other method for helping you see how to develop your main point and supporting points.

- **Consider design opportunities.** How do you want your project to look? What size and font will you use for your type? Should you use color? Will you use headings or questions to help your reader navigate? Will you include visuals or media files?

- **Write a first draft.** Gather your notes, your sources, and any outlines or organizing tools. Read through everything. Begin at the beginning or, better, with a section you feel confident about. In your introduction, forecast your main points, and establish your credibility. As you draft, ask questions: Do you need to add background information to ground your reader? Do you need counter-evidence to help you handle objections? How will you build common ground? How will you move your argument forward?

- **Integrate source materials.** As you weave your source materials into your draft, the challenge is to use sources to support your points, yet remain the author. How can you quote, paraphrase, and summarize other voices while remaining the major voice in your work? Be sure to follow guidelines for citing sources in the appropriate style for your audience and/or assignment.

- **Seek responses to your draft.** Which of your friends or classmates would be open to reading and responding to your draft? What other potential reviewers are available (your instructor, a writing center tutor)? Ask specific questions of your readers — questions about your thesis, evidence, organization, overall impact, and more.

Language, Culture, and Context

Multilingual

Asking Experienced Writers to Review a Thesis

If you speak two or more languages, you might find it helpful to ask one or two classmates who have more experience with the particular type of academic writing to look at your explicit thesis. Ask if the thesis is as direct and clear as it can be, and revise accordingly.

Quick Help

Guidelines for Revising a Research Project

- **Take responses into account.** Look at specific problems that reviewers think you need to solve or strengths you might capitalize on. For example, if they showed great interest in one point but no interest in another, consider expanding the first and deleting the second.

- **Reconsider your original purpose, audience, and stance.** Have you achieved your purpose? If not, consider how you can. How well have you appealed to your readers? Make sure you satisfy any special concerns of your reviewers. If your rhetorical stance toward your topic has changed, does your draft need to change, too?

- **Assess your research.** Think about whether you have investigated the topic thoroughly and consulted materials with more than one point of view. Have you left out any important sources? Are the sources you use reliable and appropriate for your topic? Have you synthesized your research findings and drawn warranted conclusions?

- **Assess your use of visuals and media.** Make sure that each visual or media component supports your argument, is clearly labeled, and is cited appropriately.

- **Gather additional material.** If you need to strengthen any points, first check your notes to see whether you already have the necessary information at hand. In some instances, you may need to do additional research.

- **Decide what changes you need to make.** List everything you must do to strengthen your draft. With your deadline in mind, plan your revision.

- **Rewrite your draft.** However you revise, in a file or on hard copy, be sure to save copies of each draft. Begin with the major changes, such as adding content or reorganizing. Then turn to sentence-level problems and word choice. Can you sharpen the work's dominant impression?

→

- **Reevaluate the title, introduction, and conclusion.** Is your title specific and engaging? Does the introduction capture readers' attention and indicate what the work discusses? Does your conclusion help readers see the significance of your argument?

- **Check your documentation.** Make sure you've included a citation in your text for every quotation, paraphrase, summary, visual, and media file that you incorporated, following your documentation style consistently.

- **Edit your draft.** Check grammar, usage, spelling, punctuation, and mechanics. Consider the advice of computer spell checkers and grammar checkers carefully before accepting it.

▲ **For visual analysis** This illustration shows some of the kinds of writing and presenting that are part of many careers today. What writing do you expect to do in your college courses, at work, and in social and public life?

Academic, Professional, and Public Writing

When I say work I only mean writing. Everything else is just odd jobs.

— MARGARET LAURENCE

13 Writing Well in Any Discipline or Profession

Writing well plays an important role in almost every discipline and profession. As one MBA wrote recently, "Those who advance quickly in my company are those who write and speak well — it's as simple as that." While writing is always a valuable skill, writing well means different things in different professions and disciplines. As you prepare written assignments for various courses and in different professional settings, then, you will need to become familiar with the genres, vocabularies, styles, methods of proof, and conventional formats used in each field.

13a Consider genres and formats across disciplines and professions.

Writing is central to successful communication, regardless of the discipline or profession. Whether you are explaining the results of a survey you conducted for a psychology class, working on a proposal for material sciences and engineering, or analyzing a treatise for a philosophy class, writing helps you get the job done.

One good way to learn to write well in a discipline or profession is to think carefully about the *genres,* or kinds of writing, aimed at achieving a particular goal for a particular audience. Like popular genres (think of sci-fi movies, for instance, or hip-hop music), academic and professional genres share characteristic features and conventions — but they are not lockstep, fill-in-the-blank forms. Rather, they are flexible and adaptable to different audiences and rhetorical situations. In addition, genres evolve in response to shifting linguistic and cultural contexts. For centuries, letters followed conventions established in the medieval era (they were very formal, for one thing), but more recently they evolved to include lots of subgenres (thank-you letters, rejection letters, cover letters) before shading into email and text messages and adapting to online environments.

Sometimes you will be assigned to write in a particular genre — a rhetorical analysis in first-year writing, for example, or care notes for your internship at a nursing home. You may also be expected to follow certain formats, such as the IMRAD — introduction, methods, results, and discussion — typically used in much science writing. If so, look for examples of these genres and formats, and study them to see how they work and what their features are. Whether or not you are assigned a genre or format, you will profit by thinking carefully about genre before beginning to write. Here are some ways to begin:

- ***Think about the discipline or profession the assignment is for.*** If you are writing about sustainable agriculture for a human biology class, you may be expected to write an argument presenting the debate around sustainability and offering a solution. If you're sharing results of an interview you conducted as part of your work for a nonprofit organization, you will probably choose to follow the conventions of a report.

- ***Ask: Who is the audience?*** If you are writing about sexual harassment policies on campus and your audience is the first-year class, you might use a narrative or story; while writing about the same subject for a presentation to the student governing body, you might use the features of a resolution.

- ***Determine the best medium to use.*** For a presentation on climate change in a political science class, you might choose to create an infographic, following the characteristic features of that genre. You might choose to distribute the infographic as a print document or, if you've built links into the data, you may find that digital distribution works better for your purposes.

13b Consider expectations for academic assignments.

When you receive an assignment, your first job is to be sure you understand what that assignment is asking you to do. Some assignments may be as vague as "Write a five-page essay on one aspect of the Civil War." Others may be fairly specific: "Collect, summarize, and interpret data drawn from a sample of letters to the editor published in two newspapers, one in a small rural community and one in an urban community, over a period of three months." Whatever the assignment, use the questions on the next page to analyze it.

13c Learn specialized vocabularies and styles.

Entering an academic discipline or a profession is like going to a party where you don't know anyone. At first you feel like an outsider, and you may not understand much of what you hear or see. Before you enter the conversation, you have to listen and observe carefully. Eventually, however, you will be able to join in — and if you stay long enough, participating in the conversation becomes easy and natural.

> ## Quick Help
>
> ### Analyzing an Assignment
>
> - **What is the purpose of the assignment?** Are you expected to join a discussion, demonstrate your mastery of the topic in writing, or something else?
> - **Who is the audience?** The instructor will be one audience, but are there others? If so, who are they?
> - **What does the assignment ask of you?** Look for key terms such as *summarize, explain, evaluate, interpret, illustrate,* and *define.*
> - **Do you need clarification of any terms?** If so, ask your instructor.
> - **What do you need to know or find out to complete the assignment?** You may need to do background reading, develop a procedure for analyzing or categorizing information, or carry out some other kind of preparation.
> - **What does the instructor expect in a written response?** How will you use sources? What kinds of sources should you use? How should you organize and develop the assignment? What is the expected format and length?
> - **Can you locate a model of an effective response to a similar assignment?**
> - **What do other students think the assignment requires?** Talking over an assignment with classmates is one good way to test your understanding.

To learn the routines, practices, and ways of knowing in a new field, you must also make an effort to enter into the conversation. A good way to get started is to study the vocabulary of the field you are most interested in.

Highlight the key terms in your reading or notes to learn how much specialized or technical vocabulary you will be expected to know. If you find only a small amount of specialized vocabulary, try to master the new terms quickly by reading carefully, looking up key words or phrases, and asking questions. If you find a great deal of specialized vocabulary, however, you may want to familiarize yourself with it methodically. The following strategies may help:

- Keep a log of unfamiliar words used in context. Check definitions in your textbook's glossary or index, or consult a specialized dictionary.
- See if your textbook has a glossary of terms or sets off definitions. Study pertinent sections to master the terms.
- Work with key concepts. Even if they are not yet entirely clear to you, using them will help you understand them. For example, in a statistics class, try to work out (in words) how to do an analysis of *covariance*, step by step, even if you are not sure of the precise

definition of the term. And don't forget that you can ask a tutor, TA, or instructor to help you understand the concept.

- Take special note of the ways technical language or disciplinary vocabulary is used in online information related to a particular field.

You can also learn about disciplinary and professional writing by looking closely at stylistic features. Study pieces of writing in the field with the following in mind:

- *Overall tone.* How would you describe it? (2f)
- *Title.* Are titles generally descriptive ("Findings from a Double-Blind Study of the Effect of Antioxidants"), persuasive ("Antioxidants Proven Effective"), or something else? How does the title shape your expectations?
- *Stance.* To what extent do writers in the field strive for distance and objectivity? What strategies help them to achieve this stance? (2c)
- *Sentence length.* Are sentences long and complex? simple and direct?
- *Voice.* Are verbs generally active or passive? Why? (35g)
- *Point of view.* Do writers use the first-person *I* or third-person terms such as *the investigator*? perhaps a combination? What is the effect of the choice?
- *Visuals.* Do writers typically use elements such as graphs, tables, maps, or photographs? How are visuals integrated into the text? What role, if any, do headings and other formatting elements play in the writing? (Chapter 18)
- *Documentation style.* Do writers use MLA, APA, or *Chicago* style? (Chapters 54–64)

Of course, writings within a single discipline may have different purposes and different styles. A chemist may write a grant proposal, a literature review, and a lab report, each with a different purpose and style.

Talking the Talk

The First Person

"Is it true that I should never use *I* in college writing?" In much college writing, using the first-person *I* is perfectly acceptable to most instructors. As always, think about the context. If your own experience is relevant to the topic, you are better off saying *I* than trying too hard not to. But don't overdo it, especially if the writing isn't just autobiographical. And check with your instructor if you aren't sure: in certain academic disciplines, using *I* may be seen as inappropriate.

13d Use evidence effectively.

As you grow familiar with an area of study or a professional position, you will develop a sense of what it takes to prove a point in that field or role. You can speed up this process, however, by investigating and questioning. The following questions will help you think about the use of evidence in materials you read:

- How do writers in the field use precedent and authority? What or who counts as an authority in this field? How are the credentials of an authority established? (9g)
- What kinds of quantitative data (countable or measurable items) are used, and for what purposes? How are the data gathered and presented?
- How are qualitative data (systematically observed items) used?
- How are statistics used and presented? Are tables, charts, graphs, or other visuals important, and why?
- How is logical reasoning used? How are definition, cause and effect, analogy, and example used?
- How does the field use primary materials — the firsthand sources of information — and secondary sources that are reported by others? (See 10e.) How is each type of source presented?
- What kinds of textual evidence are cited?
- How are quotations and other references to sources used and integrated into a text? (Chapter 12)

13e Pay attention to ethical issues.

Writers in all disciplines face ethical questions. Those who plan and carry out research on living people, for example, must be careful to avoid harming their subjects. Researchers in all fields must be scrupulous in presenting data to make sure that others can replicate research and test claims. In whatever discipline or field you are working, you should take into consideration your own interests, those of your collaborators, and those of your employers — but you must also responsibly safeguard the interests of the general public.

Fortunately, a growing number of disciplines have adopted guidelines for ethics. The American Psychological Association has been a pioneer in this area, and many other professional organizations and companies (the American Sociological Association, the American Educational Research

Association, Starbucks, Coca-Cola) have their own codes of conduct or standards of ethics. These guidelines can help you make decisions about day-to-day writing. Even so, you will no doubt encounter situations where the right or ethical decision is murky at best. In such situations, consult your own conscience first and then talk your choices over with colleagues you respect before coming to a decision on how to proceed.

13f Collaborate effectively and with an open mind.

In academic and professional environments, working with others is not just a highly valued skill — it is a necessity. Such collaboration happens when peers work together on a shared document, when classmates divide research and writing duties to create a multimedia presentation, when reviewers share advice on a draft, or when colleagues in an office offer their views on appropriate revisions for a companywide document.

Because people all over the world now have the ability to research, study, write, and work together, you must be able to communicate effectively within and across cultures. Conventions for academic writing (or for forms of digital communication) can vary from culture to culture, from discipline to discipline, and from one form of English to another. What is considered polite in one culture may seem rude in another, so those who communicate globally must take care to avoid giving offense — or taking it where none was intended. (For more information on writing across cultures, see Chapter 24.)

Planning goes a long way toward making any group collaboration work well. Although you will probably do much of your group work online, keep in mind that face-to-face meetings can accomplish some things that virtual meetings cannot.

TIPS FOR WORKING WELL IN A GROUP

- Establish a regular meeting time and space (whether in person or online), and exchange contact information.
- Commit to participating actively, accomplishing tasks, and meeting deadlines.
- Work backwards from the final deadline to create an overall agenda.
- Keep notes from each group meeting.
- Use group meetings to work together on difficult problems. Check with your instructor if part of the task is unclear or if members don't agree on what is required.

Talking the Talk

Collaborating—or Cheating?

"When is asking others for help and opinions acceptable, and when is it cheating?" In academic work, the difference between collaborating and cheating depends almost entirely on context. There will be times when instructors will expect you to work alone—during exams, for example. At other times, working with others may be required, and getting others' opinions on your writing is always a good habit. You draw the line, however, at having another person do your work for you. Submitting material under your name that you did not write is unacceptable in college writing. But collaboration is a key fact of life in today's digital world, so it's important to think carefully about how to collaborate effectively and ethically.

- Express opinions politely, respectfully, and with an open mind. If disagreements arise, try paraphrasing (*So what you're saying is . . .*) to see if everyone is hearing the same thing.

- Remember that the goal is not for everyone just to get along; constructive conflict is desirable. Get a spirited debate going, and discuss all available options.

- If your project requires a group-written document, assign one member to get the writing project started. Set deadlines for each part of the project. Come to an agreement about how you will edit and change each other's contributions to avoid offending any member of the group.

- Reflect on the group's effectiveness periodically. Should you make changes as you go forward? What has the group done best? What has it done less successfully? What have you learned about how to work more effectively with others on future projects?

14 Writing in the Humanities

In humanities disciplines, the nature of texts can vary widely, from poems and plays to novels, articles, philosophical treatises, films, advertisements, paintings, and so on. You can expect critical reading and textual analysis to play important roles in humanities courses, whether the texts you're studying are ancient or modern, literary or historical, verbal or visual.

14a Read texts in the humanities.

To read critically in literature, art, film, and philosophy courses, you will need to pose questions and construct hypotheses as you read. You may ask, for instance, why a writer might make some points or develop some examples but omit others. Rather than finding meaning only in the surface information that texts or artifacts convey, you should use your own questions and hypotheses to create fuller meanings and make claims about the significance of what you read.

To successfully engage texts, you must recognize that you are not a neutral observer, not an empty cup into which the meaning of a work is poured. If such were the case, writing would have exactly the same meanings for all of us, and reading would be a fairly boring affair. If you have ever gone to see a movie with a friend and each come away with a completely different understanding or response, you already have ample evidence that a text never has just one meaning.

Nevertheless, you may in the past have been willing to accept the first meaning to occur to you—to take a text at face value. Most humanities courses, however, will expect you to exercise your interpretive powers. The guidelines in this section can help you build your strengths as a close reader of humanities texts.

14b Write texts in the humanities.

As a writer in the humanities, you will use the findings from close examination of a text or artifact to develop an argument or to construct an analysis.

Assignments

Common assignments that make use of the skills of close reading, analysis, and argument include the following:

> summary
>
> personal response
>
> position paper
>
> comparison or contrast
>
> analysis of a primary source or secondary source
>
> research project

In philosophy, for example, you might need to summarize an argument, analyze a text's logic and effectiveness, or discuss a moral issue from a particular philosophical perspective. A literature assignment may ask you to

Quick Help

Guidelines for Reading Texts in the Humanities

- **Determine the purpose of the text.** The two most common purposes for works in the humanities are to provide information and to argue for a particular interpretation. Pay attention to whether the text presents opinions or facts, to what is included and omitted, and to how facts are presented to the audience.

- **Get an overall impression.** What does the work make you think about — and why? What is most remarkable or memorable? What confuses you?

- **Annotate the text.** Be prepared to "talk back," ask questions, note emerging patterns or themes, and point out anything out of place or ineffective.

- **Look at the context.** Consider the time and place represented in the work as well as when and where the writer lived. You may also consider social, political, or personal forces that may have affected the writer.

- **Think about the audience.** Who are the readers or viewers the writer seems to address? Do they include you?

- **Pay attention to genre.** What category does the work fall into (graphic novel, diary, political cartoon, sermon, argumentative essay, Hollywood western)? What is noteworthy about the form? How does it conform to, stretch, or even subvert your expectations about the genre? (2e)

- **Pay attention to visual elements and design.** How does the text look? What visual elements does it include? What contribution do these make to the overall effect or argument?

- **Note the point of view.** Whose point of view is represented? How does it affect your response?

- **Notice the major themes.** Are specific claims being advanced? How are these claims supported?

- **Understand how primary and secondary sources differ.** Primary sources provide firsthand knowledge, while secondary sources report on or analyze the research of others. (10e)

look very closely at a particular text ("Examine the role of chocolate in Toni Morrison's *Tar Baby*") or to go well beyond a primary text ("Discuss the impact of agribusiness on modernist novels"). Other disciplines may ask you to write articles, primary source analyses, or research papers.

For texts in literature, modern languages, and philosophy, writers often use the documentation style of the Modern Language Association (see Chapter 54 for advice on using MLA style). For projects in history and other areas of the humanities, writers often use the style of the University of Chicago Press (see Chapter 62 for advice on using *Chicago* style).

Critical stance

To analyze a text, you need to develop a critical stance — the approach you will take to the work — that can help you develop a thesis or major claim (see 2c and 3c). To evaluate the text and present a critical response to it, you should look closely at the text itself, including its style; at the context in which it was produced; and at the audience the text aims to reach, which may or may not include yourself.

To look closely at the text itself, consider its genre, form, point of view, and themes, and look at the stylistic features, such as word choice, use of imagery, visuals, and design. Then consider context: ask why the text was created, note its original and current contexts, and think about how attitudes and ideas of its era may have influenced it. Consider who the intended audience might be, and think about how people outside this intended group might respond to the text. Finally, think about your personal response to the text as well.

Carrying out these steps should provide you with plenty of material to work with as you begin to shape a critical thesis and write your analysis. You can begin by grounding your analysis in one or more important questions you have about the work.

Literary analysis

When you analyze or interpret a literary work, think of your thesis as answering a question about some aspect of the work. The guiding question you bring to the literary work will help you decide on a critical stance toward the work. For example, a student who is writing about Shakespeare's *Macbeth* might find her curiosity piqued by the many comic moments that appear in this tragedy. She might turn the question of why Shakespeare uses so much comedy in *Macbeth* into a thesis statement that proposes an answer.

QUESTION	What role does comedy play in *Macbeth*, one of Shakespeare's most widely read tragedies?
THESIS STATEMENT	The many unexpected comic moments in *Macbeth* emphasize how disordered the world becomes for murderers like Macbeth and his wife.

14c   A student's close reading of poetry

Following is an excerpt from student Bonnie Sillay's close reading of two poems by E. E. Cummings. This essay follows MLA style (see Chapters 54–57). Bonnie is creating her own interpretation, so the only works she cites are the poems she analyzes.

Student Writer

Bonnie Sillay

½″

Sillay 1

Bonnie Sillay

Angela Mitchell

English 1102

4 December 2018

"Life's Not a Paragraph"

Throughout his poetry, E. E. Cummings leads readers deep
into a thicket of scrambled words, missing punctuation, and
unconventional structure. Within Cummings's poetic bramble,
ambiguity leads the reader through what seems at first a confusing
and winding maze. However, this confusion actually transforms into a
path that leads the reader to the center of the thicket where
Cummings's message lies: readers should not allow their experience to
be limited by reason and rationality. In order to communicate his belief
that emotional experience should triumph over reason, Cummings
employs odd juxtapositions, outlandish metaphors, and inversions of
traditional grammatical structures that reveal the illogic of reason.
Indeed, by breaking down such formal boundaries, Cummings's poems
"since feeling is first" and "as freedom is a breakfastfood" suggest that
emotion, which provides the compositional fabric for our experience of
life, should never be defined or controlled.

In "since feeling is first," Cummings urges his reader to reject
attempts to control emotion, using English grammar as one example
of the restrictive conventions present in society. Stating that "since
feeling is first / who pays any attention / to the syntax of things"
(lines 1-3), Cummings suggests that emotion should not be forced
to fit into some preconceived framework or mold. He carries this
message throughout the poem by juxtaposing images of the
abstract and the concrete—images of emotion and of English
grammar. Cummings's word choice enhances his intentionally
strange juxtapositions, with the poet using grammatical terms that
suggest regulation or confinement. For example, in the line "And

Name,
instructor,
course
number,
date on left
margin

Title centered

Present
tense used
to discuss
poetry

Foreshadows
discussion of
work to come

Introductory
paragraph
ends with
thesis
statement

Quotation
cited
parenthetically

Double
spacing
throughout

Annotations indicate effective choices or **MLA-style formatting**.

Sillay 2

Paper header includes last name and page number

death i think is no parenthesis" (16), Cummings uses the idea that parentheses confine the words they surround in order to warn the reader not to let death confine life or emotions.

Transition sentence connects the previous paragraph to this one

The structure of the poem also rejects traditional conventions. Instead of the final stanzas making the main point, Cummings opens his poem with his primary message, that "feeling is first" (1). Again, Cummings shows that emotion rejects order and structure. How can emotion be bottled in sentences and interrupted by commas, colons, and spaces? To Cummings, emotion is a never-ending run-on sentence that should not be diagramed or dissected.

Writer uses a metaphor that captures the spirit of Cummings's point

In the third stanza of "since feeling is first," Cummings states his point outright, noting "my blood approves, / and kisses are a better fate / than wisdom" (7-9). Here, Cummings argues for reveling in the feeling during a fleeting moment such as a kiss. He continues, "the best gesture of my brain is less than / your eyelids' flutter" (11-12). Cummings wants the reader to focus on a pure emotive response (the flutter of an eyelash) — on the emotional, not the logical — on the meanings of words instead of punctuation and grammar.

Quotation integrated into writer's sentence

Cummings's use of words such as *kisses* and *blood* (8, 7) adds to the focus on the emotional. The ideas behind these words are difficult to confine or restrict to a single definition: kisses mean different things to different people, blood flows through the body freely and continually. The words are not expansive or free enough to encompass all that they suggest. Cummings ultimately paints language as more restrictive than the flowing, powerful force of emotion.

Paragraph reiterates Cummings's claim and sums up his argument

The poet's use of two grammatical terms in the last lines, "for life's not a paragraph / And death i think is no parenthesis," warns against attempts to format lives and feelings into conventional and rule-bound segments (15-16). Attempts to control, rather than feel, are rejected throughout "since feeling is first." Emotion should be limitless, free from any restrictions or rules.

Sillay 3

While "since feeling is first" argues that emotions should not be controlled, ordered, or analyzed, "as freedom is a breakfastfood" suggests the difficulty of defining emotion. In this poem, Cummings uses deliberately far-fetched metaphors such as "freedom is a breakfastfood" and "time is a tree" (1, 26). These metaphors seem arbitrary: Cummings is not attempting to make profound statements on time or freedom. Instead, he suggests that freedom and time are subjective, and attempts at narrow definition are ridiculous. Inversions of nature, such as "robins never welcome spring" and "water most encourage flame" (16, 7), underscore emotion's ability to defy reason. These inversions suggest the arbitrariness of what "since feeling is first" calls "the syntax of things" (3).

Although most of "as freedom is a breakfastfood" defies logic, Cummings shifts the tone at the end to deliver one last metaphor: "but love is the sky" (27). The word *but* separates this definition from the rest of the poem and subtly implies that, unlike the metaphors that have come before it, "love is the sky" is an accurate comparison. In order to reach this final conclusion, however, Cummings has taken his readers on a long and often ambiguous journey.

Nevertheless, the confusion has been deliberate. Cummings wants his readers to follow him through the winding path through the thicket because he believes the path of the straight and narrow limits the possibilities of experience. Through the unconventionality of his poetic structures, Cummings urges his readers to question order and tradition. He wants his readers to realize that reason and rationality are always secondary to emotion and that emotional experience is a free-flowing force that should not be constrained. Cummings's poetry suggests that in order to get at the true essence of something, one must look past the commonsensical definition and not be limited by "the syntax of things."

Clear and explicit transition from discussion of first poem

Writer returns to the image of the thicket from the introduction to create a closing that resonates with the opening

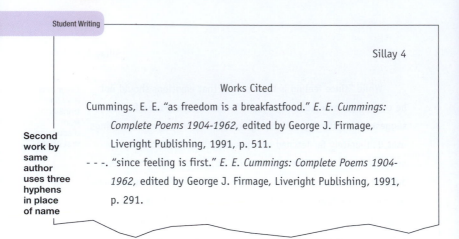

Sillay 4

Works Cited

Cummings, E. E. "as freedom is a breakfastfood." *E. E. Cummings:*
Complete Poems 1904-1962, edited by George J. Firmage,
Liveright Publishing, 1991, p. 511.

- - -. "since feeling is first." *E. E. Cummings: Complete Poems 1904-*
1962, edited by George J. Firmage, Liveright Publishing, 1991,
p. 291.

Second work by same author uses three hyphens in place of name

15 Writing in the Social Sciences

The social sciences share with the humanities an interest in what it means to be human. But the social sciences also share with the sciences the goal of engaging in a systematic, observable study of human behavior. When you write in the social sciences, you will attempt to identify, understand, and explain patterns of human behavior.

15a Read texts in the social sciences.

When you read in the social sciences, you ask questions, analyze, and interpret as you read, whether you are reading academic paper that sets forth a theory and defends it, a case study that describes a particular case and draws implications from it, or a research report that presents the results of an investigation of an important question. Most of what you read in the social sciences will attempt to prove a point, and you will need to evaluate how well that point is supported.

The social sciences, like other disciplines, often use specialized vocabulary as shorthand for complex ideas that otherwise would take paragraphs to explain.

Quantitative and qualitative studies

Different texts in the social and natural sciences may call for different methods and strategies. Texts that report the results of *quantitative* studies present numerical data drawn from surveys, polls, experiments, and tests. For example, a study of voting patterns in southern states might rely on quantitative data such as statistics. Texts that report the results of *qualitative* studies rely on non-numerical methods such as interviews and observations to reveal social patterns. A study of the way children in one kindergarten class develop rules of play, for instance, would draw on qualitative data—observations of social interaction, interviews with students and teachers, and so on. Of course, some work in the social and behavioral sciences combines quantitative and qualitative data and methods: an educational report might begin with statistical data related to a problem and then move to a qualitative case study to explore what the statistics reveal.

In the social sciences, both quantitative and qualitative researchers must determine what they are examining and measuring in order to get answers to research questions. A researcher who studies childhood aggression, for example, must first define and measure *aggression*. If the research is qualitative, a researcher may describe types of behavior that indicate aggression and then discuss observations of children and interviews with teachers and peers about those behaviors. A quantitative researcher, on the other hand, might design an experiment that asks children to rate their peers' aggression on a scale of one to ten.

It's important to recognize that both quantitative and qualitative studies have points of view, and that researchers' opinions influence everything from the hypothesis and the design of the research study to the interpretation of findings. Readers must consider whether the researchers' views are sensible and solidly supported by evidence, and they must pay close attention to the kind of data the writer is using and what those data can—and cannot—prove. For example, if researchers of childhood aggression define *aggression* in a way that readers find unpersuasive, or if they observe behaviors that readers consider playful rather than aggressive, then the readers will likely not accept their interpretation of the findings.

Conventional formats

Make use of conventional disciplinary formats to help guide your reading in the social sciences. Many such texts conform to the format and documentation style of the American Psychological Association (APA). In addition, articles often include standard features—an abstract that gives an overview of the findings, followed by headings that present the introduction, review of literature, methods, results, discussion, and references.

Readers who become familiar with such a format can easily find the information they need. (For more on APA style, see Chapters 58–61.)

15b   Write texts in the social sciences.

Perhaps because the social sciences share concerns with both the humanities and the sciences, the forms of writing within the social sciences are particularly varied. Assignments in social science classes can often be organized under five main categories:

- Writing that encourages student learning, such as reaction pieces and position papers
- Writing that demonstrates student learning, such as summaries, abstracts, and research papers
- Writing that requires students to analyze and evaluate the writings of others, such as literature reviews, book reviews, and briefs
- Writing that asks students to replicate the work of others or to engage in original research, such as quantitative research reports, case studies, and ethnographic analyses
- Writing that reflects common on-the-job communication tasks for members of a discipline, such as radio scripts, briefing notes, and informational reports

Many forms of writing in the social sciences call either explicitly or implicitly for argument (see Chapter 8). If you write an essay that reports on the results of a survey you developed about attitudes among students on your campus toward physician-assisted suicide, you will make an explicit argument about the significance of your data. But even with other forms of writing, such as summaries and book reports, you will implicitly argue that your description and analysis provide a clear, thorough overview of the text(s) you have read.

Style in the social sciences

Writing in the social sciences need not be dry and filled with jargon. While you need to understand the conventions, concepts, and habits of mind typical of a discipline, you can still write clear prose that engages readers.

When discussing research sources in a paper conforming to APA style, use the past tense or the present perfect tense for the verbs (35e): *Raditch showed* or *Raditch has shown*. Make sure that any writing you do is as clear and grammatically correct as possible so that readers see you as capable and credible.

Literature reviews

Students of the social sciences write literature reviews to find out the most current thinking about a topic, to learn what research has already been carried out on that topic (research in a field is that field's "literature"), to evaluate the work that has been done, and to set any research they will do in context. The following guidelines are designed to help you explore and question sources, looking for flaws or gaps. Such a critical review could then lead to a discussion of how your own research will avoid such flaws and advance knowledge.

- What is your topic or dependent variable (item or characteristic studied)?
- What is already known about this topic? What characteristics does the topic or dependent variable have? How have other researchers measured the item or characteristic being studied? What other factors are involved, and how are they related to each other and to your topic or variable? What theories are used to explain the way things are now?
- How has research been done so far? Who or what has been studied? How have measurements been taken?
- Has there been change over time? What has caused any changes?
- What problems do you find in the new research? What questions have not been answered? Have researchers drawn unwarranted conclusions?
- What gaps will your research fill? How is it new? What problems do you want to correct?

15c An excerpt from a student's psychology literature review

Following is an excerpt from a psychology literature review by Tawnya Redding that adheres to the conventions for social science writing in this genre and follows the guidelines of APA style (see Chapters 58–61) to document sources.

Student Writer

Tawnya Redding

1

Page number appears flush right on first line of every page

Title (boldface), writer's name, department and school, course number and title, professor, and date centered and double-spaced

Mood Music: Music Preference and the Risk for Depression and Suicide in Adolescents

Tawnya Redding

School of Psychological Science, Oregon State University

PSY 480: Clinical Research Methods

Professor Ede

February 23, 2009

2

Mood Music: Music Preference and the Risk for Depression and Suicide in Adolescents

Music is a significant part of American culture. Since the explosion of rock and roll in the 1950s, there has been a concern for the effects that music may have on listeners, and especially on young people. The genres most likely to come under suspicion in recent decades have included heavy metal, country, and blues. These genres have been suspected of having adverse effects on the mood and behavior of young listeners. But can music really alter the disposition and create self-destructive behaviors in listeners? And if so, which genres and aspects of those genres are responsible? The following review of the literature will establish the correlation between potentially problematic genres of music such as heavy metal and country and depression and suicide risk. First, correlational studies concerning music preference and suicide risk will be discussed, followed by a discussion of the literature concerning the possible reasons for this link. Finally, studies concerning the effects of music on mood will be discussed. Despite the link between genres such as heavy metal and country and suicide risk, previous research has been unable to establish the causal nature of this link.

The Correlation Between Music and Depression and Suicide Risk

Studies over the past two decades have set out to answer this question by examining the correlation between youth music preference and risk for depression and suicide. A large portion of these studies have focused on heavy metal and country music as the main genre culprits associated with youth suicidality and depression (Lacourse et al., 2001; Scheel & Westefeld, 1999; Stack & Gundlach, 1992). Stack and Gundlach (1992) examined the radio airtime devoted to country music in 49 metropolitan areas and found that the higher the percentages of country music airtime, the higher the

Full title boldface and centered

Background information about review supplied

Questions focus reader's attention

Boldface headings help organize review

Parenthetical references follow APA style

8

References
begin on
new page;
heading is
centered and
boldface

**Print journal
article**

**Journal
article with
DOI**

References

Baker, F., & Bor, W. (2008). Can music preference indicate mental health status in young people? *Australasian Psychiatry, 16*(4), 284–288. https://doi.org/10.1080/10398560701879589

George, D., Stickle, K., Rachid, F., & Wopnford, A. (2007). The association between types of music enjoyed and cognitive, behavioral, and personality factors of those who listen. *Psychomusicology, 19*(2), 32–56.

Lacourse, E., Claes, M., & Villeneuve, M. (2001). Heavy metal music and adolescent suicidal risk. *Journal of Youth and Adolescence, 30*(3), 321–332.

Lai, Y.-M. (1999). Effects of music listening on depressed women in Taiwan. *Issues in Mental Health Nursing, 20*(3), 229–246. https://doi.org/10.1080/016128499248637

Martin, G., Clark, M., & Pearce, C. (1993). Adolescent suicide: Music preference as an indicator of vulnerability. *Journal of the American Academy of Child and Adolescent Psychiatry, 32*(3), 530–535.

Scheel, K., & Westefeld, J. (1999). Heavy metal music and adolescent suicidality: An empirical investigation. *Adolescence, 34*(134), 253–273.

Siedliecki, S., & Good, M. (2006). Effect of music on power, pain, depression and disability. *Journal of Advanced Nursing, 54*(5), 553–562. https://doi.org/10.1111/j.1365-2648.2006.03860.x

Smith, J. L., & Noon, J. (1998). Objective measurement of mood change induced by contemporary music. *Journal of Psychiatric & Mental Health Nursing, 5*(5), 403–408.

Stack, S. (2000). Blues fans and suicide acceptability. *Death Studies, 24*(3), 223–231.

Stack, S., & Gundlach, J. (1992). The effect of country music on suicide. *Social Forces, 71*(1), 211–218. https://doi.org/10.2307/2579974

ABSTRACT AND RUNNING HEAD (FOR PROFESSIONAL PAPERS)

MOOD MUSIC   2

Abstract

There has long been concern for the effects that certain genres of music (such as heavy metal and country) have on youth. While a correlational link between these genres and increased risk for depression and suicide in adolescents has been established, researchers have been unable to pinpoint what is responsible for this link, and a causal relationship has not been determined. This paper will begin by discussing correlational literature concerning music preference and increased risk for depression and suicide, as well as the possible reasons for this link. Finally, studies concerning the effects of music on mood will be discussed. This examination of the literature on music and increased risk for depression and suicide points out the limitations of previous research and suggests the need for new research establishing a causal relationship for this link as well as research into the specific factors that may contribute to an increased risk for depression and suicide in adolescents.

Keywords: suicide, depression, music, adolescents

Running head (title shortened to 50 characters or fewer) in all capital letters on every page; heading centered and boldface

Abstract required for professional papers submitted for publication

Clear, straightforward description of literature under review

Text is double-spaced

Conclusions indicated

Keywords help readers find article online or in a database

16 Writing in the Natural and Applied Sciences

Natural sciences such as biology, chemistry, and physics study the natural world and its phenomena; applied sciences such as nanotechnology and the various fields of engineering apply knowledge from the natural sciences to practical problems. Whether you are working in the lab or the field, writing will play a key role in your courses in the natural and applied sciences.

16a Read texts in the natural and applied sciences.

Scientists and engineers work with evidence that can be observed, verified, and controlled. Though they cannot avoid interpretation, they still strive for objectivity by using the scientific method—observing or studying phenomena, formulating a hypothesis about the phenomena, and testing that hypothesis through controlled experiments and observations. Scientists and engineers aim to generate precise, replicable data; they develop experiments to account for extraneous factors. In this careful, precise way, scientists and engineers identify, test, and write persuasively about theoretical and real-world problems.

Argument in the sciences

As you read in the sciences, try to become familiar with disciplinary terms, concepts, and formats as soon as possible, and practice reading and listening for detail. If you are reading a first-year biology textbook, you can draw upon general critical-reading strategies. In addition, charts, graphs, illustrations, models, and other visuals often play an important role in scientific writing, so your ability to read and comprehend these visual displays of knowledge is particularly important.

When you read a science or engineering textbook, you can assume that the information presented there is authoritative and as objective as possible. When you read specialized materials, however, recognize that although scholarly reports undergo significant peer review, they nevertheless represent arguments (Chapter 8). The connection between facts and claims in the sciences, as in all subject areas, is created by the author rather than simply revealed by the data. So read both facts and claims with a questioning eye: Did the scientist choose the best method to test the hypothesis? Are there other reasonable interpretations of the experiment's results? Do other studies contradict the conclusions of this experiment? When you read specialized texts in the sciences with questions like these in mind, you are reading—and thinking—like a scientist. (For additional information on assessing a source's credibility, see 11c.)

Conventional formats

As you advance in your course work, you will need to develop reading strategies for increasingly specialized texts as well as data and diagrams. Many scientific texts include standard features—an abstract that gives an overview of the findings, followed by an introduction and literature review, a materials and methods section, the results of the research, discussion, and references, and tables of numerical data or other visuals.

An experienced reader in sciences and engineering might skim an abstract to see if an article warrants further reading. If it does—and this judgment is based on the reader's own research interest—he or she might then read the introduction to understand the rationale for the experiment and then skip to the results. A reader with a specific interest in the methods will read that section with particular care. You might expect, however, to read a journal article for a science or engineering course from start to finish, giving equal weight to each section.

16b Write texts in the natural and applied sciences.

In the sciences and engineering, you must be able to respond to a diverse range of writing and speaking tasks. Often, you must maintain lab or engineering notebooks that include careful records of experiments. You will also write memos, papers, project proposals and reports, literature reviews, and progress reports; in addition, you may develop print and web-based presentations for both expert and nonexpert audiences (Chapter 19). Particularly common writing assignments in the sciences are the literature review, research proposal, and research report.

Assignments

Most scientists spend a great deal of time writing research or grant proposals aimed at securing funds to support their research. As an undergraduate, you may have an opportunity to make similar proposals to an office of undergraduate research or to a science-based firm that supports student research. Funding agencies often have guidelines for preparing a proposal. Proposals for research funding generally include the following sections:

title page, introduction, purpose(s) and significance of the study, methods, timeline, budget, and references. You may also need to submit an abstract.

Research reports, another common writing form in the sciences, may include both literature reviews and discussions of primary research, most often experiments. Like journal articles, research reports generally follow this form: title, author(s), abstract, introduction, literature review, materials and methods, results, discussion, and references. Academic journals in many fields now expect work that they publish to follow this format, known by the shorthand "IMRAD" (for "Introduction, Methods, Results, and Discussion"). The focus of many IMRAD-format articles is on the introduction (which situates the research in the context of other work in the field) and on the discussion of the results. Many instructors will ask you to write lab reports (16c), which are briefer versions of research reports and may not include a literature review.

Today, most scientific writing is collaborative. As you move from introductory to advanced courses and then to the workplace, you will increasingly find yourself working as part of a team or group. Indeed, in such areas as engineering, collaborative projects are the norm.

Style in the sciences

In general, use the present tense for most writing you do in the natural and applied sciences. Use the past tense, however, when you are describing research already carried out (by you or others) or published in the past.

As a writer in the sciences, you will need to produce complex figures, tables, images, and models and use software designed to analyze data or run computer simulations. In addition, you must present data carefully. If you create a graph, you should provide headings for columns, label axes with numbers or units, and identify data points. Caption figures and tables with a number and descriptive title. And avoid orphan data — data that you present in a figure or table but don't comment on in your text.

Finally, make sure that any writing you do is as clear, concise, and grammatically correct as possible to ensure that readers see you as capable and credible.

16c   An excerpt from a student's chemistry lab report

Student Writer

Allyson Goldberg

Following is an excerpt from a lab report on a chemistry experiment by student Allyson Goldberg.

Goldberg 2

Introduction

The purpose of this investigation was to experimentally determine the value of the universal gas constant, R. To accomplish this goal, a measured sample of magnesium (Mg) was allowed to react with an excess of hydrochloric acid (HCl) at room temperature and pressure so that the precise amount and volume of the product hydrogen gas (H_2) could be determined and the value of R could be calculated using the ideal gas equation, $PV = nRT$.

Introduction explains purpose of lab and gives overview of results

Materials & Methods

Two samples of room temperature water, one about 250mL and the other about 400mL, were measured into a smaller and larger beaker respectively. 15.0mL of HCl was then transferred into a side arm flask that was connected to the top of a buret (clamped to a ringstand) through a 5/16" diameter flexible tube. (This "gas buret" was connected to an adjacent "open buret," clamped to the other side of the ringstand, and left open to the atmosphere of the laboratory at its wide end, by a 1/4" diameter flexible tube. These two burets were adjusted on the ringstand so that they were vertically parallel and close together.) The HCl sample was transferred to the flask such that none came in contact with the inner surface of the neck of the flask. The flask was then allowed to rest, in an almost horizontal position, in the smaller beaker.

Materials and methods section explains lab setup and procedure

Passive voice throughout is typical of writing in the natural sciences

The open buret was adjusted on the ringstand such that its 20mL mark was horizontally aligned with the 35mL mark on the gas buret. Room temperature water was added to the open buret until the water level of the gas buret was at about 34.00mL.

A piece of magnesium ribbon was obtained, weighed on an analytical balance, and placed in the neck of the horizontal side

Goldberg 3

arm flask. Next, a screw cap was used to cap the flask and form an airtight seal. This setup was then allowed to sit for 5 minutes in order to reach thermal equilibrium.

After 5 minutes, the open buret was adjusted so that the menisci on both burets were level with each other; the side arm flask was then tilted vertically to let the magnesium ribbon react with the HCl. After the brisk reaction, the flask was placed into the larger beaker and allowed to sit for another 5 minutes.

Next, the flask was placed back into the smaller beaker, and the open buret was adjusted on the ringstand such that its meniscus was level with that of the gas buret. After the system sat for an additional 30 minutes, the open buret was again adjusted so that the menisci on both burets were level.

This procedure was then repeated two more times, with the exception that HCl was not again added to the side arm flask, as it was already present in enough excess for all reactions from the first trial.

Results and calculations show measurements and calculations of final value of R

Results and Calculations

Trial #	Lab Temp. (°C)	Lab Pressure (mbar)	Mass of Mg Ribbon Used (g)	Initial Buret Reading (mL)	Final Buret Reading (mL)
1	24.4	1013	0.0147	32.66	19.60
2	24.3	1013	0.0155	33.59	N/A*
3	25.0	1013	0.0153	34.35	19.80

*See note in Discussion section.

17 Writing in Professional Settings

Today's professionals are part of a global economy that relies more than ever on clear written communication. Whether you are writing to get a job or writing on the job, keep in mind that texts you produce in professional settings will be more successful if you pay attention to your purpose and your audience and write in the genre that your readers expect.

17a Read texts in professional settings.

In business today, writers have almost unlimited access to information and to people whose expertise can be useful for a project. Somehow, you will need to negotiate and evaluate a huge stream of information.

General strategies for effective reading (Chapter 7) can help. One such strategy, keeping a clear purpose in mind when you read, is particularly important for work-related reading. Are you reading to solve a problem? to gather and synthesize information? to make a recommendation? Knowing why you are reading will increase your productivity. Time constraints and deadlines will also affect your decisions about what and how to read; the ability to identify important information quickly by skimming is a skill you should cultivate as a business reader, as is knowing when *not* to skim but to attend carefully to an entire text or message.

17b Write texts in professional settings.

Writing assignments in business classes generally serve two related functions. While their immediate goal is to help you master the theory and practice of business, these assignments also prepare you for the kinds of writing that you will one day face in the workplace. For this reason, students in *every* discipline need to know how to write effective business documents such as memos, emails, letters, proposals, reports, and résumés.

Much writing in business today is collaborative in nature. You may find that your coworkers expect you to ask for or offer comments on drafts of important documents that will present your team's work to others in the company or to the public. For more on collaboration, see 13f.

Professional writers tend to use conventional formats and academic written English. When you write to employers or prospective employers, stick to more formal communication unless you have a very good reason to do otherwise. Remember, too, that much or all of the writing you do at work is public writing as well, and that employers have easy access to — and in fact ownership of — email and other documents written by employees. As always, it's best to use discretion in all on-the-job communication.

Memos and email

Memos are a common form of communication sent within and between organizations. Today, memos are typically delivered as email messages; they tend to be brief and direct, often dealing with only one subject.

As with any writing, consider the audience for your memo carefully. Make sure to include everyone who might need the information, but be cautious about sharing it too widely, especially when the information in your document may be sensitive.

Follow these guidelines for writing effective memos and professional email:

- Clearly identify the subject.
- Begin with the most important information: depending on the memo's purpose, you may have to provide background information, define a task or problem, or clarify a goal.
- Use your opening paragraph to focus on how the information you convey affects your readers.
- Focus each of your following paragraphs on one idea pertaining to the subject.
- Relate your information concisely and in a way that is relevant to the reader.
- Emphasize exactly what you want readers to do and when.
- Use attachments for detailed supporting information.
- Adjust your style and tone to fit your audience.
- Attempt to build goodwill in your conclusion.

Following is a memo, written by students Michelle Abbott and Carina Abernathy, that presents an analysis and recommendation to help an employer make a decision.

Student Writer

Michelle Abbott

Student Writer

Carina Abernathy

MEMO

TO:	Rosa Donahue, Sales Manager
FROM:	Michelle Abbott & Carina Abernathy
SUBJECT:	Taylor Nursery Bid
DATE:	March 5, 2018

As you know, Taylor Nursery has requested bids on a 25,000-pound order of private-label fertilizer. Taylor Nursery is one of the largest distributors of our Fertikil product.

Opening provides background

The total cost for manufacturing 25,000 pounds of the private-label brand for Taylor Nursery is $44,075. This cost includes direct material, direct labor, and variable manufacturing overhead. Although our current equipment and facilities provide adequate capacity for processing this special order, the job will require overtime labor, which has been factored into our costs.

Most important information put in bold

The minimum price that Jenco could bid for this product without losing money is $44,075 (our cost). Applying our standard markup of 40% results in a price of $61,705. You could reasonably establish a price anywhere within that range.

Options presented

Taylor Nursery has requested bids from several competitors. One rival, Eclipse Fertilizers, is submitting a bid of $60,000 on this order. Therefore, our recommendation is to slightly underbid Eclipse with a price of $58,000, representing a markup of approximately 32%.

Final recommendation

Please let us know if we can be of further assistance in your decision on the bid.

Closing builds goodwill by offering further help

Proposal

In businesses and the professions, writers are often called upon to write proposals that aim to evoke some action based on the proposal's recommendations. Writers in professional settings might have the need to propose a solution for a problem or propose a study of a problem. Often, proposals have a very specific purpose and audience. While the format can vary, almost all proposals will include the following parts, usually with subheadings to direct the reader:

- an abstract or summary that clarifies the purpose of the proposal
- a background section that includes a problem statement or statement of need
- a section on desired objectives or outcomes
- methods for achieving the outcomes
- a means of evaluating those outcomes
- information about how the results will be shared with others
- a budget

The following proposal excerpt begins by addressing the problem as the writer sees it and then by stating the major objective. Following this opening, the proposal goes on to include additional sections: Previous Research and Current Knowledge; Project Design; Statistical Analysis; Health and Safety Concerns; Implications for Fire Management, Firefighters, and Policymakers; and Budget.

Here is the opening of a proposal to conduct research to help reduce the smoke inhalation firefighters are exposed to.

Wildland Firefighter Smoke Exposure

Problem Statement

Wildland firefighters work in a dynamic environment and are often faced with a variety of hazards on any given day. One of the most common, but often overlooked hazards is exposure to potentially harmful levels of contaminants in wildland smoke. This may also be one of the least understood risks of wildland firefighting. With the increased information regarding the potential health effects of vegetative smoke to respiratory and cardiovascular systems it became apparent that more work needed to be done to measure the exposure experienced by firefighters during their work shift and by personnel at fire camps. Previous National Wildfire Coordination Group (NWCG)-sponsored smoke exposure studies indicated that employees were overexposed approximately 5% of the time at wildfires and 10% of the time at prescribed fires.[1]

Unlike their counterparts who fight structural fires, wildland firefighters do not wear respiratory protective equipment. Therefore it is essential that fire managers have a good understanding of the exposures their firefighters face under various conditions. In order to understand the potential effects of this exposure, managers must also be able to understand the exposure levels for critical time periods such as instantaneous exposures, short-term exposures, and longer-term exposures, including 24-hour exposure. In order to predict long-term effects of wildland smoke exposure, it will also be necessary to predict career length exposures.

Objective

The objective of this study is to expand the current state of knowledge on wildland firefighter smoke exposure. First, it will provide important information on the levels of irritants firefighters are exposed to. In order for fire managers and safety and health managers to develop safe exposure levels and mitigation measures to protect wildland firefighters, they must be able to understand the critical factors that influence exposure levels to firefighters. This research will measure the exposure levels of carbon monoxide (CO), particulate matter (PM_4), and crystalline silica (SiO_2) on wildland and prescribed fires in several geographic areas of the United States.

---

[1]Reinhardt, Timothy E.; Ottmar, Roger D. 2000. Smoke exposure at western wildfires. Res. Pap. PNW-RP-525. Portland, OR: U.S. Department of Agriculture, Forest Service, Pacific Northwest Research Station. 72 p.

Cover letter

A cover letter, which often accompanies a résumé, aims to demonstrate how the experiences and skills you outline in your résumé have prepared you for a particular job. Remember to focus, then, on how you can benefit the company, not how the company can help you. A well-written letter can help you stand out from a pile of candidates, even if you are new to the field and don't yet have impressive qualifications, so craft your words carefully.

If you are posting a cover letter to accompany an online application, you will probably provide your contact information elsewhere, and you may not know the name or title of the person who will ultimately read the letter. Follow these guidelines for effective professional communication:

- Use a conventional format unless you have a specific reason to do otherwise.
- Whenever possible, write to a specific person (*Dear Ms. Robinson* or *Dear Mr. Otuteye*).
- Be polite — even if you have a complaint.
- Clearly state your reason for writing. Include whatever details will help your reader see your point and respond.
- If appropriate, make clear what you hope your reader will do.
- Express appreciation for your reader's attention.
- Make it easy for your reader to respond by including your contact information.

Résumé

While a cover letter usually emphasizes specific parts of the résumé, telling how your background is suited to a particular job, a résumé summarizes your experience and qualifications and provides support for your letter. An effective résumé is brief, usually one or two pages. You should be aware, though, that conventions for résumés (or CVs) may differ from country to country. Job applicants for positions outside the United States, for example, will often report more personal information than is allowed in the U.S. along with a personal photo, information about family, and exam scores. In addition, they may use a narrative style as opposed to the lists (education, experience, publications, etc.) favored in the United States. If you are applying for a position in a country other than the U.S., be sure to look for examples of résumés used in that country.

Research shows that employers in the United States generally spend less than a minute reading a résumé. Since they are reading for the purpose of fulfilling *their* needs, they expect a résumé to be easy to read. Formatting your document neatly and using clear headings and adequate spacing will work in your favor.

A well-written résumé with a standard format and typefaces is still, in many cases, the best way to distinguish yourself, but in certain contexts, a more creative résumé that includes media links, images, and other non-traditional content may help you succeed. As with any writing situation, consider your context and purpose.

Your résumé may be arranged chronologically (from most to least recent) or functionally (based on skill or expertise). Include the following information:

- ***Name, address, phone number, email address.*** You may also want to include links to a career profile page or personal website, and, if the content is professionally appropriate, to social media content such as a Twitter feed.
- ***Educational background.*** Include degrees, diplomas, majors, and special programs or courses that pertain to your field of interest.
- ***Work experience.*** Identify each job — whether a paying job, an internship, or military experience — with dates and names of organizations. Describe your duties by carefully selecting strong action verbs.
- ***Skills, personal interests, activities, awards, and honors.***
- ***References.*** Most writers simply say that references are available on request.
- ***Images.*** Some applicants also include images in their résumés. Make choices that seem appropriate for your specific situation.

Job seekers today usually upload résumés to a company website when applying for a position. In such cases, take special care to make sure that you have caught any errors or typos before submitting the form.

The following pages show student Megan N. Lange's résumé in two formats, one in traditional print style and the other in a creative format optimized for digital presentation. Like many recent college graduates, she is considering possible career paths, and having two very different résumés prepared allows her to present herself appropriately to either traditional or more creative potential employers.

Student Writer

Megan N. Lange

TRADITIONAL RÉSUMÉ

Name in
boldface
and larger
type size

Educational
background

Relevant
work
experience

Courses
relevant to
position
being
sought

Affiliations
and
experience
not listed
above

Megan N. Lange
1234 Kingston Pike • Knoxville, TN 37919
Phone: 865.643.xxxx • Email: mlange1@utk.edu

Education

Exp. May 2018   **The University of Tennessee**, Knoxville. B.A. in Technical Writing
                and Business Editing, Classical Studies

May 2013   **Lenoir City High School**

Work Experience

• **The Yankee Candle Company** – Store 433   August 2014 – present
  Sales Associate: assists guests in-store, answers phones,
  restocks floor, operates cash register

• **Holston Conference of the United Methodist Church**   June 2015 – August 2015
  Youth and Young Adult Intern: worked in-office with team,
  out-of-office with local youth workers, planned and facilitated
  youth retreats and events

• **Megan Lange Photography**   January 2015 – present
  Head Photographer: senior portraiture, weddings, maternity

Relevant Courses

• **Technical Writing 360**   Fall 2015
  Focused on proper formatting of different professional
  documents, teamwork, creative thinking

• **Technical Writing 460**   Spring 2016
  Proofreading and formatting of professional documents,
  email etiquette, international communication

Affiliations/Memberships

• **Society for Technical Communication**, East Tennessee Chapter   Spring 2016

Other Experience

• **Great Smoky Mountain Chrysalis Board**   August 2014 – present
• **University of Tennessee Singers**   August 2013 – May 2015
• **Cedar Springs Presbyterian Church Choir**   August 2015 – present

References available upon request.

Megan Lange uses this résumé to apply for most jobs. The clean, inviting, businesslike look presents the content in expected ways — her name and contact information, educational background, work experience, courses she has taken in the field she hopes to enter, and other information that may help prospective employers know more about the kind of person she is.

CREATIVE RÉSUMÉ

Megan Lange uses this résumé to apply for positions for which her creativity would be an asset. The design is still easy to read, but reveals more of her personality. Icons under "Social Media" are live links to her feeds on various sites.

18   Making Design Decisions

In the ancient Greek world, a speaker's delivery (known as *actio*) was an art every educated person needed to master: how a speaker delivered a speech — tone, pace, volume, use of gestures, and so on — had a great impact on the message and how it would be received. Writers now have many tools that writers and speakers in the ancient world did not have to help them get and hold an audience's attention, from font options to color, visuals, and sound. All these tools help bring the dimension of *visual rhetoric* to today's writing.

18a   Choose a type of text.

A text can be anything that you might "read" — not just words but also images, data, audio, video, or combinations of media. A print book, for example, may include words alone or words and visuals. Texts that go online can grow much richer with animations, video, audio, links, and interactive features. College writers today have choices that were unimaginable until quite recently.

Rhetorical contexts

Ultimately, the organization and look of any text you design should depend on your rhetorical situation. You should make decisions about layout, formatting, color, fonts (for written words), elements such as images or video, and other aspects of design based on rhetorical needs — your audience, purpose, topic, stance, genre conventions, and so on — and on practical constraints, such as the time and tools available.

Design choices for different genres

While you might still be assigned to compose traditional texts such as academic essays, you may also be asked to create coursework in many other genres. Research conducted for this textbook found that today's students are encountering assignments that range from newsletters, infographics, and poster presentations to PechaKuchas, podcasts, and video essays — and that multimodal assignments are increasingly characteristic of first-year writing courses. Whatever genre you choose for your assignment, familiarize yourself with conventions of design for that genre, and think carefully about the most appropriate and compelling design choices for your particular context.

Print or digital delivery

One of your first design decisions will involve determining whether you'll deliver your text digitally, in print, or both ways. In general, print documents are portable, easy to read without online access or technical assistance, and relatively fast to produce. Digital texts, on the other hand, can include sound, animation, and video; updates are easy to make; distribution is fast and efficient; and feedback can be swift. Design decisions may have similar goals, such as clarity and readability, no matter what medium you are working in, but the specific choices you make to achieve those goals may differ in print and digital texts.

18b Plan a visual structure.

Today, all writers need to think carefully about the look of any text they create and plan a visual structure for it. The design decisions you make will help guide readers by making the texts easier to follow and understand.

Design principles

Designer Robin Williams, in her *Non-Designer's Design Book*, points out four simple principles for designing effective texts — contrast, alignment, repetition, and proximity. These principles are illustrated here with the familiar Wikipedia page design.

Chances are that most readers will look first at either the heading or the images on this Wikipedia page. The site uses large black type against a white background for the title of each page at the upper left. On this page, color images of molecular models also draw the eye.

CONTRAST

Contrast attracts your eye to elements on a page and guides you around it, helping you follow an argument or find information. You may achieve contrast through the use of color, icons, boldface or large type size, headings, and so on. Begin with a focus point — the dominant point, image, or words where you want your reader's eye to go first — and structure the flow of your visual information from this point.

ALIGNMENT

Alignment refers to the way visuals and text on a page are lined up, both horizontally and vertically. The overall guideline is not to mix alignments arbitrarily. That is, if you begin with a left alignment, stick with it for the major parts of your page. The result will be a cleaner and more organized look. For example, the title, text, and subheadings of a Wikipedia article align with the left margin, and images align with the right margin.

REPETITION

Readers are guided by the repetition of key words and elements. Use a consistent design throughout your document for such elements as color, typeface, and images. Every Wikipedia page uses the same fonts and the same layout, so readers know what to expect.

PROXIMITY

Parts of a text that are closely related should appear together (proximate to one another). Your goal is to position related points, text, and visuals near one another and to use clear headings to identify these clusters, as the Wikipedia page does.

CONSISTENT OVERALL IMPRESSION

Aim for a visual structure and design that create the appropriate overall impression or mood for your text. For example, with an academic essay, whether print or digital, you will probably make conservative choices that strike a serious scholarly note. In a newsletter for a campus group, you might choose attention-getting images. In a website designed to introduce yourself to future employers, you might favor a mix of material drawn from your current résumé, including writing, embedded video or links to digital content that relates to your skills and career goals, and at least one image of yourself — all in one carefully organized and easy-to-comprehend structure.

Templates

If designing your writing yourself seems intimidating, consider using a template, a basic model that shows you how to lay out a particular type of text. You may have used templates in a word-processing program to create a document such as a memo or report, in presentation software to create slides, or in a blog-publishing service to design your content. Before you create a text in a genre that is new to you, it's a good idea to look for available design templates. You can use them to see typical elements and layouts for the genre, even if you decide not to follow the template's settings for color, fonts, and other details of formatting.

18c Format print and digital texts appropriately.

With so many options available, you should always spend some time thinking about appropriate formatting for elements of your text. Although the following guidelines often apply, remember that print documents, web pages, slide shows, videos, and so on all have their own formatting conventions. Keep in mind that you may be required to use MLA, APA, or *Chicago* guidelines for formatting an academic essay. See 54e, 58e, and 62c, respectively, for this help.

White space (negative space)

The parts of a page or screen left intentionally blank are called *white space* or *negative space*. Too little white space makes a page look crowded, while too much can make it seem empty. Think about the amount of white space at the page level (top and side margins), paragraph level (the space between paragraphs), and sentence level (the space between sentences). Aim for consistency. Within the page, you can also use white space around content such as an image, an embedded video, or a list to make it stand out.

Color

As you design your documents, keep in mind that some colors can evoke powerful responses, so take care that the colors you use match the message you are sending. Color can enliven texts that are mainly alphabetic, but using color poorly can also make a text seem less readable and inviting. If you decide to use color in a document, keep your color palette, or range of colors, fairly limited to avoid a jumbled or confused look. Use the following tips to carry readers through your document.

- Use color to draw attention to elements you want to emphasize: headings, text boxes, or graphs, for example.
- Be consistent in your use of color; use the same color for all of your headings, for example, or the same background color for all of your presentation slides.
- Choose color combinations that are easy to read. Ask a few peers or friends whether your text is legible against the background before presenting, submitting, or posting your work.
- Make sure visuals and text are legible in the setting in which they will be read. Colors can be sharper on a computer monitor than in a print document, and slides may look different when you project them.

Type sizes and fonts

For words in the body of a traditional report, essay, or web posting, an 11- or 12-point type size is conventional.

Choose a readable font, either a serif font (used in this sentence) or a sans serif font (used in headings on this page). Although unusual fonts might seem attractive at first glance, readers may find such styles distracting and hard to read over long stretches of material. Remember that fonts help you create the tone of a document, so consider your audience and purpose when selecting type.

Different fonts convey different feelings.
Different fonts convey different feelings.
DIFFERENT FONTS CONVEY DIFFERENT FEELINGS.
Different fonts convey different feelings.

Most important, be consistent in the size and style of typeface you use, especially for the main part of your text. Unless you are striving for some special effect, shifting sizes and fonts within a document can give an appearance of disorderliness. But purposeful use of special fonts can signal imagination, humor, and even spontaneity.

Margins and line spacing

For traditional print projects, you will probably use a single column of text with standard one-inch margins for your writing, but other kinds of projects call for text columns of variable widths or for multiple columns.

Both very short and very long text lines can be difficult to read. Online readers generally prefer short, manageable chunks of text rather than long paragraphs; consider breaking up a long online piece with headings or visuals.

By using buttons like those shown here, you can decide whether or not you want left and right margins justified, or squared off—as they are on typical book pages (including this one). Readers will often expect you to align the left margin, except in posters and other texts where

left align, center, right align, justify

you are trying to achieve a distinctive visual effect. However, most readers prefer the right margin to be "ragged," or unjustified, as it is in the Wikipedia entry in 18b.

For college writing assignments, you will usually use double-spaced type with the first line of each paragraph indented one-half inch. Letters, memos, and online texts are usually single-spaced and may use spaces between paragraphs instead of paragraph indentation. Look for samples of texts in the genre, or ask about your instructor's preference.

Headings

For brief essays and reports, you may need no headings at all. For longer texts, however, headings help readers understand the organization. Headings can help break long web texts into the short, manageable chunks that online readers expect. Some kinds of reports require conventional headings (such as *Abstract* and *Summary*), which writers must provide.

You can distinguish headings by type size and font as well as by color, as this book does. Position each level of heading consistently throughout the text. And remember that headings need to appear above the text they introduce; be careful, for example, not to put a heading at the bottom of a printed page.

For formal academic work, look for the most succinct, informative, and consistent way to word headings. Choose all nouns, for example, or all questions.

NOUN	Toxicity
NOUN PHRASE	Levels of toxicity
GERUND (-*ING*) PHRASE	Measuring toxicity
QUESTION	How can toxicity be measured?
COMMAND/ IMPERATIVE	Measure the toxicity.

Language, Culture, and Context

Multilingual

Reading Patterns

In documents written in English and other Western languages, information tends to flow from left to right and top to bottom — since that is the way English texts are written and read. In some languages, which may be written from right to left or vertically, documents may be arranged from top right to bottom left. Understanding the reading patterns of the language you are working in will help you design your documents most effectively.

18d　Consider visuals and media.

Choose visuals and other media that will help make a point more vividly and succinctly than written words alone. In some cases, visuals and media may even be your primary text.

- Choose visual and media elements that will make your text more effective for your audience.
- Consider design principles for placement of visual and media files within a text, and aim to make your media files accessible to as many readers as possible.
- Tell the audience explicitly what a visual demonstrates, especially if it presents complex information. Do not assume readers will "read" the visual the way you do; your commentary on it is important.
- Follow established conventions for documenting visual and media sources. See 54e (MLA), 58e (APA), or 62c (*Chicago*). Ask permission for use if someone else controls the rights.

Considering Disabilities

Color for Contrast

Remember when you are using color that not everyone will see it as you do. Some individuals do not perceive color at all; others perceive color in a variety of ways, especially colors like blue and green, which are close together on the color spectrum. You can learn more at the website colourblindawareness.org.

- Get responses to your visuals and media in an early draft. If readers can't follow them or are distracted by them, revise accordingly.
- If you alter or edit visuals, audio, or video to include them in your writing, be sure to do so ethically.

Visual and media selection

Consider carefully what you want visuals, audio, or video to do for your writing. What will your audience want or need you to show? Try to choose visuals and media that will enhance your credibility, allow you to make your point more emphatically, and clarify your overall text. Note that different visuals work best for different situations. Tables, for example, help make detailed numerical information easier to read; a diagram can illustrate the parts of an object or process; and a photograph can capture something meaningful about an event, object, or person.

SAMPLE TABLE

	United States		
SCHOOL ENROLLMENT	**Estimate**	**Percent**	**Percent margin of error**
Population 3 years and older enrolled in school	82,148,370	—	—
Nursery/preschool	4,959,823	6.0	+/− 0.1
Kindergarten	4,181,764	5.1	+/− 0.1
Elementary school (grades 1–8)	32,831,750	40.0	+/− 0.1
High school (grades 9–12)	16,985,786	20.7	+/− 0.1
College or graduate school	23,189,247	28.2	+/− 0.1

U.S. CENSUS BUREAU

SAMPLE DIAGRAM

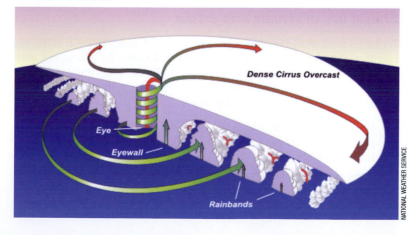

Dense Cirrus Overcast

Eye

Eyewall

Rainbands

NATIONAL WEATHER SERVICE

SAMPLE PHOTOGRAPH

LIBBY WELCH/ALAMY STOCK PHOTO

Effective media content can be your own work or materials created by others. If you are using media from another source, be sure to give appropriate credit and to get permission before making it available to the public as part of your work.

Placement

Make sure to position visuals and media clips alongside or after the text that refers to them. In formal texts, number figures and tables separately and give them informative titles. Some documentation styles ask that you include source information in a caption.

Ethical use of visuals and media

Technical tools available to writers and designers today make it relatively easy to manipulate and edit visuals, audio, and video. As you would with any source material, carefully assess any visuals you find for effectiveness, appropriateness, and validity, and identify the source for any media files you use that you have not created yourself.

- Check the context in which the visual, video, or audio appears. Is it part of an official government, school, or library site or otherwise from a credible source (11c)?
- If the visual is a photograph, is the information about the photo believable? Could it have been altered or "doctored"?

Considering Disabilities

Making Media Texts Accessible

As you create media texts, take steps to make sure that all your readers can access your content — for example, by providing alternative text for all visuals so that they will make sense when read by a screen reader, and by providing captions for sound files and transcripts of longer audio content. For details on designing accessible texts, visit the Americans with Disabilities Act site at www.ada.gov, and click on "Design Standards."

- If the visual is a chart, graph, or diagram, are the numbers and labels explained? Are the sources of the data given? Will the visual representation help readers make sense of the information, or could it mislead them?
- Can you find contact information for the creator or rightsholder?

At times, you may make certain changes to visuals that you use, such as cropping an image to show the most important detail, digitally brightening a dark image, or using a short clip from a longer audio or video file. You can make digital changes as long as you do so ethically, telling your audience what you have done and making no attempt to mislead readers.

19   Creating Presentations

When the Gallup Poll reports on what U.S. citizens say they fear most, the findings are often the same from year to year: public speaking is apparently even scarier than an attack from outer space. Nevertheless, many writing courses require you to give presentations in front of an audience, and it's safe to say that most jobs require you to present information orally in front of audiences of all kinds. People who are successful presenters point to four elements crucial to their effectiveness:

- a thorough knowledge of the subject
- careful attention to the interactive nature of speaking and thus to the needs of the audience
- careful integration of verbal and visual information
- practice, practice, and more practice

19a   Consider assignment, purpose, and audience for presentations.

You'll be wise to begin preparing for a class presentation as soon as you get the assignment. Think about how much time you have to prepare; how long the presentation is to be; whether you will use written-out text, note cards, or some other kind of cue; what kind of posters, handouts, slides, or other materials you may need; and what equipment you will need. If you are making a group presentation, you will need time to divide duties and practice. Make sure that you understand how the presentation will be graded or assessed.

Consider the purpose of your presentation (2c). Are you expected to lead a discussion? teach a lesson? give a report? engage a group in an activity? Also consider the audience (2d). What do audience members know or think about your topic? What do they need to know to follow your presentation and perhaps accept your point of view? If your presentation will be posted online, is there any reason to limit the audience who will have access to it? Finally, consider your own stance toward your topic and audience. Are you an expert? novice? well-informed observer?

Student writer Shuqiao Song got a two-part assignment for her writing class on graphic narratives: she had to write a researched argument, and then she had to turn that information into a script for a twelve-minute oral presentation with slides. After some brainstorming and talking with her instructor, Shuqiao chose her favorite graphic memoir, Alison Bechdel's *Fun Home*, as her topic.

As she thought about her assignment and topic, Shuqiao realized that she had more than one purpose. Certainly she wanted to do well on the assignment and receive a good grade. But she also wanted to convince her classmates that Bechdel's book was a complex and important one and that its power lay in the relationship between words and images. She also had to admit to at least one additional purpose: it would be great to turn in a truly *impressive* performance.

19b   Write to be heard and remembered.

Getting and keeping the attention of listeners may require you to use different strategies than the ones you generally employ when writing for a reading audience. To be *remembered* rather than simply heard, consider these features of memorable presentations.

Stories

There's nothing like a good story to get and hold audience attention. In fact, presentation expert Nancy Duarte found that stories were at the heart of hundreds of great speeches she analyzed, whether they were informative or argumentative. Many speakers prefer to use personal stories that are witty and memorable. Andrew Linderman, a storytelling coach, says that the best ones are "honest and personal . . . without emoting too much or going off the rails." But a good presentation story may also be about someone else. Shuqiao Song used several stories from the book *Fun Home* to help make her argument.

Introduction and conclusion

Remember that listeners, like readers, tend to remember beginnings and endings most readily, so work extra hard to make these elements memorable. Consider, for example, using a startling statement, opinion, or question; a dramatic anecdote; a powerful quotation; or a vivid image. Shifting

---

Quick Help

Guidelines for Presentations

- Check to make sure your presentation accomplishes the goals of the assignment.
- Be sure you are achieving your intended purpose.
- Consider your audience's expectations and knowledge about the subject of your presentation. Provide any background information necessary to help your audience follow your line of reasoning and your major points.
- Use a clear and straightforward organizational structure for your presentation.
- Check for signposts that can guide listeners, including explicit transitions and the repetition of key words and ideas.
- Rely mostly on easy-to-understand and straightforward sentences. Consider revising any long or complicated sentences to make your presentation easier to follow. Use concrete language.
- Consider marking your notes for pauses and emphasis. Also note material that you can skip if you find yourself short of time.
- Make sure that your slides and media contribute clearly to your presentation.
- Review your visuals to make sure they follow principles of good design.
- Prepare a list of sources to accompany your presentation.
- Practice your presentation so that you will appear confident and knowledgeable — and then practice it again!

language, especially into a variety of language that your audience will identify with, is another effective way to catch their attention (see 23c). Whenever you can link your subject to the experiences and interests of your audience, do so.

Shuqiao Song began her presentation this way:

> Welcome, everyone. I'm Shuqiao Song and I'm here today to talk about residents of a dys*FUN*ctional *HOME*.
>
> We meet these residents in a graphic memoir called *Fun Home*.

(Here, Shuqiao showed a three-second video clip of author Alison Bechdel saying, "I love words, and I love pictures. But especially, I love them together — in a mystical way that I can't even explain.")

> That was Alison Bechdel, author of *Fun Home*. In that clip, she conveniently introduces the topics of my presentation today: Words. Pictures. And the mystical way they work together.

Note that this presentation opened with a play on words ("dys*FUN*ctional *HOME*"), to which Shuqiao returned later on, and with a short, vivid video clip that perfectly summed up the main topic of the presentation. Also note the use of short sentences and fragments, special effects that act like drumbeats to get and hold the attention of the audience.

Signpost language

Organize your presentation clearly and carefully, and give an overview of your main points toward the beginning of your presentation. (You may wish to recall these points again toward the end of the talk.) Throughout your presentation, pause between major points, and use signpost language as you move from one topic to the next. Such signposts act as explicit transitions in your talk and should be clear and concrete: *The second crisis point in the breakup of the Soviet Union occurred hard on the heels of the first* instead of *The breakup of the Soviet Union came to another crisis point*. In addition to such explicit transitions (4d) as *next*, *on the contrary*, and *finally*, you can offer signposts by repeating key words and ideas as well as by sticking to concrete topic sentences to introduce each new idea.

At the end of Shuqiao's introduction, she set forth the structure of her presentation in a very clear, straightforward, and simple way to help her audience follow what came next:

> So, to outline the rest of my presentation: first, I'll show how *text* is insufficient — but also why it is necessary to Bechdel's story. Second, I'll

show how *images* can't be trusted, but again, why they are still necessary for Bechdel's purposes. Third and finally, I'll show how the interplay of text and image in *Fun Home* creates a more complex and comprehensive understanding of the story.

Simple syntax and memorable language

Avoid long, complicated sentences, and use straightforward sentence structure (subject-verb-object) as much as possible. Listeners prefer action verbs and concrete nouns to abstractions. You may need to deal with abstract ideas, but try to provide concrete examples for them (26a). Memorable presentations often call on the power of figures of speech and other devices of language, such as careful repetition, parallelism, and climactic order.

Shuqiao Song's presentation script included the following example:

Now, to argue my second point, I'll begin with an image. This is a René Magritte painting. The text means, *"This is not a pipe."* Is this some surrealist Jedi mind trick? Not really. Now listen to the title of the painting to grasp Magritte's point. The painting is called *The Treason of Images*. Here Magritte is showing us that "this is not a pipe" because it is an *image* of a pipe.

In a presentation on Fun Home, *Shuqiao Song uses a Magritte painting as evidence to show that "images can't be trusted."*

Shuqiao's short sentences, vivid word choice ("surrealist Jedi mind trick"), and straightforward subject-verb-object syntax all help to make the passage easy on listeners.

Script

Even though you will probably rely on some written material, you will need to adapt it for speech. Depending on the assignment, the audience, and your personal preferences, you may even speak from a full script. If so, double- or triple-space it, and use fairly large print so that it will be easy to refer to. Try to end each page with the end of a sentence so that you won't have to pause while you turn a page. In addition, you may decide to mark spots where you want to pause and to highlight words you want to emphasize.

A PARAGRAPH FROM SHUQIAO SONG'S PRINT ESSAY

Finally, we can see how image and text function together. On the one hand, image and text support each other in that each highlights the subtleties of the other; but on the other hand, the more interesting interaction comes when there is some degree of distance between what is written and what is depicted. In *Fun Home*, there is no one-to-one closure that mentally connects text and image. Rather, Bechdel pushes the boundaries of mental closure between image and text. If the words and pictures match exactly, making the same point, the story would read like a children's book, and that would be too simple for what Bechdel is trying to accomplish. However, text and image can't be so mismatched that meaning completely eludes the readers.

Note that the revised paragraph presents the same information, but this time it is written to be heard. The revision uses helpful signpost language, some repetition, simple syntax, and informal varieties of English to help listeners follow along and remain interested.

SHUQIAO SONG'S PARAGRAPH REVISED FOR ORAL PRESENTATION

Finally, image and text can work together. They support each other: each highlights the subtleties of the other. But they are even more interesting when there's a gap — some distance between the story the words tell and the story the pictures tell. In *Fun Home*, text and image are never perfectly correlated. After all, if the words and pictures matched up exactly, the story would read like a kids' book. That would be way too simple for Bechdel's purposes. But we wouldn't want a complete disconnect between words and images either, since we wouldn't be able to make sense of them.

Notes

If you decide to speak from notes rather than from a full script, here are some tips for doing so effectively:

- In general, use one note card for each point in your presentation.
- Number the cards.
- On each card, include the major point you want to make in large bold text and any subpoints in a bulleted list.
- Include signpost language (*another benefit is . . .*) on each note.
- Practice your presentation using the notes at least twice.
- Time your presentation. Use color or brackets to mark material in your notes that you can skip if you are running too long.

19c Create slides or other visuals.

Visuals are often an integral part of a presentation, carrying a lot of the message the speaker wants to convey. So think of your visuals not as add-ons but as a major means of getting your points across. Many speakers use slides created in presentation software to help keep themselves on track

---

Considering Disabilities

Accessible Presentations

Remember that some members of your audience may have trouble seeing or hearing your presentation, so do all you can to make your presentation accessible.

- Face any audience members who rely on lip-reading to understand your words. For a large audience, request an ASL (American Sign Language) interpreter.
- Do not rely on color or graphics alone to get across information.
- For presentations you publish online, provide brief textual descriptions of your visuals.
- If you use video, provide labels or captions to explain any sounds that won't be audible to some audience members, and embed spoken captions to explain images to those who cannot see them. Be sure that the equipment is caption capable.
- Provide a transcript for audio or video elements for those who need it.

and to guide the audience. In addition, posters, flip charts, chalkboards, or interactive whiteboards can also help you make strong visual statements.

Presentation tools such as PowerPoint, Google Slides, or Prezi allow you to prepare slides you want to display and even to enhance the images with sound. To choose among them, consider what the tool allows you to do and how much time you will need to learn to use it effectively. For more on design principles, see Chapter 18.

For her presentation, "Residents of a Dys*FUN*ctional *HOME*: Text and Image," Shuqiao Song developed a series of very simple slides aimed at underscoring her points and keeping her audience focused. She began by introducing the work, showing the book cover on an otherwise black slide. Throughout the presentation, she used very simple visuals — a word or two, or a large image from the book she was discussing — to keep her audience focused on what she was saying.

Quick Help

Guidelines for Slide Presentations

- Audiences can't read and listen to you at the same time, so make the slides support what you are saying as clearly and visually as possible. Just one or two words — or a visual without words — may be more effective than a list of bullet points.

- Avoid reading from your slides. Your audience can read faster than you can talk, and you will bore your listeners with this technique.

- Use your media wisely, and respect your audience's time. If you feel that you need to include more than three or four bullet points (or more than fifty words of text) on a slide, you may be trying to convey too much information and may need to rethink your presentation.

- Make sure text is large enough to read, and create a clear contrast between text or illustration and background. In general, light backgrounds work better in a darkened room, and dark backgrounds in a lighted one.

- Choose visuals that will reproduce sharply, and make sure they are large enough to be clearly visible.

- Make sure that sound or video clips are audible and that they relate directly to your topic.

- Although there are no firm rules about how many slides you should use or how long each slide should be made visible, plan length and timing with your audience's needs and your purpose in mind.

- Most important, make sure your slides engage and help your listeners rather than distract them from your message.

19d Practice and deliver the presentation.

In oral presentations, as with many other things in life, practice makes perfect. Prepare a draft of your presentation and slides or other media far enough in advance to allow you to seek feedback from friends or classmates — just as you would with an essay. If possible, make a video of yourself, and then examine the video in detail. You can also practice in front of a mirror or in front of friends.

If you are using slides or other visuals to accompany your presentation (and most students do so), make sure your use of the visuals is smooth and on track with your script.

Also, make sure you can be heard clearly. If you are soft-spoken, concentrate on projecting your voice. If your voice tends to rise when you are in the spotlight, practice lowering your pitch. If you speak rapidly, practice slowing down and enunciating words clearly. Remember that tone of voice affects listeners, so aim for a tone that conveys interest in and commitment to your topic and listeners.

Once you are comfortable giving the presentation, make sure you will stay within the allotted time. One good rule of thumb is to allow roughly two and a half minutes per double-spaced page of text. The only way to be sure about your time, however, is to time yourself as you practice. Knowing that your presentation is neither too short nor too long will help you relax and gain self-confidence; and when the members of your audience sense your self-confidence, they will become increasingly receptive to your message.

Experienced speakers always expect to feel at least some anxiety before delivering a presentation — and they develop strategies for dealing with it. Remember that a little nervousness can act to your advantage: adrenaline, after all, can help you perform well.

Having confidence in your own knowledge will go a long way toward making you a confident presenter. In addition to doing your homework, however, you may be able to use the following strategies to good advantage:

- **Consider how you will dress** and how you will move around. In each case, your choices should be appropriate for the situation. Most experienced speakers like to dress simply and comfortably for easy movement. But dressing up a little signals your pride in your appearance and your respect for your audience.

- **Check out the presentation room** and double-check to make sure you have all the equipment you might need. Go over the scene of your presentation in your mind, and think it through completely, in order to feel more comfortable during it.

- **If you are using handouts,** decide when to distribute them. Unless they include material you want your audience to use while you speak, distribute them after the presentation.

Pause before you begin your presentation, and concentrate on your opening lines. During your presentation, interact with your audience as much as possible. You can do so by facing the audience at all times and making eye contact as often as possible; avoid staring just at your laptop or at the screen behind you. Invite questions, but try to keep your answers short so that others may participate in the conversation. When you conclude, remember to thank your audience.

19e Consider other kinds of presentations.

You may want or need to think about other kinds of presentations for school or work, including poster presentations, online presentations, or PechaKuchas.

Many college courses and conferences now call on students to make *poster presentations*. During the class or conference session, the presenter uses a poster board as background while talking through the presentation and answering questions. Poster presentations give you a chance to demonstrate your knowledge about a subject "on your feet," answering questions and interacting with those who attend the session. If you are preparing for a poster presentation, remember to make sure that the information on the poster can be easily seen and read and is simply and clearly organized.

You may also have an opportunity to make presentations online, in your classes or in your job. A webcast, for example, is a presentation that is broadcast on the Internet, using streaming media to distribute the presentation to viewers, who might be anywhere in the world. As you prepare for an online presentation, you will want to develop a clear script as well as a set of slides or other visuals. Remember that you probably won't be able to make eye contact with your audience; you'll need to speak into the camera — as if you are speaking directly to them.

Another popular form of presentation is the *PechaKucha*, from Japanese for "chit chat" — a special form with a set structure: twenty slides, each of which advances automatically after twenty seconds, for a total time of 6:40. Astrid Klein and Mark Dytham, architects in Tokyo, invented PechaKucha in 2003 because they felt that "architects talk too much" about their own work; they wanted to design a way to keep the presentations succinct and crisp. From this professional presentation format grew "PechaKucha nights" where people can share their work in a relaxed and supportive, if sometimes also competitive, atmosphere. Some college instructors are now inviting students to try their hands at constructing a PechaKucha as a way of presenting ideas to classmates.

For any of these presentation types — posters, online webcasts, or PechaKuchas — remember to consider your purpose carefully and to make sure that your presentation will appeal to the audience you have chosen.

20 Communicating in Other Media

Writing instructors across the country are assigning not just slide presentations but annotated playlists, blogs, comics, live tweets, podcasts, video essays, wikis, and more. Student writers seem to like and appreciate such multimodal assignments, saying that they provide room for creative control and for self-expression. As communicating with media becomes more common and even more necessary in your life, it's important to think carefully about your goals and your audiences — as well as about how to accomplish and reach them effectively, no matter what kind of project you are creating.

20a Consider your rhetorical context.

As with any college assignment, you will want to make sure you consider time and technical constraints. Many online projects take much more time than a traditional writing assignment: one student, for example, recently spent ninety hours creating a three-minute animated video! So you need to plan carefully to make sure you have both the access to any tools you will need and the time to carry out the project (and to learn about the tools, if necessary).

As with any writing project, you will want to think about rhetorical concerns, such as your purpose for creating the text, the needs of your audience, and the main point or message you want to get across.

- *Why are you creating this text, document, or project?* How do you want viewers to use it? Considering purpose will help you determine what features you want to highlight.

- *What potential audience(s) can you identify?* Thinking about the audience for your project will help you make strong rhetorical choices about tone, word choice, graphic style and design, level of detail, and many other factors. If your intended audience is limited to people you know (such as a wiki for members of your class), you may be able to make some assumptions about their background, knowledge, and likely responses. If you are covering a particular topic, you may have ideas about the type of audience you think you'll attract. Plan your project to appeal to readers you expect — but remember that an online text may reach other, unanticipated audiences.

- *What is the topic of your project?* The topic will certainly affect the content and design of the project. If you want to focus on the latest Hong Kong film releases, for example, you might create a blog that always places your most recent posts at the top; if you want to explore the works of 1940s detective writers, you might produce a website with pages devoted to particular writers or themes. If you prefer to show information on your topic, you might consider creating an infographic or a video essay that you can post to an existing site.

- *How do you relate to your subject matter?* Your rhetorical stance determines how your audience will see you. Will you present yourself as an expert? a fan? a novice seeking input from others? What information will make you seem credible and persuasive to your audience(s)?

20b Consider types of multimodal texts.

Among the common types of multimodal assignments in college writing courses are websites and web pages, blogs, microblogs, wikis, audio and video projects, and nondigital multimodal projects like comics. The following table presents six kinds of assignments that call for multimodal work, along with characteristics and questions you should ask yourself as you undertake such assignments.

Common Multimodal Assignments

Type	Characteristics	Rhetorical considerations
Website	Websites allow a writer to organize elements as a cluster of associations. Each page may cover a single aspect of a larger topic. A menu on the page typically lets readers find related information on the site.	• What decisions will you make about layout? • How do you want visitors to navigate your site?
Blog	Blogs function like an online journal or column. Individual posts can be short or long, formal or informal — and the content can be on a single topic or a variety of topics. Bloggers often invite commentary.	• How do you want to represent yourself to readers? • How often will readers expect you to post?
Microblog (Twitter, for example)	Microblogs allow users to post brief updates and comments about a variety of topics. Users can hold individual accounts or can write officially for a company, organization, or government agency.	• What labels will you add to your posts to help readers find them? • What are expectations and conventions around sharing other people's posts?

Type	Characteristics	Rhetorical considerations
Wiki	Wikis are online texts that empower all users to contribute content. Wikis create communities where all content is evaluated by other members; they draw on the collective knowledge of many contributors.	• How will you identify your sources of information? • What responsibilities do you have to others in your community?
Audio/ Video	Audio and video content can vary as widely as the content found in written-word media. Writers who create podcasts (which can be downloaded for playback) and streaming media (which can be played without downloading) may produce episodic content united by a common host or theme.	• Will you embed your file in another type of document, such as a website or slide presentation? • What technical help do you need to achieve your purpose and reach your viewers or listeners?
Nondigital multimodal project	Projects like comics, posters, and scrapbooks offer creative ways to reach audiences without having to use digital tools.	• How will you share your work? • Why is a nondigital project right for your writing situation?

Considering Disabilities

Accessible Web Texts

Much on the web remains hard to access and read for persons with disabilities. The website for the Americans with Disabilities Act provides guidelines on designing accessible sites, which include offering textual descriptions of any visuals and captions for any sound files. For details, visit www.ada.gov, and click on "Design Standards."

20c   Plan features of texts.

Use organization, interactivity, and links to make your multimodal text work as effectively as possible.

Organization

Whether you are creating a layout for a web page or storyboarding a video essay, you should develop a clear structure for your text. Some types of on-line texts are organized in standard ways—most blogs and social media sites, for example, put the newest posts at the top. Others allow you to make choices about how to arrange materials. Choose a structure that makes sense for your purpose, audience, topic, and rhetorical stance. Arrange your text to allow readers to find what they are looking for as quickly and intuitively as possible. (For more on organizing and planning your text, see 3e.)

Interaction

The possibility of interaction with readers is one of the great opportunities of online writing, but you can consider different levels of interactivity. While wikis are full-scale collaborative efforts and allow contribution from users, you might also include something as simple as a thumbs-up/thumbs-down or LIKE button to allow users to share reactions to a text. Online texts can incorporate polls, comments, and links for contacting writers. For nondigital projects, plan out how to invite a conversation.

Links

Academic and formal writing follows guidelines that tell readers the sources of other people's ideas and research through notes and bibliographic references. Some less formal online writing includes links to external sites. You can also link to content that helps prove a point, such as complex explanations, supporting statistics, bibliographies, referenced websites, or additional readings. Links also help readers navigate from one part of a text to another.

Each link should have a clear rhetorical purpose and be in an appropriate location. If you put a link in the middle of a paragraph, be aware that readers may go to the linked content before finishing what's before them—and if that link takes them to an external site, they may never come back! If it's important for users to read the whole paragraph, you may want to move the link to the end of it.

21 Writing to Make Something Happen in the World

How do you define "good writing"? When researchers asked college students this question as part of a study, they expected fairly straightforward definitions like "writing that gets its message across," but the students kept coming back to one central idea: good writing "makes something happen in the world." The students felt particular pride in the writing they did for family and friends — and for many extracurricular activities that were meaningful to them. They produced newsletters for community action groups, nature guides for local parks, and websites for local emergency services; one student had even written an algorithm that helps to track sex traffickers on the web. Furthermore, once these students graduated from college, they continued to create and *value* these kinds of public writing. The writing that matters most to many students and citizens, then, is public writing that has an effect in the world: writing that gets up off the page or screen, puts on its working boots, and marches out to get something done!

 ## 21a Decide what should happen.

During and after your college years, you are likely to create writing that you do because you want to make a difference. You may already have found reasons for communicating with a public audience — perhaps you have

- invited others to an event you're hosting
- advertised your expertise
- reported on a project you were involved in
- advocated for a cause you believe in

Often the purpose for doing this kind of writing may seem obvious to you — you have a clear idea of *what* the writing needs to accomplish. Now take

---

Quick Help

Characteristics of Writing That Makes Something Happen

- Public writing has a clear **purpose** (to promote a cause; to explain a problem; or to persuade others to act, for example). (21a)
- It is intended for a specific **audience** and addresses those people directly. (21b)
- It uses the **genre** most suited to its purpose and audience (a poster to alert people to an upcoming fund drive, a newsletter to inform members of a group, or a social media post to promote an upcoming performance). (21b)
- It appears in a **medium** (print, online, or both) where the intended audience will see it. (21b)
- It generally uses straightforward, everyday **language**.
- It generally uses **design** to get and hold the audience's attention.

the time to consider *how* to get the results that you want. As with any writing, be sure to get feedback from friends and others who may be affected by your plan.

21b Connect with your audience.

When you have clarified the actions you want your readers to take in response to your writing, think about the people you most want to reach — audiences today can be your immediate neighbors or like-minded people around the country or the globe. Who will be interested in the topic you are writing about? For example, if you want to encourage your elementary school to plant a garden, you might try to interest local parents, teachers, and PTA members; if you are planning to suggest a boycott of a particular national brand, you might start with social media followers.

With a target audience in mind, think carefully about where and how you are likely to find them, how you can get their attention, and what you can say to achieve your purpose.

Appeals to an audience

What do you know about your audience's values and interests? Why should they appreciate what you want to communicate? If you want to convince neighbors to contribute resources to build a local playground, then you may have a head start: knowing the neighbors and their children, and understanding local concerns about safety, can help you think of effective appeals to get their attention and convince them to join in this project. However, if you want to create a flash mob to publicize ineffective security at chemical plants near your city, you will need to reach as many people as possible, most of whom you will not know. Finding ways to reach appropriate audiences and convince them to join your project may require you to do some research. (For more on emotional, ethical, and logical appeals, see 8c.)

Genre and media

Even if you know the members of your audience, you still need to think about the genre and media that will be most likely to reach them. To get neighbors involved in a playground project, you might decide that a colorful print flyer delivered door to door and posted at neighborhood gathering places would work best, or you may put together a neighborhood Facebook page or email list in order to share information digitally. To gather a flash mob, an easily forwarded message — text, tweet, or email — will probably work best.

Appropriate language

For all public writing, think carefully about the audience you *want* to reach — as well as unintended audiences your message *might* reach. Doing so can help you craft writing that will be persuasive without being offensive.

Timing

When you want to make something happen, timing is crucial to the success of your project. If you want people to plan to attend an event, present your text to them two weeks ahead of time. If you are issuing a blog or newsletter, make sure that you create content frequently enough to keep people interested (but not so often that readers can't or won't bother to keep up). If you are reporting information based on something that has already happened, make it available as soon as possible so that your audience won't consider your report "old news."

21c Sample writing to make something happen in the world

On the following pages are some examples of the forms that public writing can take.

RALLY SPEECH

Eleven-year-old Naomi Wadler speaks at the youth-led March for Our Lives in Washington, D.C., in March 2018, organized as a call to action about gun violence in America. See the text of her speech on p. 222.

We Know Life Isn't Equal for Everyone

I am here today to acknowledge and represent the African American girls whose stories don't make the front page of every national newspaper, whose stories don't lead on the evening news. I represent the African American women who are victims of gun violence, who are simply statistics instead of vibrant, beautiful girls full of potential.

It is my privilege to be here today, I am indeed full of privilege. My voice has been heard. I am here to acknowledge their stories, to say they matter, to say their names, because I can, and I was asked to be. For far too long, these names, these black girls and women, have been just numbers. I'm here to say, "Never again" for those girls, too. I am here to say that everyone should value those girls, too.

People have said that I am too young to have these thoughts on my own. People have said that I am a tool of some nameless adult. It's not true. My friends and I might still be eleven, and we might still be in elementary school, but we know. We know life isn't equal for everyone, and we know what is right and wrong. We also know that we stand in the shadow of the Capitol, and we know that we have seven short years until we, too, have the right to vote. So I am here today to honor the words of Toni Morrison: "If there is a book that you want to read but it hasn't been written yet, you must be the one to write it." I urge everyone here and everyone who hears my voice to join me in telling the stories that aren't told, to honor the girls, the women of color who are murdered at disproportionate rates in this nation. I urge each of you to help me write the narrative for this world and understand, so that these girls and women are never forgotten.

PURPOSE	Fifth-grade student Naomi Wadler joined the youth-led protest called March for Our Lives, held just five weeks after the shootings at Marjorie Stoneman Douglas High School in Parkland, Florida. She spoke at the rally to convince listeners to remember that African American girls and women are victims of gun violence "at disproportionate[ly higher] rates" than any other racial group in America. She informed her audience about black female students who had been killed in gun violence events that had not been reported in national news stories.
AUDIENCE	Attendees of the March 24, 2018, rally "March for Our Lives" and those following the event on social media
GENRE	Speech
DELIVERY	Live delivery to a live audience at a Washington, D.C., rally

FUNDRAISING WEB PAGE

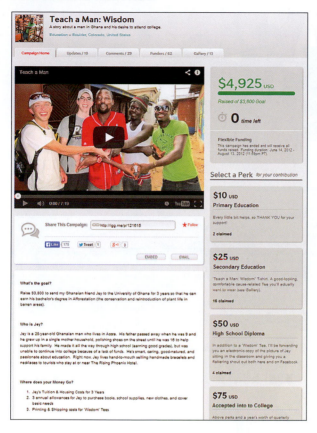

PURPOSE	Student Justin Dart created a fundraising web page to crowd-source funding to help Jey, a young street vendor in Accra, Ghana, get a college education.
AUDIENCE	Justin, a marketing student at the University of Colorado, aimed this campaign, "Teach a Man: Wisdom," at friends and acquaintances.
GENRE	Using the Indiegogo template, Justin posted a video about the recipient's background and purpose of the fundraiser; a short description of the project, designed for easy reading; and a list of perks for donors at various levels. Other tabs offered updates that Justin posted over the course of the fundraising project, comments from donors, photos, and more.
DELIVERY	Justin delivered his text online and urged friends to share the campaign on other social media sites. He and his team ended up raising enough to pay for Jey's university tuition and housing.

WEB COMIC

PURPOSE   Student Zack Karas worked with a team of classmates to do field research in a public space and then present a critical analysis of the environment they studied, a local coffee shop.

AUDIENCE   Zack and his team initially presented to their classmates. The secondary audience included blog readers who share Zack's interest in humor and online comics.

GENRE   Zack used his team's coffee shop experience as the basis for a comic, the final panels of which include a twist: his comic avatar fails to recognize that he, like many of the customers, is also a "post-ironic hipster . . . with facial hair, a hoodie, and an iPhone."

DELIVERY   After a traditional class presentation, Zack posted the comic on a blog created to host his artwork.

PITCH PACKAGE

Strange Fruit
The Hip-Hopera 15

AMERICA LOVES MUSICALS!!!

With hit shows like *Glee* and *Smash,* musicals are becoming a bigger phenomenon and more popular than ever. Now more gritty and raw, musicals are used to explore many different elements of life. *Strange Fruit* is no exception. Using the most popular musical art form today, hip-hop, *Strange Fruit* bravely goes into uncharted territory through innovative means. *Strange Fruit* is a film that digs up the deep roots of our American past, discovering how slavery affects interracial relationships today. It's a powerful and poignant film, full of music, drama, humor, and passion. It's aimed to be a musical sensation.

SAMPLE BOX OFFICE GROSS COMPARISONS

MOVIE	COST	GROSS
The Help	25 million	169 million
Dreamgirls	70 million	100 million
The Color Purple	15 million	98 million
Chicago	45 million	306 million
Back to the Future	19 million	350 million
Precious	10 million	47 million

PURPOSE	Deborah Jane and Jamie Burke collaborated to create a pitch package to encourage investment in a film based on Deborah's play *Strange Fruit: The Hip-Hopera.*
AUDIENCE	Local theater and film executives and enthusiasts
GENRE	The pitch package, a PDF, included a combination of traditional pages: a synopsis, cast list, character analyses, biographies of the production team, and a financial analysis — alongside the theater poster.
DELIVERY	The team assembled the pitch package digitally for easy email distribution.

▲ **For visual analysis** This image shows a person using language to claim identities. It's important to make careful choices in the language you use to present yourself and to represent others. What words or phrases would you use to capture aspects of your identity?

Language and Style

Many people think of language as a set of rules; break them, and you're wrong. But that's not how language works.

— ROBERT LANE GREENE

22   Language and Identity

Draw a circle in the middle of a piece of paper or screen and put your name in it. Then add spokes pointing out from all around that circle and take some time to list words that identify you —

> your relationship to family and others (sister, brother, mentor, friend)
>
> your major interests (sports fan, runner, reader, gardener, gamer)
>
> your background (nationality, birthplace or hometown, race, religion, sexual orientation)
>
> personal attributes you claim or that others use to label you (good student, friendly, shy)

Some of the words you've written are bits of language that help you to construct your identity. Others may be words that other people have used to identify you, words you may or may not agree with or accept.

Identity is a familiar word, but it's worth pausing to think a bit about what it means. Most scholars would define identity as a web of relationships built up through language: how you understand your relationship to the world around you and use that understanding to imagine possibilities for your future. And language is the scaffold we use to name these relationships.

Parts of your identity are stable — your age, for example, or your birthplace. But much of identity is constructed through social interactions with other people and with institutions and is thus flexible, subject to change and evolution. So identities can be multiple and shifting. They can also be imposed on you by other people or institutions that use language to label you in a way that is inappropriate, unfair, or unacceptable to you. In these ways, language works to construct who you are and who you can be.

22a   Recognize how the language of others can shape identity.

Look back at the circle and spokes you drew and the words you attached to the spokes. Underline the ones that you think may be labels others would put on you. If you've found any words like "clumsy" or "bad at math" or "outsider" or "immigrant" or "top of the class," are these descriptors ones *you have chosen* as part of your identity? Research has shown that children who are put into groups labeled according to ability levels tend to simply adapt to that label. Mike Rose, now a professor at UCLA, has written about being placed in a non-college-bound track as a young person: "I lived down to expectations." In Rose's case, he was eventually able to resist and reject that label, with the help of a teacher. But until he did so, that label — *non-college-bound* — was a part of his identity.

It's worth taking time to ask how you use language (especially labels) to "identify" other people, those you know and those you don't know. While all people tend to categorize others as a way to understand them (she's a *sorority girl*; he's a *hipster*), those labels may not be accurate or important to the other person's own understanding of themselves — and may indeed be oversimplifications or stereotypes. Open-minded, ethical college writers take care not to impose identities on others, just as they resist letting others impose identities on them.

22b Use language to shape your own identity.

One of your main goals as a college writer is not only to be aware of how the language of other people and groups can shape your identity but to resist such efforts by making sure that you are the person doing that shaping as much as possible. Professor Mike Rose had a chance to reject the label of lower-track student, but what's even more important is that he seized the opportunity to begin defining himself as a high-performing honors student who would eventually earn a PhD. Poet and artist Gloria Anzaldúa often asked her students "who is the *you* you want to be in ten years?" because she knew that the language choices they were making were going to shape that distant identity.

In addition, college writers need to think about whose voices are heard and whose may be ignored in certain situations. For example, a student speaking or writing from the identity of a beginner or novice may not get the respect that one writing from an identity of expertise does. A student writing about mental health issues among college students, for example, might draw on her experience and expertise as an activist for mental health

resources on campus, or as a double major in biology and psychology, or as a suicide attempt survivor. Or perhaps all of these aspects of her identity may help to establish her *ethos*, or her credibility (see also 9g). As a college writer, aim to be confident in your own identity, to communicate from an identity of your own choosing, and to imagine and pursue other identities you want to embrace.

23 Language Varieties

When Pulitzer Prize–winning author Junot Díaz spoke to a group of college students in California, he used colloquial English and Spanish, plus more than a few four-letter words — and the students loved every minute of it. When he was interviewed later on National Public Radio, however, Díaz addressed his nationwide audience in more formal English. As a college student, you will need to think carefully about how to make appropriate choices. Since academic English is still expected for most of your classes, you will want to use it effectively. But you may also want to be open to using another language, a combination of languages, or one of the many rich varieties of English in your college writing. Strong writers understand how to mix languages and dialects or varieties of English as they use their entire language repertoire to create effective and compelling messages across a range of rhetorical situations.

23a Practice language awareness.

Recognizing the crucial role language plays in shaping identity has led some writers to conclude that "I am my language." Gloria Anzaldúa certainly makes that case when she says that she wants all of her languages to be recognized *and accepted* as part of her identity: the academic English and Spanish she has learned, working class/slang English, the northern Mexican Spanish dialect, and Tex-Mex, the regional Spanish of Texas and New Mexico.

Think for a moment about the languages and dialects and varieties of languages that are part of your background and who you are. Today nearly 25 percent of people in the U.S. speak a language other than English at home. But even if you think of yourself as speaking only English, you probably also know and use a number of dialects. If you come from Boston, Minnesota, Appalachia, or many other regions of the country, you probably speak the regional dialect common to that area. In addition, you may be learning a professional dialect (like the specialized language of computer programmers) or using one associated with groups you belong to (surfers or political activists). The dialects and languages you have at your disposal are what allow you to communicate effectively and powerfully with a wide range of audiences.

Taking such a broad, inclusive, and accepting view of the rich varieties of language available to writers and speakers today is what scholars call

Talking the Talk

What Does It Mean to Have a *Translingual Approach* to Writing?

As a way to further explain this approach, a group of scholars note the following characteristics:

- Understanding that languages are never fixed but rather flexible and changing across time and from genre to genre
- Having respect for differences within and across languages and dialects
- Paying careful attention to how writers use words, sentences, and stylistic features that push against boundaries and are experimental
- Understanding that "breaking" rules doesn't always indicate a mistake or an error

— adapted from Bruce Horner, Min-Zhan Lu, Jacqueline Royster, and John Trimbur, "Language Difference in Writing: Toward a Translingual Approach," *College English* vol. 73, no. 3, Jan 2011, pp. 303–21.

having "translingual dispositions," or a "translingual approach" that views language varieties more open-mindedly than ever before.

23b Use academic English appropriately.

How do writers decide when to mix languages or dialects? The key to answering this question is appropriateness — what is most effective and fitting for a writer's particular purpose and audience. Used appropriately and wisely, *all* varieties of English can help to get your messages across in compelling ways.

One variety of English, often referred to as "edited academic English," is taught in schools, represented in this and most other textbooks, used in much of the national media, and written and spoken widely by those holding social and economic power. As the language used in business and most public institutions, this variety of English is one you probably want to be completely familiar with. But even "edited academic English" is not static: like all language varieties, it encompasses a wide range of choices, from the formal style used in much of the writing you will do in college to the informal style characteristic of conversation.

> ### Quick Help
>
> **Language Varieties**
>
> You can use different languages and dialects to good effect for the following purposes:
>
> - to repeat someone's exact words, precisely and respectfully
> - to evoke a person, place, or activity
> - to establish your credibility and build common ground
> - to make a strong point
> - to connect with an audience

23c Use varieties of English to evoke a place or community.

Using the language of a local community is an effective way to evoke a character or place. See how author John Steinbeck uses dialect to let readers hear the language spoken by community members in his classic novel, *The Grapes of Wrath*:

> "Ever'body says words different," said Ivy. "Arkansas folks says 'em different from Oklahomy folks says 'em different. And we seen a lady from Massachusetts, an' she said 'em differentest of all. Couldn' hardly make out what she was sayin'."
>
> – JOHN STEINBECK, *The Grapes of Wrath*

Weaving together regionalisms and more formal English can also be effective in creating a sense of place. Here, an anthropologist writing about one Carolina community chooses not to paraphrase; she takes care to let the residents speak their minds — and in their own words:

> For Roadville, schooling is something most folks have not gotten enough of, but everybody believes will do something toward helping an individual "get on." In the words of one oldtime resident, "Folks that ain't got no schooling don't get to be nobody nowadays."
>
> – SHIRLEY BRICE HEATH, *Ways with Words*

23d Build credibility within a community.

Whether you are Native American or trace your ancestry to Europe, Asia, Latin America, Africa, or elsewhere, your heritage probably lives on in the language you use.

See how one Hawaiian writer uses Hawaiian pidgin language to paint a picture of young teens hearing a "chicken skin" story from their grandmother.

> " — So, rather dan being rid of da shark, da people were stuck with many little ones, for dere mistake."
>
> Then Grandma Wong wen' pause, for dramatic effect, I guess, and she wen' add, "Dis is one of dose times. . . . Da time of da sharks."
>
> Those words ended another of Grandma's chicken skin stories. The stories she told us had been passed on to her by her grandmother, who had heard them from her grandmother. Always skipping a generation.
>
> – RODNEY MORALES, "When the Shark Bites"

Notice how the narrator of the story presents information necessary to the story line mostly in formal English while using terms characteristic of Hawaiian pidgin to represent spoken language. Mixing languages in this way demonstrates that the writer is a member of the community whose language he is representing and thus able to build credibility with others in the community.

Take care, however, in using the language of communities other than your own. When used inappropriately, such language can have an opposite effect, perhaps destroying credibility and alienating your audience.

23e Bring in other languages.

You might use a language other than English for the same reasons you might use different dialects of English: to represent the actual words of a speaker, to make a point, to connect with your audience, or to get their attention. See how Gerald Haslam uses Spanish to capture his great-grandmother's words and to make a point about his relationship to her.

"*Expectoran su sangre!*" exclaimed Great-grandma when I showed her the small horned toad I had removed from my breast pocket. I turned toward my mother, who translated: "They spit blood."

"*De los ojos,*" Grandma added. "From their eyes," mother explained, herself uncomfortable in the presence of the small beast.

– GERALD HASLAM, *California Childhood*

And here, a student writer uses her native Spanish as she writes a literacy narrative about her experience growing up in Puerto Rico and learning English.

"Todo se ve bien . . ." my father would start and look at me with his right eyebrow raised. The same gesture I forced myself to learn, staring at a mirror for a month, just so I could prove to him that it didn't intimidate me. "¿Qué pasó con Inglés?" I would simply look away and shrug my shoulders, desperately avoiding the gaze of disappointment that his eyes would try to burn on me. After all, I was his first born, and there were a lot of expectations to meet. "¿Voy a ver un cambio para el próximo semestre, verdad?" And without glancing back at him, I would answer a soft, "Sí."

In elementary school, I got A's and B's in every course except one: English. As a young and naive mind, born and raised on a Spanish-speaking island, I never understood why I needed another language.

– Paola García-Muñiz

Note that García-Muñiz includes Spanish in her narrative without translating it. In this case, the student deliberately chose to include the phrases in Spanish because she wanted to represent her two worlds (two languages) in the essay so that "the audience would better understand what I was talking about: it wasn't about making it simpler or harder for readers to read, but allowing them to visualize the story exactly as it happened."

Another student describes how he combines multiple languages as part of his learning process. Taking notes in multiple languages, he says, "helps [him] save time."

[F]rom my personal experiences, I think that note-taking activities play a significant role in the retention of ideas in a systematic and efficient manner. Using multiple languages such as Hindi, Sanskrit, and English increases the speed of this activity and helps me retain knowledge of these languages for a long time. I mainly use Hindi to present my ideas briefly and Sanskrit to describe the actions of the subject. Suresh Canagarajah, in his chapter, "World Englishes as Code-Meshing," explains that code-meshing is a process of combining different languages to communicate an idea in a more efficient manner (273). When I do code-meshing, I use multiple languages because it helps me save time during note-taking, as well as retain knowledge about Hindi and Sanskrit languages.

Fig. 1 Sample of my note-taking activity during my Florida History Class

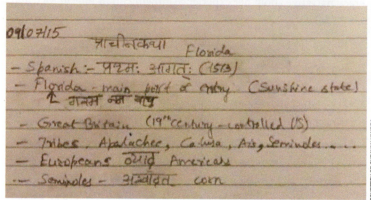

– Shravan Yandra

Like these students, you may want to bring other languages into your writing, using them to help you communicate more efficiently and effectively with your audiences.

24 Writing to the World

Writers today often communicate instantaneously across vast distances and cultures. Businesspeople complete multinational transactions with a single click, students in Ohio take online classes at MIT or chat with hundreds of Facebook friends, and tweets from Tehran find readers in Atlanta. When the whole world can be your potential audience, it's time to step back and think about how to communicate successfully with such a diverse group — how to become a world writer. In addition to adopting an open mind about language varieties (see Chapter 23), there are other ways you can make sure you are communicating well with diverse audiences.

24a   Think about what seems "normal."

Your judgment on what's "normal" may be based on assumptions you are not even aware of. But remember: behavior that is considered out of place in one context may appear perfectly normal in another. What's considered "normal" in a text message would be anything but in a request for an internship with a law firm. If you want to communicate with people across cultures, try to learn something about the norms in those cultures and be aware of the norms that guide your own behavior.

Like most people, you may tend to see your own way as the "normal" way to do things. How do your own values and assumptions guide your thinking and behavior? Keep in mind that if your ways seem inherently right, then — even without thinking about it — you may assume that other ways are somehow not right. These tips may help:

- Know that most ways of communicating are influenced by cultural contexts and differ widely from one culture to the next.
- Pay close attention to the ways that people from cultures other than your own communicate, and be flexible.
- Once you tune in to differences, keep an open mind: don't assume that all members of a community behave in the same way or value the same things.
- Remember that your audience may be made up of people from many backgrounds who have very different concepts about what is appropriate or "normal."

Quick Help

Communicating across Cultures

- Recognize what you consider "normal." Examine your own customary behaviors and assumptions with an open mind, and think about how they may affect what you think and say (and write). (24a)
- Listen closely to someone from another culture, and ask for clarification if necessary. Carefully define your terms. (24b)
- Think about your audience's expectations. How much authority should you have? What kind of evidence will count most with your audience? (24c)
- Organize your writing with your audience's expectations in mind. If in doubt, use formal style. (24c)

24b Clarify meaning.

When an instructor called for "originality" in his students' essays, what did he mean? A Filipina student thought *originality* meant going to an original source and explaining it; a student from Chicago thought *originality* meant coming up with an idea entirely on her own. The professor, however, expected students to read multiple sources and develop a critical point of their own about those sources. In subsequent classes, this professor defined *originality* as he was using it in his classes, and he gave examples of student work he judged original.

This brief example points to the challenges all writers face in trying to communicate across space, across languages, across cultures. While there are no foolproof rules, here are some tips for communicating with people from cultures other than your own:

- Listen carefully. Ask people to explain or even repeat a point if you're not absolutely sure you understand.
- Take care to be explicit about the meanings of the words you use.
- Invite response — ask whether you're making yourself clear. This kind of back-and-forth is particularly easy (and necessary) in email.
- Remember that a visual may help make your meaning clearer.

24c Meet audience expectations.

When you do your best to meet an audience's expectations about how a text should work, your writing is more likely to have the desired effect. In practice, figuring out what audiences want, need, or expect can be difficult — especially when you are writing in public spaces online and your audiences can be composed of anyone, anywhere. If you do know something about your readers' expectations, use what you know to present your work effectively. If you know little about your potential audiences, however, carefully examine your assumptions about your readers.

Expectations about your authority as a writer

In the United States, students are often asked to establish authority in their writing — by drawing on personal experience, by reporting on research, or by taking a position for which they can offer evidence and support. But this expectation about writerly authority is by no means universal. Indeed, some cultures view student writers as novices whose job is to reflect what they learn from their teachers. One Japanese student, for example, said he was taught that it's rude to challenge a teacher: "Are you ever so smart that you should challenge the wisdom of the ages?"

As a world writer, remember that those you're addressing may hold a wide range of attitudes about authority. Ask these questions:

- What is your relationship to those you are addressing?
- What knowledge are you expected to have? Is it appropriate for or expected of you to demonstrate that knowledge — and, if so, how?
- What tone is appropriate? If in doubt, show respect: politeness is rarely if ever inappropriate.
- What level of control do you have over your writing? In a report, you may have the final say. But if you are writing on a wiki, where you share control with others, sensitivity to communal standards is key.

Expectations about persuasive evidence

How do you decide what evidence will best support your ideas? The answer depends, in large part, on the audience you want to persuade. Americans generally give great weight to factual evidence.

Differing concepts of what counts as evidence can lead to arguments that go nowhere. Consider, for example, how rare it is for a believer in creationism to be persuaded by what the theory of evolution presents as evidence — or for a supporter of evolutionary theory to be convinced by what creationists present as evidence. Think carefully about how you use evidence in writing, and pay attention to what counts as evidence to members of other groups you are trying to persuade. The following questions can be useful:

- Should you rely on facts? concrete examples? firsthand experience? religious or philosophical texts? other sources?
- Should you include the testimony of experts? Which experts are valued most, and why?
- When does evidence from unedited websites such as blogs offer credible support, and when should you question or reject it?

Once you determine what counts as evidence in your own thinking and writing, think about where you learned to use and value this kind of evidence. You can ask these same questions about the use of evidence by members of other cultures.

Expectations about organization

As you make choices about how to organize your writing, remember that the patterns you find pleasing are likely to be ones that are deeply embedded in your own culture. For example, the following organizational pattern is probably familiar to many U.S. students: introduction and thesis, necessary background, overview of the parts to follow, systematic presentation of evidence, consideration of other viewpoints, and conclusion. If a piece of writing follows this pattern, American academic readers ordinarily find it well organized and coherent.

In the United States, many audiences expect a writer to get to the point as directly as possible. But not all audiences have such expectations. For instance, a Chinese student with an excellent command of English heard from her U.S. teachers that her writing was "vague," with too much "beating around the bush." As it turned out, her teachers in China had prized this kind of indirectness, expecting audiences to read between the lines.

When writing for audiences who may not share your expectations, then, think about how you can organize material to get your message across effectively. There are no hard and fast rules to help you organize your writing for effectiveness across cultures, but here are a few options to consider:

- Determine if and when you should state a thesis (3c).

- Consider whether digressions are a good idea, a requirement, or best avoided with your intended audience.

- In online postings, place the most important information first and be as succinct as possible. When submitting a résumé online or creating a blog, you may need to follow a template.

Expectations about style

As with beauty, style is most definitely in the eye of the beholder — and thus is always affected by language, culture, and rhetorical tradition. In fact, what constitutes effective style varies broadly across cultures and depends on the rhetorical situation — purpose, audience, and so on (see Chapter 2). Even so, there is one important style question to consider when writing across cultures: what level of formality is most appropriate? In most writing to a general audience in the United States, a fairly informal style is often acceptable, even appreciated. Many cultures, however, tend to value a more formal approach. When in doubt, it may be wise to err on the side of formality in writing to people from other cultures, especially to those in authority. These tips may help:

- Be careful to use proper titles: Dr. Atul Gawande, Professor Jaime Mejía

- Avoid slang and other expressions or sentence structures that may be unfamiliar to those in your audience.

- Do not use first names of people you do not know unless invited to do so. Note, however, that an invitation to use a first name could come indirectly; if someone signs a message to you with his or her first name, you are implicitly invited to use the first name as a term of address.

- For professional communication, use complete sentences. Open with a greeting that includes the person's full name ("Dear Sasha Vrebalov") or the person's title ("Dear Professor Otuteye") if you know it.

Beyond formality, other stylistic preferences vary widely, and context matters. Long, complex sentences and ornate language may be exactly what some audiences are looking for. On Twitter, on the other hand, writers have to limit their message to 140 or 280 characters — so using abbreviated words, symbols, and fragments is expected, even desirable.

World writers, then, should take very little about language for granted. To be an effective world writer, aim to recognize and respect stylistic differences as you move from community to community and to meet expectations whenever you can.

25 Language That Builds Common Ground

The words we select have power: they can praise, delight, inspire — and also hurt, offend, or even destroy. Words that offend prevent others from identifying with you and thus damage your credibility. Few absolute guidelines exist for using words that respect differences and build common ground. Two rules, however, can help: consider carefully the sensitivities and preferences of others, and watch for words that betray your assumptions, even when you have not directly stated them.

Quick Help

Using Language That Builds Common Ground

- Check for stereotypes and other assumptions that might come between you and your readers. Look, for instance, for language implying approval or disapproval and for the ways you use *we*, *you*, and *they*. (25a)

- Be careful to respect the pronoun preferences of those you are speaking with or writing to; some people reject *he*, *she*, *him*, and *her* as noninclusive. (25b)

- Avoid sexist language. (25b)

- Make sure your references to race, religion, sexual orientation, and so on are relevant or necessary to your discussion. If they are not, leave them out. (25c and d)

- Check that the terms you use to refer to groups are accurate and acceptable. (25c and d)

25a Examine assumptions and avoid stereotypes.

Unstated assumptions that enter into thinking and writing can destroy common ground by ignoring important differences between others and ourselves. For example, a student in a religion seminar who uses *we* to refer to Christians and *they* to refer to members of other religions had better be sure that everyone in the class identifies as Christian, or some may feel left out of the discussion.

At the same time, don't overgeneralize about or stereotype a group of people. Because stereotypes are often based on half-truths, misunderstandings, and hand-me-down prejudices, they can lead to intolerance, bias, and bigotry.

Sometimes stereotypes and assumptions lead writers to call special attention to a group affiliation when it is not relevant, as in *a woman plumber* or *a white basketball player*. Even positive stereotypes — for example, *Jewish doctors are the best* — or neutral ones — *all college students like pizza* — can hurt, for they ignore the uniqueness of an individual. Careful writers make sure their language doesn't stereotype any group or individual.

25b Examine assumptions about gender.

Powerful gender-related words can subtly affect our thinking and our behavior. For instance, at one time many young women were discouraged from pursuing careers in medicine or engineering at least partially because speakers commonly referred to hypothetical doctors or engineers as *he* (and then labeled a woman who worked as a doctor *a woman doctor*, as if to say, "She's an exception; doctors are normally men"). Similarly, a label like *male nurse* may offend by reflecting stereotyped assumptions about proper roles for men. Equally problematic is the traditional use of *man* and *mankind* to refer to people of both sexes and the use of *he* and *him* to refer generally to any human being.

Today, some people reject the simple binary between male/female and do not wish to identify with either of those terms, being referred to not as *he* or *she* but as *they* (using *they* as singular) or as an alternative, neutral term such as *ze*.

25c Examine assumptions about race and ethnicity.

Generalizations about racial and ethnic groups can result in especially harmful stereotyping. To build common ground, then, avoid language that ignores differences not only among individual members of a race or ethnic group but also among subgroups. Writers must be aware, for instance, of the diverse places from which Americans of Spanish-speaking ancestry have come.

When writing about an ethnic or racial group, how can you refer to that group in terms that its members actually desire? Doing so is sometimes not an easy task, for terms can change often and vary widely.

The word *colored*, for example, was once widely used in the United States to refer to Americans of African ancestry. By the 1950s, the preferred term had become *Negro*. This changed in the 1960s, however, as *black* came to be preferred by most, though certainly not all, members of that community. Since the late 1980s, both *black* — sometimes capitalized (*Black*) — and *African American* have been widely used.

Once widely preferred, the term *Native American* has been challenged by those who argue that the most appropriate way to refer to indigenous peoples is by the specific name of the tribe or pueblo, such as *Chippewa* or *Zuni*. Many people once referred to as *Eskimos* prefer *Inuit* or a specific term such as *Tlingit*. It has also become fairly common for tribal groups to refer to themselves as *American Indians*. In international contexts, the broader *indigenous peoples* is preferred.

The terms *Latino* and *Hispanic* are often interchanged. *Latino* and *Latina* (and the gender-neutral *Latinx*) are geographic references; these words describe people who trace their ancestry to any country in Latin America — that is, Mexico, Central America, South America, or the Caribbean. *Hispanic*, on the other hand, describes people who trace their ancestry to a Spanish-speaking country. For example, Native Brazilians, who speak Portuguese as their first language, are Latino but not Hispanic.

Ethnic terminology changes often enough to challenge the most careful writers — including writers who belong to the groups they are writing about. Consider your words carefully and seek information about ways members of groups refer to themselves (or ask about preferences), but don't expect one person to speak for all members of a group or expect unanimity on such terms.

Consider other kinds of difference.

Age

Mention age if it is relevant, but be aware that age-related terms (*matronly*, *well-preserved*, and so on) can carry derogatory connotations. Describing Mr. Fry as *elderly but still active* may sound polite to you, but chances are Mr. Fry would prefer being called *an active seventy-eight-year-old* — or just *a seventy-eight-year-old*, which eliminates the unstated assumption of surprise that he is active at his age.

Class

Take special care to examine your words for assumptions about socio-economic status or class. As a writer, you should not assume that all your readers share your background or values — that your classmates all own cars, for instance. And avoid using any words — *redneck*, *blueblood*, and the like — that might alienate members of an audience.

Geographical area

You should not assume that geography determines personality or lifestyle. New Englanders are not all thrifty and tight-lipped; people in "red states" may hold liberal views; midwesterners are not always polite. Be careful not to make simplistic assumptions.

Physical ability or health

When writing about a person with a serious illness or physical disability, ask yourself whether mentioning the disability is relevant to your discussion and whether the words you use carry negative connotations. You might choose, for example, to say someone *uses* a wheelchair rather than to say he or she is *confined to* one. Similarly, you might note a subtle but meaningful difference in calling someone a *person with paraplegia* rather than a *paraplegic*, or a *sexual assault survivor* rather than *victim*. Mentioning the person first and the disability second, such as referring to a *child with diabetes* rather than a *diabetic child* or a *diabetic*, is always a good idea.

Religion

Assumptions about religious groups are very often inaccurate and unfair. For example, Roman Catholics hold a wide spectrum of views on abortion, Muslim women do not all wear veils, and many Baptists are not fundamentalists. In fact, many people do not believe in or practice a religion at all, so be careful of such assumptions. As in other cases, do not use religious labels without considering their relevance to your point.

Sexual orientation

If you wish to build common ground, do not assume that readers all share one sexual orientation. As with any label, reference to sexual orientation should be governed by context. Someone writing about Senator Tammy Baldwin's economic views would probably have no reason to refer to her sexual orientation. On the other hand, someone writing about diversity in U.S. government might find it important to note that, in 2012, Baldwin became the first openly gay person elected to the Senate.

> ## Considering Disabilities
>
> ### Knowing Your Readers
>
> Nearly 10 percent of first-year college students identify themselves as having one or more disabilities. That's no small number. Effective writers consider their own and their readers' disabilities so that they can find ways to build common ground.

26 Style Matters!

In an age of information overload, how do writers get and hold the attention of an audience? Research shows that the answer to that question can be summed up in one word: *style*. As media critic Howard Rheingold argues, when we are inundated with information from every imaginable source 24/7, it's not so much *what* you say that gets attention but *how* you say it. So it's well worth thinking about style — which encompasses the words and images you choose, how you arrange them, and how you design them to create an overall impression that will attract and hold audiences.

Style in writing is as varied as style in dress or music or the moves of baseball pitchers, so there's no one-size-fits-all style and no set of hard and fast rules for how to create an effective style. The following tips can help you, however, as you consider how to use style to your advantage as a writer.

26a Use effective words.

The words you choose help to define the style of anything you write. For much of your writing in college, your style may be fairly formal, like the following passage from a report on the Global Climate Action Summit held in San Francisco during September 2018:

> Political and government leaders at all levels must bring society together to collectively and urgently address climate change and identify innovative measures to do so. They should set national, regional, sectoral and city-level targets; put forward bold policies; and create the necessary frameworks to establish predictable economic and socially-conscious environments.

For the report, the reporter chooses words appropriate for a major newspaper along with a fairly serious tone. Note the use of words that signal the importance of the message: *must*, *urgently*, *bold* stress the importance of the message, but without in any way going "over the top." Compare the passage on p. 245 to the following speech excerpt, delivered by California Governor Jerry Brown at the same meeting:

> With science still under attack and the climate threat growing, we're launching our own damn satellite. . . . This groundbreaking initiative will help governments, businesses and landowners pinpoint— and stop—destructive emissions with unprecedented precision, on a scale that's never been done before.

Brown is speaking to those in attendance at the climate summit. Known for his fiery speaking style and aware that he is facing a friendly audience, he opens with a very dramatic statement, using very informal language (including a curse) before shifting into a more formal, moderate style. But note too his use of vivid words: *attack*, *threat*, *groundbreaking*, *pinpoint*, and *destructive*. In his rhetorical situation and with this audience, he knows his words matter — and he chooses them carefully.

Slang and colloquial language

Slang, or extremely informal language, is often confined to a relatively small group of people and usually becomes obsolete rather quickly, though some slang gains wide use (*selfie, duh*). Colloquial language, such as *in a bind* or *snooze*, is less informal, more widely used, and longer lasting than most slang.

Writers who use slang and colloquial language may not be understood. If you are writing for a general audience about gun-control legislation, for example, and you use the term *gat* to refer to a weapon, some readers may not know what you mean, and others may be irritated by what they see as a frivolous reference to a deadly serious subject.

Jargon

Jargon is the special vocabulary of a trade or profession, enabling members to speak and write concisely to one another. Reserve jargon for an audience that will understand your terms. The example that follows, from a blog about fonts and typefaces, uses jargon appropriately for an interested and knowledgeable audience.

> The Modern typeface classification is usually associated with Didones and display faces that often have too much contrast for text use. The Ingeborg family was designed with the intent of producing a Modern face that was readable at any size. Its roots might well be historic, but its approach is very contemporary. The three text weights (Regular, Bold, and Heavy) are functional and discreet while the Display weights (Fat and Block) catch

the reader's eye with a dynamic form and a whole lot of ink on the paper.

– FONTSHOP.COM BLOG

Depending on the needs of the audience, jargon can be irritating and incomprehensible—or extremely helpful. Terms that begin as jargon for specialists (*asynchronous,* for example) can quickly become part of the mainstream if they provide a useful shorthand for an otherwise lengthy explanation. Before you use technical jargon, remember your readers: if they will not understand the terms, or if you don't know readers well enough to judge, then use everyday language.

RISQUÉ

Filmfax №18

CLASSIC SHOWMANSHIP

Mr. Ed Wood

ED WOOD JR. was an American film director, screenwriter, producer, actor, author, and editor, who often performed in many of these functions simultaneously. In the 1950s, he made a run of many cheap and poorly produced *genre films,* humorously celebrated for their technical errors, dialogue, poor special effects, and outlandish plot elements.

Béla Lugosi

Pompous language, euphemisms, and doublespeak

Stuffy or pompous language is unnecessarily formal for the purpose, audience, or topic. It often gives writing an insincere or unintentionally humorous tone, making a writer's ideas seem insignificant or even unbelievable.

POMPOUS

Pursuant to the August 9 memorandum regarding petroleum pricing, it is incumbent upon us to endeavor to make maximal utilization of alternate methods of communication in lieu of personal visitation.

REVISED

As noted in the August 9 memo, gas costs are still high, so please use email, texting, and phone calls rather than personal visits whenever possible.

As this example illustrates, some writers use words in an attempt to sound expert, and these puffed-up words can easily backfire.

Language, Culture, and Context

Multilingual

Avoiding Fancy Language

In writing academic English, which is fairly formal, students are often tempted to use many "big words" instead of simple language. Although learning impressive words can be a good way to expand your vocabulary, it is usually best to avoid flowery or fancy language in college writing. Writing at U.S. universities values clear, concise prose.

Quick Help

Editing for Appropriate Language

- Check to see that your language reflects the appropriate level of formality for your audience, purpose, and topic.
- Unless you are writing for a specialized audience that will understand jargon, either define technical terms or replace them with words that are easy to understand.
- Revise pompous language, inappropriate euphemisms, and doublespeak.
- Consider the connotations of words carefully. If you say someone is *pushy*, be sure you mean to be critical; otherwise, use a word like *assertive*.
- Use both general and specific words. If you are writing about the general category *beds*, for example, do you give enough concrete detail (*an antique four-poster bed*)?

Talking the Talk

Texting Abbreviations

"Can I use text-message slang when I contact my teacher?" In a chat or text message, abbreviations such as *u* for *you* may be conventional, but using such shortcuts when communicating with an instructor can be a mistake. At least some of your instructors are likely to view them as disrespectful, unprofessional, or simply sloppy writing. Unless you are working to create a special effect for a special purpose and audience, keep to the conventions of academic English for college writing — and for contacting your instructor.

Euphemisms are words and phrases that make unpleasant ideas seem less harsh. *Your position is being eliminated* seeks to soften the blow of being fired or laid off. Other euphemisms include *pass on* or *pass away* for die and *plus-sized* for fat. Although euphemisms can sometimes appeal to an audience by showing that you are considerate of people's feelings, they can also sound insincere or evasive.

Doublespeak is language used to hide or distort the truth. During massive layoffs and cutbacks in the business world, companies speak of firings as *employee repositioning* or *proactive downsizing*, and of unpaid time off as a *furlough*. The public — and particularly those who lose their jobs — recognize these terms for what they are.

Denotation and connotation

Thinking of a stone tossed into a pool and ripples spreading out from it can help you understand the distinction between *denotation*, the dictionary meaning of a word (the stone), and *connotation*, the associations that accompany the word (the ripples). The words *enthusiasm*, *passion*, and *obsession*, for instance, all carry roughly the same denotation. But the connotations are quite different: an *enthusiasm* is a pleasurable and absorbing interest; a *passion* has a strong emotional component and may affect someone positively or negatively; an *obsession* is an unhealthy attachment that excludes other interests.

Note the differences in connotation among the following three statements:

- Students against Racism (SAR) erected a temporary barrier on the campus oval. They say it symbolizes "the many barriers to those discriminated against by university policies."

- Left-wing agitators threw up an eyesore on the oval to stampede the university into giving in to their demands.

- Supporters of human rights for all students challenged the university's investment in racism by erecting a protest barrier on campus.

The first statement is the most neutral, merely stating facts; the second, using words with negative connotations (*agitators*, *eyesore*, *stampede*), is strongly critical; the third, using a phrase with positive connotations (*supporters of human rights*) and presenting assertions as facts (*the university's investment in racism*), gives a favorable slant to the story.

General and specific language

Effective writers balance general words, which name or describe groups or classes, with specific words, which identify individual and particular things. Some general words are abstract; they refer to things we cannot perceive through our five senses. Specific words are often concrete; they name things we can see, hear, touch, taste, or smell. We can seldom draw a clear-cut line between general or abstract words on the one hand and specific or concrete words on the other. Instead, most words fall somewhere in between.

GENERAL	LESS GENERAL	SPECIFIC	MORE SPECIFIC
book	dictionary	abridged dictionary	*The American Heritage College Dictionary*

ABSTRACT	LESS ABSTRACT	CONCRETE	MORE CONCRETE
culture	visual art	painting	van Gogh's *Starry Night*

Strong writing usually provides readers with both an overall picture and specific examples or concrete details to fill in that picture. In the following passage, the author might have simply made a general statement—*their breakfast was always liberal and good*—or simply given the details of the breakfast. Instead, he employs both general and specific language.

> There would be a brisk fire crackling in the hearth, the old smoke-gold of morning and the smell of fog, the crisp cheerful voices of the people and their ruddy competent morning look, and the cheerful smells of breakfast, which was always liberal and good, the best meal that they had: kidneys and ham and eggs and sausages and toast and marmalade and tea.
>
> – THOMAS WOLFE, *Of Time and the River*

26b   Use figurative language.

Figurative language, or figures of speech, paint pictures in readers' minds, allowing them to "see" a point readily and clearly. Far from being merely decorative, such language is often crucial to readers' understanding. As such, figurative language will help you develop a style that gets your readers' attention.

Similes, metaphors, and analogies

Similes use *like*, *as*, *as if*, or *as though* to make explicit the similarity between two seemingly different things.

▶ You can tell the graphic-novels section in a bookstore from afar, by the young bodies sprawled around it like casualties of a localized disaster.
> – PETER SCHJELDAHL

▶ The comb felt as if it was raking my skin off.
> – MALCOLM X, "My First Conk"

Metaphors are implicit comparisons, omitting the *like*, *as*, *as if*, or *as though* of similes.

▶ The Internet is the new town square.   – JEB HENSARLING

Analogies compare similar features of two dissimilar things; they explain something unfamiliar by relating it to something familiar.

▶ People are like stained-glass windows. They sparkle and shine when the sun is out, but when the darkness sets in, their true beauty is revealed only if there is a light from within.   – ELISABETH KÜBLER-ROSS

▶ One Hundred and Twenty-fifth Street was to Harlem what the Mississippi was to the South, a long traveling river always going somewhere, carrying something.   – MAYA ANGELOU, *The Heart of a Woman*

Patterns of repetition: alliteration, anaphora, antithesis

There are a number of figures of speech that use repetition to good effect. Alliteration, the repetition of sounds (repetition of vowels is called "assonance" and repetition of consonants is called "consonance"), can be used for emphasis:

▶ Four score and seven years ago our fathers brought forth upon this continent a new nation. . . .
> – ABRAHAM LINCOLN, "Gettysburg Address"

Anaphora refers to the repetition of a word or words at the beginning of successive sentences: it acts like a drumbeat to hammer a point home. See it at work in Martin Luther King's "I Have a Dream" speech:

▶ Go back to Mississippi, go back to Alabama, go back to South Carolina, go back to Georgia, go back to Louisiana, go back to the slums and ghettos of our northern cities, knowing that somehow this situation can and will be changed.

Antithesis uses parallel structures to mark a sharp contrast or opposition:

▶ Those who kill people are called murderers; those who kill animals, sportsmen.

▶ Write quickly and you will never write well; write well and you will soon write quickly.
> – QUINTILIAN

26c Use powerful verbs.

Verbs are the action words of sentences; they carry readers along and evoke movement. So it's worth paying close attention to the verbs you use. Take a look at the verbs in the following brief passage:

> When Sean Parker was young, he *cofounded* Napster and *changed* the way we *listen* to music. In his twenties, he *helped jump-start* Facebook and *changed* the way we *interact* with each other. Now, at age 38, he's *set on*

Language, Culture, and Context

Multilingual

Learning Idioms

Why do you wear a diamond *on* your finger but *in* your ear? See 41a for more on using prepositions idiomatically.

changing something else: the way we *treat* disease. The Parker Institute for Cancer Immunotherapy, which he *founded* in 2016, has *dedicated* $250 million toward *using* new technologies like Crispr *to teach* the human body *to vanquish* cancer.

–MEGAN MOLTENI, "Why DNA Is
the Most Exciting Programming Language Today"

These everyday verbs establish the forward movement and rhythm of this passage, and the repetition of *change* works like a drumbeat to lead up to the climax of the sentence: to *teach* us to *vanquish* cancer. The writer could have said "using new technologies to end cancer." But that wouldn't have evoked the active, urgent sense that the other verbs create.

Here's another brief example that describes the scene at the 1968 Olympics when Tommie Smith and John Carlos mounted the podium as medal-winners:

The Star-Spangled Banner blaring over the stadium speakers, each bowed his head and raised a black-gloved fist — Smith's right, Carlos's left. Around the stadium, *jaws dropped* and *cameras flashed*.
– TIK ROOT, "The Price of Protest," *The Atlantic*, October 2018

Root could have written "The action got a big response," but saying that wouldn't paint the picture for us that dropping jaws and flashing cameras created.

In addition to choosing strong verbs, you should favor active voice over passive voice verbs in most cases. The verbs in the preceding sentences are all active: in the sentence about Sean Parker, for example, the writer says that he cofounded Napster (active voice) rather than Napster was cofounded by him (passive voice). While writers in the sciences often need to use passive voice, because readers can process active verbs more easily than passive ones it's wise to stick to active voice unless it's inappropriate to do so. (See 35g.)

Research also shows that writers who depend overly on forms of the verb "to be" (*is*, *was*, *were*, and so on) produce writing that can sound flat and even boring. So if you find you're using these verbs a lot — say for about 30 percent of all the verbs you use — that's probably a clue to revise.

26d Vary sentence length and sentence openings.

Is there a "just right" length for a particular sentence or idea? The answer depends partly on your purpose, intended audience, and topic. But note that after one or more long sentences with complex ideas or images, the punch of a short sentence — like the one at the end of the following passage — can be refreshing.

> To become a doctor, you spend so much time in the tunnels of preparation — head down, trying not to screw up, just going from one day to the next — that it is a shock to find yourself at the other end, with someone offering you a job. *But the day comes.*
>
> — ATUL GAWANDE, *Better*

Now take a look at another passage, written about the upcoming twenty-third season of *The Simpsons*:

> Let's make a pact. The next person who whines about how *The Simpsons* sucks gets flung in a well. The rest of us can tailgate. Spare us your blustery, pedantic indignation. There's nothing to add. No petition long enough, no outcry loud enough. Winter is coming and so is the Fox series' twenty-third season and 500th episode. If this really upsets you . . . Just. Quit. Watching.
>
> — MARY H. K. CHOI

Choi opens with a four-word sentence, speaking directly to readers, which aims to get their attention. The next somewhat longer sentence is then followed by two short sentences and then another longer sentence. The passage ends with a five-word sentence followed by three single words punctuated as sentences. Choi makes the most of these very short sentences, which stop readers, almost like holding up a sign that says "pay attention to this." The allusions to *Game of Thrones* ("Winter is coming") and a Marvin Gaye ballad ("No petition long enough") create echoes for readers, and the verbs are generally strong (*whines*, *sucks*, *spare*). Overall, this is a passage readers will probably remember.

Because the opening of a sentence is often its most memorable part, writers work especially hard to create engaging and varied openings. One student opened an essay on problems facing teenagers in her hometown with this dramatic sentence: "Rachel struck me as an honest thief." That is a sentence that invites readers to keep reading! The sentence begins with the subject of the sentence, Rachel, and it works very well in this instance. But if sentence after sentence begins with a subject, a passage may become monotonous or hard to read, as in the following case.

> The way football and basketball are played is as interesting as the players.
> ~~Football~~ Because football is a game of precision/, ~~Each~~ each play is diagrammed to accomplish a certain goal. Basketball, however, is a game of endurance. ~~A~~ In fact, a basketball game looks like a track meet; the team that drops of exhaustion first, loses.
> Basketball players are often compared to artists/; ~~The players'~~ their graceful moves and slam dunks are their masterpieces.

The editing adds variety by using a subordinating word (*Because*) and a prepositional phrase (*In fact*) and by linking sentences. Varying sentence openings prevents the passage from seeming to jerk or lurch along.

You can also add variety to your sentence openings by using transitions, various kinds of phrases, and dependent clauses.

TRANSITIONAL EXPRESSIONS

▶ *In contrast,* our approach will save time and money.

▶ *However,* the report is accurate.

▶ *Additionally,* my client insists on immunity from prosecution.

PHRASES

▶ *Before dawn,* tired commuters drink their first cups of coffee.

▶ *Frustrated by the delays,* the drivers started honking their horns.

▶ *To qualify for flight training,* one must be in excellent physical condition.

DEPENDENT CLAUSES

▶ *Because the hills were dry,* the fire spread rapidly.

▶ *When the police appeared wearing riot gear,* the protesters stopped chanting, stared for a moment, and then scattered.

▶ *Although you may not consider a cell phone a necessity,* a homeless veteran will not be able to find a job without one.

Talking the Talk

Style in Technical Writing

For some types of writing, varying sentence structure and length is not always appropriate. Many technical writers, particularly those who write manuals that will be translated into other languages, must follow stringent rules for sentence structure and length. One computer company, for example, requires writers to adhere to a strict subject-verb-object order and limit all of their sentences to no more than fifteen words. Learn the style conventions of your field as fully as possible, and then bring them to bear on your own sentence revisions.

27 Coordination, Subordination, and Emphasis

Coordination and subordination are ways of joining ideas in sentences that show relationships between ideas and emphasize more important ideas. In speech, people tend to use *and* and *so* as all-purpose connectors.

> I've requested that information for you, and I will get back in touch shortly to let you know what's going on.

If you said this sentence aloud, you could provide clues about which parts of the sentence were most important by stressing certain words and phrases and by using facial expressions and gestures to provide hints about your meaning. But if you wrote the sentence rather than saying it, your reader might not be certain what you wanted to emphasize.

Quick Help

Editing for Coordination, Subordination, and Emphasis

How do your ideas flow from one sentence to another? Do they connect smoothly and clearly? Are the more important ideas given more emphasis than less important ones?

- Look for strings of short sentences that might be combined to join related ideas. (27a)

  ▶ The report was short, ~~It~~ was persuasive, ~~It~~ changed my mind.
  (edits: "but it" replacing "It"; "it" replacing "It")

- If you use *and* excessively, decide whether all the ideas are equally important. If they are not equal, edit to subordinate the less important ones. (27b)

- Make sure that the most important ideas appear in independent clauses that can stand alone as complete sentences. (27b)

  ▶ ~~The~~ report was short, ~~even though~~ it changed my mind.
  (edit: "Even though the" replacing "The"; "even though" deleted)

- Identify the word or words you want to receive special emphasis. If those words are buried in the middle of a sentence, edit the sentence to change their position. The end and the beginning are generally the most emphatic. (27c)

- If a sentence includes a series of three or more words, phrases, or clauses, try to arrange the items in the series in climactic order, with the most important item last. (27c)

By choosing subordination, you convey that one part of the sentence or the other is more important. The emphasis here is on the promise to get back in touch, not on the request that has already happened:

> Having requested that information for you, I will get back in touch shortly to let you know what's going on.

You can also use other coordinating conjunctions to clarify the relationships between equally important ideas. Notice the different impression you would give by using *but* instead of *and*:

> I've requested that information for you, but I will get back in touch shortly to let you know what's going on.

All these sentences are grammatically correct, but all of them mean slightly different things. Choosing appropriate coordination and subordination allows your meaning to come through clearly.

27a   Use coordination to relate equal ideas.

When used well, coordination relates separate but equal ideas. The element that links the ideas, usually a coordinating conjunction (*and, but, for, nor, or, so, yet*) or a semicolon, makes the precise relationship clear. The following sentences by N. Scott Momaday all use coordination, but the relationship between independent clauses differs in each sentence:

> ▶ They acquired horses, *and* their ancient nomadic spirit was suddenly free of the ground.
>
> ▶ There is perfect freedom in the mountains, *but* it belongs to the eagle and the elk, the badger and the bear.
>
> ▶ No longer were they slaves to the simple necessity of survival; they were a lordly and dangerous society of fighters and thieves, hunters and priests of the sun.   – N. SCOTT MOMADAY, *The Way to Rainy Mountain*

Momaday uses coordination in these sentences carefully in order to achieve very specific effects. In the first sentence, for example, the use of *and* gives a sense of adding on: "They acquired horses" *and*, of equal importance, "their ancient nomadic spirit was suddenly free." Momaday might have made other, equally correct choices, but they would have resulted in slightly different sentences. Compare these altered versions with Momaday's sentences. How do the changes affect your understanding?

> ▶ They acquired horses, *so* their ancient nomadic spirit was suddenly free of the ground.
>
> ▶ There is perfect freedom in the mountains; it belongs to the eagle and the elk, the badger and the bear.

In your own writing, think about exactly what information you want to convey with coordination. You, too, may have several correct options — so make the choice that works best for your situation and audience.

Coordination can help make explicit the relationship between two ideas.

▶ **Generations have now grown up with *The Simpsons*/; Bart, Lisa, and Maggie never get older, but today's college students may have been watching the show since before they could talk.**

Connecting these two sentences with a semicolon strengthens the connection between two closely related ideas.

When you connect ideas within a sentence, make sure the relationship between the ideas is clear.

▶ **Surfing the Internet is a common way to spend leisure time, ~~and~~ but it should not replace human contact.**

What does a common form of leisure have to do with replacing human contact? Changing *and* to *but* better relates the two ideas.

27b Use subordination to distinguish main ideas.

Subordination allows you to distinguish major points from minor points or to bring in supporting details. If, for instance, you put your main idea in an independent clause — words that could stand alone as a sentence (34e) — you might then put any less significant ideas in dependent clauses, phrases, or even single words. The following sentence italicizes the subordinated point:

▶ **Mrs. Viola Cullinan was a plump woman *who lived in a three-bedroom house somewhere behind the post office.***

— MAYA ANGELOU, "My Name Is Margaret"

The dependent clause adds important information about Mrs. Cullinan, but it is subordinate to the independent clause.

Choices about subordination

Notice that the choice of what to subordinate rests with the writer and depends on the intended meaning. Angelou might have given the same basic information differently.

▶ **Mrs. Viola Cullinan, *a plump woman*, lived in a three-bedroom house somewhere behind the post office.**

Subordinating the information about Mrs. Cullinan's size to that about her house would suggest a slightly different meaning, of course. When you write, think carefully about what you want to emphasize and subordinate information accordingly.

Subordination also establishes logical relationships among ideas. These relationships are often specified by relative pronouns—such as *which*, *who*, and *that*—and by subordinating conjunctions.

COMMON SUBORDINATING CONJUNCTIONS

after	if	unless
although	once	until
as	since	when
as if	so that	where
because	than	while
before		

The following sentence italicizes the subordinate clause and underlines the subordinating word:

▶ She usually rested her smile until late afternoon <u>*when*</u> *her women friends dropped in and Miss Glory, the cook, served them cold drinks on the closed-in porch.* – MAYA ANGELOU, "My Name Is Margaret"

Excessive coordination

Using too many coordinate structures can be monotonous and can make it hard for readers to recognize the most important ideas. Subordinating lesser ideas can help highlight the main ideas.

▶ Many people check email in the evening, and so they grab their smartphone. ~~They~~ Though they may intend to respond only to urgent messages, a friend sends a link to a blog post, ~~and~~ which they decide to read ~~it~~ for just a short while~~.~~/. ~~and~~ Eventually, they get engrossed in Facebook, and they end up spending the whole evening in front of the screen.

▶ ~~Our~~ Although our new boss can be difficult, ~~although~~ she has revived and maybe even saved the division.

The editing puts the more important information—that she has saved part of the company—in an independent clause and subordinates the rest.

Excessive subordination

When too many subordinate clauses are strung together, readers may have trouble keeping track of the main idea.

TOO MUCH SUBORDINATION

▶ Philip II sent the Spanish Armada to conquer England, which was ruled by Elizabeth, who had executed Mary because she was plotting to overthrow Elizabeth, who was a Protestant, whereas Mary and Philip were Roman Catholics.

REVISED

▶ Philip II sent the Spanish Armada to conquer England, which was ruled by Elizabeth, a Protestant. She had executed Mary, a Roman Catholic like Philip, because Mary was plotting to overthrow her.

Putting the facts about Elizabeth executing Mary into an independent clause makes key information easier to recognize.

27c Use closing and opening positions for emphasis.

When you read a sentence, the part you are most likely to remember is the ending. This part of the sentence should move the writing forward by providing new information, as it does in the following example:

▶ Employers today expect college graduates to have *excellent writing skills.*

A less emphatic but still important position in a sentence is the opening, which often connects the new sentence with what has come before.

▶ Today's employers want a college-educated workforce that can communicate well. *Excellent writing skills* are high on the list of qualifications.

If you place relatively unimportant information in the memorable closing position of a sentence, you may undercut what you want to emphasize or give more emphasis to the closing words than you intend.

▶ Last month, she ~~She~~ gave ~~$500,000 to~~ the school capital campaign $500,000. ~~last month.~~

Moving *$500,000* to the end of the sentence emphasizes the amount.

Talking about Style

Anticlimax and Humor

Sometimes it's fun to turn the principle of climactic order upside down, opening with grand or exaggerated language only to end anticlimactically, with everyday words.

> He is a writer for the ages — the ages of four to eight.
> — DOROTHY PARKER

Parker builds up expectations at the beginning of the sentence — only to undercut them unexpectedly by shifting the meaning of *ages.* Having led readers to expect something dramatic, she makes us laugh, or at least smile, with words that are decidedly undramatic.

When you arrange ideas in order of increasing importance, power, or drama, your writing builds to a climax. Consider the following sentence:

▶ After they've finished with the pantry, the medicine cabinet, and the attic, [neat people] will throw out the red geranium (too many leaves), sell the dog (too many fleas), and send the children off to boarding school (too many scuffmarks on the hardwood floors).
> — SUSANNE BRITT, "Neat People vs. Sloppy People"

Would Britt's words have the same effect if *throw out the red geranium* appeared after *sell the dog* or *send the children off to boarding school*? By saving the most dramatic item for last, she makes her point forcefully and memorably.

28 Consistency and Completeness

In conversation, you will hear inconsistent and incomplete structures all the time. For instance, during an interview with journalist Bill Moyers, Jon Stewart discussed the supposed objectivity of news reporting.

> But news has never been objective. It's always . . . what does every newscast start with? "Our top stories tonight." That's a list. That's a subjective . . . some editor made a decision: "Here's our top stories. Number one: There's a fire in the Bronx."

Because Stewart is talking casually, tossing out examples and ideas as they come to mind, some of his sentences begin one way but then move in another direction. The mixed structures pose no problem for the viewer — they sound like conversations we hear every day — but sentences such as these can often be confusing in writing. Because of social media, writing is getting more conversational — even academic writing. As a result, writers are free to develop a conversational and even experimental style. But in formal academic writing, it's still wise to stick with consistent and complete structures.

28a Revise faulty sentence structure.

Faulty sentence structure causes problems for readers and writers alike. One common type of faulty structure is a mixed structure, which results from beginning a sentence with one grammatical pattern and then switching to another one.

> **MIXED** The fact that I get up at 5:00 AM, a wake-up time that explains why I'm always tired in the evening.

The sentence starts out with a subject (*The fact*) followed by a dependent clause (*that I get up at 5:00 AM*). The sentence needs a predicate to complete the independent clause, but instead it moves to another phrase followed by a dependent clause (*a wake-up time that explains why I'm always tired in the evening*), and what results is a sentence fragment.

> **REVISED** *The fact* that I get up at 5:00 AM *explains* why I'm always tired in the evening.

Deleting *a wake-up time that* changes the rest of the sentence into a predicate.

> **REVISED** *I get up* at 5:00 AM, a wake-up time that explains why I'm always tired in the evening.

Deleting *The fact that* turns the beginning of the sentence into an independent clause.

(For information about subjects and predicates, see 34b and c; for information about independent and dependent clauses, see 34e.)

28b Match up subjects and predicates.

Another kind of mixed structure, called faulty predication, occurs when a subject and predicate do not fit together grammatically or simply do not make sense together. Many cases of faulty predication result from using forms of *be* when another verb would be stronger.

> ▶ A characteristic that I admire is ~~a person who is generous.~~ generosity.

A person is not a characteristic.

> ▶ The rules of the corporation ~~expect~~ require employees to be on time.

Rules cannot expect anything.

Constructions using *is when*, *is where*, and *the reason . . . is because* are used frequently in informal contexts, but they may be inappropriate in academic writing because they describe a noun using an adverb clause (34e).

> ▶ A stereotype is ~~when someone characterizes~~ an unfair characterization of a group.~~unfairly.~~

> ▶ A confluence is ~~where~~ a place two rivers join to form one.

> ▶ ~~The reason~~ I like to play soccer ~~is~~ because it provides aerobic exercise.

28c Use elliptical structures carefully.

Sometimes writers omit a word in a compound structure. This type of structure, known as an elliptical structure, is appropriate when the word omitted later in the compound is exactly the same as the word earlier in the compound.

> ▶ That bell belonged to the figure of Miss Duling as though it grew directly out of her right arm, as wings grew out of an angel or a tail [grew] out of the devil. — EUDORA WELTY, *One Writer's Beginnings*

If the omitted word does not match a word in the other part of the compound, readers might be confused, so the omission is inappropriate in formal writing.

Quick Help

Editing for Consistency and Completeness

- If you find an especially confusing sentence, check to see whether it has a subject and a predicate. If not, revise as necessary. (28a) If you find both a subject and a predicate, and you are still confused, see whether the subject and verb make sense together. (28b)

- Revise any *is when*, *is where*, and *the reason . . . is because* constructions. (28b)

  ▶ Spamming is ~~where companies send~~ electronic junk mail.

  the practice of sending

- Check all comparisons for completeness. (28e)

  ▶ We like Lisa better than Margaret.

  we like

▶ His skills are weak, and his performance only average.

is

The verb *is* does not match the verb in the other part of the compound (*are*), so the writer needs to include it.

28d Check for missing words.

The best way to catch inadvertent omissions is to proofread carefully.

▶ The new website makes it easier to look and choose from the company's inventory.

at

28e Make comparisons complete, consistent, and clear.

When you compare two or more things, the comparison must be complete, logically consistent, and clear.

▶ I was embarrassed because my parents were so different/

from my friends' parents.

Different from what? Adding *from my friends' parents* tells readers what the comparison is being made with.

UNCLEAR	Aneil always felt more affection for his brother than his sister.
CLEAR	Aneil always felt more affection for his brother than his sister did.
CLEAR	Aneil always felt more affection for his brother than he did for his sister.

29 Parallelism

Parallel grammatical structures show up in many familiar phrases: *sink or swim, rise and shine, shape up or ship out.* If you look and listen for these structures, you will see parallelism in everyday use. Bumper stickers often use parallel grammatical structures to make their messages memorable (*Minds are like parachutes; both work best when open*), but the pleasing effects of parallel structures can benefit any kind of writing, from tweets to academic essays.

29a Make items in a series parallel.

Parallelism makes a series both graceful and easy to follow.

▶ In the eighteenth century, armed forces could fight *in open fields* and *on the high seas.* Today, they can clash *on the ground anywhere, on the sea, under the sea*, and *in the air.*
     – DONALD SNOW AND EUGENE BROWN, *The Contours of Power*

The parallel phrases, as well as the parallel structure of the sentences themselves, highlight the contrast between warfare in the eighteenth century and warfare today.

In the following sentences, note how the revisions make all items in the series parallel:

▶ The quarter horse skipped, pranced, and ~~was sashaying.~~ sashayed.

> ### Quick Help
>
> #### Editing for Parallelism
>
> - Look for any series of three or more items, and make all of the items parallel in structure. (29a)
> - Be sure items in lists and in related headings are parallel. (29a)
> - Check for places where two ideas are paired in the same sentence. Often these ideas will appear on either side of *and*, *but*, *or*, *nor*, *for*, *so*, or *yet*, or after each part of *both . . . and*, *either . . . or*, *neither . . . nor*, *not only . . . but also*, *whether . . . or*, or *just as . . . so*. Edit to make the two ideas parallel in structure. (29b)
> - Check any parallel structures to make sure that you have included all necessary words — prepositions, the *to* of the infinitive, and so on.

> The children ran down the hill, skipped over the lawn, and ~~into~~ the swimming pool. ^{*jumped*}

> The duties of the job include babysitting, housecleaning, and *preparing* ~~preparation of~~ meals.

Items in a list, in a formal outline, and in headings in a writing project should be parallel.

> Kitchen rules: (1) Coffee to be made only by library staff. (2) Coffee service to be closed at 4:00 P.M. (3) Doughnuts to be kept in cabinet. (4) *Coffee materials not to be handled by faculty.* ~~No faculty members should handle coffee materials.~~

29b Make paired ideas parallel.

Parallel structures can help you pair two ideas effectively. The more nearly parallel the two structures are, the stronger the connection between the ideas will be.

> *History became* popular, and *historians became* alarmed.
> — WILL DURANT

> *I type* in one place, but *I write* all over the house. — TONI MORRISON

▶ Writers are often more interesting on the page than they are in ~~person.~~ the flesh.

In these examples, the parallel structures help readers see an important contrast between two ideas or acts.

Coordinating conjunctions

When you link ideas with a coordinating conjunction — *and, but, or, nor, for, so,* or *yet* — try to make the ideas parallel in structure.

▶ Consult a friend in your class or who is good at math. *(who is)*

▶ The wise politician promises the possible and ~~should accept~~ *accepts* the inevitable.

In both sentences, the editing links the two ideas by making them parallel.

Correlative conjunctions

Use the same structure after both parts of a correlative conjunction: *either . . . or, both . . . and, neither . . . nor, not . . . but, not only . . . but also, just as . . . so,* and *whether . . . or.*

▶ I wanted not only to go away to school but also to *live in* New England.

Balancing *to go* with *to live* links the two ideas and makes the sentence easier to read.

30 Shifts

A shift in writing is an abrupt change that results in inconsistency. Sometimes a writer or speaker will shift deliberately, as linguist Geneva Smitherman does in this passage from *Word from the Mother*: "There are days when I optimistically predict that Hip Hop will survive — and thrive. . . . In the larger realm of Hip Hop culture, there is cause for optimism as we witness Hip Hop younguns tryna git they political activist game togetha."

Smitherman's shift from formal academic language to vernacular, or everyday, speech is a stylistic choice that calls out for and holds our attention. Although writers make shifts for good rhetorical reasons, unintentional shifts in verb tenses, pronouns, and tone can be confusing to readers.

Shifts are also often used to create humorous effects. Here's Dave Barry describing the English language:

> English spelling is unusual because our language is a rich verbal tapestry woven together from the tongues of the Greeks, the Latins, the Angles, the Klaxtons, the Celtics, the 76ers, and many other ancient peoples, all of whom had severe drinking problems.

Shifting from ancient peoples to modern basketball teams to drinking problems aims to get a laugh from readers. Barry and many other comedians use such abrupt shifts to good effect in their routines. But in most of your college writing, you'll be well advised to use such shifts cautiously.

30a Revise unnecessary shifts in verb tense.

If the verbs in a passage refer to actions occurring at different times, they may require different tenses. Be careful, however, not to change tenses for no reason.

▶ A few countries produce almost all of the world's illegal drugs, but
       affects
addiction ~~affected~~ many countries.

30b Revise unnecessary shifts in mood.

Be careful not to shift from one mood to another without good reason. The mood of a verb can be indicative (he *closes* the door), imperative (*close* the door), or subjunctive (if the door *were closed*) (35h).

▶ Keep your eye on the ball, and ~~you should~~ bend your knees.

30c Revise unnecessary shifts in voice.

Do not shift without reason between the active voice (she *sold* it) and the passive voice (it *was sold*). Sometimes a shift in voice is justified, but often it only confuses readers (35g).

                                   me
▶ Two youths approached me/and ~~I was~~ asked for my wallet.

> The original sentence shifts from the active (*youths approached*) to the passive (*I was asked*), so it is unclear who asked for the wallet. Making both verbs active clears up the confusion.

> ## Quick Help
>
> ### Confusing Shifts
>
> - Make sure you have a reason for shifting from one verb tense to another. (30a)
> - Revise any shifts in mood — perhaps from an indicative statement to an imperative — that are not necessary. (30b)
> - Check for shifts from active (*She asks questions*) to passive voice (*Questions are asked*). Are they intentional? (30c)
> - Make sure you have good reasons for any shifts in person or number — from *we* to *you*, for example. (30d)
> - Check your writing for consistency in tone and word choice. (30f)

30d Revise unnecessary shifts in person and number.

Unnecessary shifts in point of view among first person (*I, we*), second person (*you*), and third person (*he, she, it, they*), or between singular and plural subjects, can be very confusing to readers.

> You
> ▶ ~~Someone~~ can do well on this job if you budget your time.
>   ^

> Is the writer making a general statement or giving advice? Eliminating the shift eliminates this confusion.

30e Revise shifts between direct and indirect discourse.

Multilingual

When you quote someone's exact words, you are using direct discourse: *She said, "I'm an editor."* When you report what someone says without repeating the exact words, you are using indirect discourse: *She says she is an editor.* Shifting between direct and indirect discourse in the same sentence can cause problems, especially with questions.

>   he
> ▶ Viet asked what could ~~he~~ do to help?.
>   ^   ^

> The editing eliminates an awkward shift by reporting Viet's question indirectly. It could also be edited to quote Viet directly: *Viet asked, "What can I do to help?"*

30f Revise shifts in tone and word choice.

Tone, a writer's attitude toward a topic or audience, is related to word choice and to overall formality or informality. Watch out for tone or diction shifts that can confuse readers and leave them wondering what your real attitude is (2f).

INCONSISTENT TONE

The problem of student debt affects not only college students and their families, but the whole darn economy. With the average debt upon graduation hovering close to $40,000, how many recent grads will earn enough to pony up without robbing a bank? In the past, young earners have contributed to the US economy with home purchases, auto purchases, and other spending, but now they're stuck at home freeloading with parents and riding the bus.

In this version, both the topic of student debt and the opening are fairly serious. But the writer shifts suddenly to sarcasm (*robbing a bank*) and to informal language like *stuck* and *freeloading*. Readers cannot tell whether the writer is presenting a serious analysis or preparing for a humorous satire. The revision makes the tone consistently formal.

REVISED

The problem of student debt affects not only college students and their families, but the entire economy. With the average debt upon graduation hovering close to $40,000, how many recent grads will earn enough to pay their bills? In the past, young earners have contributed to the US economy with home purchases, auto purchases, and other spending, but such milestone purchases are being delayed today — or avoided entirely.

31 Conciseness

If you have a Twitter account, you know a lot about being concise — that is, about getting messages across without wasting words (Twitter limits writers to 140 or 280 characters). Recently, *New York Times* editor Bill Keller decided to start a discussion by tweeting, "Twitter makes you stupid. Discuss." That little comment drew a large number of responses, including one from his wife that read, "I don't know if Twitter makes you stupid, but it's making you late for dinner. Come home."

No matter how you feel about the effects of Twitter on the brain (or stomach!), you can make any writing more effective by using clear structures and choosing words that convey exactly what you mean to say.

31a Eliminate unnecessary words.

Sometimes writers say that something is large *in size* or red *in color* or that two ingredients should be combined *together*. The italicized words are unnecessarily repetitive; delete such redundant words.

> ▶ ~~Compulsory attendance~~ at assemblies is required.
> ^Attendance^

> ▶ Many different forms of hazing occur, such as physical ~~abuse~~ and mental abuse.

Meaningless modifiers

Many modifiers are so overused that they have little meaning.

MEANINGLESS MODIFIERS

absolutely, awfully, definitely, fine, great, interesting, quite, really, very

Wordy phrases

Wordy phrases can be reduced to a word or two with no loss in meaning.

WORDY	CONCISE
at that point in time	then
at the present time	now/today
due to the fact that	because
for the purpose of	for
in order to	to
in spite of the fact that	although

Quick Help

Editing for Conciseness

- Look for redundant words. If you are unsure about a certain word, read the sentence without it; if meaning is not affected, leave the word out. (31a)
- Take out empty words — words like *aspect* or *factor*, *definitely* or *very*. (31a)
- Replace wordy phrases with a single word. Instead of *because of the fact that*, try *because*. (31a)
- Reconsider any sentences that begin with *it is* or *there is/are*. Unless they create special emphasis, try recasting the sentences without these words. (31b)

31b Simplify sentence structure.

Using simple grammatical structures can strengthen your sentences considerably.

▶ Hurricane Katrina, ~~which was certainly~~ one of the most powerful storms
                      widespread
  ever to hit the Gulf Coast, caused damage.~~to a very wide area.~~

Deleting unnecessary words and replacing five words with one tightens the sentence and makes it easier to read.

▶ When ~~she was~~ questioned about her previous job, she seemed
        and
  nervous/~~She also~~ tried to change the subject.

Combining two sentences produces one concise sentence.

There is, there are, and *it is*

Sometimes expletive constructions — *there is, there are,* and *it is* — can introduce a topic effectively; often, however, your writing will be better without them.

        Many
▶ ~~There are many~~ people ~~who~~ fear success because they believe they do not
  deserve it.

            Presidential   need
▶ ~~It is necessary for presidential~~ candidates to perform well on television.

Active voice

Some writing situations call for the passive voice (35g), but it is always wordier than the active — and often makes for dull or even difficult reading.

     Gower
▶ ~~In Gower's research, it was~~ found that pythons often dwell in trees.

Wordy noun forms

Forming nouns from verbs, a process sometimes called *nominalization*, can help make prose more concise — for example, using *abolition* instead of *the process of abolishing* — but it can also make a sentence wordy and hard to read.

> The firm is now ~~engaged in an assessment of~~ ^{assessing} its procedures for ~~the development of~~ ^{developing} new products.

The original sentence sounds pretentious, and the noun phrases cloud the message. In contrast, the edited version is clear and forceful.

▲ **For visual analysis** This illustration shows Scrabble players trying to make the best possible choices as they create words. Effective communicators must also make careful choices, including when to follow "the rules" and when to move beyond them. What language choices have you had to make most recently in your writing?

The Top Twenty: A Quick Guide to Editing Your Writing

Mistakes are a fact of life: It is the response to the error that counts.

— NIKKI GIOVANNI

32 The Top Twenty
A Quick Guide to Editing Your Writing

Mistakes in grammar, punctuation, word choice, and other small-scale matters don't always disturb readers. Whether your instructor marks an error in any particular assignment will depend on personal judgments about how serious and distracting it is and about what you should be focusing on in the draft. In addition, not all grammar and punctuation errors are consistently viewed as errors: some of the patterns identified in the research for this book are considered errors by some but as stylistic options by others. Moreover, so-called "errors" can sometimes create powerful effects.

Such differing opinions don't mean that there is no such thing as correctness in writing — only that *correctness always depends on some context*, on whether the choices a writer makes seem appropriate to readers.

All writers want to be considered competent and careful. You know that readers often judge you by your control of the conventions you have agreed to use, even if the conventions change from time to time. It's good news, then, that producing writing that is conventionally correct is a goal you can achieve. In fact, if you become familiar with the twenty most common error patterns among U.S. college students today, you will have taken care of many of the issues that instructors are concerned with. In this section, you'll find those twenty mistakes, listed in order of frequency (based on our findings from the research project in which we studied thousands of pieces of writing by first-year students), with brief explanations, examples of each, and cross-references to additional help in this book.

Wrong word

▶ Religious texts, for them, take ~~prescience~~ *precedence* over other kinds of sources.

Prescience means "foresight," and *precedence* means "priority."

▶ The child suffered from a severe ~~allegory~~ *allergy* to peanuts.

Allegory is a spell checker's replacement for a misspelling of *allergy*.

▶ The panel discussed the ethical implications ~~on~~ *of* the situation.

Wrong-word errors can involve using a word with the wrong shade of meaning, using a word with a completely wrong meaning, or using a wrong preposition or another wrong word in an idiom. Selecting a word from

Quick Help

The Top Twenty

1. Wrong word
2. Missing comma after an introductory element
3. Incomplete or missing documentation
4. Vague pronoun reference
5. Spelling (including homonyms)
6. Mechanical error with a quotation
7. Unnecessary comma
8. Unnecessary or missing capitalization
9. Missing word
10. Confusing sentence structure
11. Missing comma with a nonrestrictive element
12. Unnecessary shift in verb tense
13. Missing comma in a compound sentence
14. Unnecessary or missing apostrophe (including *its/it's*)
15. Fused (run-on) sentence
16. Comma splice
17. Lack of pronoun-antecedent agreement
18. Poorly integrated quotation
19. Unnecessary or missing hyphen
20. Sentence fragment

a thesaurus without knowing its meaning, or allowing a spell checker to correct spelling automatically, can lead to wrong-word errors, so use these tools with care. If you have trouble with prepositions and idioms, memorize the standard usage. See Chapter 26 on word choice and Chapter 41 on prepositions and idioms.

2 Missing comma after an introductory element

▶ Determined to get the job done **,** we worked all weekend.

▶ Although the study was flawed **,** the results may still be useful.

Readers usually need a small pause — signaled by a comma — between an introductory word, phrase, or clause and the main part of the sentence. Use a comma after every introductory element. When the introductory element is very short, you don't always need a comma, but including it is never wrong. (See 44a.)

3 Incomplete or missing documentation

▶ Satrapi says, "When we're afraid, we lose all sense of analysis and reflection." **(263).**

This quotation comes from a print source, so a page number is needed.

▶ Some experts agree that James Joyce wrote two of the five best novels of all time. **("100 Best Novels").**

The source of this information should be identified (this online source has no page numbers).

Cite each source you refer to in the text, following the guidelines of the documentation style you are using. (The preceding examples follow MLA style — see Chapters 54–57; for other styles, see Chapters 58–64.) Omitting documentation can result in charges of plagiarism (see Chapter 12).

4 Vague pronoun reference

POSSIBLE REFERENCE TO MORE THAN ONE WORD

▶ Transmitting radio signals by satellite is a way of overcoming the problem of scarce airwaves and limiting how ~~they~~ **the airwaves** are used.

In the original sentence, *they* could refer to the signals or to the airwaves.

REFERENCE IMPLIED BUT NOT STATED

▶ The company prohibited smoking, ~~which~~ **a policy** many employees resented.

What does *which* refer to? The editing clarifies what employees resented.

A pronoun should refer clearly to the word or words it replaces (called the *antecedent*) elsewhere in the sentence or in a previous sentence. If more than one word could be the antecedent, or if no specific antecedent is present, edit to make the meaning clear. (See Chapter 38.)

5   Spelling (including homonyms)

▶ Ronald ~~Regan~~ won the election in a landslide.
     Reagan

▶ ~~Every where~~ we went, we saw crowds of tourists.
     Everywhere

The most common misspellings today are those that spell checkers cannot identify. The categories that spell checkers are most likely to miss include homonyms, compound words incorrectly spelled as separate words, and proper nouns, particularly names. After you run the spell checker, proofread carefully for errors such as these — and be sure to run the spell checker to catch other kinds of spelling mistakes.

6   Mechanical error with a quotation

▶ "I grew up the victim of a disconcerting confusion,"/ Rodriguez says (249).

The comma should be placed *inside* the quotation marks.

Follow conventions when using quotation marks with commas (44h), colons (49d), and other punctuation (48f). Always use quotation marks in pairs, and follow the guidelines of your documentation style for block quotations (48b). Use quotation marks for titles of short works (48c), but use italics for titles of long works (52a).

7   Unnecessary comma

BEFORE CONJUNCTIONS IN COMPOUND CONSTRUCTIONS THAT ARE NOT COMPOUND SENTENCES

▶ This conclusion applies to the United States/ and to the rest of the world.

No comma is needed before *and* because it is joining two phrases that modify the same verb, *applies*.

WITH RESTRICTIVE ELEMENTS

▶ Many parents⁄ of gifted children⁄ do not want them to skip a grade.

No commas are needed to set off the restrictive phrase *of gifted children*, which is necessary to indicate which parents the sentence is talking about.

Do not use commas to set off restrictive elements that are necessary to the meaning of the words they modify. Do not use a comma before a coordinating conjunction (*and, but, for, nor, or, so, yet*) when the conjunction does not join parts of a compound sentence. Do not use a comma before the first or after the last item in a series, between a subject and verb, between a verb and its object or complement, or between a preposition and its object. (See 44j.)

8 Unnecessary or missing capitalization

▶ Some ~~Traditional~~ Chinese ~~Medicines~~ containing ~~Ephedra~~ remain legal.
(traditional) (medicines) (ephedra)

Capitalize proper nouns and proper adjectives, the first words of sentences, and important words in titles, along with certain words indicating directions and family relationships. Do not capitalize most other words. When in doubt, check a dictionary. (See Chapter 50.)

9 Missing word

▶ The site foreman discriminated against women and promoted men with less experience.

Proofread carefully for omitted words, including prepositions (41a), parts of two-part verbs (41b), and correlative conjunctions (33g). Be particularly careful not to omit words from quotations.

10 Confusing sentence structure

▶ ~~The information which high~~ school athletes are presented with ~~mainly~~ includes information on what credits ~~they~~ needed to graduate, ~~and thinking about the college~~ which ~~athletes are trying~~ to play for, and apply.
(High) ... (they) ... (colleges to try) ... (how to)

A sentence that starts out with one kind of structure and then changes to another kind can confuse readers. Make sure that each sentence contains a subject and a verb (34a), that subjects and predicates make sense together (28b), and that comparisons have clear meanings (28e). When you join elements (such as subjects or verb phrases) with a coordinating conjunction, make sure that the elements have parallel structures (see Chapter 29).

11 Missing comma with a nonrestrictive element

▶ Marina, who was the president of the club, was first to speak.

The clause *who was the president of the club* does not affect the basic meaning of the sentence: Marina was first to speak.

A nonrestrictive element gives information not essential to the basic meaning of the sentence. Use commas to set off a nonrestrictive element (44c).

12 Unnecessary shift in verb tense

▶ Priya was watching the great blue heron. Then she ~~slips~~ slipped and ~~falls~~ fell into the swamp.

Verbs that shift from one tense to another with no clear reason can confuse readers (30a).

13 Missing comma in a compound sentence

▶ Meredith waited for Samir, and her sister grew impatient.

Without the comma, a reader may think at first that Meredith waited for both Samir and her sister.

A compound sentence consists of two or more parts that could each stand alone as a sentence. When the parts are joined by a coordinating conjunction, use a comma before the conjunction to indicate a pause between the two thoughts (44b).

14 Unnecessary or missing apostrophe (including *its/it's*)

▶ Overambitious parents can be very harmful to a ~~childs~~ ^{child's} well-being.

▶ The car is lying on ~~it's~~ *its* side in the ditch. ~~Its~~ *It's* a white 2012 Passat.

To make a noun possessive, add either an apostrophe and an *-s* (*Ed's book*) or an apostrophe alone (*the boys' gym*). Do not use an apostrophe in the possessive pronouns *ours, yours,* and *hers.* Use *its* to mean *belonging to it;* use *it's* only when you mean *it is* or *it has.* (See Chapter 47.)

15 Fused (run-on) sentence

▶ Klee's paintings seem simple, *but* they are very sophisticated.

▶ ~~She~~ *Although she* doubted the value of meditation, she decided to try it once.

A fused sentence (also called a *run-on*) joins clauses that could each stand alone as a sentence with no punctuation or words to link them. Fused sentences must either be divided into separate sentences or joined by adding words or punctuation. (See Chapter 42.)

16 Comma splice

▶ I was strongly attracted to her, *for* she was beautiful and funny.

▶ We hated the meat loaf*, that* the cafeteria served ~~it~~ every Friday.

A comma splice occurs when only a comma separates clauses that could each stand alone as a sentence. To correct a comma splice, you can insert a semicolon or period, connect the clauses with a word such as *and* or *because,* or restructure the sentence. (See Chapter 42.)

17 **Lack of pronoun-antecedent agreement**

> *its*
> ► Each of the proposals has ~~their~~ merits.
>   ^

> *All students*   *uniforms.*
> ► ~~Every student~~ must provide their own ~~uniform.~~
>   ^   ^

In formal academic writing, pronouns must agree with their antecedents both in gender (male or female) and in number (singular or plural). Traditionally, indefinite pronouns such as *every, everyone,* and *each* have been treated as singular antecedents and have required singular pronouns such as *his or her, his, her,* or *its.* Some writers choose to rewrite the sentence in plural, as in the second example above. However, the use of *they/their/them* is becoming increasingly acceptable with singular indefinite pronouns—to include people who do not identify as *he/his* or *she/her.* (See 38f.)

> ► Everyone should check their passport's expiration date before the trip.

When antecedents are joined by *or* or *nor,* the pronoun should always agree with the closer antecedent. A collective noun such as *team* can be either singular or plural, depending on whether the members are seen as a group or as individuals.

18 **Poorly integrated quotation**

> *showed how color affects taste:*
> ► Schlosser cites a 1970s study that ‿“Once it became apparent that the steak
>   ^
>
> was actually blue and the fries were green, some people became ill” (565).

> *According to Lars Eighner,*
> ► ‿“Dumpster diving has serious drawbacks as a way of life” (~~Eighner~~ 383).
>   ^
>
> Finding edible food is especially tricky.

Quotations should fit smoothly into the surrounding sentence structure. They should be linked clearly to the writing around them (usually with a signal phrase) rather than dropped abruptly into the writing. (See Chapter 12.)

> ### Quick Help
>
> #### Taking a Writing Inventory
>
> One way to learn from your mistakes is to take a writing inventory. It can help you think critically and analytically about how to improve your writing skills.
>
> 1. Collect two or three pieces of your writing to which either your instructor or other students have responded.
>
> 2. Read through these writings, adding your own comments about their strengths and weaknesses. How do your comments compare with those of others?
>
> 3. Group all the comments into three categories — *broad content issues* (use of evidence and sources, attention to purpose and audience, and overall impression), *organization and presentation* (overall and paragraph-level organization, sentence structure and style, and formatting), and *surface errors* (problems with wrong words, spelling, grammar, punctuation, and mechanics).
>
> 4. Make an inventory of your own strengths in each category.
>
> 5. Study your errors. Mark every instructor and peer comment that suggests or calls for an improvement, and put all these comments in a list. Consult the relevant part of this book or speak with your instructor if you don't understand a comment.
>
> 6. Make a list of the top problem areas you need to work on. How can you make improvements? Then note at least two strengths that you can build on in your writing. Reflect on your findings in a writing log that you can add to as the class proceeds.

19   Unnecessary or missing hyphen

▶ This paper looks at fictional and real life examples.

A compound adjective modifying a noun that follows it requires a hyphen.

▶ The buyers want to fix up the house and resell it.

A two-word verb should not be hyphenated.

A compound adjective that appears before a noun needs a hyphen. However, be careful not to hyphenate two-word verbs or word groups that serve as subject complements. (See Chapter 53.)

20　Sentence fragment

NO SUBJECT

▶ Marie Antoinette spent huge sums of money on herself and her favorites. Her extravagance

~~And~~ helped bring on the French Revolution.
　^

NO COMPLETE VERB

was
▶ The old aluminum boat sitting on its trailer.
　　　　　　　　　　　^

BEGINNING WITH A SUBORDINATING WORD

where
▶ We returned to the drugstore/, ~~Where~~ we waited for our buddies.
　　　　　　　　　　　　　^

A sentence fragment is part of a sentence that is written as if it were a complete sentence. Reading your draft out loud, backwards, sentence by sentence, will help you spot sentence fragments. (See Chapter 43.)

▲ **For visual analysis** This illustration shows ingredients being combined into a salad—one of many possible metaphors for the way elements of language combine to form grammatical sentences. How well does this metaphor fit with your understanding of the conventions of grammar?

Sentence Grammar

Most of us don't know a gerund from a gerbil and don't care, but we'd like to speak and write as though we did.

— PATRICIA T. O'CONNER

33 Parts of Speech

Grammatical correctness is certainly not enough to ensure that a sentence is effective and artful—or even that it serves an appropriate purpose in your writing; to achieve these goals you'll need to develop a powerful and persuasive style. Understanding grammatical structures can, however, help you produce sentences that are appropriate and effective as well as grammatically correct. The English language includes eight different categories of words called the *parts of speech*—verbs, nouns, pronouns, adjectives, adverbs, prepositions, conjunctions, and interjections. Many English words can function as more than one part of speech. When you *book an airplane flight*, the word *book* is a verb; when you *take a good book to the beach*, it is a noun; and when you have *book knowledge*, it is an adjective.

33a Verbs

Verbs move the meaning of sentences along by showing action (*glance*, *speculate*), occurrence (*become*, *happen*), or being (*be*, *seem*). Verbs change form to show *time*, *person*, *number*, *voice*, and *mood* (Chapter 35).

TIME	we *work*, we *worked*
PERSON	I *work*, she *works*
NUMBER	one person *works*, two people *work*
VOICE	she *asks*, she *is asked*
MOOD	we *see*, if I *were to see*

Helping verbs (also called *auxiliary verbs*) combine with main verbs to create verb phrases. Auxiliaries include the forms of *be*, *do*, and *have*, which are also used as main verbs, and *can*, *could*, *may*, *might*, *must*, *shall*, *should*, *will*, and *would* (35b).

► I *could have danced* all night.

► She *would prefer* to learn Italian rather than Spanish.

► When *do* you *need* the spreadsheet?

> ## Language, Culture, and Context
>
> Multilingual
>
> ### Count and Noncount Nouns
>
> Do people conduct *research* or *researches*? See 36a for a discussion of count and noncount nouns.

33b Nouns

Nouns name persons (*aviator, child*), places (*lake, library*), things (*truck, suitcase*), or concepts (*happiness, balance*). Proper nouns, which are capitalized, name specific persons, places, things, or concepts: *Bill, Iowa, Supreme Court, Buddhism*. Collective nouns (37d) name groups: *flock, jury*.

Most nouns change from singular (one) to plural (more than one) when you add *-s* or *-es*: *horse, horses; kiss, kisses*. Some nouns, however, have irregular plural forms: *woman, women; mouse, mice; deer, deer*. Noncount nouns (36a) cannot be made plural because they name things that cannot easily be counted: *dust, peace, prosperity*.

The possessive form of a noun shows ownership. Possessive forms add an apostrophe plus *-s* to most singular nouns or just an apostrophe to most plural nouns: *the horse's owner, the boys' department*.

Nouns are often preceded by the article (or determiner) *a, an*, or *the*: *a rocket, an astronaut, the launch* (36b).

33c Pronouns

Pronouns often take the place of nouns or other words functioning as nouns so that you do not have to repeat words that have already been mentioned. A word or word group that a pronoun replaces or refers to is called the antecedent of the pronoun (38f).

ANTECEDENT   PRONOUN
▶ Caitlin refused the invitation even though *she* wanted to go.

Pronouns fall into several categories.

PERSONAL PRONOUNS

Personal pronouns refer to specific persons or things. Each can take several forms (*I, me, my, mine*) depending on its function in the sentence (38a).

▶ When Keisha saw the dogs again, **she** called **them**, and **they** ran to **her**.

Note: For a discussion of using pronouns in inclusive and nonsexist ways, see 38f.

POSSESSIVE PRONOUNS

Possessive pronouns (*my, mine, your, yours, her, hers, his, its, our, ours, their, theirs*) are personal pronouns that indicate ownership (38a and 47a). For a discussion of using plural *they* with a singular noun or pronoun, see 38f.

▶ *My* roommate lost *her* keys.

REFLEXIVE PRONOUNS

Reflexive pronouns refer to the subject of the sentence or clause in which they appear. They end in *-self* or *-selves*: *myself, yourself, himself, herself, itself, oneself, ourselves, yourselves, themselves.*

▶ The seals sunned *themselves* on the warm rocks.

INTENSIVE PRONOUNS

Intensive pronouns have the same form as reflexive pronouns. They emphasize a noun or another pronoun.

▶ He decided to paint the apartment *himself.*

INDEFINITE PRONOUNS

Indefinite pronouns do not refer to specific nouns, although they may refer to identifiable persons or things. The following is a partial list:

all, another, anybody, both, each, either, everything, few, many, most, neither, none, no one, nothing, one, some, something

▶ *Everybody* screamed, and *someone* fainted, when the lights went out.

DEMONSTRATIVE PRONOUNS

Demonstrative pronouns (*this, that, these, those*) identify or point to specific nouns.

▶ *These* are Peter's books.

INTERROGATIVE PRONOUNS

Interrogative pronouns (*who, which, what*) are used to ask questions.

▶ *Who* can help set up the chairs for the meeting?

RELATIVE PRONOUNS

Relative pronouns (*who, which, that, what, whoever, whichever, whatever*) introduce dependent clauses and relate the dependent clause to the rest of the sentence (34e). The interrogative pronoun *who* and the relative pronouns *who* and *whoever* have different forms depending on how they are used in a sentence (38b).

▶ Maya, *who* hires interns, is the manager *whom* you should contact.

RECIPROCAL PRONOUNS

Reciprocal pronouns (*each other, one another*) refer to individual parts of a plural antecedent.

▶ The business failed because the partners distrusted *each other.*

33d Adjectives

Adjectives modify (limit the meaning of) nouns and pronouns, usually by describing, identifying, or quantifying those words (see Chapter 39). Adjectives that identify or quantify are sometimes called *determiners* (36b).

▶ The *red* Corvette ran off the road. [describes]
▶ *That* Corvette needs to be repaired. [identifies]
▶ We saw *several other* Corvettes race by. [quantifies]

In addition to their basic forms, most descriptive adjectives have other forms that allow you to make comparisons: *small, smaller, smallest; foolish, more foolish, most foolish, less foolish, least foolish.*

▶ This year's attendance was *smaller* than last year's.

Adjectives usually precede the words they modify, though they may follow linking verbs: *The car was defective.* Many pronouns (33c) can function as identifying adjectives when they are followed by a noun.

▶ *That* is a dangerous intersection. [pronoun]
▶ *That* intersection is dangerous. [identifying adjective]

Other kinds of adjectives that identify or quantify are the articles *a, an,* and *the* (36b) and numbers (*three, sixty-fifth, five hundred*).

Proper adjectives, which are capitalized (50b), are formed from or relate to proper nouns (*Egyptian, Emersonian*).

33e Adverbs

Adverbs modify verbs, adjectives, other adverbs, or entire clauses (see Chapter 39). Many adverbs end in *-ly,* though some do not (*always, never, very, well*), and some words that end in *-ly* are not adverbs but adjectives (*friendly, lovely*). One of the most common adverbs is *not.*

▶ Business writers *frequently* communicate with strangers. [modifies the verb *communicate*]

▶ How can they attract customers in an *increasingly* difficult economy? [modifies the adjective *difficult*]

▶ They must work *especially* hard to avoid offending readers. [modifies the adverb *hard*]

▶ *Obviously*, they need to weigh their words with care. [modifies the independent clause that makes up the rest of the sentence]

Adverbs often answer the questions *when? where? why? how? to what extent?*

Many adverbs, like many adjectives, take different forms when making comparisons: *forcefully, more forcefully, most forcefully, less forcefully, least forcefully.*

Conjunctive adverbs modify an entire clause, and they express the connection in meaning between that clause and the preceding clause (or sentence). Common conjunctive adverbs include *however, furthermore, therefore,* and *likewise.*

 ## 33f Prepositions

Prepositions express relationships — in space, time, or other senses — between nouns or pronouns and other words in a sentence.

▶ We did not want to leave *during* the game.

▶ The contestants waited nervously *for* the announcement.

A prepositional phrase (see Chapter 41) begins with a preposition and ends with the noun or pronoun it connects to the rest of the sentence.

▶ Drive *across* the bridge and go *down* the avenue *past* three stoplights.

SOME COMMON PREPOSITIONS

about	below	in	over
above	beside	inside	past
after	between	into	since
against	beyond	near	through
along	by	of	under
among	down	off	until
around	during	on	up
at	for	onto	with
before	from	out	

SOME COMPOUND PREPOSITIONS

according to	in addition to	instead of
as well as	in front of	next to
because of	in place of	out of
except for	in spite of	with regard to

Research for this book shows that many writers—including native speakers of English—have trouble choosing appropriate prepositions. If you are not sure which preposition to use, consult your dictionary, or use search engines or online databases to choose one.

33g Conjunctions

Conjunctions connect words or groups of words to each other and tell something about the relationship between these words.

Coordinating conjunctions

Coordinating conjunctions (27a) join equivalent structures, such as two or more nouns, pronouns, verbs, adjectives, adverbs, prepositions, conjunctions, phrases, or clauses.

▶ A strong *but* warm breeze blew across the desert.

▶ Please print *or* type the information on the application form.

▶ Taiwo worked two shifts today, *so* she is tired tonight.

COORDINATING CONJUNCTIONS

and	but	for	nor	or	so	yet

Correlative conjunctions

Correlative conjunctions join equal elements, and they come in pairs.

▶ *Both* Bechtel *and* Kaiser submitted bids on the project.

▶ Maisha *not only* sent a card *but also* visited me in the hospital.

CORRELATIVE CONJUNCTIONS

both . . . and	just as . . . so	not only . . . but also
either . . . or	neither . . . nor	whether . . . or

Subordinating conjunctions

Subordinating conjunctions (27b) introduce adverb clauses and signal the relationship between the adverb clause and another clause, usually an independent clause. For instance, in the following sentence, the subordinating conjunction *while* signals a time relationship, letting us know that the two events in the sentence happened simultaneously:

▶ **Sweat ran down my face *while* I frantically searched for my child.**

SOME COMMON SUBORDINATING CONJUNCTIONS

after	once	until
although	since	when
as	so that	where
because	than	whether
before	that	while
how	though	who
if	unless	why

Conjunctive adverbs

Conjunctive adverbs connect independent clauses and often act as transitional expressions (44e) that show how the second clause relates to the first clause. As their name suggests, conjunctive adverbs can act as both adverbs and conjunctions because they modify the second clause in addition to connecting it to the preceding clause.

▶ **The cider tasted bitter; *however*, each of us drank a tall glass of it.**
▶ **The cider tasted bitter; each of us, *however*, drank a tall glass of it.**

SOME CONJUNCTIVE ADVERBS

also	however	nevertheless	still
besides	indeed	next	then
certainly	instead	now	therefore
finally	meanwhile	otherwise	thus
furthermore	moreover	similarly	undoubtedly

33h Interjections

Interjections express surprise or emotion: *oh, ouch, hey.* Interjections often stand alone. Even when they are included in a sentence, they do not relate grammatically to the rest of the sentence.

▶ *Hey,* **no one suggested that we would find an easy solution to this problem.**

34 Parts of Sentences

The grammar of your first language comes to you almost automatically. Listen in on a conversation between two four-year-olds:

AUDREY: My new bike that Aunt A got me has a red basket and a loud horn, and I love it.

LILA: Can I ride it?

AUDREY: Yes, as soon as I take a turn.

This simple conversation features sophisticated grammar—the subordination of one clause to another, a compound object, and a number of adjectives—used effortlessly. If you are like many English speakers, you may never really have reflected on the details of how the language works. Paying close attention to how you put sentences together can help you understand the choices available to you whenever you write.

The basic grammar of sentences

A sentence is a grammatically complete group of words that expresses a thought. Words in a sentence can be identified by parts of speech (see Chapter 33), but you should also understand how words and phrases function in sentences.

Subjects and predicates

To be grammatically complete, a sentence must contain both a subject, which identifies what the sentence is about, and a predicate, which says or asks something about the subject or tells the subject to do something.

SUBJECT	PREDICATE
I	have a dream.
The rain in Spain	stays mainly in the plain.
Skill as an archer	makes Julia a formidable opponent.

Talking the Talk

Understanding Grammatical Terms

"I never learned any grammar." You may lack *conscious* knowledge of grammar and grammatical terms (and if so, you are not alone — American students today rarely study English grammar). But you probably understand the ideas that grammatical terms such as *auxiliary verb* and *direct object* represent, even if the terms themselves are unfamiliar. Brushing up on the terms commonly used to talk about grammar will make it easier for you and your instructor to share a common language when you discuss the best ways to get your ideas across clearly.

Some sentences contain only a one-word predicate with an implied subject; for example, *Stop!* is a complete sentence, with the unspoken subject *you*. Most sentences, however, contain some words that expand upon the basic subject and predicate.

The central elements of subjects and predicates are <u>nouns</u> (33b) and <u>verbs</u> (33a).

```
 ┌──── SUBJECT ────┬──── PREDICATE ────┐
         NOUN   VERB
```
▶ A solitary <u>figure</u> <u>waited</u> on the platform.

```
 ┌──── SUBJECT ────┬──────── PREDICATE ────────┐
 NOUN                  VERB
```
▶ <u>Skill</u> as an archer <u>makes</u> Julia a formidable opponent.

Conventional English word order

Multilingual

In general, subjects, verbs, and objects must all be placed in specific positions within a sentence.

SUBJECT VERB OBJECT   ADVERB
▶ Mario left Venice reluctantly.

The only word in this sentence that you can move is the adverb *reluctantly* (*Mario reluctantly left Venice* or *Reluctantly, Mario left Venice*). The three key elements of subject, verb, and object rarely move out of their normal order.

Quick Help

Basic Sentence Patterns

1. Subject / verb

   ┌ **S** ┐┌ **V** ┐
   ► Babies drool.

2. Subject / verb / subject complement

   ┌ **S** ┐┌ **V** ┐┌ **SC** ┐
   ► Babies smell sweet.

3. Subject / verb / direct object

   ┌ **S** ┐┌ **V** ┐┌ **DO** ┐
   ► Babies drink milk.

4. Subject / verb / indirect object / direct object

   ┌ **S** ┐┌ **V** ┐┌───── **IO** ─────┐┌── **DO** ──┐
   ► Babies give grandparents pleasure.

5. Subject / verb / direct object / object complement

   ┌ **S** ┐┌ **V** ┐┌ **DO** ┐┌ **OC** ┐
   ► Babies keep parents awake.

Sentence patterns

Knowing a word's part of speech (see Chapter 33) helps you understand how to use it, but you also have to look at the part it plays in a particular sentence. In the following sentences, the noun *description* plays different roles:

> SUBJECT
> ► This *description* conveys the ecology of the Everglades.

> DIRECT OBJECT
> ► I read a *description* of the ecology of the Everglades.

In the first sentence, *description* serves as the subject of the verb *conveys*, while in the second it serves as the direct object of the verb *read*.

34b Subjects

The subject of a sentence identifies what the sentence is about. The simple subject consists of one or more nouns (33b) or pronouns (33c); the complete subject consists of the simple subject with all its modifiers.

▶ <u>Baseball</u> is a summer game.

┌── **COMPLETE SUBJECT** ──┐
▶ Sailing over the fence, the <u>ball</u> crashed through Mr. Wilson's window.

┌── **COMPLETE SUBJECT** ──┐
▶ <u>Those</u> who sit in the bleachers have the most fun.

A compound subject contains two or more <u>simple subjects</u> joined with a coordinating conjunction (*and, but, or*) or a correlative conjunction (*both . . . and, either . . . or, neither . . . nor, not only . . . but also*). (See 33g.)

▶ <u>Baseball</u> *and* <u>softball</u> developed from cricket.
▶ *Both* <u>baseball</u> *and* <u>softball</u> developed from cricket.

Subject positions

The subject usually comes before the predicate (34a), but sometimes writers reverse this order to achieve a particular effect.

▶ Up to the plate stepped *Casey*.

In questions, the subject appears between the helping verb and the main verb.

▶ Can *statistics* lie?
▶ How did the *manager* turn these players into a winning team?

In sentences beginning with *there* or *here* followed by a form of the verb *be*, the subject always follows the verb. *There* and *here* are never the subject.

▶ There was no *joy* in Mudville.

Explicit subjects

Multilingual

While many languages can omit a sentence subject, English very rarely allows this. You might write *Responsible for analyzing data* on a résumé, but in most varieties of spoken and written English, you must state the subject explicitly. In fact, with only a few exceptions, all clauses in English must have an explicit subject.

it
▶ They took the Acela Express to Boston because ⌃ was fast.

English even requires a kind of "dummy" subject to fill the subject position in certain kinds of sentences.

▶ *It* is raining.
▶ *There* is a strong wind.

Imperative sentences (34f), which express requests or commands, are an exception to the rule of explicit subjects; the subject *you* is usually implied rather than stated.

▶ *(You)* Keep your eye on the ball.

34c Predicates

In addition to a subject, every sentence has a predicate, which asserts or asks something about the subject or tells the subject to do something. The key word of most predicates is a verb. The simple predicate of a sentence consists of the main verb and any auxiliaries; the complete predicate includes the simple predicate and any modifiers of the verb and any objects or complements (34a) and their modifiers.

```
     ┌─── COMPLETE PREDICATE ───┐
```
▶ Both of us are planning to major in history.

A compound predicate contains two or more verbs that have the same subject, usually joined by a coordinating or a correlative conjunction (33g).

▶ Omar shut the book, put it back on the shelf, *and* sighed.

On the basis of how they function in predicates, verbs can be divided into three categories: linking, transitive, and intransitive.

Linking verbs

A linking verb connects a subject with a subject complement (sc), a word or word group that identifies or describes the subject.

```
     S      V   ┌──── SC ────┐
```
▶ Christine *is* an excellent teacher.

```
     S  V   SC
```
▶ She *is* patient.

A subject complement can be either a noun or pronoun (*teacher*) or an adjective (*patient*).

The forms of *be*, when used as main verbs, are common linking verbs. Other verbs, such as *appear, become, feel, grow, look, make, seem, smell,* and *sound*, can also function as linking verbs, depending on the sense of the sentence.

```
     ┌──── S ────┐   V     SC
```
▶ The neighborhood *looked* prosperous.

Transitive verbs

Multilingual

A transitive verb expresses action that is directed toward a noun or pronoun called the *direct object* (DO).

    S   V   ⌐——— DO ———⌐
▶ Sven *peeled* all the rutabagas.

Here, the subject and verb do not express a complete thought. The direct object completes the thought by saying *what* he peeled.

    A direct object may be followed by an object complement (OC), a word or word group that describes or identifies the direct object. Object complements may be adjectives, as in the first example below, or nouns, as in the second example.

    S V ⌐——————— DO ——————⌐⌐—— OC ——⌐
▶ I *find* cell-phone conversations in restaurants very annoying.

    S   V   DO   ⌐—— OC ——⌐
▶ Alana *considers* Keyshawn her best friend.

Some transitive verbs may also be followed by an indirect object (IO), which is the recipient of the direct object. The indirect object tells to whom or what, or for whom or what, the verb does its action.

  ⌐————— S —————⌐ V IO ⌐——— DO ———⌐
▶ The sound of the traffic *gave* me a splitting headache.

    Transitive verbs typically require you to state the object explicitly. For example, you can't just say *Give!* even if it is clear that you mean *Give me the phone.*

Intransitive verbs

Multilingual

An intransitive verb does not have a direct object.

  ⌐—— S ——⌐   V
▶ The Red Sox *persevered*.

  ⌐—— S ——⌐ V
▶ Their fans *watched* anxiously.

The verb *persevered* has no object (it makes no sense to ask, *persevered what?*), and the verb *watched* is directed toward an object that is implied but not expressed.

    Some verbs that express action can be only transitive or only intransitive, but most can be used either way, with or without a direct object.

  ⌐— S —⌐ V ⌐ DO ⌐
▶ The butler *opened* the door. [transitive]

  ⌐— S —⌐ V
▶ The door *opened* silently. [intransitive]

34d Phrases

A phrase is a group of words that lacks a subject or a predicate or both.

Noun phrases

Made up of a noun and all its modifiers, a noun phrase can function in a sentence as a subject, object, or complement.

▶ *Delicious, gooey peanut butter* is surprisingly healthful.
     ┌──────── SUBJECT ────────┐

▶ I craved *a green salad with plenty of fresh vegetables.*
     ┌──────────── OBJECT ────────────┐

▶ Soup is *a popular lunch.*
    ┌ COMPLEMENT ┐

Verb phrases

A main verb and its auxiliary verbs make up a verb phrase, which can function in a sentence only as a verb.

▶ Frank *can swim* for a long time.

▶ His headaches *might have been caused* by tension.

Prepositional phrases

A prepositional phrase begins with a preposition and includes a noun or pronoun (the object of the preposition) and any modifiers of the object. Prepositional phrases usually function as adjectives or adverbs.

▶ Our house *in Maine* was a cabin.
     ADJECTIVE

▶ *From Cadillac Mountain*, you can see the northern lights.
  ┌──── ADVERB ────┐

Verbal phrases

Verbals look like verbs, but they function as nouns, adjectives, or adverbs. There are three kinds of verbals: participles, gerunds, and infinitives.

PARTICIPLES AND PARTICIPIAL PHRASES

The present participle is the *-ing* form of a verb (*spinning*). The past participle of most verbs ends in *-ed* (*accepted*), but some verbs have an irregular past participle (*worn*, *frozen*). Participles function as adjectives (39a).

▶ A kiss awakened the *dreaming* princess.

▶ The cryptographers deciphered the *hidden* meaning in the message.

Participial phrases, which also act as adjectives, consist of a present or past participle and any modifiers, objects, or complements.

▶ *Irritated by the delay*, Luisa complained.

▶ A dog *howling at the moon* kept me awake.

GERUNDS AND GERUND PHRASES

The gerund has the same *-ing* form as the present participle but functions as a noun.

    SUBJECT
▶ *Writing* takes practice.

    DIRECT OBJECT
▶ The organization promotes *recycling*.

Gerund phrases, which function as nouns, consist of a gerund and any modifiers, objects, or complements.

    ⌐——— SUBJECT ———¬
▶ *Opening their eyes to the problem* was not easy.

    ⌐——— DIRECT OBJECT ———¬
▶ They suddenly heard *a loud wailing from the sandbox.*

INFINITIVES AND INFINITIVE PHRASES

The infinitive is the *to* form of a verb (*to dream*, *to be*). An infinitive can function as a noun, an adjective, or an adverb.

    ⌐ NOUN ¬
▶ She wanted *to write.*

    ADJECTIVE
▶ They had no more time *to waste.*

    ⌐ ADVERB ¬
▶ The corporation was ready *to expand.*

Infinitive phrases consist of an infinitive and any modifiers, objects, or complements. Like infinitives, they function as nouns, adjectives, or adverbs.

▶ My goal is *to be a biology teacher.* — NOUN

▶ A party *to end the semester* would be a good idea. — ADJECTIVE

▶ *To perfect a draft,* always proofread carefully. — ADVERB

INFINITIVE-GERUND CONFUSION

Multilingual

In general, infinitives indicate intentions, desires, or expectations, and gerunds indicate facts. Knowing whether to use an infinitive or a gerund in a sentence can be challenging.

Infinitives to state intentions

▶ Kumar *expected to get* a good job after graduation.

▶ Last year, Fatima *decided to change* majors.

Verbs such as *expect* and *decide*, which indicate intentions, must always be followed by an infinitive.

Gerunds to state facts

▶ Jerzy *enjoys going* to the theater.

▶ Kim *appreciated getting* a card from Sean.

Verbs like *enjoy* and *appreciate*, which indicate that something has actually happened, can be followed only by gerunds, not by infinitives.

Other rules and guidelines A few verbs can be followed by either an infinitive or a gerund. With some, such as *begin* and *continue*, the choice doesn't affect the meaning. With others, however, the difference is important.

▶ Carlos was working as a medical technician, but he *stopped to study* English.

The infinitive shows that Carlos quit because he intended to study English.

▶ When Carlos left the United States, he *stopped studying* English.

The gerund indicates that Carlos gave up his English studies when he left.

You can use only a gerund — never an infinitive — right after a preposition.

▶ This fruit is safe for ~~to eat.~~ ^*eating.*^

▶ This fruit is safe ~~for~~ to eat.

▶ This fruit is safe for ^*us*^ to eat.

Consult a learner's dictionary for more information on whether to follow a verb with an infinitive or a gerund.

Absolute phrases

An absolute phrase usually includes a noun or pronoun and a participle. It modifies an entire sentence rather than a particular word and is usually set off from the rest of the sentence with commas (44c).

▶ I stood on the deck, *the wind whipping my hair.*
▶ *My fears laid to rest,* I set off on my first solo flight.

Appositive phrases

An appositive phrase is a noun phrase that renames the noun or pronoun that immediately precedes it (44c).

▶ The report, *a hefty three-volume work,* included more than ninety recommendations.
▶ We had a single desire, *to change the administration's policies.*

34e Clauses

A clause is a group of words containing a subject and a predicate. There are two kinds of clauses: independent and dependent. Independent clauses (also known as main clauses) can stand alone as complete sentences.

▶ The window is open.

Pairs of independent clauses may be joined with a comma and a coordinating conjunction (*and, but, for, nor, or, so, yet*).

▶ The window is open, so the room feels cool.

Like independent clauses, <u>dependent clauses</u> (also referred to as subordinate clauses) contain a subject and a predicate. They cannot stand alone as complete sentences, however, for they begin with a subordinating word — a subordinating conjunction (33g) or a relative pronoun (33c) — that connects them to an independent clause.

▶ <u>Because the window is open</u>, <u>the room feels cool</u>.

The subordinating conjunction *because* transforms the independent clause *the window is open* into a dependent clause. In doing so, it indicates a causal relationship between the two clauses.

Dependent clauses function as nouns, adjectives, or adverbs.

Noun clauses

Multilingual

Noun clauses are always contained within another clause. They usually begin with a relative pronoun (*that, which, what, who, whom, whose, whatever, whoever, whomever, whichever*) or with *when, where, whether, why,* or *how.*

┌──────── SUBJECT ────────┐
▶ *What the archeologists found* was startling.

┌──────── DIRECT OBJECT ────────┐
▶ Rita explained *that the research was necessary.*

┌──────── SUBJECT COMPLEMENT ────────┐
▶ The mystery was *why the ancient city had been abandoned.*

┌──────── OBJECT OF PREPOSITION ────────┐
▶ They were looking for *whatever information was available.*

Like a noun, a noun clause is an integral part of the sentence; for example, in the second sentence the independent clause is not just *Rita explained* but *Rita explained that the research was necessary.* This complex sentence is built out of two sentences; one of them (*The research was necessary*) is embedded in the other (*Rita explained [something]*). The relative pronoun *that* introduces the noun clause that is the object of *explained.*

A *that* clause can serve as the subject of a sentence, but the effect is very formal.

┌──────── SUBJECT ────────┐
▶ *That the city had been abandoned* was surprising.

In less formal contexts, and in spoken English, a long noun clause is usually moved to the end of the sentence and replaced with the "dummy subject" *it.*

▶ *It* was surprising *that the city had been abandoned.*

Adjective clauses

Multilingual

Adjective clauses modify nouns and pronouns in another clause. Usually, they immediately follow the words they modify.

► The surgery, *which took three hours*, was a complete success.

► It was performed by the surgeon *who had developed the procedure.*

► The hospital was the one *where I was born.*

Sometimes the relative pronoun introducing an adjective clause may be omitted, as in the following examples:

► That is one book [*that*] *I intend to read.*

► The company [*that*] *the family had invested in* grew rapidly.

To see how the adjective clause fits into this sentence, rewrite it as two sentences: *The company grew rapidly. The family had invested in it.* To make *The family had invested in it* a relative clause, change *it* to a relative pronoun and move it to the beginning of the clause: *The family had invested in it* becomes *that the family had invested in.* Then position the new clause after the word it describes (in this case, *company*): *The company that the family had invested in grew rapidly.*

In very formal writing, when the pronoun you are changing is the object of a preposition, select *which* (or *whom* for people) and move the whole prepositional phrase to the beginning of the clause: *The company in which the family had invested grew rapidly.* In many American English contexts, however, such constructions may sound too formal, so consider your audience carefully.

Adverb clauses

Adverb clauses modify verbs, adjectives, or other adverbs. They begin with a subordinating conjunction (33g). Like adverbs, they usually tell when, where, why, how, or to what extent.

► We hiked *where few other hikers went.*

► My backpack felt heavier *than it ever had.*

► Climbers ascend Mount Everest *because it is there.*

34f Types of sentences

Just like words, sentences can be categorized both grammatically and functionally.

Grammatical sentence structure

Grammatically, sentences may be classified as simple, compound, complex, or compound-complex.

SIMPLE SENTENCES

A simple sentence consists of one independent clause and no dependent clause. The subject or the verb, or both, may be compound.

┌──────────── INDEPENDENT CLAUSE ────────────┐
▶ The trailer is surrounded by a wooden deck.

┌──────────────────── INDEPENDENT CLAUSE ────────────────────┐
▶ Pompeii and Herculaneum disappeared under tons of lava and ash.

COMPOUND SENTENCES

A compound sentence consists of two or more independent clauses and no dependent clause. The clauses may be joined by a comma and a coordinating conjunction (33g) or by a semicolon.

┌──────── INDEPENDENT CLAUSE ────────┐   ┌ INDEPENDENT CLAUSE ┐
▶ Occasionally a car goes up the dirt trail, and dust flies everywhere.

┌──── INDEPENDENT CLAUSE ────┐ ┌──── INDEPENDENT CLAUSE ────┐
▶ Alberto is obsessed with soccer; he eats, breathes, and lives the game.

COMPLEX SENTENCES

A complex sentence consists of one independent clause and at least one dependent clause.

┌INDEPENDENT CLAUSE┐┌──── DEPENDENT CLAUSE ────┐
▶ Many people believe that anyone can earn a living.

┌──── DEPENDENT CLAUSE ────┐ ┌──── INDEPENDENT CLAUSE ────┐
▶ As I awaited my interview, I sat with another candidate
┌ DEPENDENT CLAUSE ┐
who smiled nervously.

COMPOUND-COMPLEX SENTENCES

A compound-complex sentence consists of two or more independent clauses and at least one dependent clause.

INDEPENDENT CLAUSE ⌐ DEPENDENT CLAUSE ⌐   INDEPENDENT CLAUSE
▶ I complimented Luis when he finished the job, and he seemed pleased.

⌐ INDEPENDENT CLAUSE ⌐   ⌐ INDEPENDENT CLAUSE ⌐
▶ The actors performed well, but the audience hated the play,
⌐————— DEPENDENT CLAUSE —————⌐
which was confusing and far too long.

Sentence function

In terms of function, sentences can be declarative (making a statement), interrogative (asking a question), imperative (giving a command), or exclamatory (expressing strong feeling).

DECLARATIVE	Willy sings with the Grace Church Boys' Choir.
INTERROGATIVE	How long has he sung with them?
IMPERATIVE	Comb his hair before the performance starts.
EXCLAMATORY	What voices those boys have!

35   Verbs and Verb Phrases

Restaurant menus often spotlight verbs in action. One famous place in Boston, for instance, offers to bake, broil, pan-fry, deep-fry, poach, sauté, fricassée, blacken, or scallop any of the fish entrées on its menu. To someone ordering — or cooking — at this restaurant, the important distinctions lie entirely in the verbs.

When used skillfully, verbs can be the heartbeat of prose, moving it along, enlivening it, carrying its action. (See Chapter 37 for advice on subject-verb agreement.)

Quick Help

Editing the Verbs in Your Own Writing

- Check verb endings that cause you trouble. (35a and c)
- Double-check forms of *lie* and *lay*, *sit* and *set*, *rise* and *raise*. See that the words you use are appropriate for your meaning. (35d)
- If you are writing about a literary work, remember to refer to the action in the work in the present tense. (35e)
- If you have problems with verb tenses, use the guidelines in 35e to check your verbs.
- Check all uses of the passive voice for appropriateness. (35g)
- Check all verbs used to introduce quotations, paraphrases, and summaries. (12b) If you rely on *say*, *write*, and other very general verbs, try substituting more vivid, specific verbs (*claim*, *insist*, and *wonder*, for instance).

35a   Understand the five forms of verbs.

Except for *be*, all English verbs have five forms.

BASE FORM	PAST TENSE	PAST PARTICIPLE	PRESENT PARTICIPLE	-S FORM
talk	talked	talked	talking	talks
adore	adored	adored	adoring	adores

BASE FORM	We often *go* to Legal Sea Foods.
PAST TENSE	Grandpa always *ordered* bluefish.
PAST PARTICIPLE	Grandma *has tried* the oyster stew.
PRESENT PARTICIPLE	Juanita *is getting* the shrimp platter.
-S FORM	The chowder *needs* salt and pepper.

-s *and* -es *endings*

Except with *be* and *have*, the *-s* form consists of the base form plus *-s* or *-es*. In standard English, this form indicates action in the present for third-person singular subjects. All singular nouns; the personal pronouns *he*, *she*, and *it*; and many other pronouns (such as *this*, *anyone*, *everything*, and *someone*) are third-person singular.

	SINGULAR	PLURAL
FIRST PERSON	I wish	we wish
SECOND PERSON	you wish	you wish
THIRD PERSON	he/she/it *wishes*	they wish
	Joe *wishes*	children wish
	someone *wishes*	many wish

For a discussion of using plural *they* with a singular noun or pronoun, see 38f.

Forms of be

Be has three forms in the present tense and two in the past tense.

BASE FORM	be
PAST PARTICIPLE	been
PRESENT PARTICIPLE	being
PRESENT TENSE	I *am*, he/she/it *is*, we/you/they *are*
PAST TENSE	I/he/she/it *was*, we/you/they *were*

35b Form verb phrases appropriately.

English sentences must have at least one verb or verb phrase that is not simply an infinitive (*to write*), a gerund (*writing*), or a participle (*written*) without any helping verbs. Use helping (also called *auxiliary*) verbs with a main verb—a base form, present participle, or past participle—to create verb phrases.

Talking about Style

Everyday Use of *Be*

Spoken varieties of English may follow rules for the use of *be* that differ from the rules of most academic English. For instance, you may have heard speakers say "She ain't here now" (instead of *She isn't here now*) or "He be at work every Saturday" (instead of *He is at work every Saturday*). You may sometimes want to quote dialogue featuring such spoken usages when you write or to use what linguists refer to as "habitual *be*" in writing to particular audiences. In most academic and professional writing, however, you will want to follow the conventions of academic English. (For help with using varieties of English, see Chapter 23.)

The most common auxiliaries are forms of *be*, *have*, and *do*. *Have* is used to form perfect tenses that indicate completed action (35e); *be* is used with progressive forms that show continuing action (35e) and to form the passive voice (35g).

▶ The engineers *have considered* possible problems. [completed action]
▶ The college *is building* a new dormitory. [continuing action]
▶ The activists *were warned* to stay away. [passive voice]

As an auxiliary, *do* is used to show emphasis, to form questions, and to make negative statements.

▶ I *do respect* my opponent's viewpoint. [emphasis]
▶ *Do* you *know* the answer? [question]
▶ He *does* not *like* wearing a tie. [negative statement]

Helping (auxiliary) verb order

Multilingual

Verb phrases can be built up out of a main verb and one or more auxiliaries.

▶ Immigration figures *have been rising* every year.

Verb phrases have strict rules of order. The only permissible change to word order is to form a question, moving the first auxiliary to the beginning of the sentence: *Have immigration figures been rising every year?*
    When two or more auxiliaries appear in a verb phrase, they must follow a particular order based on the type of auxiliary:

1. A modal (*can, could, may, might, must, shall, should, will, would*, or *ought to*)
2. A form of *have* used to indicate a perfect tense (35e)
3. A form of *be* used to indicate a progressive tense (35e)
4. A form of *be* used to indicate the passive voice, followed by a past participle (35g)

▶ The invitation *must have been sent* through the mail.

Modals

Multilingual

The modal auxiliaries — *can, could, may, might, shall, should, will, would, must*, and *ought to* — indicate future action, possibility, necessity, or obligation.

▶ They *will explain* the procedure. [future action]
▶ You *can see* three states from the top of the mountain. [possibility]
▶ Students *must manage* their time wisely. [necessity]
▶ They *should examine* the results of the study. [obligation]

No verb phrase can include more than one modal.

> ▶ Jackie will ~~can~~ speak Czech much better soon.
>
> be able to

USING MODALS FOR REQUESTS OR INSTRUCTIONS

Modals are often used in requests and instructions. If you use a modal such as *could* or *would*, you are politely acknowledging that the person you are talking to may be unable or unwilling to do what you ask.

> ▶ *Could* you bring me a pillow?

Modals appearing in instructions usually indicate whether an action is suggested or required:

1. You *can* / You *may* post your work online. [Posting online is allowed.]
2. You *should* submit your report electronically. [Posting online is recommended or required.]
3. You *must* / You *will* submit your report electronically. [Posting online is required.]

USING MODALS TO SHOW DOUBT OR CERTAINTY

Modals can also indicate how confident the writer is about his or her claims. Using *may* or *might* results in a tentative suggestion, while *will* indicates complete confidence:

> ▶ The study *might help explain* the findings of previous research.
> ▶ The study *will help explain* the findings of previous research.

Phrases with modals

Multilingual

Use the base form of a verb after a modal.

> ▶ Alice *can read* Latin.
> ▶ Sanjay *should have studied* for the test.

In some languages, modals like *can* and *must* are followed by an infinitive (*to* + base form). In English, only the base form follows a modal.

> ▶ Alice can ~~to~~ read Latin.

Notice that a modal auxiliary never changes form to agree with the subject.

For the most part, modals refer to present or future time. When you want to use a modal to refer to the past, you follow the modal with a perfect form of the main verb (see 35e).

▶ If you have a fever, you *should see* a doctor.

▶ If you had a fever, you *should have seen* a doctor.

The modal *must* is a special case. The past tense of *must* is *had to* or *needed to.*

▶ You *must renew* your visa by the end of this week.

▶ You *had to renew* / You *needed to renew* your visa by last Friday.

Note, too, the different meanings of the negative forms *must not* and *don't have to.*

▶ You *must not go* to the party. [You are forbidden to go.]

▶ You *don't have to go* to the party. [You are not required to go, but you may.]

35c Use appropriate forms of irregular verbs.

A verb is regular when its past tense and past participle are formed by adding -*ed* or -*d* to the base form.

BASE FORM	PAST TENSE	PAST PARTICIPLE
love	loved	loved
honor	honored	honored
obey	obeyed	obeyed

A verb is irregular when it does not follow the -*ed* or -*d* pattern. If you are not sure whether a verb form is regular or irregular, or what the correct form is, consult the following list or a dictionary. Dictionaries list any irregular forms under the entry for the base form.

Some common irregular verbs

BASE FORM	PAST TENSE	PAST PARTICIPLE
be	was/were	been
become	became	become
begin	began	begun
bite	bit	bitten, bit
break	broke	broken
bring	brought	brought
build	built	built
buy	bought	bought
choose	chose	chosen

BASE FORM	PAST TENSE	PAST PARTICIPLE
come	came	come
cost	cost	cost
do	did	done
draw	drew	drawn
dream	dreamed, dreamt	dreamed, dreamt
drive	drove	driven
eat	ate	eaten
fall	fell	fallen
feel	felt	felt
fight	fought	fought
find	found	found
forget	forgot	forgotten, forgot
get	got	gotten, got
give	gave	given
go	went	gone
grow	grew	grown
hang (suspend)[1]	hung	hung
have	had	had
hear	heard	heard
hide	hid	hidden
know	knew	known
lay	laid	laid
lead	led	led
leave	left	left
lie (recline)[2]	lay	lain
lose	lost	lost
make	made	made
mean	meant	meant
prove	proved	proved, proven
read	read	read
ride	rode	ridden
rise	rose	risen
run	ran	run

---

[1]*Hang* meaning "execute by hanging" is regular: *hang, hanged, hanged.*
[2]*Lie* meaning "tell a falsehood" is regular: *lie, lied, lied.*

BASE FORM	PAST TENSE	PAST PARTICIPLE
say	said	said
see	saw	seen
send	sent	sent
shoot	shot	shot
show	showed	showed, shown
sing	sang	sung
sit	sat	sat
sleep	slept	slept
speak	spoke	spoken
spend	spent	spent
stand	stood	stood
steal	stole	stolen
strike	struck	struck, stricken
take	took	taken
tear	tore	torn
throw	threw	thrown
wake	woke, waked	waked, woken
write	wrote	written

35d   Choose between *lie* and *lay*, *sit* and *set*, *rise* and *raise*.

These pairs of verbs cause confusion because both verbs in each pair have similar-sounding forms and related meanings. In each pair, one of the verbs is transitive, meaning that it is followed by a direct object (*I laid the cloth on the table*). The other is intransitive, meaning that it does not have an object (*He lay on the floor when his back ached*). The best way to avoid confusing these verbs is to memorize their forms and meanings.

BASE FORM	PAST TENSE	PAST PARTICIPLE	PRESENT PARTICIPLE	-S FORM
lie (recline)	lay	lain	lying	lies
lay (put)	laid	laid	laying	lays
sit (be seated)	sat	sat	sitting	sits
set (put)	set	set	setting	sets
rise (get up)	rose	risen	rising	rises
raise (lift)	raised	raised	raising	raises

lie

▶ The doctor asked the patient to ~~lay~~ on his side.
      ^

set

▶ Jason ~~sat~~ the vase on the table.
   ^

rose

▶ Sami ~~raised~~ up in bed and glared at us.
   ^

35e Use verb tenses appropriately.

Multilingual

Verb tenses show when the action takes place. The three simple tenses are the present tense, the past tense, and the future tense.

PRESENT TENSE	I *ask*, I *write*
PAST TENSE	I *asked*, I *wrote*
FUTURE TENSE	I *will ask*, I *will write*

More complex aspects of time are expressed through progressive, perfect, and perfect progressive forms of the simple tenses.

PRESENT PROGRESSIVE	I *am asking*, I *am writing*
PAST PROGRESSIVE	I *was asking*, I *was writing*
FUTURE PROGRESSIVE	I *will be asking*, I *will be writing*
PRESENT PERFECT	I *have asked*, I *have written*
PAST PERFECT	I *had asked*, I *had written*
FUTURE PERFECT	I *will have asked*, I *will have written*
PRESENT PERFECT PROGRESSIVE	I *have been asking*, I *have been writing*
PAST PERFECT PROGRESSIVE	I *had been asking*, I *had been writing*
FUTURE PERFECT PROGRESSIVE	I *will have been asking*, I *will have been writing*

The simple tenses locate an action only within the three basic time frames of present, past, and future. Progressive forms express continuing actions; perfect forms express actions completed before another action or time in the present, past, or future; perfect progressive forms express actions that continue up to some point in the present, past, or future.

Present tense

SIMPLE PRESENT

Use the simple present to indicate actions occurring now and those occurring habitually.

▶ I *eat* breakfast every day at 8:00 AM.

▶ Love *conquers* all.

Use the simple present when writing about action in literary works.

▶ *Moby Dick*'s Ishmael slowly ~~realized~~ ^{realizes} all that ~~was~~ ^{is} at stake in the search for the white whale.

General truths or scientific facts should be in the simple present, even when the predicate of the sentence is in the past tense.

▶ Pasteur demonstrated that his boiling process ~~made~~ ^{makes} milk safe.

When you are quoting, summarizing, or paraphrasing a work, in general use the present tense.

▶ Keith Walters ~~wrote~~ ^{writes} that the "reputed consequences and promised blessings of literacy are legion."

But in an essay using APA (American Psychological Association) style, report your experiments or another researcher's work in the past tense (*wrote, noted*) or the present perfect (*has reported*). (See Chapter 58.)

▶ Comer (1995) ~~notes~~ ^{noted} that protesters who deprive themselves of food are seen as "caring, sacrificing, even heroic" (p. 5).

PRESENT PROGRESSIVE

Use the present progressive form when an action is in progress now. The present progressive uses a present form of *be* (*am, is, are*) and the *-ing* form of the main verb.

▶ He *is directing* a new film.

In contrast, use the simple present tense for actions that frequently occur in the present, but that are not necessarily happening now.

    SIMPLE PRESENT   PRESENT PROGRESSIVE
▶ My sister *drives* a bus. She *is taking* a vacation now.

With an appropriate expression of time, you can use the present progressive to indicate a scheduled event in the future.

▶ We *are having* friends over for dinner tomorrow night.

Some verbs are rarely used in progressive forms in formal writing. These verbs are said to express unchanging conditions or mental states: *believe, belong, hate, know, like, love, need, own, resemble, understand.* However, in spoken and informal written English, progressive forms like *I'm loving this* and *You're not understanding me correctly* are becoming increasingly common.

PRESENT PERFECT

The present perfect tense indicates actions begun in the past and either completed at some unspecified time in the past or continuing into the present. To form the present perfect, use a present form of *have* (*has, have*) and a perfect participle such as *talked.*

▶ Uncontrolled logging *has destroyed* many tropical forests.

PRESENT PERFECT PROGRESSIVE

Use the present perfect progressive form to indicate continuous actions begun in the past and continuing into the present. To form the present perfect progressive, use the present perfect form of *be* (*have been, has been*) and the *-ing* form of the main verb.

▶ Since September, he *has been writing* a novel in his spare time.

Past tense

In the past tense, you can use simple past, past progressive, past perfect, and past perfect progressive forms.

SIMPLE PAST

Use the simple past to indicate actions or conditions that occurred at a specific time and do not extend into the present.

▶ Germany *invaded* Poland on September 1, 1939.

PAST PROGRESSIVE

Use the past progressive when an action was in progress in the past. It is used relatively infrequently in English, and it focuses on duration or calls attention to a past action that went on at the same time as something else. The past progressive uses a past form of *be* (*was, were*) and the *-ing* form of the main verb.

▶ Lenin *was living* in exile in Zurich when the tsar was overthrown.

PAST PERFECT

Use the past perfect to indicate actions or conditions completed by a specific time in the past or before some other past action occurred. To form the past perfect, use *had* and a perfect participle such as *talked*.

▶ By the fourth century, Christianity *had become* the state religion.

PAST PERFECT PROGRESSIVE

Use the past perfect progressive form to indicate a continuing action or condition in the past that had already been happening when some other past action happened. (You will probably need the simple past tense for the other past action.) To form the past perfect progressive, use the past perfect form of *be* (*had been*) and the *-ing* form of the main verb.

▶ Carter *had been planning* a naval career until his father died.

Future tense

The future tense includes simple, progressive, perfect, and perfect progressive forms.

SIMPLE FUTURE

Use the simple future (*will* plus the base form of the verb) to indicate actions or conditions that have not yet begun.

▶ The exhibition *will come* to Washington in September.

FUTURE PROGRESSIVE

Use the future progressive to indicate continuing actions or conditions in the future. The future progressive uses the future form of *be* (*will be*) and the *-ing* form of the main verb.

▶ The loans *will be coming* due over the next two years.

FUTURE PERFECT

Use the future perfect to indicate actions or conditions that will be completed by or before some specified time in the future. To form the future perfect, use *will have* and a perfect participle such as *talked*.

▶ By next summer, she *will have published* the results of the research study.

FUTURE PERFECT PROGRESSIVE

Use the future perfect progressive to indicate continuing actions or conditions that will be completed by some specified time in the future. To form

> ## Quick Help
>
> ### Editing Verb Tenses
>
> If you have trouble with verb tenses in standard English, make a point of checking for these common trouble spots as you proofread.
>
> - Problems with verb form: writing *seen* for *saw*, for example, which confuses the past-participle and past-tense forms. (35c)
> - Problems with tense: using the simple past (*Uncle Charlie arrived*) when meaning requires the present perfect (*Uncle Charlie has arrived*). (35e)
> - Think carefully before using a regional or ethnic variety of English in situations calling for academic English. (See Chapter 23.)

the future perfect progressive, use the future perfect form of *be* (*will have been*) and the *-ing* form of the main verb.

▶ As of May 1, I *will have been living* in Tucson for five years.

35f Sequence verb tenses effectively.

Careful and accurate use of tenses is important for clear writing. Even the simplest narrative describes actions that take place at different times; when you use the appropriate tense for each action, readers can follow such time changes easily.

▶ By the time he *lent* her the money, she *had declared* bankruptcy.

Use an infinitive (*to* plus a base form: *to go*) to indicate actions occurring at the same time as or later than the action of the predicate verb.

▶ Each couple *hopes to win* the dance contest.

The hoping is in the present; the winning is in the future.

Use a present participle (base form plus *-ing*) to indicate actions occurring at the same time as that of the predicate verb.

▶ *Seeking to relieve unemployment,* Roosevelt established several public works programs.

A past participle or a present-perfect participle (*having* plus a past participle) indicates actions occurring before that of the predicate verb.

▶ ~~Flying~~ **Flown** to the front, the troops joined their hard-pressed comrades.

The past participle *flown* shows that the flying occurred before the joining.

▶ ~~Crushing~~ **Having crushed** all opposition at home, he launched a war of conquest.

He launched the war after he crushed the opposition.

One common error is to use *would* in both clauses of a sentence with an *if* clause. Use *would* only in one clause.

▶ If I ~~would have~~ **had** played harder, I would have won.

35g Use active and passive voice effectively.

Voice tells whether the subject is acting (*he questions us*) or being acted upon (*he is questioned*). When the subject is acting, the verb is in the active voice; when the subject is being acted upon, the verb is in the passive voice.

ACTIVE VOICE   The storm *uprooted* huge pine trees.

PASSIVE VOICE   Huge pine trees *were uprooted* by the storm.

The passive voice uses the appropriate form of the auxiliary verb *be* followed by the past participle of the main verb: *he is being questioned, he was questioned, he will be questioned, he has been questioned.*

While passive voice is often appropriate and necessary in scientific writing, most contemporary writers use the active voice as much as possible because it livens up their prose. Passive-voice verbs often make a passage hard to understand and remember. In addition, writers sometimes use the passive voice to avoid taking responsibility for what they have written. A government official who admits that "mistakes were made" skirts the question: who made them?

To shift a sentence from the passive to the active voice, make the performer of the action the subject of the sentence, and make the recipient of the action an object.

▶ ~~The~~ **My sister took the** prizewinning photograph. ~~was taken by my sister.~~

The passive voice can work well in some situations. Journalists often use the passive voice when the performer of an action is unknown or less important than the recipient.

▶ Colonel Muammar el-Qaddafi *was killed* during an uprising.

Much technical and scientific writing uses the passive voice to highlight what is being studied.

▶ The volunteers' food intake *was* closely *monitored.*

35h Understand mood and conditional sentences.

The mood of a verb indicates the attitude of the writer. The indicative mood states facts and opinions or asks questions. The imperative mood gives commands and instructions. The subjunctive mood (used mainly in clauses beginning with *that* or *if*) expresses wishes or conditions that are contrary to fact.

INDICATIVE	I *did* the right thing.
IMPERATIVE	*Do* the right thing.
SUBJUNCTIVE	If I *had done* the right thing, I would not be in trouble now.

Subjunctives

The present subjunctive uses the base form, no matter what the subject of the verb is.

▶ It is important that children *be* psychologically ready for a new sibling.

The past subjunctive is the same as the simple past except for the verb *be*, which uses *were* for all subjects.

▶ He spent money as if he *had* infinite credit.
▶ If the store *were* better located, it would attract more customers.

Subjunctive mood

Because the subjunctive can create a rather formal tone, many people today tend to substitute the indicative mood in informal conversation.

▶ If I *was* a better swimmer, I would try out for the team. [informal]

For academic and professional writing, use the subjunctive in the following contexts:

CLAUSES EXPRESSING A WISH
▶ He wished that his mother *were* still living nearby.

AS IF AND AS THOUGH CLAUSES

▶ He started down the trail as if he *were* walking on ice.

THAT CLAUSES EXPRESSING A REQUEST OR DEMAND

▶ The job requires that the employee *be* in good physical condition.

IF CLAUSES EXPRESSING A CONDITION THAT DOES NOT EXIST

▶ If the sale of tobacco *were* banned, tobacco companies would suffer.

One common error is to use *would* in both clauses. Use the subjunctive in the *if* clause and *would* in the main clause.

    had
▶ If I ~~would have~~ played harder, I would have won.
    ^

Conditional sentences

Multilingual

Sentences that use an *if* clause don't always require subjunctive forms. Each of the following conditional sentences makes different assumptions about whether or not the *if* clause is true.

▶ If you *practice* writing frequently, you *know* what your chief problems are.

This sentence assumes that what is stated in the *if* clause is probably true. Any tense that is appropriate may be used in both the *if* clause and the main clause.

▶ If you *practice* writing for the rest of this term, you *will understand* the process better.

This sentence makes a prediction. The main clause uses the future tense (*will understand*) or a modal that can indicate future time (*may understand*). The *if* clause uses the present tense.

▶ If you *practiced* writing every single day, it *would* eventually *seem* much easier to you.

This sentence indicates doubt. In the *if* clause, the verb is past subjunctive, even though it refers to future time. The main clause contains *would* + the base form of the main verb.

▶ If you *practiced* writing on Mars, you *would find* no one to read your work.

This sentence imagines an impossible situation. The past subjunctive is used in the *if* clause, although past time is not being referred to, and *would* + the base form is used in the main clause.

▶ If you *had practiced* writing in ancient Egypt, you *would have used* hieroglyphics.

This sentence shifts the impossibility to the past; obviously, you aren't going to find yourself in ancient Egypt. But a past impossibility demands a form that is "more past": the past perfect in the *if* clause and *would* + the perfect form of the verb in the main clause.

36   Nouns and Noun Phrases

Although all languages have nouns, English nouns differ from those in some other languages in various ways, such as their division into count and noncount nouns and the use of plural forms, articles, and other modifiers.

36a   Use count and noncount nouns appropriately.

Multilingual

Nouns in English can be either count nouns or noncount nouns. Count nouns refer to distinct individuals or things that can be directly counted: *a doctor, an egg, a child; doctors, eggs, children.* Noncount nouns refer to masses, collections, or ideas without distinct parts: *milk, rice, courage.* You cannot count noncount nouns except with a preceding phrase: *a glass of milk, three grains of rice, a little courage.*

Count nouns usually have singular and plural forms: *tree, trees.* Noncount nouns usually have only a singular form: *grass.*

COUNT	NONCOUNT
people (plural of person)	humanity
tables, chairs, beds	furniture
letters	mail
pebbles	gravel
suggestions	advice

Some English nouns can be either count or noncount, depending on their meaning.

COUNT	Before video games, children played with *marbles.*
NONCOUNT	The palace floor was made of *marble.*

When you learn a new noun in English, you need to determine whether it is count, noncount, or both. Many dictionaries provide this information.

36b Use determiners appropriately.

Multilingual

Determiners are words that identify or quantify a noun, such as <u>this</u> study, <u>all</u> people, <u>his</u> suggestions.

COMMON DETERMINERS

- the articles *a, an, the*
- *this, these, that, those*
- *my, our, your, his, her, its, their*
- possessive nouns and noun phrases (<u>*Sheila's*</u> paper, <u>*my friend's*</u> book)
- *whose, which, what*
- *all, both, each, every, some, any, either, no, neither, many, much, (a) few, (a) little, several, enough*
- the numerals *one, two,* etc.

These determiners . . .	. . . can precede these noun types	Examples
a, an, each, every	singular count nouns	*a* book *an* American *each* word *every* Buddhist
this, that	singular count nouns noncount nouns	*this* book *that* milk
(a) little, much	noncount nouns	*a little* milk *much* affection
some, any, enough	noncount nouns plural count nouns	*some* milk *any* fruit *enough* trouble *some* books *any* questions *enough* problems
the	singular count nouns plural count nouns noncount nouns	*the* doctor *the* doctors *the* information
these, those, (a) few, many, both, several	plural count nouns	*these* books *those* plans *a few* ideas *many* students *both* hands *several* trees

Determiners with singular count nouns

Every singular count noun must be preceded by a determiner. Place any adjectives between the determiner and the noun.

▶ <u>my</u> sister
      ^

▶ <u>the</u> growing population
      ^

▶ <u>that</u> old neighborhood
      ^

Determiners with plural or noncount nouns

Noncount and plural nouns sometimes have determiners and sometimes do not. For example, *This research is important* and *Research is important* are both acceptable but have different meanings.

36c Use articles conventionally.

Multilingual

Articles (*a, an,* and *the*) are a type of determiner. In English, choosing which article to use — or whether to use an article at all — can be challenging. Although there are exceptions, the following general guidelines can help.

The articles a or an

Use the indefinite articles *a* and *an* with singular count nouns. Use *a* before a consonant sound (*a car*) and *an* before a vowel sound (*an uncle*). Consider sound rather than spelling: *a house, an hour.*

  A or *an* tells readers they do not have enough information to identify specifically what the noun refers to. Compare these sentences:

▶ I need *a* new coat for the winter.

▶ I saw *a* coat that I liked at Dayton's, but it wasn't heavy enough.

The coat in the first sentence is hypothetical. Since it is indefinite to the writer and the reader, it is used with *a*, not *the*. The second sentence refers to an actual coat, but since the writer cannot expect the reader to know which one, it is used with *a* rather than *the*.

If you want to speak of an indefinite quantity rather than just one indefinite thing, use *some* or *any* with a noncount noun or a plural count noun. Use *any* in negative sentences and questions.

▶ This stew needs *some* more salt.

▶ I saw *some* plates that I liked at Gump's.

▶ This stew doesn't need *any* more salt.

▶ Do you have *any* sandwiches left?

The article the

Use the definite article *the* with both count and noncount nouns whose identity is known or is about to be made known to readers. The necessary information for identification can come from the noun phrase itself, from elsewhere in the text, from context, from general knowledge, or from a superlative.

▶ Let's meet at the fountain in front of Dwinelle Hall.

The phrase *in front of Dwinelle Hall* identifies the specific fountain.

▶ Last Saturday, a fire that started in a restaurant spread to a nearby clothing store. The store ~~Store~~ was saved, although it suffered water damage.

The word *store* is preceded by *the*, which directs our attention to the information in the previous sentence, where the store is first identified.

▶ She asked him to shut the door when he left her office.

The context shows that she is referring to her office door.

▶ Bill is now the best singer in the choir.

The superlative *best* identifies the noun *singer*.

No article (the zero article)

Noncount and plural count nouns can be used without an article or any other determiner when making generalizations:

▶ In this world nothing is certain but death and taxes.
— BENJAMIN FRANKLIN

Franklin refers not to a particular death or specific taxes but to death and taxes in general, so no article is used with *death* or with *taxes*.

English differs from many other languages that use the definite article to make generalizations. In English, a sentence like *The ants live in colonies* can refer only to particular, identifiable ants, not to ants in general.

It is sometimes possible to make general statements with *the* or *a/an* and singular count nouns.

▶ **First-year college students** are confronted with many new experiences.

▶ **A first-year student** is confronted with many new experiences.

▶ **The first-year student** is confronted with many new experiences.

These sentences all make the same general statement, but the emphasis of each sentence is different. The first sentence refers to first-year students as a group, the second focuses on a hypothetical student taken at random, and the third sentence, which is characteristic of formal written style, projects the image of a typical student as representative of the whole class.

37 Subject-Verb Agreement

In everyday terms, the word *agreement* refers to an accord of some sort: friends agree to go to a movie; the United States and Russia negotiate an agreement about reducing nuclear arms. In most sentences, making subjects and verbs agree is fairly simple; only a few subject-verb constructions cause confusion.

Understand subject-verb agreement.

In academic varieties of English, verbs must agree with their subjects in number (singular or plural) and in person (first, second, or third).

To make a <u>verb</u> in the present tense agree with a third-person singular <u>subject</u>, add *-s* or *-es* to the base form.

▶ A vegetarian <u>diet</u> <u>lowers</u> the risk of heart disease.

To make a verb in the present tense agree with any other subject, use the base form of the verb.

▶ I *miss* my family.

▶ They *live* in another state.

> ## Quick Help
>
> ### Editing for Subject-Verb Agreement
>
> - Identify the subject that goes with each verb. Cover up any words between the subject and the verb to identify agreement problems more easily. (37b)
> - Check compound subjects. Those joined by *and* usually take a plural verb form. With those subjects joined by *or* or *nor*, however, the verb agrees with the part of the subject closest to the verb. (37c)
> - Check collective-noun subjects. These nouns take a singular verb form when they refer to a group as a single unit but a plural form when they refer to the multiple members of a group. (37d)
> - Check indefinite-pronoun subjects. Most take a singular verb form. *Both*, *few*, *many*, *others*, and *several* take a plural form; and *all*, *any*, *enough*, *more*, *most*, *none*, and *some* can be either singular or plural, depending on the noun they refer to. (37e)

The verbs *have* and *be* do not follow the *-s* or *-es* pattern with third-person singular subjects. *Have* changes to *has*; *be* has irregular forms in both the present and past tenses and in the first person as well as the third person. (See Chapter 35.)

▶ War *is* hell.

▶ The soldier *was* brave beyond the call of duty.

In some varieties of correct African American or regional English, third-person singular verb forms do not end with *-s* or *-es*: *She go to work every day.* In most academic writing, however, your audience will expect third-person singular verb forms to end in *-s* or *-es* (35a).

37b Make separated subjects and verbs agree.

Make sure the <u>verb</u> agrees with the <u>subject</u> and not with another noun that falls in between.

▶ A <u>vase</u> of flowers <u>makes</u> a room attractive.

▶ Many books on the best-seller list ~~has~~ little literary value.
               have

The simple subject is *books*, not *list*.

Be careful when you use phrases beginning with *as well as, along with, in addition to, together with*, or similar prepositions. They do not make a singular subject plural.

▶ A passenger, as well as the driver, ~~were~~ injured in the accident.
$\overset{\text{was}}{}$

> Though this sentence has a grammatically singular subject, it suggests the idea of a plural subject. The sentence makes better sense with a compound subject: *The driver and a passenger were injured in the accident.*

37c   Make verbs agree with compound subjects.

Two or more subjects joined by *and* generally require a plural verb form.

▶ Tony and his friend commute from Louisville.

▶ A backpack, a canteen, and a rifle ~~was~~ issued to each recruit.
$\overset{\text{were}}{}$

When subjects joined by *and* are considered a single unit or refer to the same person or thing, they take a singular verb form.

▶ George W. Bush's older brother and political ally was the governor of

Florida.

▶ Drinking and driving ~~remain~~ a major cause of highway fatalities.
$\overset{\text{remains}}{}$

> In this sentence, *drinking and driving* is considered a single activity, and a singular verb is used.

If the word *each* or *every* precedes subjects joined by *and*, the verb form is singular.

▶ Each boy and girl chooses one gift to take home.

With subjects joined by *or* or *nor*, the verb agrees with the part closest to the verb.

▶ Neither my roommate nor my neighbors *like* my loud music.

▶ Either the witnesses or the defendant ~~are~~ lying.
$\overset{\text{is}}{}$

If you find such sentences awkward, put the underline{plural noun} closest to the underline{verb}: *Either the defendant or the* underline{*witnesses*} underline{*are*} *lying.*

37d   Make verbs agree with collective nouns.

Collective nouns — such as *family, team, audience, group, jury, crowd, band, class,* and *committee* — refer to a group. Collective nouns can take either singular or plural verb forms, depending on whether they refer to the group as a single unit or to the multiple members of the group. The meaning of a sentence as a whole is your guide to whether a collective noun refers to a unit or to the multiple parts of a unit.

▶ After deliberating, the jury *reports* its verdict.

The jury acts as a single unit.

▶ The jury still *disagree* on a number of counts.

The members of the jury act as multiple individuals.

scatter
▶ The duck family ~~scatters~~ when the cat approaches.

Family here refers to the many ducks; they cannot scatter as one.

Treat fractions that refer to singular nouns as singular and those that refer to plural nouns as plural.

SINGULAR	Two-thirds of the park *has* burned.
PLURAL	Two-thirds of the students *were* commuters.

Even though *eyeglasses, scissors, pants,* and other such words refer to single items, they take plural verbs because they are made up of pairs.

▶ Where *are* my reading glasses?

Treat phrases starting with *the number of* as singular and with *a number of* as plural.

SINGULAR	The number of applicants for the internship *was* amazing.
PLURAL	A number of applicants *were* put on the waiting list.

37e Make verbs agree with indefinite pronouns.

Indefinite pronouns do not refer to specific persons or things. Most take singular verb forms.

SOME COMMON INDEFINITE PRONOUNS

another	anything	everything	nothing
any	either	much	somebody
anybody	everybody	nobody	someone
anyone	everyone	no one	something

▶ Of the two jobs, neither *holds* much appeal.

▶ Each of the plays ~~depict~~ *depicts* a hero undone by a tragic flaw.

Both, *few*, *many*, *others*, and *several* are plural.

▶ Though many *apply*, few *are* chosen.

All, *any*, *enough*, *more*, *most*, *none*, and *some* can be singular or plural, depending on the noun they refer to.

▶ All of the cake *was* eaten.

▶ All of the candidates *promise* to improve the schools.

37f Make verbs agree with *who*, *which*, and *that*.

When the relative pronouns *who*, *which*, and *that* are used as a subject, the verb agrees with the antecedent of the pronoun.

▶ Fear is an ingredient that *goes* into creating stereotypes.

▶ Guilt and fear are ingredients that *go* into creating stereotypes.

Problems often occur with the words *one of the*. In general, *one of the* takes a plural verb, while *only one of the* takes a singular verb.

▶ Carla is one of the employees who always ~~works~~ overtime.
　　　　　　　　　　　　　　　　　work

Some employees always work overtime. Carla is among them. Thus *who* refers to *employees*, and the verb is plural.

▶ Ming is the only one of the employees who always ~~work~~ overtime.
　　　　　　　　　　　　　　　　　　　works

Only one employee always works overtime, and that employee is Ming. Thus *one*, and not *employees*, is the antecedent of *who*, and the verb form is singular.

37g　Make linking verbs agree with subjects.

A linking verb should agree with its subject, which usually precedes the verb, not with the subject complement, which follows it (34a).

▶ Three key treaties ~~is~~ the topic of my talk.
　　　　　　　　　　are

The subject is *treaties*, not *topic*.

▶ Nero Wolfe's passion ~~were~~ orchids.
　　　　　　　　　　　was

The subject is *passion*, not *orchids*.

37h　Make verbs agree with subjects ending in *-s*.

Some words that end in *-s* appear plural but are singular and thus take singular verb forms.

▶ Measles still ~~strike~~ many Americans.
　　　　　　strikes

Some nouns of this kind (such as *statistics* and *politics*) may be either singular or plural, depending on context.

SINGULAR	Statistics *is* a course I really dread.
PLURAL	The statistics in that study *are* highly questionable.

37i Make verbs agree with subjects that follow.

In English, verbs usually follow subjects. When this order is reversed, make the verb agree with the subject, not with a noun that happens to precede it.

▶ Beside the barn ~~stands~~ *stand* silos filled with grain.

The subject is *silos*; it is plural, so the verb must be *stand*.

In sentences beginning with *there is*, *there are*, *there was*, or *there were*, the word *there* serves only as a placeholder; the subject follows the verb.

▶ There are five basic positions in classical ballet.

The subject, *positions*, is plural, so the verb must also be plural.

37j Make verbs agree with titles and words used as words.

▶ *One Writer's Beginnings* ~~describe~~ *describes* Eudora Welty's childhood.

▶ *Steroids* ~~are~~ *is* a little word that packs a big punch in the world of sports.

38 Pronouns

As words that stand in for nouns, pronouns carry a lot of weight in everyday language. These directions show one of the reasons why it's important to use pronouns clearly:

> When you see a dirt road turning left off Winston Lane, follow it for two more miles.

The listener may not know whether *it* means the dirt road or Winston Lane. Pronouns can improve understanding, but only when they're used carefully and accurately.

38a Consider a pronoun's role in the sentence.

Most speakers of English know intuitively when to use *I*, *me*, and *my*. Our choices reflect differences in case, the form a pronoun takes to indicate how it acts in a sentence. Pronouns acting as subjects are in the subjective case (*I*); those acting as objects are in the objective case (*me*); those acting as possessives are in the possessive case (*my*).

SUBJECTIVE PRONOUNS	OBJECTIVE PRONOUNS	POSSESSIVE PRONOUNS
I	me	my/mine
we	us	our/ours
you	you	your/yours
he/she/it	him/her/it	his/her/hers/its
they	them	their/theirs
who/whoever	whom/whomever	whose

Subjective case

A pronoun should be in the subjective case (*I*, *we*, *you*, *he/she/it*, *they*, *who*, *whoever*) when it is a subject, a subject complement, or an appositive renaming a subject or subject complement.

> **SUBJECT**
>
> *She* was passionate about recycling.

> **SUBJECT COMPLEMENT**
>
> The main supporter of the recycling program was *she*.

> **APPOSITIVE RENAMING A SUBJECT OR SUBJECT COMPLEMENT**
>
> Three colleagues — Peter, John, and *she* — worked on the program.

Americans routinely use the objective case for subject complements, especially in conversation: *Who's there? It's me.* If the subjective case for a subject complement sounds stilted or awkward (*It's I*), try rewriting the sentence using the pronoun as the subject (*I'm here*).

> ► ~~The~~ ^She was the^ first person to see Kishore after the awards. ~~was she.~~

Objective case

Use the objective case (*me*, *us*, *you*, *him/her/it*, *them*) when a pronoun functions as a direct or indirect object, an object of a preposition, an appositive renaming an object, or a subject of an infinitive.

DIRECT OBJECT

The boss surprised *her* with a big raise.

INDIRECT OBJECT

The owner gave *him* a reward.

OBJECT OF A PREPOSITION

Several friends went with *me*.

APPOSITIVE RENAMING AN OBJECT

The students elected two representatives, Joan and *me*.

SUBJECT OF AN INFINITIVE

The students convinced *him* to vote for the school bond.

Possessive case

Use the possessive case when a pronoun shows possession or ownership. The adjective forms of possessive pronouns (*my, our, your, his/her/its, their, whose*) are used before nouns or gerunds, and noun forms (*mine, ours, yours, his/hers/its, theirs, whose*) take the place of a possessive noun. Possessive pronouns do not include apostrophes (47a).

BEFORE A NOUN

The sound of *her* voice came right through the walls.

IN PLACE OF A POSSESSIVE NOUN

The responsibility is *hers*.

Pronouns before a gerund should be in the possessive case.

▶ I remember ~~him~~ his singing.

His modifies the gerund *singing*.

38b Use *who, whoever, whom,* and *whomever* appropriately.

A common problem with pronoun case is deciding whether to use *who* or *whom*. Even when traditional grammar requires *whom*, many Americans use *who* instead, especially in informal writing and speech. Nevertheless, you should understand the difference between *who* and *whom* so that you can make informed choices in situations such as formal college writing. The most common confusion with *who* and *whom* occurs when they begin a question and when they introduce a dependent clause.

Talking the Talk

Correctness or Stuffiness?

"I think *Everyone has their opinion* sounds better than *Everyone has his or her opinion*. And nobody says *whom*. Why should I write that way?" Over time, the conventions governing certain usages — such as *who* versus *whom*, or *their* versus *his or her* when it refers to an indefinite pronoun like *everyone* — have become much more relaxed. In fact, many resist the use of binary terms like *his/her* completely, preferring to use a non-gendered term like *they* or *zir*. It's also common now to see writers announcing their pronoun preferences in blog posts and in email signatures. To many Americans, *Whom did you talk to?* sounds unpleasantly fussy. However, other people object to less formal constructions such as *Who did you talk to?* and *No one finished their test*. Unfortunately, you can't please everyone. Use whatever you are most comfortable with in speaking, but be more careful in formal writing. If you don't know whether your audience will prefer more or less formality, try recasting your sentence.

Questions

You can determine whether to use *who* or *whom* at the beginning of a question by answering the question using a personal pronoun. If the answer is *he*, *she*, or *they*, use *who*; if it is *him*, *her*, or *them*, use *whom*.

> Whom
> ▶ ~~Who~~ did you visit?
>   ^
>
> I visited *them*. *Them* is objective; thus *whom* is correct.

> Who
> ▶ ~~Whom~~ do you think wrote the story?
>   ^
>
> I think *she* wrote the story. *She* is subjective; thus *who* is correct.

Dependent clauses

The case of a pronoun in a dependent clause is determined by its purpose in the clause, no matter how that clause functions in the sentence. If the pronoun acts as a subject or subject complement in the clause, use *who* or *whoever*. If the pronoun acts as an object in the clause, use *whom* or *whomever*.

> whoever
> ▶ The center is open to ~~whomever~~ wants to use it.
>   ^
>
> *Whoever* is the subject of the clause *whoever wants to use it*. (The clause is the object of the preposition *to*, but the clause's function in the sentence does not affect the case of the pronoun.)

▶ The new president was not ~~who~~ she had expected.
    ^whom

> Here, *whom* is the object of the verb *had expected* in the clause *whom she had expected.*

If you are not sure which case to use, try separating the dependent clause from the rest of the sentence. Rewrite the clause as a new sentence, and substitute a personal pronoun for *who(ever)* or *whom(ever)*. If the pronoun is in the subjective case, use *who* or *whoever*; if it is in the objective case, use *whom* or *whomever*.

▶ The minister glared at (*whoever/whomever*) made any noise.

> Isolate the clause *whoever/whomever made any noise*. Substituting a personal pronoun gives you *they made any noise*. *They* is in the subjective case; therefore, *The minister grimaced at whoever made any noise.*

▶ The minister glared at whoever ~~she thought~~ made any noise.

> Ignore such expressions as *he thinks* and *she says* when you isolate the clause.

38c Consider case in compound structures.

When a pronoun is part of a compound subject, complement, object, or appositive, put it in the same case you would use if the pronoun were alone.

▶ When ~~him~~ and Zelda were first married, they lived in New York.
    ^he

▶ The boss invited ~~she~~ and her family to dinner.
    ^her

▶ This morning saw yet another conflict between my sister and ~~I.~~
    ^me.

▶ Both panelists — Javonne and ~~me~~ — were stumped.
    ^I

To decide whether to use the subjective or objective case in a compound structure, mentally delete the rest of the compound and try the pronoun alone.

▶ Come to the park with Anh and ~~I.~~
    ^me.

> Mentally deleting *Anh and* results in *Come to the park with I.* Rewrite as *Come to the park with Anh and me.*

38d Consider case in elliptical constructions.

In elliptical constructions, some words are understood but left out. When an elliptical construction ends in a pronoun, put the pronoun in the case it would be in if the construction were complete.

▶ His sister has always been more athletic than *he* [is].

In some elliptical constructions, the case of the pronoun depends on the meaning intended.

▶ Willie likes Lily more than *she* [likes Lily].

She is the subject of the omitted verb *likes*.

▶ Willie likes Lily more than [he likes] *her*.

Her is the object of the omitted verb *likes*.

38e Use *we* and *us* appropriately before a noun.

If you are unsure about whether to use *we* or *us* before a noun, recast the sentence without the noun. Use whichever pronoun would be correct if the noun were omitted.

▶ <del>Us</del> We fans never give up hope.

Without *fans*, *we* would be the subject.

▶ The Rangers depend on <del>we</del> us fans.

Without *fans*, *us* would be the object of a preposition.

38f Make pronouns agree with antecedents.

The antecedent of a pronoun is the word the pronoun refers to. The antecedent usually appears before the pronoun — earlier in the sentence or in the prior sentence. Pronouns and antecedents are said to agree when they match up in person, number, and gender.

SINGULAR   The choirmaster raised *his* baton.

PLURAL   The boys picked up *their* music.

Compound antecedents

Compound antecedents joined by *and* require plural pronouns.

▶ *My parents and I* tried to resolve *our* disagreement.

When *each* or *every* precedes a compound antecedent, however, it takes a singular pronoun.

▶ *Every plant* and *animal* has *its* own ecological niche.

With a compound antecedent joined by *or* or *nor*, the pronoun agrees with the nearer or nearest antecedent. If the parts of the antecedent are of different genders, however, this kind of sentence can be awkward or ambiguous and may need to be revised.

AWKWARD	Neither Annie nor Barry got *his* work done.
REVISED	Annie didn't get *her* work done, and neither did Barry.

When a compound antecedent contains both singular and plural parts, the sentence may sound awkward unless the plural part comes last.

▶ Neither the newspaper nor the radio stations would reveal *their* sources.

Collective-noun antecedents

A collective noun that refers to a single unit (*herd, team, audience*) requires a singular pronoun.

▶ The audience fixed *its* attention on center stage.

When such an antecedent refers to the multiple parts of a unit, however, it requires a plural pronoun.

▶ The director chose this cast for the play because *they* had experience in

the roles.

Indefinite-pronoun antecedents

Indefinite pronouns are those that do not refer to specific persons or things. Most indefinite pronouns are always singular; a few are always plural. Some can be singular or plural depending on the context.

▶ *One* of the ballerinas lost *her* balance.

▶ *Many* in the audience jumped to *their* feet.

SINGULAR Some of the furniture was showing *its* age.

PLURAL Some of the farmers abandoned *their* land.

Sexist and noninclusive pronouns

Indefinite pronouns often serve as antecedents that may be either male or female. Writers used to use a masculine pronoun, known as the generic *he*, to refer to such indefinite pronouns. However, such wording ignores females and excludes those who choose not to identify as *he* or *she*.

When the antecedent is *anybody*, *each*, *everybody*, or *everyone*, some people avoid the generic *he* by using a plural pronoun.

▶ Each student should check *their* account by midnight tonight.

If you are writing for situations in which formal choices are expected, be aware that some people believe that it's a mistake to use the plural *their* with singular antecedents such as *anybody*, *each*, and *everyone*. However, you will hear such sentences in conversation and see them in more and more writing.

Quick Help

Editing Out Generic *He*, *His*, *Him*

Everyone should know his *legal rights.*

Here are three ways to express the same idea without *his*:

1. Revise to make the antecedent a plural noun.
   All citizens should know their *legal rights.*

2. Revise the sentence altogether.
   Everyone should have some knowledge of basic legal rights.

3. Use both masculine and feminine pronouns.
   Everyone should know his *or* her *legal rights.*

4. Use *they* as a gender-neutral solution.
   Everyone should know their *legal rights.*

The third option can be seen as awkward and noninclusive. The fourth option, though considered informal by some, is increasingly acceptable in formal writing.

38g Make pronouns refer to clear antecedents.

The antecedent of a pronoun is the word the pronoun substitutes for. If a pronoun is too far from its antecedent, readers will have trouble making the connection between the two.

Ambiguous antecedents

Readers have trouble when a pronoun can refer to more than one antecedent.

▶ The car went over the bridge just before ~~it~~ *the bridge* fell into the water.

What fell into the water — the car or the bridge? The revision makes the meaning clear.

▶ Kerry told Ellen, "~~she~~ *I* should be ready soon."

Reporting Kerry's words directly, in quotation marks, eliminates the ambiguity.

Vague use of it, this, that, and which

The words *it*, *this*, *that*, and *which* often function as a shortcut for referring to something mentioned earlier. But such shortcuts can cause confusion. Like other pronouns, each must refer to a specific antecedent.

▶ When the senators realized the bill would be defeated, they tried to postpone the vote but failed. ~~It~~ *The entire effort* was a fiasco.

▶ Nancy just found out that she won the lottery, ~~which~~ *and that news* explains her sudden resignation from her job.

Indefinite use of you, it, and they

In conversation, we frequently use *you*, *it*, and *they* in an indefinite sense in such expressions as *you never know*; *in the paper, it said*; and *they say*. In academic and professional writing, however, use *you* only to mean "you, the reader," and *they* or *it* only to refer to a clear antecedent.

▶ Commercials try to make ~~you~~ ^people^ buy without thinking.

▶ ~~On the~~ ^The^ Weather Channel, ~~it~~ reported that an earthquake devastated parts of Pakistan.

▶ ~~In France, they~~ ^Many restaurants in France^ allow dogs. ~~in many restaurants.~~

Possessive antecedents

A possessive may *suggest* a noun antecedent but does not serve as a clear antecedent.

▶ In ~~Alexa's~~ ^her^ formal complaint, ~~she~~ ^Alexa^ showed why the test question was wrong.

39 Adjectives and Adverbs

As words that describe other words, adjectives and adverbs can add liveliness and color to writing, helping writers show rather than just tell. In addition, adjectives and adverbs often provide indispensable meanings to the words they modify. In basketball, for example, there is an important difference between a *flagrant* foul and a *technical* foul, or an *angry* coach and an *abusively angry* coach. In each instance, the modifiers are crucial to accurate communication.

39a Understand adjectives and adverbs.

Adjectives modify nouns and pronouns, answering the question *which? how many?* or *what kind?* Adverbs modify verbs, adjectives, other adverbs, or entire clauses; they answer the question *how? when? where?* or *to what extent?* Many adverbs are formed by adding *-ly* to adjectives (*slight, slightly*), but many are not (*outdoors, very*). And some words that end in *-ly* are adjectives (*lovely, homely*). To tell adjectives and adverbs apart, identify the word's function in the sentence.

39b Use adjectives after linking verbs.

When adjectives come after linking verbs, they usually describe the subject: *I am patient*. Note that in specific sentences, some verbs may or may not act as linking verbs — *look, appear, sound, feel, smell, taste, grow,* and *prove,* for instance. When a word following one of these verbs modifies the subject, use an adjective; when the word modifies the verb, use an adverb.

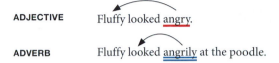

| **ADJECTIVE** | Fluffy looked angry. |
| **ADVERB** | Fluffy looked angrily at the poodle. |

Linking verbs suggest a state of being, not an action. In the preceding examples, *looked angry* suggests the state of being angry; *looked angrily* suggests an angry action.

Quick Help

Editing Adjectives and Adverbs

- Scrutinize each adjective and adverb. Consider synonyms for each one to see whether you have chosen the best word possible.
- See if a more specific noun would eliminate the need for an adjective (*mansion* rather than *enormous house,* for instance); do the same with verbs and adverbs.
- Consider adding an adjective or adverb that might make your writing more vivid or specific.
- Make sure that all adjectives modify nouns or pronouns and that all adverbs modify verbs, adjectives, or other adverbs. Check especially for the proper use of *good* and *well, bad* and *badly, real* and *really.* (39c)
- Make sure all comparisons are complete. (39d)
- If English is not your first language, check that adjectives are in the right order. (39g)
- Avoid using too many adverbs and adjectives in your writing. (39h)

39c Use adverbs to modify verbs, adjectives, and adverbs.

In everyday conversation, you will often hear (and perhaps use) adjectives in place of adverbs. When you write in formal academic English, however, use adverbs to modify verbs, adjectives, and other adverbs.

▶ You can feel the song's meter if you listen ~~careful.~~ carefully.

▶ The audience was ~~real~~ really disappointed by the show.

Good *and* well, bad *and* badly

The modifiers *good*, *well*, *bad*, and *badly* cause problems for many writers because the distinctions between *good* and *well* and between *bad* and *badly* are often not observed in conversation. *Good* and *bad* are always adjectives, and both can be used after a linking verb. In formal writing, do not use them to modify a verb, an adjective, or an adverb; use *well* or *badly* instead.

▶ The weather looks *good* today.

▶ He plays the trumpet ~~good~~ well and the trombone ~~bad.~~ badly.

Badly is an adverb and can modify a verb, an adjective, or another adverb. Do not use it after a linking verb in formal writing; use *bad* instead.

▶ I feel ~~badly~~ bad for the Cubs' fans.

Problems also arise because *well* can function as either an adjective or an adverb. As an adjective, *well* means "in good health"; as an adverb, it means "in a good manner" or "thoroughly."

ADJECTIVE	After a week of rest, Julio felt *well* again.
ADVERB	They play *well* enough to make the team.

*Regional modifiers (*right *smart,* wicked *fun)*

Most regions have certain characteristic adjectives and adverbs. Some of the most colorful are intensifiers, adverbs meaning *very* or *absolutely*. In parts of the South, for example, and particularly in Appalachia, you are likely to hear the following: *He paid a right smart price for that car* or *She*

> ## Language, Culture, and Context
> **Multilingual**
>
> ### Adjectives with Plural Nouns
>
> In Spanish, Russian, and many other languages, adjectives agree in number with the nouns that they modify. In English, however, adjectives do not change their number this way: *her kittens are cute* (not *cutes*).

was plumb tuckered out. In New England, you might hear *That party was wicked fun*. In each of these cases, the adverb (*right, plumb, wicked*) acts to intensify the meaning of the adjective (*smart, tuckered out, fun*).

As with all language, use regional adjectives and adverbs when they are appropriate (23c). In writing about a family member in Minnesota, for example, you might well quote her, bringing midwestern expressions into your writing. For most academic writing, however, you should use academic English.

39d Choose appropriate comparative and superlative forms.

Most adjectives and adverbs have three forms: positive, comparative, and superlative.

POSITIVE	COMPARATIVE	SUPERLATIVE
large	larger	largest
early	earlier	earliest
careful	more careful	most careful
delicious	more delicious	most delicious

▶ Canada is *larger* than the United States.

▶ My son needs to be *more careful* with his money.

▶ This is the *most delicious* coffee we have tried.

The comparative and superlative of most short (one-syllable and some two-syllable) adjectives are formed by adding *-er* and *-est*. With some two-syllable adjectives, longer adjectives, and most adverbs, use *more* and *most*: *scientific, more scientific, most scientific; elegantly, more elegantly, most elegantly*. If you are not sure whether a word has *-er* and *-est* forms, consult the dictionary entry for the simple form.

Irregular forms

A number of adjectives and adverbs have irregular comparative and superlative forms.

POSITIVE	COMPARATIVE	SUPERLATIVE
good	better	best
well	better	best
bad	worse	worst
badly	worse	worst
little (quantity)	less	least
many, some, much	more	most

Comparatives or superlatives

In academic writing, use the comparative to compare two things; use the superlative to compare three or more.

▶ Rome is a much *older* city than New York.

▶ Damascus is one of the ~~older~~ *oldest* cities in the world.

▶ Which of the two candidates is the ~~strongest~~ *stronger* for the job?

Double comparatives and superlatives

Double comparatives and superlatives, used in some informal contexts, use both *more* or *most* and the *-er* or *-est* ending. Occasionally they can act to build a special emphasis, as in the title of Spike Lee's movie *Mo' Better Blues*. In college writing, however, double comparatives and superlatives may count against you. Make sure not to use *more* or *most* before adjectives or adverbs ending in *-er* or *-est* in formal situations.

▶ Paris is the ~~most~~ loveliest city in the world.

Incomplete comparisons

Even if you think your audience will understand an implied comparison, you will be safer if you make sure that comparisons in formal writing are complete and clear (28e).

▶ The patients taking the drug appeared healthier/ *than those receiving a placebo.*

Absolute concepts

Some readers consider modifiers such as *perfect* and *unique* to be absolute concepts; according to this view, a construction such as *more unique* is illogical because a thing is either unique or it isn't, so modified forms of the concept don't make sense. However, many seemingly absolute words have multiple meanings, all of which are widely accepted as correct. For example, *unique* may mean *one of a kind* or *unequaled*, but it can also simply mean *distinctive* or *unusual*.

If you think your readers will object to a construction such as *more perfect* (which appears in the U.S. Constitution) or *somewhat unique*, then avoid such uses.

Multiple negatives

Multiple negatives such as *I can't hardly see you* have a long history in English (and in other languages) and can be found in the works of Chaucer and Shakespeare. In the eighteenth century, however, in an effort to make English more logical, double negatives came to be labeled as incorrect. In college writing, you may well have reason to quote passages that include them (whether from Shakespeare, Toni Morrison, or your grandmother), but it is safer to avoid other uses of double negatives in academic writing.

 39e **Consider nouns as modifiers.**

Sometimes a noun can function as an adjective by modifying another noun, as in *chicken soup* or *money supply*. If noun modifiers pile up, however, they can make your writing harder to understand.

AWKWARD	The cold war–era Rosenberg espionage trial and execution continues to arouse controversy.
REVISED	The Rosenbergs' trial and execution for espionage during the cold war continues to arouse controversy.

 39f **Understand adjectives ending in -*ed* and -*ing*.**
Multilingual

Many verbs refer to feelings — for example, *bore, confuse, excite, frighten, interest*. The present participles of such verbs, which end in -*ing*, and the past participles, which end in -*ed*, can be used as adjectives (33d).

Use the *-ed* (past participle) form to describe a person having the feeling.

▶ The *frightened* boy started to cry.

Use the *-ing* (present participle) form to describe the thing or person causing the feeling.

▶ The *frightening* movie gave him nightmares.

Be careful not to confuse the two types of adjectives.

interested
▶ I am ~~interesting~~ in African literature.
            ^

                                    interesting.
▶ African literature seems ~~interested.~~
                            ^

39g Put adjectives in order.

Multilingual

Modifiers are words that give more information about a noun; that is, they *modify* the meaning of the noun in some way. Some modifiers precede the noun, and others follow it, as indicated in the chart on p. 349.

If there are two or more adjectives, their order is variable, but English has strong preferences, described below.

- Subjective adjectives (those that show the writer's opinion) go before objective adjectives (those that merely describe): *these old-fashioned kitchen tiles.*

- Adjectives of size generally come early: *these large old-fashioned kitchen tiles.*

- Adjectives of color generally come late: *these beautiful blue kitchen tiles.*

- Adjectives derived from proper nouns or from nouns that refer to materials generally come after color terms and right before noun modifiers: *these beautiful blue Portuguese ceramic kitchen tiles.*

- All other objective adjectives go in the middle, separated by commas (see 44d): *these decorative, heat-resistant, old-fashioned blue Portuguese ceramic kitchen tiles.*

Very long noun phrases are usually out of place in most kinds of writing. Academic and professional writing tends to avoid long strings of adjectives.

Modifier Type	Arrangement	Examples
determiners	at the beginning of the noun phrase	*these* old-fashioned tiles
all or *both*	before any other determiners	*all* these tiles
numbers	after any other determiners	these *six* tiles
noun modifiers	directly before the noun	these *kitchen* tiles
adjectives	between determiners and noun modifiers	these *old-fashioned* kitchen tiles
phrases or clauses	after the noun	the tiles *on the wall* the tiles *that we bought*

39h Avoid overuse of adverbs and adjectives.

In formal academic writing, expert writers tend to use adverbs and adjectives sparingly. So take a tip from the experts: using fewer modifiers can ensure that each adjective or adverb has a greater impact.

Adverbs

In his memoir *On Writing*, novelist Stephen King says, "I believe the road to hell is paved in adverbs, and I will shout it from the rooftops." Note that he doesn't say he will shout it *loudly*, since readers already know that shouting is loud. Many adverbs are simply redundant:

▶ Tourists meandered ~~aimlessly~~ in the garden.

   The verb *meandered* means "wandered aimlessly," so *aimlessly* is
   unnecessary.

In academic writing, avoid redundant adverbs, and omit adverbs that are so overused that they have little meaning anymore, such as *definitely*, *absolutely*, and *extremely*.

Adjectives

Adjectives can also lead to redundancy. Ask yourself whether you need to say "the *large* mountain" or whether your readers will know that a mountain is large. When you overuse adjectives, you can simply bog down readers.

▶ The author responded to the ~~wonderful cheery~~ smiles lighting up all of the ~~happy, delighted~~ faces in the ~~listening~~ audience.

Adjectives and adverbs in informal writing

As always, consider the context when deciding whether you are overusing adjectives and adverbs. Repetition that would be inappropriate in formal contexts can add effective emphasis in informal writing, as in the hashtag *#sosososcared* or a status update saying "I'm massively, insanely psyched for the show tonight."

40 Modifier Placement

Consider the following notice in a guidebook:

> Visit the old Dutch cemetery where early settlers are buried from noon to five daily.

Does the old cemetery really bury early settlers for five hours every day? Repositioning the modifier *from noon to five daily* eliminates the confusion

---

Quick Help

Editing for Misplaced or Dangling Modifiers

1. Identify all the modifiers in each sentence, and draw an arrow from each modifier to the word it modifies.
2. If a modifier is far from the word it modifies, try to move the two closer together. (40a)
3. Does any modifier seem to refer to a word other than the one it is intended to modify? If so, move the modifier so that it refers clearly to only the intended word. (40a and b)
4. If you cannot find the word to which a modifier refers, revise the sentence: supply such a word, or revise the modifier itself so that it clearly refers to a word already in the sentence. (40c)

and makes it clear when the cemetery is open: *From noon to five daily, you may visit the old Dutch cemetery where early settlers are buried.* To be effective, modifiers should refer clearly to the words they modify and be placed close to those words.

40a Revise misplaced modifiers.

Modifiers can cause confusion or ambiguity if they are not close enough to the words they modify or if they seem to modify more than one word in the sentence.

▶ She teaches a seminar this term _{on voodoo} ~~on voodoo~~ at Skyline College.

> The voodoo is not at the college; the seminar is.

▶ ~~Billowing from every window,~~ _{He} he saw clouds of smoke_{, billowing from every window.}/

> People cannot billow from windows.

▶ _{After he lost the 1962 governor's race,} Nixon told reporters that he planned to get out of politics. ~~after he lost the 1962 gubernatorial race.~~

> The unedited sentence implies that Nixon planned to lose the race.

Limiting modifiers

Be especially careful with the placement of limiting modifiers such as *almost, even, just, merely,* and *only.* In general, these modifiers should be placed right before or after the words they modify. Putting them in other positions may produce not just ambiguity but a completely different meaning.

AMBIGUOUS	The court *only* hears civil cases on Tuesdays.
CLEAR	The court hears *only* civil cases on Tuesdays.
CLEAR	The court hears civil cases on Tuesdays *only.*

In the first sentence, placing *only* before *hears* makes the meaning ambiguous. Does the writer mean that civil cases are the only cases heard on Tuesdays or that those are the only days when civil cases are heard?

▶ The city _{almost} ~~almost~~ spent $20 million on the new stadium.

> The original sentence suggests the money was almost spent; moving *almost* makes clear that the amount spent was almost $20 million.

Squinting modifiers

If a modifier can refer to either the word before it or the word after it, it is a squinting modifier. Put the modifier where it clearly relates to only a single word.

SQUINTING	Students who practice writing *often* will benefit.
REVISED	Students who *often* practice writing will benefit.
REVISED	Students who practice writing will *often* benefit.

40b Revise disruptive modifiers.

Disruptive modifiers interrupt the connections between parts of a grammatical structure or a sentence, making it hard for readers to follow the progress of the thought.

▶ <u>If they are cooked too long, vegetables will</u>
~~Vegetables will, if they are cooked too long,~~ lose most of their nutritional value.

A modifier placed between the *to* and verb of an infinitive (*to boldly go*) is known as a split infinitive. Once considered a serious writing error, split infinitives are no longer taboo. Few readers will object to a split infinitive in a clear and understandable sentence.

▶ **Students need to *really* know the material to pass the exam.**

Sometimes, however, split infinitives can be distracting to readers — especially when more than one word comes between the parts of the infinitive. In such cases, move the modifier before or after the infinitive, or reword the sentence, to remove the distracting interruption.

▶ Hitler expected the British to fairly quickly *surrender*. ~~surrender.~~

40c Revise dangling modifiers.

Dangling modifiers modify nothing in particular in the rest of a sentence. They often *seem* to modify something that is implied but not actually present in the sentence. Dangling modifiers frequently appear at the beginnings or ends of sentences.

DANGLING	Driving nonstop, Salishan Lodge is located two hours from Portland.
REVISED	Driving nonstop from Portland, you can reach Salishan Lodge in two hours.

To revise a dangling modifier, often you need to add a subject that the modifier clearly refers to. In some cases, however, you have to revise the modifier itself, turning it into a phrase or a clause.

▶ Reluctantly, ~~the hound was given away~~ to a neighbor.
our family gave away

In the original sentence, was the dog reluctant, or was someone else who is not mentioned reluctant?

▶ ~~As~~ a young boy, his grandmother told stories of her years as a country schoolteacher.
When he was

His grandmother was never a young boy.

▶ ~~Thumbing through the magazine, my~~ eyes automatically noticed the perfume ads.
My ... *as I was thumbing through the magazine.*

Eyes cannot thumb through a magazine.

41 Prepositions and Prepositional Phrases

Words such as *to*, *from*, *over*, and *under* show the relations between other words; these words are prepositions, and they are one of the more challenging elements of English writing. You will need to decide which preposition to use for your intended meaning and understand how to use verbs that include prepositions, such as *take off*, *pick up*, and *put up with*.

41a Use prepositions idiomatically.

Multilingual

Even if you know where to use a preposition, it can be difficult to determine which preposition to use. Each of the most common prepositions has a wide range of applications, and this range never coincides exactly from one language to another. See, for example, how *in* and *on* are used in English.

▶ The peaches are *in* the refrigerator.
▶ The peaches are *on* the table.
▶ Is that a diamond ring *on* your finger?

The Spanish translations of these sentences all use the same preposition (*en*), a fact that might lead you astray in English.

Quick Help

Using Prepositions Idiomatically

1. **Keep in mind typical examples of each preposition.**

   IN The peaches are *in* the refrigerator.

   There are still some pickles *in* the jar.

   The book you are looking for is *in* the bookcase.

   Here the object of the preposition *in* is a container that encloses something.

   ON The peaches are *on* the table.

   There are still some pickles *on* the plate.

   The book you are looking for is *on* the top shelf.

   Here the object of the preposition *on* is a horizontal surface with which something is in direct contact.

2. **Learn other examples that show some similarities and some differences in meaning.**

   IN You shouldn't drive *in* a snowstorm.

   Here there is no container, but like a container, the falling snow surrounds the driver. The preposition *in* is used for other weather-related expressions as well: *in a tornado, in the sun, in the rain*.

   ON Is that a diamond ring *on* your finger?

   The preposition *on* is used to describe things we wear: *the hat on his head*, *the shoes on her feet*, *the tattoo on his back*.

3. **Use your imagination to create mental images that can help you remember figurative uses of prepositions.**

   IN Michael is *in* love.

   The preposition *in* is often used to describe a state of being: *in love*, *in pain*, *in a panic*. As a way to remember this, you might imagine the person immersed *in* this state of being.

4. **Try to learn prepositions not in isolation but as part of a system.**
For example, in identifying the location of a place or an event, you can use the three prepositions *at*, *in*, and *on*. *At* specifies the exact point in space or time.

AT   There will be a meeting tomorrow *at* 9:30 AM *at* 160 Main Street.

Expanses of space or time within which a place is located or an event takes place might be seen as containers and so require *in*.

IN   I arrived *in* the United States *in* January.

On must be used in two cases: with the names of streets (but not the exact address) and with days of the week or month.

ON   The airline's office is *on* Fifth Avenue.

I'll be moving to my new apartment *on* September 30.

▶ Is that a ruby ring ~~in~~ ^{on} your finger?

There is no easy solution to the challenge of using English prepositions idiomatically. Search engines and online databases of English usage can, however, help you see how other writers have expressed a particular idiom. You can also try the strategies in the box in this section.

41b Use two-word verbs idiomatically.

Multilingual

Some words that look like prepositions do not always function as prepositions. Consider the following two sentences:

▶ The balloon rose *off* the ground.
▶ The plane took *off* without difficulty.

In the first sentence, *off* is a preposition that introduces the prepositional phrase *off the ground*. In the second, *off* does not function as a preposition. Instead, it combines with *took* to form a two-word verb with its own meaning. Such a verb is called a phrasal verb, and the word *off*, when used this way, is called an adverbial particle. Many prepositions can function as particles to form phrasal verbs.

Phrasal verbs

The verb + particle combination that makes up a phrasal verb is a single entity that often cannot be torn apart.

>   *off*
> ▶ The plane took ^ without difficulty. ~~off.~~
>   ^

However, when a phrasal verb takes a direct object (34a), the particle may sometimes be separated from the verb by the object.

> ▶ I *picked up my baggage* at the terminal.
> ▶ I *picked my baggage up* at the terminal.

If a personal pronoun (such as *it*, *her*, or *him*) is used as the direct object, that pronoun must separate the verb from its particle.

> ▶ I *picked it up* at the terminal.

Prepositional verbs

Some idiomatic two-word verbs are not phrasal verbs.

> ▶ We *ran into* our neighbor on the train.

Here, *into* is a preposition, and *our neighbor* is its object. You can't separate the verb from the preposition (*We ran our neighbor into on the train* does not make sense in English). Verbs like *run into* are called prepositional verbs.

Notice that *run into our neighbor* is different from a normal verb and prepositional phrase, such as *run into a room*. The combination *run + into* has a special meaning, "meet by chance," that you could not guess from the meanings of *run* and *into*.

English has many idiomatic prepositional verbs. Here is a small sample.

PREPOSITIONAL VERB	MEANING
take after	resemble (usually a parent or older relative)
get over	recover from
count on	trust

Other prepositional verbs have predictable meanings but require you to use a particular preposition that you should learn along with the verb: *depend on*, *look at*, *listen to*, *approve of*.

Finally, look out for phrasal-prepositional verbs such as the following, which include a verb, a particle, and a preposition in a set order.

PHRASAL-PREPOSITIONAL VERB	MEANING
put up with	tolerate
look forward to	anticipate with pleasure
get away with	avoid punishment for

42 Comma Splices and Fused Sentences

Writers sometimes use comma splices to create powerful special effects. In advertising and other slogans, comma splices can provide a catchy rhythm.

> Dogs have owners, cats have staff.   – BUMPER STICKER

42a Identify comma splices and fused sentences.

A comma splice results from placing only a comma between two independent clauses, as in this tweet:

> One thing is certain, girls everywhere need education.

A related construction is a fused, or run-on, sentence, which results from joining two independent clauses with no punctuation or connecting word between them. As a fused sentence, the tweet above would read *One thing is certain girls everywhere need education.*

Using comma splices is increasingly common in writing that aims for a casual, informal feel, but comma splices and fused sentences in formal academic writing are likely to draw an instructor's criticism. If you use comma splices and fused sentences in formal writing, be sure your audience can tell that you are doing so for a special effect.

42b Separate the clauses into two sentences.

The simplest way to revise comma splices or fused sentences is to separate them into two sentences.

COMMA SPLICE	My mother spends hours tilling the soil and moving manure/. ~~this~~ **This** part of gardening is nauseating.

FUSED SENTENCE	My mother spends hours tilling the soil and moving manure. ~~this~~ **This** part of gardening is nauseating.

If the two clauses are very short, making them two sentences may sound abrupt and terse, so some other method of revision is probably preferable.

357

Quick Help

Editing for Comma Splices and Fused Sentences

If you find no punctuation between two independent clauses — groups of words that can stand alone as sentences — you have identified a fused sentence. If you find two such clauses joined only by a comma, you have identified a comma splice. Revise comma splices and fused sentences with one of these methods.

1. Separate the clauses into two sentences. (42b)

   ▶ Education is an elusive idea. ~~it~~ It means different things to different people.

2. Link the clauses with a comma and a coordinating conjunction (*and*, *but*, *or*, *nor*, *for*, *so*, or *yet*). (42c)

   ▶ Education is an elusive idea, for it means different things to different people.

3. Link the clauses with a semicolon. (42d)

   ▶ Education is an elusive idea; it means different things to different people.

   If the clauses are linked with only a comma and a conjunctive adverb — a word like *however*, *then*, *therefore* — add a semicolon.

   ▶ Education is an elusive idea; indeed, it means different things to different people.

4. Recast the two clauses as one independent clause. (42e)

   ▶ ~~Education is an elusive idea, it~~ An elusive idea, education means different things to different people.

5. Recast one independent clause as a dependent clause. (42f)

   ▶ Education is an elusive idea because it means different things to different people.

6. In informal writing, link the clauses with a dash. (42g)

   ▶ Education is an elusive idea — it means different things to different people.

42c Link the clauses with a comma and a coordinating conjunction.

If the two clauses are closely related and equally important, join them with a comma and a coordinating conjunction (*and, but, or, nor, for, so,* or *yet*). (See 27a.)

COMMA SPLICE
I got up feeling bad, *and* I feel even worse now.

FUSED SENTENCE
I should pay my tuition, *but* I need a new car.

Language, Culture, and Context
Multilingual

Judging Sentence Length

In U.S. academic contexts, readers sometimes find a series of short sentences "choppy" and undesirable. If you want to connect two independent clauses into one sentence, be sure to join them using one of the methods discussed in this chapter so that you avoid creating a comma splice or fused sentence. Another useful tip for writing in American English is to avoid writing several very long sentences in a row. If you find this pattern in your writing, try breaking it up by including a shorter sentence occasionally.

Talking about Style

Comma Splices in Context

Spliced and fused sentences appear frequently in literary and journalistic writing, where they can create momentum with a breathless rush of details:

> Bald eagles are common, ospreys abound, we have herons and mergansers and kingfishers, we have logging with Percherons and Belgians, we have park land and nature trails, we have enough oddballs, weirdos, and loons to satisfy anybody. – ANNE CAMERON

Context is critical. Depending on audience, purpose, and situation, structures commonly considered errors can actually be appropriate and effective.

42d Link the clauses with a semicolon.

If the ideas in the two clauses are closely related and you want to give them equal emphasis, link them with a semicolon.

COMMA SPLICE   This photograph is not at all realistic; it even uses dreamlike images to convey its message.

FUSED SENTENCE   The practice of journalism is changing dramatically; advances in technology have sped up news cycles.

Be careful when you link clauses with a conjunctive adverb or a transitional phrase. You must precede such words and phrases with a semicolon (see 45a), with a period, or with a comma combined with a coordinating conjunction (27a).

COMMA SPLICE   Many developing countries have very high birthrates; therefore, most of their citizens are young.

FUSED SENTENCE   Many developing countries have very high birthrates. Therefore, most of their citizens are young.

FUSED SENTENCE   Many developing countries have very high birthrates, and therefore, most of their citizens are young.

SOME CONJUNCTIVE ADVERBS AND TRANSITIONAL PHRASES

also	indeed	similarly
anyway	in fact	still
besides	instead	then
certainly	likewise	therefore
finally	moreover	thus
furthermore	namely	undoubtedly
however	nevertheless	
in addition	next	
in contrast	now	

42e Rewrite the clauses as one independent clause.

Sometimes you can reduce two spliced or fused independent clauses to a single independent clause.

> COMMA SPLICE
> ~~A large part~~ **Most** of my mail is advertisements~~,~~ **and** ~~most of the rest is~~ bills.

42f Rewrite one independent clause as a dependent clause.

When one independent clause is more important than the other, try converting the less important one to a dependent clause (27b).

> COMMA SPLICE
> The arts and crafts movement, **which reacted against mass production,** called for handmade objects~~. it reacted against mass production.~~

In the revision, the writer chooses to emphasize the first clause, the one describing what the movement advocated, and to make the second clause, the one describing what it reacted against, into a dependent clause.

> FUSED SENTENCE
> **Although** Zora Neale Hurston is regarded as one of America's major novelists, she died in obscurity.

In the revision, the writer chooses to emphasize the second clause and to make the first one into a dependent clause by adding the subordinating conjunction *although*.

42g Link the two clauses with a dash.

In informal writing, you can use a dash to join the two clauses, especially when the second clause elaborates on the first clause.

> COMMA SPLICE
> Exercise trends come and go— this year yoga is hot.

43 Sentence Fragments

Sentence fragments are often used to make writing sound conversational, as in this Facebook status update:

> Realizing that there are no edible bagels in this part of Oregon. Sigh.

Fragments — groups of words that are punctuated as sentences but are not sentences — are often seen in intentionally informal writing and in public writing, such as advertising, that aims to attract attention or give a phrase special emphasis. But you should think carefully before using fragments in academic or professional writing, where some readers might regard them as errors.

43a Identify sentence fragments.

A group of words must meet three criteria to form a complete sentence. If it does not meet all three, it is a fragment. Revise a fragment by combining it with a nearby sentence or by rewriting it as a complete sentence.

1. A sentence must have a subject (34b).
2. A sentence must have a verb, not just a verbal. A verbal cannot function as a sentence's verb without an auxiliary verb (34d).

   VERB   The terrier is *barking*.

   VERBAL   The terrier *barking*.

3. Unless it is a question, a sentence must have at least one clause that does not begin with a subordinating word (33g). Following are some common subordinating words:

although	though
as	unless
because	when
before	where
how	whether
if	which
since	who
that	

43b Revise phrase fragments.

Phrases are groups of words that lack a subject, a verb, or both (34d). When verbal phrases, prepositional phrases, noun phrases, and appositive phrases are punctuated like sentences, they become fragments. To revise these fragments, attach them to an independent clause, or make them a separate sentence.

▶ NBC is broadcasting the debates/ ~~With~~ discussions afterward. [with]

> *With discussions afterward* is a prepositional phrase, not a sentence. The editing combines the phrase with an independent clause.

▶ The town's growth is controlled by zoning laws/ ~~A~~ strict set of regulations for builders and corporations. [a]

> *A strict set of regulations for builders and corporations* is an appositive phrase renaming the noun *zoning laws*. The editing attaches the fragment to the sentence containing that noun.

▶ Kamika stayed out of school for three months after Linda was born. [She did so to] ~~To~~ recuperate and to take care of the baby.

> *To recuperate and to take care of the baby* includes verbals, not verbs. The revision — adding a subject (*she*) and a verb (*did*) — turns the fragment into a separate sentence.

Fragments beginning with transitions

If you introduce an example or explanation with one of the following transitions, be certain you write a sentence, not a fragment.

also	for example	like
as a result	for instance	such as
besides	instead	that is

▶ Joan Didion has written on many subjects/ ~~Such~~ as the Hoover Dam and migraine headaches. [such]

> The second word group is a phrase, not a sentence. The editing combines it with an independent clause.

43c Revise compound-predicate fragments.

A compound predicate consists of two or more verbs, along with their modifiers and objects, that have the same subject. Fragments occur when one part of a compound predicate lacks a subject but is punctuated as a separate sentence. These fragments usually begin with *and, but,* or *or.* You can revise them by attaching them to the independent clause that contains the rest of the predicate.

▶ They sold their house/ ~~And~~ *and* moved into an apartment.

43d Revise dependent-clause fragments.

Dependent clauses contain both a subject and a verb, but they cannot stand alone as sentences; they depend on an independent clause to complete their meaning. Dependent clauses usually begin with words such as *after, because, before, if, since, though, unless, until, when, where, while, who, which,* and *that.* You can usually combine dependent-clause fragments with a nearby independent clause.

▶ When I decided to work part-time/, I gave up a lot of my earning potential.

If you cannot smoothly attach a clause to a nearby independent clause, try deleting the opening subordinating word and turning the dependent clause into a sentence.

▶ The majority of injuries in automobile accidents occur in two ways.
   ~~When an~~ *An* occupant either is hurt by something inside the car or is thrown from the car.

▲ **For visual analysis** This illustration shows tools in use. Writers use punctuation and mechanical devices such as capital letters to connect and separate information. How can you use these tools effectively?

Punctuation and Mechanics

The function of most punctuation . . . is to add precision and complexity to meaning. It increases the information potential of strings of words.

— LOUIS MENAND

44 Commas

Commas often play a crucial role in meaning. See how important the comma is in the following directions for making hot cereal:

> Add Cream of Wheat slowly, stirring constantly.

That sentence tells the cook to *add the cereal slowly*. If the comma came before the word *slowly*, however, the cook might add all of the cereal at once and *stir slowly*. Using commas correctly can help you communicate more effectively.

44a Use commas to set off introductory words, phrases, and clauses.

▶ However, health care costs keep rising.

▶ In the end, only you can decide.

▶ Wearing new running shoes, Logan prepared for the race.

▶ To win the contest, Connor needed skill and luck.

▶ Pencil poised in anticipation, Audrey waited for the drawing contest to begin.

▶ While friends watched, Lila practiced a gymnastics routine.

▶ If candidates expect to be taken seriously, they should suggest solutions for the problems of ordinary Americans.

Some writers omit the comma if the introductory element is short and does not seem to require a pause after it.

▶ *At the racetrack* Henry lost his entire paycheck.

However, you will seldom be wrong if you use a comma after an introductory element.

> ## Quick Help
>
> ### Editing for Commas
>
> Research for this book shows that five of the twenty most common errors in college writing involve commas. Check your writing for the following errors:
>
> 1. Check every sentence that doesn't begin with the subject to see whether it opens with an introductory element (a word, phrase, or clause that describes the subject or tells when, where, how, or why the main action of the sentence occurs). In these cases, use a comma to separate the introductory material from the main part of the sentence. (44a)
>
> 2. Look at every sentence that contains one of the conjunctions *and*, *but*, *or*, *nor*, *for*, *so*, or *yet*. If the groups of words both before and after the conjunction function as complete sentences, you have a compound sentence. Make sure to use a comma before the conjunction. (44b)
>
> 3. Look at each adjective clause beginning with *which*, *who*, *whom*, *whose*, *when*, or *where*, and at each phrase and appositive. (34e) Is the element essential to the meaning of the sentence? If the sentence would be unclear without it, do not set off the element with commas. (44c)
>
> 4. Make sure that adjective clauses beginning with *that* are not set off with commas. Do not use commas between subjects and verbs, verbs and objects or complements, or prepositions and objects; to separate parts of compound constructions other than compound sentences; to set off restrictive clauses; or before the first or after the last item in a series. (44c and d)
>
> 5. Do not use a comma alone to separate sentences; this would create a comma splice (see Chapter 42).

44b Use commas with conjunctions that join clauses in compound sentences.

A comma usually precedes a coordinating conjunction (*and, but, or, nor, for, so,* or *yet*) that joins two independent clauses in a compound sentence (34e).

▶ The title sounds impressive, but *administrative clerk* is just another word for *photocopier.*

▶ The show started at last, and the crowd grew quiet.

With very short clauses, you can sometimes omit the comma.

▶ **She saw her chance and she took it.**

Always use the comma if there is any chance the sentence will be misread without it.

▶ **I opened the junk drawer, and the cabinet door jammed.**
                                    ^

Use a semicolon rather than a comma when the clauses are long and complex or contain their own commas.

▶ **When these early migrations took place, the ice was still confined to the lands in the far north; but eight hundred thousand years ago, when man was already established in the temperate latitudes, the ice moved southward until it covered large parts of Europe and Asia.**
                                    – ROBERT JASTROW, *Until the Sun Dies*

44c Use commas to set off nonrestrictive elements.

Nonrestrictive elements are word groups that do not limit, or restrict, the meaning of the noun or pronoun they modify. Setting nonrestrictive elements off with commas shows your readers that the information is not essential to the meaning of the sentence. Restrictive elements, on the other hand, *are* essential to meaning and should *not* be set off with commas. The same sentence may mean different things with and without the commas:

▶ **The bus drivers rejecting the management offer remained on strike.**
▶ **The bus drivers, rejecting the management offer, remained on strike.**

The first sentence says that only *some* bus drivers, the ones rejecting the offer, remained on strike. The second says that *all* the drivers did.

Since the decision to include or omit commas affects how readers interpret your sentence, you should think especially carefully about what you mean to say and then use commas (or omit them) accordingly.

RESTRICTIVE   Drivers *who have been convicted of drunken driving* should lose their licenses.

In the preceding sentence, the clause *who have been convicted of drunken driving* is essential because it explains that only drivers who have been convicted of drunken driving should lose their licenses. Therefore, it is *not* set off with commas.

NONRESTRICTIVE	The two drivers involved in the accident, *who have been convicted of drunken driving,* should lose their licenses.

In the second sentence, however, the clause *who have been convicted of drunken driving* is not essential to the meaning because it merely provides more information about what it modifies, *The two drivers involved in the accident.* Therefore, the clause is set off with commas.

To decide whether an element is restrictive or nonrestrictive, read the sentence without the element, and see if the deletion changes the meaning of the rest of the sentence.

- If the deletion does change the meaning of the sentence, the element is probably restrictive, and you should not set it off with commas.
- If it does not change the meaning, the element is probably nonrestrictive and requires commas.

Adjective and adverb clauses

An adjective clause that begins with *that* is always restrictive; do not set it off with commas. An adjective clause beginning with *which* may be either restrictive or nonrestrictive; however, some writers prefer to use *which* only for nonrestrictive clauses, which they set off with commas.

RESTRICTIVE CLAUSES

▶ The claim *that men like seriously to battle one another to some sort of finish* is a myth.
–   JOHN MCMURTRY, "Kill 'Em! Crush 'Em! Eat 'Em Raw!"

The *that* clause is necessary to the meaning because it explains which claim is a myth; therefore, the clause is not set off with commas.

▶ The man‚ who rescued Jana's puppy‚ won her eternal gratitude.

The *who* clause is necessary to the meaning because only the man who rescued the puppy won the gratitude; therefore, the clause takes no commas.

NONRESTRICTIVE CLAUSES

▶ I borrowed books from the rental library of Shakespeare and Company, *which was the library and bookstore of Sylvia Beach at 12 rue de l'Odeon.*
–   ERNEST HEMINGWAY, *A Moveable Feast*

The clause describing Shakespeare and Company is not necessary to the meaning of the sentence and therefore is set off with a comma.

In general, set off an adverb clause that follows a main clause only if it begins with *although, even though, while,* or another subordinating conjunction expressing contrast.

▶ Johan uses semicolons frequently, while Cheryl prefers periods and short
sentences.
‸

The clause *while Cheryl prefers periods and short sentences* expresses contrast;
therefore, it is set off with a comma.

Do *not* set off any other adverb clause that follows a main clause.

▶ Remember to check your calculations, before you submit the form.

Phrases

Participial phrases may be restrictive or nonrestrictive. Prepositional
phrases are usually restrictive, but sometimes they are not essential to the
meaning of a sentence and are set off with commas (34d).

NONRESTRICTIVE PHRASES

▶ Frédéric Chopin, in poor health, still composed prolifically.
‸   ‸

The phrase *in poor health* does not limit the meaning of *Frédéric Chopin* and so
is set off with commas.

Appositives

An appositive renames a nearby noun (34d). When an appositive is not
essential to identify what it renames, it is set off with commas.

NONRESTRICTIVE APPOSITIVES

▶ Jon Stewart, an actor and comic, became a respected political
‸   ‸
commentator.

Jon Stewart's name identifies him; the appositive *an actor and comic* provides
extra information.

RESTRICTIVE APPOSITIVES

▶ Mozart's opera, *The Marriage of Figaro*, was considered revolutionary.

The appositive is restrictive because Mozart wrote more than one opera.

44d Use commas with items in a series.

▶ He has plundered our seas, ravaged our coasts, burnt our towns, and
destroyed the lives of our people.   – Declaration of Independence

You may see a series with no comma after the next-to-last item, particularly in newspaper writing. Occasionally, however, omitting the comma can cause confusion.

> ▶ All the cafeteria's vegetables — broccoli, green beans, peas, and
>   carrots — were cooked to a gray mush.
>   ^
>
> Without the comma after *peas,* you wouldn't know if there were three choices (the third being a *mixture* of peas and carrots) or four.

When the items in a series contain commas of their own or other punctuation, separate them with semicolons rather than commas (45b).

Coordinate adjectives, those that relate equally to the noun they modify, should be separated by commas.

> ▶ The long, twisting, muddy road led to a shack in the woods.
>   ^   ^

In a sentence like *The cracked bathroom mirror reflected his face,* however, *cracked* and *bathroom* are not coordinate because *bathroom mirror* is the equivalent of a single word, which is modified by *cracked*. Hence, they are *not* separated by commas.

You can usually determine whether adjectives are coordinate by inserting *and* between them. If the sentence makes sense with the *and,* the adjectives are coordinate and should be separated by commas.

> ▶ They are sincere *and* talented *and* inquisitive researchers.
>
> The sentence makes sense with the *and*s, so the adjectives should be separated by commas: *They are sincere, talented, inquisitive researchers.*
>
> ▶ Byron carried an elegant *and* pocket watch.
>
> The sentence does not make sense with *and,* so the adjectives *elegant* and *pocket* should not be separated by a comma: *Byron carried an elegant pocket watch.*

44e Use commas to set off parenthetical and transitional expressions.

Parenthetical expressions add comments or information. Because they often interrupt the flow of a sentence, they are usually set off with commas.

> ▶ Some studies have shown that chocolate, of all things, helps to prevent
>   ^   ^
>   tooth decay.
>
> ▶ Roald Dahl's stories, it turns out, were often inspired by his own
>   ^   ^
>   childhood.

Transitional expressions, conjunctive adverbs (words such as *however* and *furthermore*), and other words and phrases used to connect parts of sentences are usually set off with commas (4d).

▶ **Ozone is a by-product of dry cleaning, for example.**

44f Use commas to set off contrasting elements, interjections, direct address, and tag questions.

CONTRASTING ELEMENTS

▶ On official business it was she, *not my father*, one would usually hear on the phone or in stores.

       – RICHARD RODRIGUEZ, "Aria: A Memoir of a Bilingual Childhood"

INTERJECTIONS

▶ *My God*, who wouldn't want a wife?

       – JUDY BRADY, "I Want a Wife"

DIRECT ADDRESS

▶ Remember, *sir*, that you are under oath.

TAG QUESTIONS

▶ The governor did not veto the unemployment bill, *did she*?

44g Use commas with dates, addresses, titles, and numbers.

Dates

Use a comma between the day of the week and the month, between the day of the month and the year, and between the year and the rest of the sentence, if any.

▶ **The attacks on the morning of Tuesday, September 11, 2001, took the**

   United States by surprise.

Do not use commas with dates in inverted order or with dates consisting of only the month and the year.

▶ She dated the letter *26 August 2015.*

▶ Thousands of Germans swarmed over the Berlin Wall in *November 1989.*

Addresses and place-names

Use a comma after each part of an address or place-name, including the state if there is no ZIP code. Do not precede a ZIP code with a comma.

▶ Forward my mail to the Department of English, The Ohio State University, Columbus, Ohio 43210.

▶ Portland, Oregon, is much larger than Portland, Maine.

Titles

Use commas to set off a title such as *MD* or *PhD* from the name preceding it and from the rest of the sentence. The titles *Jr.* and *Sr.,* however, often appear without commas.

▶ Oliver Sacks, MD, wrote about the way the mind works.

▶ Martin Luther King Jr. was one of the twentieth century's greatest orators.

Numbers

In numerals of five digits or more, use a comma between each group of three, starting from the right.

▶ The city's population rose to *158,000* in the 2000 census.

The comma is optional within numerals of four digits but never occurs in four-digit dates, street addresses, or page numbers.

▶ The college had an enrollment of *3,789* [or *3789*] in the fall of 2018.

▶ My grandparents live at *2428* Loring Place.

▶ Turn to page *1566.*

44h Use commas to set off most quotations.

Commas set off a quotation from words used to introduce or identify the source of the quotation. A comma following a quotation goes inside the closing quotation mark. (See 49d for advice about using colons instead of commas to introduce quotations.)

▶ A German proverb warns, "Go to law for a sheep, and lose your cow."

▶ "All I know about grammar," said Joan Didion, "is its infinite power."

Do not use a comma after a question mark or exclamation point.

▶ "What's a thousand dollars?" asks Groucho Marx in *The Cocoanuts.* "Mere chicken feed. A poultry matter."

▶ "Out, damned spot!" cries Lady Macbeth.

Do not use a comma when you introduce a quotation with *that*.

▶ The writer of Ecclesiastes concludes that "all is vanity."

Do not use a comma before an indirect quotation — one that does not use the speaker's exact words.

▶ Patrick Henry declared that he wanted either liberty or death.

44i   Use commas to prevent confusion.

Sometimes commas are necessary to make sentences easier to read or understand.

▶ The members of the dance troupe strutted in, in matching costumes.

▶ Before, I had planned to major in biology.

44j   Eliminate unnecessary commas.

Excessive use of commas can spoil an otherwise fine sentence.

Around restrictive elements

Do not use commas to set off restrictive elements — elements that limit, or define, the meaning of the words they modify or refer to (44c).

▶ I don't let my children watch films that are violent.

▶ A law reforming campaign financing was passed in 2002.

▶ The actor Chiwetel Ejiofor might win this award.

Between subjects and verbs, verbs and objects or complements, and prepositions and objects

Do not use a comma between a subject and its verb, a verb and its object or complement, or a preposition and its object. This rule holds true even if the subject, object, or complement is a long phrase or clause.

▶ Watching movies late at night⁄ is a way for me to relax.

▶ Parents must decide⁄ how much television their children may watch.

▶ The winner of⁄ the community-service award stepped forward.

In compound constructions

In compound constructions (other than compound sentences — see 44b), do not use a comma before or after a coordinating conjunction that joins the two parts.

▶ Improved health care⁄ and more free trade were two of the administration's goals.

The *and* here joins parts of a compound subject, which should not be separated by a comma.

▶ Donald Trump was born rich⁄ and used his money to make more money.

The *and* here joins parts of a compound predicate, which should not be separated by a comma.

Before the first or after the last item in a series

▶ The auction included⁄ furniture, paintings, and china.

▶ The swimmer took slow, elegant, powerful⁄ strokes.

45 Semicolons

The following public-service announcement, posted in New York City subway cars, reminded commuters what to do with a used newspaper at the end of the ride:

Please put it in a trash can; that's good news for everyone.

The semicolon in the subway announcement separates two clauses that could have been written as separate sentences. Semicolons, which create a pause stronger than that of a comma but not as strong as the full pause of a period, show close connections between related ideas.

45a   Use semicolons to link independent clauses.

Though a comma and a coordinating conjunction often join independent clauses, semicolons provide writers with subtler ways of signaling closely related clauses. The clause following a semicolon often restates an idea expressed in the first clause; it sometimes expands on or presents a contrast to the first.

> ▶ **Immigration acts were passed; newcomers had to prove, besides moral correctness and financial solvency, their ability to read.**
> – Mary Gordon, "More Than Just a Shrine"

Gordon uses a semicolon to join the two clauses, giving the sentence an abrupt rhythm that suits the topic: laws that imposed strict requirements.

A semicolon should link independent clauses joined by conjunctive adverbs such as *therefore*, *however*, and *indeed* or transitional expressions such as *in fact*, *in addition*, and *for example* (33g).

> ▶ **The circus comes as close to being the world in microcosm as anything I know; in a way, it puts all the rest of show business in the shade.**
> – E. B. White, "The Ring of Time"

If two independent clauses joined by a coordinating conjunction contain commas, you may use a semicolon instead of a comma before the conjunction to make the sentence easier to read.

> ▶ **Every year, whether the Republican or the Democratic party is in office, more and more power drains away from the individual to feed vast reservoirs in far-off places; and we have less and less say about the shape of events which shape our future.**
> – William F. Buckley Jr., "Why Don't We Complain?"

> ### Quick Help
>
> **Editing for Semicolons**
>
> - If you use semicolons, be sure they appear only between independent clauses — groups of words that can stand alone as sentences (45a) — or between items in a series. (45b)
> - If you find few or no semicolons in your writing, ask yourself whether you should add some. Would any closely related ideas in two sentences be better expressed in one sentence with a semicolon? (45a)

45b Use semicolons to separate items in a series containing other punctuation.

Ordinarily, commas separate items in a series (44d). But when the items themselves contain commas or other marks of punctuation, using semicolons to separate the items will make the sentence clearer and easier to read.

▶ **Anthropology encompasses archeology, the study of ancient civilizations through artifacts; linguistics, the study of the structure and development of language; and cultural anthropology, the study of language, customs, and behavior.**

45c Revise misused semicolons.

A comma, not a semicolon, should separate an independent clause from a dependent clause or phrase.

▶ **The police found fingerprints;, which they used to identify the thief.**

▶ **The new system would encourage students to register for courses online;, thus streamlining registration.**

A colon, not a semicolon, should introduce a series or list.

▶ **The reunion tour includes the following bands;: Urban Waste, Murphy's Law, Rapid Deployment, and Ism.**

46   End Punctuation

Periods, question marks, and exclamation points often appear in advertising to create special effects or draw readers along from line to line.

> You have a choice to make.
> Where can you turn for advice?
> Ask our experts today!

End punctuation tells us how to read each sentence—as a matter-of-fact statement, a query, or an emphatic request. Making appropriate choices with end punctuation allows readers to understand exactly what you mean.

46a   Use periods appropriately.

Use a period to close sentences that make statements or give mild commands.

▶ **All books are either dreams or swords.**   – AMY LOWELL

▶ **Don't use a fancy word if a simpler word will do.**
         – GEORGE ORWELL, "Politics and the English Language"

A period also closes indirect questions, which report rather than ask questions.

▶ **We all wonder who will win the election.**

Until recently, periods have been used with most abbreviations in American English (see Chapter 51). However, more and more abbreviations are appearing without periods.

Mr.	MD	BC *or* B.C.
Ms.	PhD	BCE *or* B.C.E.
Mrs.	MBA	AD *or* A.D.
Jr.	RN	AM *or* a.m.
Dr.	Sen.	PM *or* p.m.

Some abbreviations rarely if ever appear with periods. These include the postal abbreviations of state names, such as *FL* and *TN* (though the traditional abbreviations, such as *Fla.* and *Tenn.,* do call for periods), and most groups of initials (*GE, CIA, AIDS, UNICEF*). If you are not sure whether a particular abbreviation should include periods, check a dictionary, or follow the style guidelines (such as those of the Modern Language Association) you are using in a research paper.

46b   Use question marks appropriately.

Use a question mark to close sentences that ask direct questions.

▶   **Have you finished the essay, or do you need more time?**

Question marks do not close *indirect* questions, which report rather than ask questions.

▶   **She asked whether I opposed his nomination?.**

Do not use a comma or a period immediately after a question mark that ends a direct quotation (48f).

▶   **"Am I my brother's keeper?/" Cain asked.**

▶   **Cain asked, "Am I my brother's keeper?"/**

Questions in a series may have question marks even when they are not separate sentences.

▶   **I often face a difficult choice: should I go to practice? finish my homework? spend time with my friends?**

A question mark in parentheses can be used to indicate that a writer is unsure of a date, a figure, or a word.

▶   **Quintilian died in 96 CE (?).**

46c   Use exclamation points appropriately.

Use an exclamation point to show surprise or strong emotion.

▶   **In those few moments of geologic time will be the story of all that has happened since we became a nation. And what a story it will be!**
        – JAMES RETTIE, "But a Watch in the Night"

Today, we live in a world of many exclamations. But use exclamation points sparingly in academic work because they can distract your readers or suggest that you are exaggerating. In general, try to create emphasis through word choice and sentence structure rather than with exclamation points.

▶ This university is so large, so varied, that attempting to tell someone everything about it would take three years**.**

Do not use a comma or a period after an exclamation point that ends a direct quotation.

▶ On my last visit, I looked out the sliding glass doors and ran breathlessly to Connor in the kitchen: "There's a *huge* black pig in the backyard!"

– ELLEN ASHDOWN, "Living by the Dead"

46d Consider end punctuation in informal writing.

In informal writing, especially texts and tweets with character limits, writers today are increasingly likely to omit end punctuation entirely. In informal writing that does use end punctuation, research shows that ellipses (. . .), or "dots," are on the rise; they can signal a trailing off of a thought or leave open the possibility of further communication. Exclamation marks can convey an excited or a chatty tone, so they are used more frequently in social media and other informal writing situations than in academic writing. And some writers have argued that ending informal writing with a period rather than no punctuation at all can suggest that the writer is irritated. The meaning of end punctuation is changing in informal contexts, so pay attention to how others communicate, and use what you learn in your own social writing.

47 Apostrophes

The little apostrophe can make a big difference in meaning. The following sign at a neighborhood swimming pool, for instance, says something different from what the writer probably intended:

Please deposit your garbage (and your guests) in the trash receptacles before leaving the pool area.

Adding a single apostrophe would offer a more neighborly statement: *Please deposit your garbage (and your guests') in the trash receptacles before leaving the pool area* asks that the guests' garbage, not the guests themselves, be thrown away.

> ## Quick Help
>
> ### Editing for Apostrophes
>
> - Check each noun that ends in -*s* and shows possession. Is the apostrophe in the right place, either before or after the -*s*? (47a)
> - Check the possessive form of each indefinite pronoun, such as *someone's*. Be sure the apostrophe comes before the -*s*. (47a)
> - Check each personal pronoun that ends with -*s* (*yours*, *his*, *hers*, *its*, *ours*, *theirs*) to make sure it does not include an apostrophe. (47a)
> - Does each *it's* mean *it is* or *it has*? If not, then remove the apostrophe. (47b)
> - Make sure other contractions use apostrophes correctly. (47b)

47a   Use apostrophes appropriately to show possession.

The possessive case denotes ownership or possession of one thing by another.

Singular nouns and indefinite pronouns

Add an apostrophe and -*s* to form the possessive of most singular nouns, including those that end in -*s,* and of indefinite pronouns (33c). Do not use apostrophes with the possessive forms of personal pronouns: *yours, his, hers, its, ours, theirs.*

▶ The *bus's* fumes overpowered her.

▶ *Star Wars* made George *Lucas's* fortune.

▶ *Anyone's* guess is as good as mine.

Plural nouns

To form the possessive case of plural nouns not ending in -*s,* add an apostrophe and -*s.*

▶ The *men's* department sells business attire.

For plural nouns ending in -*s,* add only the apostrophe.

▶ The three *clowns'* costumes were bright green and orange.

Compound nouns

For compound nouns, make the last word in the group possessive.

▶ The *secretary of state's* speech was televised.

▶ My *in-laws'* disapproval dampened our enthusiasm for the new house.

Two or more nouns

To signal individual possession by two or more owners, make each noun possessive.

▶ Great differences exist between *Jerry Bruckheimer's* and *Ridley Scott's* films.

Bruckheimer and Scott have produced different films.

To signal joint possession, make only the last noun possessive.

▶ *Wallace and Gromit's* creator is Nick Park.

Wallace and Gromit have the same creator.

47b Use apostrophes in contractions.

Contractions are two-word combinations formed by leaving out certain letters, which are indicated by an apostrophe.

it is, it has/it's	you will/you'll	do not/don't
was not/wasn't	I would, I had/I'd	let us/let's
I am/I'm	would not/wouldn't	cannot/can't

Contractions are common in conversation and informal writing. Academic and professional work, however, often calls for greater formality.

Use of it's and its

Its is the possessive form of *it*. *It's* is a contraction for *it is* or *it has*.

▶ This disease is unusual; *its* symptoms vary from person to person.

▶ *It's* a difficult disease to diagnose.

8888

47c Avoid apostrophes in most plural forms.

Many style guides now advise against using apostrophes for any plurals.

▶ The gymnasts need scores of *8s* and *9s* to qualify for the finals.

Others use an apostrophe and *-s* to form the plural of numbers, letters, and words referred to as terms.

▶ The five *Shakespeare's* in the essay were spelled five different ways.

Check your instructor's preference.

48 Quotation Marks

As a way of bringing other people's words into your own, quotations can be a powerful writing tool.

> Mrs. Macken encourages parents to get books for their children, to read to them when they are "li'l," and when they start school to make certain they attend regularly. She holds herself up as an example of "a millhand's daughter who wanted to be a schoolteacher and did it through sheer hard work."
> – SHIRLEY BRICE HEATH, *Ways with Words*

The writer lets her subject speak for herself—and lets readers hear Mrs. Macken's voice.

48a Use quotation marks to identify direct quotations.

▶ The president asked Congress to "try common sense."
▶ She smiled and said, "Son, this is a day I will never forget."

Use quotation marks to enclose the words of each speaker within running dialogue. Mark each shift between speakers with a new paragraph.

> "I want no proof of their affection," said Elinor; "but of their engagement I do."
> "I am perfectly satisfied of both."
> "Yet not a syllable has been said to you on the subject, by either of them."
> – JANE AUSTEN, *Sense and Sensibility*

> ## Quick Help
>
> ### Editing for Quotation Marks
>
> - Use quotation marks around direct quotations and titles of short works. (48a and c)
> - Do not use quotation marks around set-off quotations of more than four lines of prose or more than three lines of poetry, or around titles of long works. (48b and c)
> - Use quotation marks to signal irony and invented words, but do so sparingly. (48e)
> - Check other punctuation used with closing quotation marks. (48f)
>
>   Periods and commas should be *inside* the quotation marks.
>
>   Colons, semicolons, and footnote numbers should be *outside*.
>
>   Question marks, exclamation points, and dashes should be *inside* if they are part of the quoted material, *outside* if they are not.
> - Never use quotation marks around indirect quotations. (48g)
> - Do not use quotation marks just to add emphasis to words. (48g)

Use single quotation marks for a quotation within a quotation. Open and close the quoted passage with double quotation marks, and change any quotation marks that appear *within* the quotation to single quotation marks.

▶ Baldwin says, "The title 'The Uses of the Blues' does not refer to music; I don't know anything about music."

48b Punctuate block quotations and poetry appropriately.

If the prose passage you wish to quote is more than four typed lines, set the quotation off by starting it on a new line and indenting it one-half inch from the left margin. This format, known as block quotation, does not require quotation marks.

> In "Suspended," Joy Harjo tells of her first awareness of jazz as a child:
>
> > My rite of passage into the world of humanity occurred then, via jazz. The music made a startling bridge between the familiar and strange lands, an appropriate vehicle, for . . . we were there when jazz was born. I recognized it, that humid afternoon in my formative years, as a way to speak beyond the confines of ordinary language. I still hear it. (84)

This block quotation, including the ellipsis dots and the page number in parentheses at the end, follows the style of the Modern Language Association (MLA). The American Psychological Association (APA) has different guidelines for setting off block quotations. (See Chapters 54 and 58.)

When quoting poetry, if the quotation is brief (fewer than four lines), include it within your text. Separate the lines of the poem with slashes, each preceded and followed by a space, in order to tell the reader where one line of the poem ends and the next begins.

> In one of his best-known poems, Robert Frost remarks, "Two roads diverged in a yellow wood, and I — / I took the one less traveled by / And that has made all the difference" (lines 18–20).

To quote more than three lines of poetry, indent the block one-half inch from the left margin. Do not use quotation marks. Take care to follow the spacing, capitalization, punctuation, and other features of the original poem.

> The duke in Robert Browning's poem "My Last Duchess" is clearly a jealous, vain person, whose arrogance is illustrated through this statement:
>
> > She thanked men — good! but thanked
> >
> > Somehow — I know not how — as if she ranked
> >
> > My gift of a nine-hundred-years-old name
> >
> > With anybody's gift. (lines 31–34)

48c　Use quotation marks for titles of short works.

Quotation marks are used to enclose the titles of short poems, short stories, articles, essays, songs, sections of books, and episodes of television and radio programs.

- ▶ "Dover Beach" moves from calmness to sadness. [poem]
- ▶ Alice Walker's "Everyday Use" is about more than just quilts. [short story]
- ▶ The *Atlantic* published an article entitled "Illiberal Education." [article]
- ▶ In "Photography," Susan Sontag considers the role of photography in our society. [essay]
- ▶ The *Nature* episode "Echo of the Elephants" portrays ivory hunters unfavorably. [television series episode]

Use italics rather than quotation marks for the titles of television series, magazines, movies, and other long works (see 52a).

48d Use quotation marks appropriately for definitions.

 In social science, the term *sample size* means "the number of individuals being studied in a research project."
>   – KATHLEEN STASSEN BERGER AND ROSS A. THOMPSON,
>   *The Developing Person through Childhood and Adolescence*

Use italics for words used as a term, like *sample size* above (see 52b).

48e Use quotation marks to identify irony and invented terms.

To show readers that you are using a word or phrase ironically or that you made it up, enclose it in quotation marks.

 The "banquet" consisted of dried-out chicken and canned vegetables.

The quotation marks suggest that the meal was not a banquet.

▶ Your whole first paragraph or first page may have to be guillotined in any case after your piece is finished: it is a kind of "forebirth."
>   – JACQUES BARZUN, "A Writer's Discipline"

The writer made up the term *forebirth*.

48f Follow conventions for other punctuation with quotation marks.

Periods and commas go *inside* closing quotation marks.

▶ "Don't compromise yourself," said Janis Joplin. "You are all you've got."

When you follow MLA style for documenting a short quotation, place the period *after* the parentheses with source information (see Chapter 55).

▶ In places, de Beauvoir "sees Marxists as believing in subjectivity" (Whitmarsh 63).

For more information on using a comma with a quotation, see 44h.

Colons, semicolons, and footnote numbers go *outside* closing quotation marks.

▶ I felt one emotion after finishing "Eveline": sorrow.

▶ Everything is dark, and "a visionary light settles in her eyes"; this vision, this light, is her salvation.

▶ Tragedy is defined by Aristotle as "an imitation of an action that is serious and of a certain magnitude."[1]

Question marks, exclamation points, and dashes go *inside* if they are part of the quoted material, *outside* if they are not.

PART OF THE QUOTATION

▶ The cashier asked, "Would you like to super-size that?"

▶ "Jump!" one of the firefighters shouted.

NOT PART OF THE QUOTATION

▶ What is the theme of "The Birth-Mark"?

▶ "Break a leg" — that phrase is supposed to bring good luck.

48g Revise misused quotation marks.

Do not use quotation marks for indirect quotations — those that do not use someone's exact words.

▶ Our mother told us that ⸂she was sure she would never forget the incident.⸃

Do not use quotation marks just to add emphasis to particular words or phrases.

▶ Much time was spent speculating about their ⸂relationship.⸃

Do not use quotation marks around slang or colloquial language; they create the impression that you are apologizing for using those words. If you have a good reason to use slang or a colloquial term, use it without quotation marks.

▶ After our twenty-mile hike, we were ready to ⸂turn in.⸃

Language, Culture, and Context

Multilingual

Quoting in American English

Remember that the way you mark quotations in American English (" ") may not be the same as in other languages. In French, for example, quotations are marked with *guillemets* or angle quotes (« »), while in German, quotations take split-level marks („ "). Writers of British English use single quotation marks first and, when necessary, double quotation marks for quotations within quotations. If you are writing for an American audience, be careful to follow the U.S. conventions governing quotation marks.

49 Other Punctuation Marks

Parentheses, brackets, dashes, colons, slashes, and ellipses are everywhere. Every URL includes colons and slashes, and dashes and ellipses are increasingly common in writing that expresses conversational informality.

You can also use these punctuation marks for more formal purposes: to signal relationships among parts of sentences, to create particular rhythms, and to help readers follow your thoughts.

49a Use parentheses appropriately.

Use parentheses to enclose material that is of minor or secondary importance in a sentence — material that supplements, clarifies, comments on, or illustrates what precedes or follows it.

▶ During my research, I found problems with the flat-rate income tax (a single-rate tax with no deductions).

Textual citations

▶ Freud and his followers have had a most significant impact on the ways abnormal functioning is understood and treated (Joseph, 1991).

— RONALD J. COMER, *Abnormal Psychology*

▶ Zamora notes that Kahlo referred to her first self-portrait, given to a close friend, as "your Botticelli" (110).

The first in-text citation shows the style of the American Psychological Association (APA); the second, the style of the Modern Language Association (MLA).

Numbers or letters in a list

▶ Five distinct styles can be distinguished: (1) Old New England, (2) Deep South, (3) Middle American, (4) Wild West, and (5) Far West or Californian.   – ALISON LURIE, *The Language of Clothes*

Other punctuation marks with parentheses

A period may be placed either inside or outside a closing parenthesis, depending on whether the parenthetical text is part of a larger sentence. A comma, if needed, is always placed *outside* a closing parenthesis (and never before an opening one).

▶ Gene Tunney's single defeat in an eleven-year career was to a flamboyant and dangerous fighter named Harry Greb ("The Human Windmill"), who seems to have been, judging from boxing literature, the dirtiest fighter in history.   – JOYCE CAROL OATES, "On Boxing"

Parentheses, commas, and dashes

In general, use commas when the material to be set off is least interruptive (Chapter 44), parentheses when it is more interruptive, and dashes when it is the most interruptive (49c).

 49b Use brackets appropriately.

Use brackets to enclose parenthetical elements in material that is itself within parentheses and to enclose explanatory words or comments that you are inserting into a quotation.

Material within parentheses

▶ Eventually the investigation had to examine the major agencies (including the previously sacrosanct National Security Agency [NSA]) that were conducting covert operations.

Material within quotations

▶ Massing notes that "on average, it [Fox News] attracts more than eight
million people daily — more than double the number who watch CNN."

The bracketed words clarify *it* in the original quotation.

In the quotation in the following sentence, the artist Gauguin's name
is misspelled. The bracketed word *sic,* which means "so," tells readers
that the person being quoted — not the writer who has picked up the
quotation — made the mistake.

▶ One admirer wrote, "She was the most striking woman I'd ever seen — a
sort of wonderful combination of Mia Farrow and one of Gaugin's [*sic*]
Polynesian nymphs."

49c Use dashes appropriately.

Dashes give more emphasis than parentheses to the material they enclose.

▶ The pleasures of reading itself — who doesn't remember? — were like
those of Christmas cake, a sweet devouring.
— EUDORA WELTY, "A Sweet Devouring"

Explanatory material

▶ Indeed, several of modern India's greatest scholars — such as the Mughal
historian Muzaffar Alam of the University of Chicago — are madrasa
graduates.   — WILLIAM DALRYMPLE

Material at the end of a sentence

▶ In the twentieth century it has become almost impossible to moralize
about epidemics — except those which are transmitted sexually.
— SUSAN SONTAG, *AIDS and Its Metaphors*

A sudden change in tone

▶ New York is a catastrophe — but a magnificent catastrophe.
— LE CORBUSIER

49d Use colons appropriately.

Use a colon to introduce explanations or examples and to separate some elements from one another.

Explanation, example, or appositive

▶ The men may also wear the getup known as Sun Belt Cool: a pale beige suit, open-collared shirt (often in a darker shade than the suit), cream-colored loafers and aviator sunglasses.
  – ALISON LURIE, *The Language of Clothes*

Series, list, or quotation

▶ At the baby's one-month birthday party, Ah Po gave him the Four Valuable Things: ink, inkslab, paper, and brush.
  – MAXINE HONG KINGSTON, *China Men*

▶ The teachers wondered: "Do boys and girls really learn differently?"

The preceding example could have taken a comma instead of a colon (see 44h). Use a colon rather than a comma to introduce a quotation when the lead-in is a complete sentence on its own.

▶ The State of the Union address contained one surprising statement: "America is addicted to oil."

Colons with other elements

SALUTATIONS IN FORMAL LETTERS
▶ Dear Dr. Chapman:

HOURS, MINUTES, AND SECONDS
▶ 4:59 PM
▶ 2:15:06

RATIOS
▶ a ratio of 5:1

BIBLICAL CHAPTERS AND VERSES
▶ I Corinthians 3:3–5

TITLES AND SUBTITLES
▶ *The Joy of Insight: Passions of a Physicist*

CITIES AND PUBLISHERS IN BIBLIOGRAPHIC ENTRIES
▶ Boston, MA: Bedford, 2020

Unnecessary colons

Do not put a colon between a verb and its object or complement.

▶ Some natural fibers are: cotton, wool, silk, and linen.

Do not put a colon between a preposition and its object or after such expressions as *such as, especially,* and *including.*

▶ In poetry, additional power may come from devices such as/ simile, metaphor, and alliteration.

49e Use slashes appropriately.

Use slashes to mark line divisions between two or three lines of poetry quoted within running text. When using a slash to separate lines of poetry, precede and follow it with a space (48b).

▶ In Sonnet 29, the persona states, "For thy sweet love rememb'red such wealth brings / That then I scorn to change my state with kings."

Slashes also separate parts of fractions and Internet addresses.

49f Use ellipses appropriately.

Ellipses, or ellipsis points, are three equally spaced dots. Ellipses usually indicate that something has been omitted from a quoted passage, but they can also signal a pause in speech. Ellipses are rampant on social media: too much of a good thing isn't so good after all!

Omissions

Just as you should carefully use quotation marks around any material that you quote directly from a source, so you should carefully use ellipses to indicate that you have left out part of a quotation that otherwise appears to be a complete sentence.

The ellipses in the following example (see p. 394) indicate two omissions — one in the middle of the sentence and one at the end. When you omit the last part of a quoted sentence, add a period after the ellipses, for a total of four dots. Be sure a complete sentence comes before and after the four points. If you are adding your own ellipses to a quotation that already has other ellipses, enclose yours in brackets.

ORIGINAL TEXT

▶ The quasi-official division of the population into three economic classes called high-, middle-, and low-income groups rather misses the point, because as a class indicator the amount of money is not as important as the source. — PAUL FUSSELL, "Notes on Class"

WITH ELLIPSES

▶ As Paul Fussell argues, "The quasi-official division of the population into three economic classes . . . rather misses the point. . . ."

If your shortened quotation ends with a source (such as a page number, a name, or a title), follow these steps:

1. Use three ellipsis points but no period after the quotation.
2. Add the closing quotation mark, closed up to the third ellipsis point.
3. Add the source documentation in parentheses.
4. Use a period to indicate the end of the sentence.

▶ Packer argues, "The Administration is right to reconsider its strategy . . ." (34).

Hesitation

▶ Then the voice, husky and familiar, came to wash over us — "The winnah, and still heavyweight champeen of the world . . . Joe Louis."
                        – MAYA ANGELOU, *I Know Why the Caged Bird Sings*

50   Capital Letters

Capital letters are a key signal in everyday life. Look around any store to see their importance: you can shop for Levi's or *any* blue jeans, for Coca-Cola or *any* cola, for Kleenex or *any* tissue. As these examples show, one of the most common reasons for capitalizing a word is to indicate that it is part of a name or title — of a brand, person, article, or something else.

 ## 50a   Capitalize the first word of a sentence or line of poetry.

Capitalize the first word of a sentence. If you are quoting a full sentence, capitalize the first word of the quotation.

▶ Kennedy said, "Let us never negotiate out of fear."

Quick Help

Editing for Capitalization

- Capitalize the first word of each sentence. If you quote a poem, follow its original capitalization. (50a)
- Check to make sure you have appropriately capitalized proper nouns and proper adjectives. (50b)
- Review where you have used titles of people or of works to be sure you have capitalized them correctly. (50b and c)
- Double-check the capitalization of geographical directions (*north* or *North*?), family relationships (*dad* or *Dad*?), and seasons of the year (*winter*, not *Winter*). (50d)

Capitalization of a sentence following a colon is optional.

▶ Gould cites the work of Darwin: The [*or* the] theory of natural selection incorporates the principle of evolutionary ties among all animals.

Capitalize a sentence within parentheses unless the parenthetical sentence is inserted into another sentence.

▶ Gould cites the work of Darwin. (Other researchers cite more recent evolutionary theorists.)

▶ Gould cites the work of Darwin (see page 150).

When citing poetry, follow the capitalization of the original poem. Though most poets capitalize the first word of each line in a poem, some poets do not.

▶ Morning sun heats up the young beech tree
  leaves and almost lights them into fireflies

    – June Jordan, "Aftermath"

50b Capitalize proper nouns and proper adjectives.

Capitalize proper nouns (those naming specific persons, places, and things) and most proper adjectives (those formed from proper nouns). All other nouns are common nouns and are not capitalized unless they begin a sentence or are used as part of a proper noun.

Proper nouns and adjectives	Common nouns and adjectives
PEOPLE	
Ang Lee	the film's director
Nixonian	political
NATIONS, NATIONALITIES, ETHNIC GROUPS, AND LANGUAGES	
Brazil, Brazilian	their native country, his citizenship
Italian American	an ethnic group
PLACES	
Pacific Ocean	an ocean
Hawaiian Islands	tropical islands
STRUCTURES AND MONUMENTS	
the Lincoln Memorial	a monument
the Eiffel Tower	a landmark
SHIPS, TRAINS, AIRCRAFT, AND SPACECRAFT	
the *Queen Mary*	a cruise ship
the *City of New Orleans*	the 6:00 train
ORGANIZATIONS, BUSINESSES, AND GOVERNMENT INSTITUTIONS	
United Auto Workers	a trade union
Library of Congress	certain federal agencies
ACADEMIC INSTITUTIONS AND COURSES	
University of Maryland	a state university
Political Science 102	my political science course
HISTORICAL EVENTS AND ERAS	
the Easter Uprising	a rebellion
the Renaissance	the fifteenth century
RELIGIONS AND RELIGIOUS TERMS	
God	a deity
the Qur'an	a holy book
Catholicism, Catholic	a religion, their religious affiliation
TRADE NAMES	
Nike	running shoes
Cheerios	cereal

Product names

Some contemporary companies use capitals called *InterCaps* in the middle of their own or their products' names. Follow the style you see in company advertising or on the product itself — *eBay, FedEx, iTunes.*

Titles of individuals

Capitalize titles used before a proper name. When used alone or following a proper name, most titles are not capitalized. One common exception is the word *president,* which many writers capitalize whenever it refers to the president of the United States.

Chief Justice Roberts	John Roberts, the chief justice
Professor Lisa Ede	my English professor
Dr. Cheryl Gold	Cheryl Gold, our doctor

50c Capitalize titles of works.

Capitalize most words in titles of books, articles, stories, speeches, essays, plays, poems, documents, films, paintings, and musical compositions. Do not capitalize an article (*a, an, the*), a preposition, a conjunction, or the *to* in an infinitive unless it is the first or last word in a title or subtitle.

Walt Whitman: A Life	Declaration of Independence
"As Time Goes By"	*Charlie and the Chocolate Factory*
"Shooting an Elephant"	*Rebel without a Cause*

Language, Culture, and Context

Multilingual

Learning English Capitalization

Capitalization systems vary considerably among languages, and some languages (Arabic, Chinese, Hindi, and Hebrew, for example) do not use capital letters at all. English may be the only language to capitalize the first-person singular pronoun (*I*), but Dutch and German capitalize some forms of the second-person pronoun (*you*). German capitalizes all nouns; English used to capitalize more nouns than it does now (see, for instance, the Declaration of Independence).

50d Revise unnecessary capitalization.

Do not capitalize a compass direction unless the word designates a specific
geographic region.

▶ Voters in the South and much of the West tend to favor socially
conservative candidates.

▶ John Muir headed ~~West,~~ *west,* motivated by the need to explore.

Do not capitalize a word indicating a family relationship unless the word is
used as part of the name or as a substitute for the name.

▶ I could always tell when Mother was annoyed with Aunt Rose.

▶ When she was a child, my ~~Mother~~ *mother* shared a room with my ~~Aunt.~~ *aunt.*

Do not capitalize seasons of the year and parts of the academic or financial
year.

spring	fall semester
winter	winter term
autumn	third-quarter earnings

Capitalizing entire words and phrases in online writing gives them
emphasis. On social media, writers may capitalize a few words or phrases
for comic effect (*"I am shocked, SHOCKED to hear you say that!"*). But
note that using all capital letters makes writing in digital environments feel
like shouting. In email and professional writing, use italics, boldface, or
underlining for emphasis.

51 Abbreviations and Numbers

Any time you look up an address, you see an abundance of abbreviations
and numbers, as in the following movie theater listing from a Google map
of Berkeley, California:

Oaks Theater	1875 Solano Av	Brk

Abbreviations and numbers allow writers to present detailed information
in a small amount of space.

51a Abbreviate some titles before and all titles after proper names.

Ms. Siphiwe Ndlovu	Henry Louis Gates Jr.
Mr. Adam Banks	Karen Lancry, MD
Dr. Atma Vermulakonda	Bronwyn LaMay, PhD

Other titles — including religious, academic, and government titles — should be spelled out in academic writing. In other writing, they can be abbreviated before a full name but should be written out when used with only a last name.

Rev. Fleming Rutledge	Reverend Rutledge
Prof. Vershawn Young	Professor Young
Gen. Colin Powell	General Powell

Do not use both a title and an academic degree with a person's name. Use one or the other. Instead of *Dr. Beverly Moss, PhD,* write *Dr. Beverly Moss* or *Beverly Moss, PhD.* (Note that academic degrees such as *RN* and *PhD* often appear without periods; see 46a.)

51b Abbreviate years and hours appropriately.

You can use the following abbreviations with numerals. Notice that AD precedes the numeral; all other abbreviations follow the numeral. Today, BCE and CE are generally preferred over BC and AD, and periods in all four of these abbreviations are optional.

399 BCE ("before the common era") *or* 399 BC ("before Christ")

49 CE ("common era") *or* AD 49 (*anno Domini,* Latin for "year of our Lord")

11:15 AM (*or* a.m.)

9:00 PM (*or* p.m.)

51c Abbreviate some business, government, and science terms.

As long as you can be sure your readers will understand them, use common abbreviations such as *PBS, NASA, DNA,* and *CIA.* If an abbreviation may be unfamiliar, however, spell out the full term the first time you use it, and give the abbreviation in parentheses. After that, you can use the abbreviation by itself.

▶ The Comprehensive Test Ban (CTB) Treaty was first proposed in the 1950s. For those nations signing it, the CTB would bring to a halt all nuclear weapons testing.

51d Use abbreviations in official company names.

Use such abbreviations as *Co.*, *Inc.*, *Corp.*, and *&* if they are part of a company's official name. Do not, however, use these abbreviations in most other contexts.

▶ Sears, Roebuck & Co. was the only large ~~corp.~~ in town.
corporation

▶ Paola has a part-time job at the Warner ~~Brothers~~ store in the mall.
Bros.

51e Use Latin abbreviations appropriately.

In general, avoid these Latin abbreviations except when citing sources:

e.g.	for example (*exempli gratia*)
etc.	and so forth (*et cetera*)
i.e.	that is (*id est*)
N.B.	note well (*nota bene*)
P.S.	postscript (*postscriptum*)

▶ Many firms have policies to help working parents — ~~e.g.,~~ flexible hours, parental leave, and day care.
for example,

▶ Before the conference began, Haivan unpacked the name tags, programs, pens, ~~etc.~~
and so forth.

51f   Use symbols and unit abbreviations appropriately.

Symbols such as %, +, $, and = are acceptable in charts and graphs. Dollar signs are acceptable with figures: *$11* (but not with words: *eleven dollars*). Units of measurement can be abbreviated in charts and graphs (*4 in.*) but not in the body of a paper (*four inches*).

Talking about Style

Abbreviations and Numbers in Different Fields

Use of abbreviations and numbers varies in different fields. See a typical example from a biochemistry textbook:

> The energy of a green photon . . . is 57 kilocalories per mole (kcal/mol). An alternative unit of energy is the joule (J), which is equal to 0.239 calorie; 1 kcal/mol is equal to 4.184 kJ/mol.
>
> – Lubert Stryer, *Biochemistry*

These two sentences demonstrate how useful figures and abbreviations can be; reading the same sentences would be very difficult if the numbers and units of measurement were all written out.

Become familiar with the conventions governing abbreviations and numbers in your field. The following books provide guidelines:

MLA Handbook for Writers of Research Papers for literature and the humanities

Publication Manual of the American Psychological Association for the social sciences

Scientific Style and Format: The CSE Manual for Authors, Editors, and Publishers for the natural sciences

The Chicago Manual of Style for the humanities

AIP Style Manual for physics and the applied sciences

51g   Use other abbreviations according to convention.

Some abbreviations required in notes and in source citations are not appropriate in the body of a paper.

CHAPTER AND PAGES	chapter, page, pages (*not* ch., p., pp.)
MONTHS	January, February (*not* Jan., Feb.)
STATES AND NATIONS	California, Mexico (*not* Calif., Mex.)

51h   Spell out numbers expressed in one or two words.

If you can write out a number in one or two words, do so. Use figures for longer numbers.

▶ Her screams were heard by 38̶ people, none of whom called the police.
      thirty-eight

▶ A baseball is held together by ~~two hundred sixteen~~ red stitches.
      216

If one of several numbers *of the same kind* in the same sentence requires a figure, you should use figures for all the numbers in that sentence.

▶ An audio system can range in cost from ~~one hundred dollars~~ to $2,599.
      $100

51i   Spell out numbers that begin sentences.

When a sentence begins with a number, either spell out the number or rewrite the sentence.

▶ ~~119~~ years of CIA labor cost taxpayers sixteen million dollars.
      One hundred nineteen

Most readers find it easier to read figures than three-word numbers; thus the best solution may be to rewrite this sentence: *Taxpayers spent sixteen million dollars for 119 years of CIA labor.*

Language, Culture, and Context

Multilingual

Using the Term *Hundred*

The term *hundred* is used idiomatically in English. When it is linked with numbers like two, eight, and so on, the word *hundred* remains singular: *Eight hundred years have passed and still old animosities run deep.* Add the plural -s to *hundred* only when no number precedes the term: *Hundreds of priceless books were lost in the fire.*

51j   Use figures according to convention.

ADDRESSES	23 Main Street; 175 Fifth Avenue
DATES	September 17, 1951; 4 BCE; the 1860s
DECIMALS AND FRACTIONS	65.34; 8½
PERCENTAGES	77 percent (*or* 77%)
EXACT AMOUNTS OF MONEY	$7,348; $1.46 trillion; $2.50; thirty-five (*or* 35) cents
SCORES AND STATISTICS	an 8–3 Red Sox victory; a verbal score of 600; an average age of 22; a mean of 53
TIME OF DAY	6:00 AM (*or* a.m.)

52   Italics

The slanted type known as *italics* is more than just a pretty typeface. Indeed, italics give words special meaning or emphasis. In the sentence "Many people read *People* on the subway every day," the italics (and the capital letter) tell readers that *People* is a publication.

52a   Italicize titles of long works.

In general, use italics for titles of long works; use quotation marks for shorter works (48c).

BOOKS	*Black Panther 1*
CHOREOGRAPHIC WORKS	Agnes de Mille's *Rodeo*
FILMS AND VIDEOS	*BlacKKKlansman*
LONG MUSICAL WORKS	*Brandenburg Concertos*
LONG POEMS	*Bhagavad Gita*
MAGAZINES AND JOURNALS	*Ebony*, the *New England Journal of Medicine*

NEWSPAPERS	the *Cleveland Plain Dealer*
PAINTINGS AND SCULPTURE	Kristen Visbal's *Fearless Girl*
PAMPHLETS	Thomas Paine's *Common Sense*
PLAYS	*Angels in America*
RADIO SERIES	*All Things Considered*
RECORDINGS	*Landfall*
TELEVISION SERIES	*House of Cards*

52b Italicize words, letters, and numbers used as terms.

▶ On the back of his jersey was the famous *24*.

▶ One characteristic of some New York speech is the absence of postvocalic *r* — for example, pronouncing the word *four* as "fouh."

52c Italicize non-English words and certain scientific terms.

Italicize words from other languages unless they have become part of English — like the Spanish "fiesta," for example. If a word is in an English dictionary, it does not need italics.

▶ At last one of the phantom sleighs gliding along the street would come to a stop, and with gawky haste Mr. Burness in his fox-furred *shapka* would make for our door.

— VLADIMIR NABOKOV, *Speak, Memory*

Use italics for the scientific names of plants and animals. Note that the first word in the name is also capitalized:

▶ *Canis latrans,* more commonly known as the coyote, is native to North America.

53   Hyphens

Hyphens are confusing to many people—hyphen problems are now one of the twenty most common surface errors in student writing. The confusion is understandable. Over time, the conventions for hyphen use in a given word can change (*tomorrow* was once spelled *to-morrow*). New words, even compounds such as *firewall,* generally don't use hyphens, but controversy continues to rage over whether to hyphenate *ebook* (or is it *e-book*?). And some words are hyphenated when they serve one kind of purpose in a sentence and not when they serve another.

53a   Use hyphens with compound words.

Some compounds are one word (*rowboat, pickup*), some are separate words (*hard drive*), and some require hyphens (*sister-in-law*). You should consult a dictionary to be sure. However, the following conventions can help you decide when to use hyphens with compound words.

Compound adjectives

Hyphenate most compound adjectives that precede a noun but not those that follow a noun.

a *well-liked* boss	My boss is *well liked.*
a *six-foot* plank	The plank is *six feet long.*

In general, the reason for hyphenating compound adjectives is to facilitate reading.

► Designers often use potted plants as living-room dividers.

                                          ^

Without the hyphen, *living* may seem to modify *room dividers.*

Never hyphenate an *-ly* adverb and an adjective.

► They used a widely/distributed mailing list.

Fractions and compound numbers

Use a hyphen to write out fractions and to spell out compound numbers from twenty-one to ninety-nine.

one-seventh	thirty-seven
two and seven-sixteenths	three hundred fifty-four thousand

53b Use hyphens with prefixes and suffixes.

Most words containing prefixes or suffixes are written without hyphens: *antiwar, gorillalike.* Here are some exceptions:

BEFORE CAPITALIZED BASE WORDS	un-American, non-Catholic
WITH FIGURES	pre-1960, post-1945
WITH CERTAIN PREFIXES AND SUFFIXES	all-state, ex-partner, self-possessed, quasi-legislative, mayor-elect, fifty-odd
WITH COMPOUND BASE WORDS	pre-high school, post-cold war
FOR CLARITY OR EASE OF READING	re-cover, anti-inflation, troll-like

Re-cover means "cover again"; the hyphen distinguishes it from the word *recover,* meaning "get well." In *anti-inflation* and *troll-like,* the hyphens separate confusing clusters of vowels and consonants.

53c Avoid unnecessary hyphens.

Unnecessary hyphens are at least as common a problem as omitted ones. Do not hyphenate the parts of a two-word verb such as *depend on, turn off,* or *tune out* (41b).

▶ Every player must pick⁄up a medical form before football tryouts.

The words *pick up* act as a verb and should not be hyphenated.

However, be careful to check that two words do indeed function as a verb in the sentence (33a); if they function as an adjective, a hyphen may be needed.

▶ Let's sign up for the early class.

The verb *sign up* should not have a hyphen.

▶ Where is the sign-up sheet?

The compound adjective *sign-up,* which modifies the noun *sheet,* needs a hyphen.

Do not hyphenate a subject complement — a word group that follows a linking verb (such as a form of *be* or *seem*) and describes the subject.

▶ Audrey is almost fifteen⁄years⁄old.

▲ **For visual analysis** This illustration suggests just a few possibilities for sources — from reference works to live performances — that you might cite in MLA style. Which sources will you include?

MLA Documentation

Careful citation shows your reader that you've done your homework. . . . It amounts to laying your intellectual cards on the table.

— JACK LYNCH

List of Examples

In-text citations in MLA style (Chapter 55)

Works-cited entries in MLA style (Chapter 56)

Guidelines for author listings

Print books

Print periodicals

Source maps are visual guides to citing common sources.

54 The Basics of MLA Style

Different rhetorical situations call for different approaches to citing sources — that is, for different ways of answering the question "Says who?" If you're reading a popular magazine, you probably won't expect the writer to provide careful source citations or a list of references at the end of an article. If you're posting material on a blog, you might follow conventions for citation by simply linking to the material you're talking about. But in other situations, including most academic writing, you will be expected to follow a more rigorous system for citing the information you use. Many courses in English ask writers to follow MLA style, the system developed by the Modern Language Association. For further reference, consult Chapters 55–57 or the *MLA Handbook,* Eighth Edition (2016).

54a Think about what readers need from you.

Why does academic work call for very careful citation practices when writing for the general public may not? The answer is that readers of your academic work expect to get certain information from source citations:

- Source citations demonstrate that you've done your homework on your topic and that you are a part of the conversation surrounding it. Careful citation shows your readers what you know, where you stand, and what you think is important.

- Source citations show that you understand the need to give credit when you make use of someone else's intellectual property. Especially in academic writing, when it's better to be safe than sorry, include a citation for any source you think you might need to cite. (See Chapter 12 for details.)

- Source citations give explicit directions to guide readers who want to look for themselves at the works you're using.

The guidelines for MLA style help you with this last purpose, giving you instructions on exactly what information to include in your citation and how to format that information.

54b Consider the context of your sources.

New kinds of sources crop up regularly. As the *MLA Handbook* confirms, there are often several "correct" ways to cite a source, so you will need to think carefully about *your own context* for using the source so you can identify the pieces of information that you should emphasize or include and any other information that might be helpful to your readers.

Elements of MLA citations

The first step is to identify elements that are commonly found in most works writers cite.

AUTHOR AND TITLE

The first two elements, both of which are needed for many sources, are the author's name and the title of the work. Each of these elements is followed by a period.

> **Author. Title.**

Even in these elements, your context is important. The author of a novel may be obvious, but who is the "author" of a television episode? The director? The writer? The show's creator? The star? The answer may depend on the focus of your own work. If an actor's performance is central to your discussion, then MLA guidelines ask you to identify the actor as the author. If the plot is your focus, you might name the writer of the episode as the author.

CONTAINER

The next step is to identify elements of what the MLA calls the "container" for the work. The context in which you are discussing the source and the context in which you find the source will help you determine what counts as a container in each case. If you watch a movie in a theater, you won't identify a separate container after the film title. But if you watch the same movie as part of a DVD box set of the director's work, the container title is the name of the box set. If you read an article in a print journal, the first container will be the journal that the article appears in. If you read it online, the journal may also be part of a second, larger container, such as a database. Thinking about a source as nested in larger containers may help you to visualize how a citation works.

The elements you may include in the "container" part of your citation include the following, in this order: the title of the larger container, if it's different from the title of the work; the names of any contributors such as editors or translators; the version or edition; the volume and issue numbers; the publisher or sponsor; the date of publication; and a location such as the page numbers, DOI, permalink, or URL. These elements are separated by commas, and the end of the container is marked with a period.

Author. Title. Container title, contributor names, version or edition, volume and issue numbers, publisher, date, location.

Most sources won't include all these pieces of information, so include only the elements that are available and relevant to create an acceptable citation. If you need a second container — for instance, if you are citing an article from a journal you found in a database — you simply add it after the first one, beginning with the container title and including as many of the same container elements as you can find. The rest of this chapter offers many examples of how elements and containers are combined to create citations.

One student researching messaging technologies found a potentially useful journal article by searching a library database, Academic Search Premier, through his library's website. The journal is the first container of the article, and the database is the second container.

Counts, Scott, and Karen E. Fisher. "Mobile Social Networking as Information Ground: A Case Study." *Library and Information Science Research*, vol. 32, no. 2, Apr. 2010, pp. 98-115. *Academic Search Premier*, doi:10.1016/ j.lisr.2009.10.003.

Notice that the first container includes just four relevant elements — the journal title, number (here, that means the volume and issue numbers), date, and page numbers; and the second container includes just two — the database title and location.

Types of sources

Refer to the List of Examples on pp. 409–10 to locate guidelines on citing various types of sources, including print books, print periodicals (journals, magazines, and newspapers), digital written-word sources, and other sources (films, artwork) that consist mainly of material other than written words. A digital version of a source may include updates or corrections that the print version of the same work lacks, so MLA guidelines ask you to indicate where you found the source. If you can't find a model exactly like the source you've selected, see the checklist on p. 422.

 ## Plan and connect your citations.

MLA citations appear in two connected parts — the brief in-text citation, usually in parentheses in the body of your written text, and the full citation in the list of works cited, to which the in-text citation directs your readers.

The most straightforward in-text citations include the author's name and the page number, but many variations on this basic format are discussed in Chapter 55.

In the text of her research essay (see Chapter 57), Julia Sakowitz paraphrases material from a journal article by anthropologist Arlene Dávila. As shown, she cites the article page on which the original information appears in a parenthetical reference that points readers to the entry for "Dávila, Arlene" in her list of works cited. She also cites portions of a personal interview she has conducted with Seth Kamil, which has no page numbers. These examples show just two of the many ways to cite sources using in-text citations and a list of works cited. You'll need to make case-by-case decisions based on the types of sources you include.

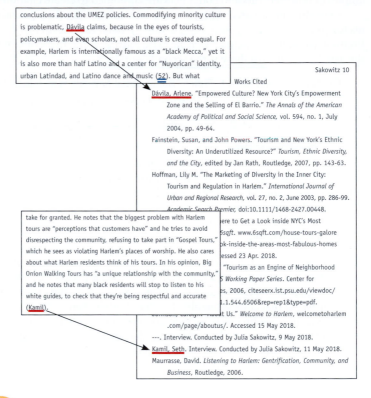

conclusions about the UMEZ policies. Commodifying minority culture is problematic, Dávila claims, because in the eyes of tourists, policymakers, and even scholars, not all culture is created equal. For example, Harlem is internationally famous as a "black Mecca," yet it is also more than half Latino and a center for "Nuyorican" identity, urban Latindad, and Latino dance and music (52). But what

Sakowitz 10

Works Cited

Dávila, Arlene. "Empowered Culture? New York City's Empowerment Zone and the Selling of El Barrio." *The Annals of the American Academy of Political and Social Science,* vol. 594, no. 1, July 2004, pp. 49-64.

Fainstein, Susan, and John Powers. "Tourism and New York's Ethnic Diversity: An Underutilized Resource?" *Tourism, Ethnic Diversity, and the City,* edited by Jan Rath, Routledge, 2007, pp. 143-63.

Hoffman, Lily M. "The Marketing of Diversity in the Inner City: Tourism and Regulation in Harlem." *International Journal of Urban and Regional Research,* vol. 27, no. 2, June 2003, pp. 286-99. *Academic Search Premier,* doi:10.1111/1468-2427.00448.

take for granted. He notes that the biggest problem with Harlem tours are "perceptions that customers have" and he tries to avoid disrespecting the community, refusing to take part in "Gospel Tours," which he sees as violating Harlem's places of worship. He also cares about what Harlem residents think of his tours. In his opinion, Big Onion Walking Tours has "a unique relationship with the community," and he notes that many black residents will stop to listen to his white guides, to check that they're being respectful and accurate (Kamil).

ere to Get a Look inside NYC's Most
sqft. www.6sqft.com/house-tours-galore
k-inside-the-areas-most-fabulous-homes
essed 23 Apr. 2018.

"Tourism as an Engine of Neighborhood
5 *Working Paper Series.* Center for
es, 2006, citeseerx.ist.psu.edu/viewdoc/
1.1.544.6506&rep=rep1&type=pdf.

t Us." *Welcome to Harlem,* welcometoharlem .com/page/aboutus/. Accessed 15 May 2018.

---. Interview. Conducted by Julia Sakowitz, 9 May 2018.

Kamil, Seth. Interview. Conducted by Julia Sakowitz, 11 May 2018.

Maurrasse, David. *Listening to Harlem: Gentrification, Community, and Business,* Routledge, 2006.

54d   Include notes as needed.

MLA citation style asks you to include explanatory notes for information or comments that don't readily fit into your text but are needed for clarification or further explanation. In addition, MLA permits bibliographic notes for offering information about or evaluation of a source, or to list multiple sources that relate to a single point. Use superscript numbers in the text to refer readers to the notes, which may appear as endnotes (under the heading *Notes* on a separate page immediately before the list of works cited) or as footnotes at the bottom of each page where a superscript number appears.

EXAMPLE OF SUPERSCRIPT NUMBER IN TEXT

Although such communication relies on the written word, many messagers disregard standard writing conventions. For example, here is a snippet from an IM conversation between two teenage girls:[1]

EXAMPLE OF EXPLANATORY NOTE

1. This transcript of an IM conversation was collected on 20 Nov. 2014. The teenagers' names are concealed to protect privacy.

54e Follow MLA format.

The MLA recommends the following format for the manuscript of a research paper. However, check with your instructor before preparing your final draft.

For a sample student essay in MLA style, see Chapter 57.

- *First page and title page.* The MLA does not require a title page. Type each of the following items on a separate line on the first page, beginning one inch from the top and flush with the left margin: your name, the instructor's name, the course name and number, and the date. Double-space between each item; then double-space again and center the title. Double-space between the title and the beginning of the text.

- *Margins and spacing.* Leave one-inch margins at the top and bottom and on both sides of each page. Double-space the entire text, including set-off quotations, notes, and the list of works cited. Indent the first line of a paragraph one-half inch.

- *Page numbers.* Include your last name and the page number on each page, one-half inch below the top and flush with the right margin.

- *Long quotations.* Set off a long quotation (one with more than four typed lines) in block format by starting it on a new line and indenting each line one-half inch from the left margin. Do not enclose the passage in quotation marks (12b).

- *Headings.* MLA style allows, but does not require, headings. Many students and instructors find them helpful.

- **Visuals.** Place tables, photographs, drawings, charts, graphs, and other figures as near as possible to the relevant text. (See 12c for guidelines on incorporating visuals into your text.) Tables should have a label and number (*Table 1*) and a clear caption. The label and caption should be aligned on the left, on separate lines. Give the source information below the table. All other visuals should be labeled *Figure* (abbreviated *Fig.*), numbered, and captioned. The label and caption should appear on the same line, followed by the source information. Remember to refer to each visual in your text, indicating how it contributes to the point you are making.

55 MLA Style for In-Text Citations

In MLA style, a citation in the text of an essay is required for every quotation, paraphrase, summary, or other material requiring documentation (see 12b). In-text citations document material from other sources with both signal phrases and parenthetical references. Parenthetical references should include the information your readers need to locate the full reference in the list of works cited at the end of the text (Chapter 56). An in-text citation in MLA style aims to give the reader two kinds of information: (1) it indicates *which source* on the works-cited page the writer is referring to, and (2) it explains *where in the source* the material quoted, paraphrased, or summarized can be found, if the source has page numbers or other numbered sections.

The basic MLA in-text citation includes the author's last name either in a signal phrase introducing the source material (12b) or in parentheses at the end of the sentence. For sources with stable page numbers, it also includes the page number in parentheses at the end of the sentence.

SAMPLE CITATION USING A SIGNAL PHRASE

In his discussion of Monty Python routines, Crystal notes that the group relished "breaking the normal rules" of language (107).

SAMPLE PARENTHETICAL CITATION

A noted linguist explains that Monty Python humor often relied on "bizarre linguistic interactions" (Crystal 108).

(For digital sources without stable page numbers, see model 2.)

Note in the examples on the following pages where punctuation is placed in relation to the parentheses. We have used underlining in some examples only to draw your attention to important elements. Do not underline anything in your own citations.

1. BASIC FORMAT FOR A QUOTATION

The MLA recommends using the <u>author's name</u> in a signal phrase to introduce the material and citing the <u>page number(s)</u> in parentheses.

> <u>Lee</u> claims that his comic-book creation, Thor, was "the first regularly published superhero to speak in a consistently archaic manner" (<u>199</u>).

When you do not mention the author in a signal phrase, include the author's last name before the page number(s), if any, in the parentheses. Use no punctuation between the author's name and the page number(s).

> The word *Bollywood* is sometimes considered an insult because it implies that Indian movies are merely "a derivative of the American film industry" (<u>Chopra 9</u>).

2. DIGITAL OR NONPRINT SOURCE

Give enough information in a signal phrase or in parentheses for readers to locate the source in your list of works cited. Many works found online or in electronic databases lack stable page numbers; you can omit the page number in such cases. However, if you are citing a work with stable pagination, such as an article in PDF format, include the page number in parentheses.

> **DIGITAL SOURCE WITHOUT STABLE PAGE NUMBERS**
>
> As a *Slate* analysis explains, "Prominent sports psychologists get praised for their successes and don't get grief for their failures" (<u>Engber</u>).

> **DIGITAL SOURCE WITH STABLE PAGE NUMBERS**
>
> According to <u>Whitmarsh</u>, the British military had experimented with using balloons for observation as far back as 1879 (<u>328</u>).

If the source includes numbered sections, paragraphs, or screens, include that number preceded by the abbreviation *sec.*, *par.*, or *scr.* in parentheses.

3. TWO AUTHORS

Use both authors' last names in a signal phrase or in parentheses.

> <u>Gilbert and Gubar</u> point out that in the Grimm version of "Snow White," the king "never actually appears in this story at all" (<u>37</u>).

4. THREE OR MORE AUTHORS

Use the first author's name and *et al.* ("and others"), unless your instructor asks you to list every name.

> Similarly, as <u>Belenky et al.</u> assert, examining the lives of women expands our understanding of human development (<u>7</u>).

5. ORGANIZATION AS AUTHOR

Give the group's full name in a signal phrase; in parentheses, abbreviate any common words in the name.

> Any study of social welfare involves a close analysis of "the impacts, the benefits, and the costs" of its policies (Social Research Corp. iii).

6. UNKNOWN AUTHOR

Use the full title, if it is brief, in your text — or a shortened version of the title in parentheses.

> One analysis defines *hype* as "an artificially engendered atmosphere of hysteria" (*Today's* 51).

7. AUTHOR OF TWO OR MORE WORKS CITED IN THE SAME PROJECT

If your list of works cited has more than one work by the same author, include the title of the work you are citing in a signal phrase or a shortened version of the title in parentheses to prevent reader confusion.

> Gardner shows readers their own silliness in his description of a "pointless, ridiculous monster, crouched in the shadows, stinking of dead men, murdered children, and martyred cows" (*Grendel* 2).

8. TWO OR MORE AUTHORS WITH THE SAME LAST NAME

Include the author's first *and* last names in a signal phrase or first initial and last name in a parenthetical reference.

> Children will learn to write if they are allowed to choose their own subjects, James Britton asserts, citing the Schools Council study of the 1960s (37-42).

9. MULTIVOLUME WORK

In a parenthetical reference, note the volume number first and then the page number(s), with a colon and one space between them.

> Modernist writers prized experimentation and gradually even sought to blur the line between poetry and prose, according to Forster (3: 150).

If you name only one volume of the work in your list of works cited, include only the page number in the parentheses.

10. LITERARY WORK

Because literary works are usually available in many different editions, cite the page number(s) from the edition you used followed by a semicolon, and then give other identifying information that will lead readers to the passage in any edition. Indicate the act and/or scene in a play (*37; sc. 1*). For a novel, indicate the part or chapter (*175; ch. 4*).

> In utter despair, Dostoyevsky's character Mitya wonders aloud about the "terrible tragedies realism inflicts on people" (376; bk. 8, ch. 2).

For a poem, cite the part (if there is one) and line(s), separated by a period. If you are citing only line numbers, use the word *line(s)* in the first reference (*lines 33-34*).

> Whitman speculates, "All goes onward and outward, nothing collapses, / And to die is different from what anyone supposed, and luckier" (6.129-30).

For a verse play, give only the act, scene, and line numbers, separated by periods.

> The witches greet Banquo as "lesser than Macbeth, and greater" (1.3.65).

11. WORK IN AN ANTHOLOGY OR COLLECTION

For an essay, short story, or other piece of prose reprinted in an anthology, use the name of the author of the work, not the editor of the anthology, but use the page number(s) from the anthology.

> Narratives of captivity play a major role in early writing by women in the United States, as demonstrated by Silko (219).

12. SACRED TEXT

To cite a sacred text such as the Qur'an or the Bible, give the title of the edition you used, the book, and the chapter and verse (or their equivalent) separated by a period. In your text, spell out the names of books. In parenthetical references, use abbreviations for books with names of five or more letters (*Gen.* for *Genesis*).

> He ignored the admonition "Pride goes before destruction, and a haughty spirit before a fall" (*New Oxford Annotated Bible*, Prov. 16.18).

13. ENCYCLOPEDIA OR DICTIONARY ENTRY

An entry from a reference work — such as an encyclopedia or a dictionary — without an author will appear on the works-cited list under the entry's title. Enclose the entry title in quotation marks, and place it in parentheses. Omit the page number for print reference works that arrange entries alphabetically.

> The term *prion* was coined by Stanley B. Prusiner from the words *proteinaceous* and *infectious* and a suffix meaning *particle* ("Prion").

14. GOVERNMENT SOURCE WITH NO AUTHOR NAMED

Because entries for sources authored by government agencies will appear on your list of works cited under the name of the country (see Chapter 56, model 63), your in-text citation for such a source should include the name of the country as well as the name of the agency responsible for the source.

> To reduce the agricultural runoff into the Chesapeake Bay, the United States Environmental Protection Agency has argued that "[h]igh nutrient loading crops, such as corn and soybean, should be replaced with alternatives in environmentally sensitive areas" (2-26).

15. ENTIRE WORK

Include the reference in the text, without any page numbers.

> Krakauer's *Into the Wild* both criticizes and admires the solitary impulses of its young hero, which end up killing him.

16. INDIRECT SOURCE (AUTHOR QUOTING SOMEONE ELSE)

Use the abbreviation *qtd. in* to indicate that you are quoting from someone else's report of a source.

> As Arthur Miller says, "When somebody is destroyed everybody finally contributes to it, but in Willy's case, the end product would be virtually the same" (qtd. in Martin and Meyer 375).

17. TWO OR MORE SOURCES IN ONE CITATION

Separate the information with semicolons.

> Economists recommend that *employment* be redefined to include unpaid domestic labor (Clark 148; Nevins 39).

18. VISUAL

When you include an image in your text, number it (*Fig. 2*) and include a parenthetical reference (*see fig. 2*). Number figures (photos, drawings, cartoons, maps, graphs, and charts) and tables separately. Each visual should include a caption with the figure or table number and information about the source—either a complete citation or enough information to direct readers to the works-cited entry.

> This trend is illustrated in a chart distributed by the College Board as part of its 2011 analysis of aggregate SAT data (see fig. 1).

Soon after the preceding sentence, readers find the following figure and a caption referring them to the entry in the list of works cited:

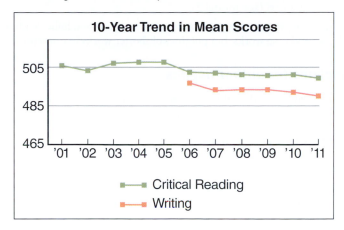

Fig. 1. Ten-year trend in mean SAT reading and writing scores (2001–2011). Data source: "SAT Trends 2011."

An image that you create might appear with a caption like this:

Fig. 4. Young women reading magazines. Personal photograph by author.

56 MLA Style for a List of Works Cited

A list of works cited is an alphabetical list of the sources you have referred to in your essay. (If your instructor asks you to list everything you have read as background, call the list *Works Consulted*.)

Formatting a list of works cited

- Start your list on a separate page after the text of your document and any notes.
- Center the heading *Works Cited* (not italicized or in quotation marks) one inch from the top of the page. See the example on p. 457.
- Begin each entry flush with the left margin, but indent subsequent lines of each entry one-half inch. Double-space the entire list.
- List sources alphabetically by the first word. Start with the author's name, if available, or the editor's name. If no author or editor is given, start with the title.

- List the author's last name first, followed by a comma and the first name. If a source has two authors, the second author's name appears first name first (see model 2).
- Capitalize every important word in titles and subtitles. Italicize titles of books and long works, but put titles of shorter works in quotation marks.

Guidelines for author listings

The list of works cited is always arranged alphabetically. The in-text citations in your writing point readers toward particular sources on the list.

NAME CITED IN SIGNAL PHRASE IN TEXT

Crystal explains . . .

NAME IN PARENTHETICAL CITATION IN TEXT

. . . (Crystal 107).

BEGINNING OF ENTRY ON LIST OF WORKS CITED

Crystal, David.

Models 1–5 explain how to arrange author names. The information that follows the name depends on the type of work you are citing. Consult the List of Examples on pp. 409–10 and choose the model that most closely resembles the source you are using.

Quick Help

Citing Sources That Don't Match Any Model Exactly

What should you do if your source doesn't match any of the models exactly? Suppose, for instance, your source is a translated essay appearing in the fifth edition of an anthology.

- Identify a basic model to follow. For example, if you decide that your source looks most like an essay in an anthology, you would start with a citation that looks like model 9.
- After listing author and title information (if given), enter as many of the elements of the container as you can find (see 54b): title of the larger container, if any; other contributors, such as editor or translator; version or edition; volume; publisher; date; and page numbers or other location information such as a URL or DOI. End the container with a period. If the container is nested in a larger container, collect the information from the second container as well.
- If you aren't sure which model to follow or how to create a combination model with multiple containers, ask your instructor or a consultant in the writing center.

1. ONE AUTHOR

Put the last name first, followed by a comma, the first name (and middle name or initial, if any), and a period.

> Crystal, David.

2. MULTIPLE AUTHORS

For two authors, list the first author with the last name first. Follow this with a comma, the word *and*, and the name of the second author with the first name first.

> Gilbert, Sandra M., and Susan Gubar.

For three or more authors, list the first author followed by a comma and *et al.* ("and others") or list all authors.

> Belenky, Mary Field, et al.
>
> Belenky, Mary Field, Blythe McVicker Clinchy, Nancy Rule Goldberger, and Jill
> Mattuck Tarule.

3. ORGANIZATION OR GROUP AUTHOR

Give the name of the group, government agency, corporation, or other organization listed as the author.

> Getty Trust.
>
> United States. Government Accountability Office.

4. UNKNOWN AUTHOR

When the author is not identified, begin the entry with the title, and alphabetize by the first important word. Italicize titles of books and long works, but put titles of articles and other short works in quotation marks.

> *New Concise World Atlas.*
>
> "California Sues EPA over Emissions."

5. TWO OR MORE WORKS BY THE SAME AUTHOR

Arrange the entries alphabetically by title. Include the author's name in the first entry, but in subsequent entries, use three hyphens followed by a period.

> Chopra, Anupama. "Bollywood Princess, Hollywood Hopeful." *The New York
> Times*, 10 Feb. 2008, nyti.ms/1QEtNpF.
>
> ---. *King of Bollywood: Shah Rukh Khan and the Seductive World of Indian
> Cinema.* Warner Books, 2007.

Note: Use three hyphens only when the work is by *exactly* the same author(s) as the previous entry.

Print books

6. BASIC FORMAT FOR A BOOK

Begin with the <u>author name(s)</u>. (See models 1–5.) Then include the title and subtitle, the <u>publisher</u>, and the year of publication. The source map on pp. 426–27 shows where to find this information in a typical book.

> <u>Rubery, Matthew</u>. *The Untold Story of the Talking Book*. <u>Harvard UP</u>,
>   2016.

7. AUTHOR AND EDITOR BOTH NAMED

> Bangs, Lester. *Psychotic Reactions and Carburetor Dung*. <u>Edited by Greil</u>
>   <u>Marcus</u>, Alfred A. Knopf, 1988.

Note: To cite the editor's contribution, begin with the editor's name.

> <u>Marcus, Greil, editor</u>. *Psychotic Reactions and Carburetor Dung*. By Lester
>   Bangs, Alfred A. Knopf, 1988.

8. EDITOR, NO AUTHOR NAMED

> <u>Wall, Cheryl A., editor</u>. *Changing Our Own Words: Essays on Criticism, Theory,*
>   *and Writing by Black Women*. Rutgers UP, 1989.

9. SELECTION IN AN ANTHOLOGY OR CHAPTER IN A BOOK WITH AN EDITOR

List the author(s) of the selection; the <u>selection title</u>, in quotation marks; the title of the book, italicized; the words *edited by* and the name(s) of the editor(s); the publisher; the year; and the abbreviation *pp.* with the <u>selection's page numbers</u>.

> Bird, Gloria. <u>"Autobiography as Spectacle: An Act of Liberation or the Illusion</u>
>   <u>of Liberation?"</u> *Here First: Autobiographical Essays by Native Americans*,
>   edited by Arnold Krupat and Brian Swann, Random House, 2000,
>   <u>pp. 63-74</u>.

Note: To provide original publication information for a reprinted selection, use the <u>original publication information</u> as a second container (see 54b):

> Byatt, A. S. "The Thing in the Forest." *The O. Henry Prize Stories 2003*, edited
>   by Laura Furman, Anchor Books, 2003, pp. 3-22. <u>Originally published in</u>
>   *The New Yorker*, 3 June 2002, pp. 80-89.

10. TWO OR MORE ITEMS FROM THE SAME ANTHOLOGY

List the anthology as one entry. Also list each selection separately with a cross-reference to the anthology. In the example below, the first two citations are for the selections used and the third is for the anthology.

> Estleman, Loren D. "Big Tim Magoon and the Wild West." Walker, pp. 391-404.

> Salzer, Susan K. "Miss Libbie Tells All." Walker, pp. 199-212.

> Walker, Dale L., editor. *Westward: A Fictional History of the American West.*
> Forge Books, 2003.

11. TRANSLATION

> Bolaño, Roberto. *2666.* Translated by Natasha Wimmer, Farrar, Straus and
> Giroux, 2008.

If the book has an editor and a translator, list both names after the title, in the order they appear on the title page.

> Kant, Immanuel. *"Toward Perpetual Peace" and Other Writings on Politics,*
> *Peace, and History.* Edited by Pauline Kleingeld, translated by David L.
> Colclasure, Yale UP, 2006.

If different translators have worked on various parts of the book, identify the translator of the part you are citing.

> García Lorca, Federico. "The Little Mad Boy." Translated by W. S. Merwin. *The*
> *Selected Poems of Federico García Lorca,* edited by Francisco García Lorca
> and Donald M. Allen, Penguin, 1969, pp. 51-53.

12. BOOK IN A LANGUAGE OTHER THAN ENGLISH

Include a translation of the title in brackets, if necessary.

> Benedetti, Mario. *La borra del café [The Coffee Grind].* Editorial Sudamericana,
> 2000.

13. GRAPHIC NARRATIVE OR COMIC

If the words and images are created by the same person, cite a graphic narrative just as you would a book (model 6).

> Bechdel, Alison. *Are You My Mother? A Comic Drama.* Houghton Mifflin
> Harcourt, 2012.

If the work is a collaboration, indicate the author or illustrator who is most important to your research before the title of the work. List

MLA SOURCE MAP

Books

Take information from the book's title page and copyright page (on the reverse side of the title page), not from the book's cover or a library catalog.

❶ Author. List the last name first. End with a period. For variations, see models 2–5.

❷ Title. Italicize the title and any subtitle; capitalize all major words. End with a period.

❸ Publisher. Identify the publisher's name as given on the book's title page. If more than one publisher appears on the title page, separate the names with a slash, leaving a space before and after the slash. If no publisher is listed on the title page, check the copyright page. Abbreviate *University* and *Press* as *U* and *P* (*Oxford UP*). Omit terms such as *Company* and *Incorporated*. Follow the publisher's name with a comma.

❹ Year of publication. If more than one copyright date is given, use the most recent one. End with a period.

A citation for the book on p. 427 would look like this:

❶   ❷

Patel, Raj. *The Value of Nothing: How to Reshape Market Society and Redefine*

❸ ❹

Democracy. Picador, 2009.

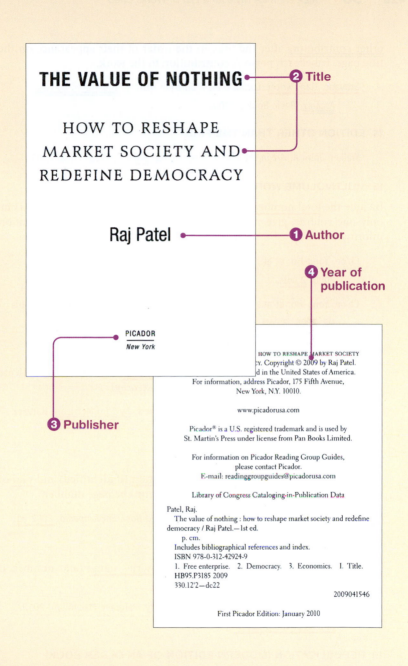

THE VALUE OF NOTHING

HOW TO RESHAPE MARKET SOCIETY AND REDEFINE DEMOCRACY

Raj Patel

2 Title

1 Author

4 Year of publication

PICADOR
New York

3 Publisher

Library of Congress Cataloging-in-Publication Data

Patel, Raj.
   The value of nothing : how to reshape market society and redefine
democracy / Raj Patel.—1st ed.
      p. cm.
   Includes bibliographical references and index.
   ISBN 978-0-312-42924-9
   1. Free enterprise.   2. Democracy.   3. Economics.   I. Title.
   HB95.P3185 2009
   330.12′2—dc22

                                                    2009041546

First Picador Edition: January 2010

other contributors after the title, in the order of their appearance on the title page. Label each person's contribution to the work.

> Stavans, Ilan, writer. *Latino USA: A Cartoon History.* Illustrated by Lalo
> Arcaraz, Basic Books, 2000.

14. EDITION OTHER THAN THE FIRST

> Walker, John A. *Art in the Age of Mass Media.* 3rd ed., Pluto Press, 2001.

15. MULTIVOLUME WORK

Include the total number of volumes after the publication date. If you cite only one volume, give the number of the volume before the publication information.

> Ch'oe, Yong-Ho, et al., editors. *Sources of Korean Tradition.* Columbia UP,
> 2000. 2 vols.

> Ch'oe, Yong-Ho, et al., editors. *Sources of Korean Tradition.* Vol. 2, Columbia
> UP, 2000. 2 vols.

16. PREFACE, FOREWORD, INTRODUCTION, OR AFTERWORD

After the writer's name, describe the contribution. After the title, indicate the book's author (with *by*) or editor (with *edited by*).

> Coates, Ta-Nehisi. Foreword. *The Origin of Others,* by Toni Morrison, Harvard
> UP, 2017, pp. vii-xvii.

17. ENTRY IN A REFERENCE BOOK

For a well-known encyclopedia, note the edition (if identified) and year of publication. If the entries are alphabetized, omit the page number.

> Kettering, Alison McNeil. "Art Nouveau." *World Book Encyclopedia,* 2002 ed.

18. BOOK THAT IS PART OF A SERIES

After the publication information, list the series name (and number, if any) from the title page.

> Denham, A. E., editor. *Plato on Art and Beauty.* Palgrave Macmillan, 2012.
> Philosophers in Depth.

19. REPUBLICATION (MODERN EDITION OF AN OLDER BOOK)

Indicate the original publication date after the title.

> Austen, Jane. *Sense and Sensibility.* 1813. Dover, 1996.

20. MORE THAN ONE PUBLISHER'S NAME

If the title page gives two publishers' names, separate them with a slash. Include spaces on both sides of the slash.

> Hornby, Nick. *About a Boy*. Riverhead / Penguin Putnam, 1998.

21. BOOK WITH A TITLE WITHIN THE TITLE

Do not italicize the title of a book or other long work within an italicized book title. For an article title within a title, italicize as usual and place the article title in quotation marks.

> Masur, Louis P. *Runaway Dream: Born to Run and Bruce Springsteen's American Vision*. Bloomsbury, 2009.

> Lethem, Jonathan. *"Lucky Alan" and Other Stories*. Doubleday, 2015.

22. SACRED TEXT

To cite any individual published editions of sacred books, begin the entry with the title.

> *Qur'an: The Final Testament (Authorized English Version) with Arabic Text*. Translated by Rashad Khalifa, Universal Unity, 2000.

Print periodicals

Begin with the author name(s). (See models 1–5.) Then include the article title, the title of the periodical, the volume and issue information, the date of publication, and the page numbers. The source map on pp. 430–31 shows where to find information in a typical periodical.

> Altschuler, Sari. "The Gothic Origins of Global Health." *American Literature*, vol. 89, no. 3, Sept. 2017, pp. 557-90.

23. ARTICLE IN A PRINT JOURNAL

Include the volume number, the issue number, and the date.

> Beckwith, Sarah. "Reading for Our Lives." *PMLA*, vol. 132, no. 2, Mar. 2017, pp. 331-36.

24. ARTICLE IN A PRINT MAGAZINE

Provide the date from the magazine cover instead of volume or issue numbers.

> Surowiecki, James. "The Stimulus Strategy." *The New Yorker*, 25 Feb. 2008, p. 29.

> Tran, Diep. "Wide Awake in America." *American Theatre*, Nov. 2017, pp. 26-28.

MLA SOURCE MAP

Articles in Print Periodicals

1 **Author.** List the last name first. End with a period. For variations, see models 2–5.

2 **Article title.** Put the title and any subtitle in quotation marks; capitalize all major words. Place a period inside the closing quotation mark.

3 **Periodical title.** Italicize the title; capitalize all major words. End with a comma.

4 **Volume and issue.** For journals, give the abbreviation *vol.* and the volume number, and the abbreviation *no.* and the issue number, if the journal provides them. Put commas after the volume and issue. (Do not include volume and issue for magazines or newspapers.)

5 **Date of publication.** List day (if given), month (abbreviated except for May, June, and July), and year, or season and year, of publication. Put a comma after the date.

6 **Page numbers.** Give the abbreviation *p.* (for "page") or *pp.* (for "pages") and the inclusive page numbers. If the article skips pages, put the first page number and a plus sign. End with a period.

A citation for the article on p. 431 would look like this:

Quart, Alissa. "Lost Media, Found Media: Snapshots from the Future of Writing." *Columbia Journalism Review*, May/June 2008, pp. 30-34.

③ Periodical title

④ No volume number

⑤ Date of publication
May/June 2008

COLUMBIA
JOURNALISM
REVIEW

May / June 2008 • cjr.org

The Future of
Writ

Nonfiction's d
ALISSA QUART

Kindle isn't it,
EZRA KLEIN

UNDER THE
A reporter re
that got him t
CAMERON MCV

LOVE THY N
The religion b
TIM TOWNSEN

COLUMBIA JOURNALISM REVIEW

② Article title

Lost Media, Found Media

Snapshots from the future of writing

BY ALISSA QUART

① Author
ALISSA QUART

If there were an ashram for people who worship contemplative long-form journalism, it would be the Nieman Conference on Narrative Journalism. This March, at the Sheraton Boston Hotel, hundreds of journalists, authors, students, and aspirants came for the weekend event. Seated on metal chairs in large conference rooms, we learned about muscular storytelling (the Q-shaped narrative structure—who knew?). We sipped cups of coffee and

become like the people at the ashram after the guru has died.

Right now, journalism is more or less divided into two camps, which I will call Lost Media and Found Media. I went to the Nieman conference partially because I wanted to see how the forces creating this new division are affecting and afflicting the Lost Media world that I love best, not on the institutional level, but for reporters and writers themselves. This world includes people who write for all the newspapers and magazines that are currently struggling with layoffs, speedups, hiring freezes, buyouts, the death or shrinkage of film- and book-review sections, limits on expensive investigative work, the erasure of foreign bureaus, and the general narrowing of institutional ambition. It includes freelance writers competing with hordes of ever-younger competitors willing to write and publish online for free, the fade-out of established journalistic career paths, and, perhaps most crucially, a muddled sense of the meritorious, as blogs level and scramble the value and status of print publications, and of professional writers. The glamour and influence once associated with a magazine elite seem to have faded, becoming a sort of pastiche of winsome articles about yearning and boxers and dinners at Elaine's.

Found Media-ites, meanwhile, are the bloggers, the contributors to Huffington Post-type sites that aggregate blogs, as well as other work that somebody else paid for, and the new nonprofits and pay-per-article schemes that aim to save journalism from 20 percent

ate bagels and heard about reporting history through letters and public documents and how to evoke empathy for our subjects, particularly our most marginal ones. As we listened to reporters discussing great feats—exposing Walter Reed's fetid living quarters for wounded soldiers, for instance—we also renewed our pride in our profession. In short, the conference exemplified the best of the older media models, the ones that have so recently fallen into economic turmoil.

Yet even at the weekend's strongest lectures on interview techniques or the long-form profile, we couldn't ignore the digital elephant in the room. We all knew as writers that the kinds of pieces we were discussing require months of work to be both deep and refined, and that we were all hard-pressed for the time and the money to do that. It was always hard for nonfiction writers, but something seems to have changed. For those of us who believed in the value of the journalism and literary nonfiction of the past, we had

profit-margin demands. Although these elements are often disparate, together they compose the new media landscape. In economic terms, I mean all the outlets for nonfiction writing that seem to be thriving in the new era or striving to fill niches that Lost Media is giving up in a new order. Stylistically, Found Media tends to feel spontaneous, almost accidental. It's a domain dominated by the young, where writers get points not for following traditions or burnishing them but for amateur and hybrid vigor, for creating their own venues and their own genres. It is about public expression and community—not quite John Dewey's Great Community, which the critic Eric Alterman alluded to in a recent *New Yorker* article on newspapers, but rather a fractured form of Dewey's ideal: call it Great Communities.

To be a Found Media journalist or pundit, one need not be elite, expert, or trained; one must simply produce punchy intellectual property that is in conversation with groups of

Illustration by Tomer Hanuka

⑥ Page numbers
30-34

25. ARTICLE IN A PRINT NEWSPAPER

Include the <u>edition</u> (if listed) and the <u>section number or letter</u> (if listed).

> Fackler, Martin. "Japan's Foreign Minister Says Apologies to Wartime Victims
>
> Will Be Upheld." *The New York Times,* 9 Apr. 2014, <u>late ed., p. A6</u>.

Note: For locally published newspapers, add the city in brackets after the name if it is not part of the name: *Globe and Mail [Toronto].*

26. ARTICLE THAT SKIPS PAGES

When an article skips pages, give only the <u>first page number and a plus sign</u>.

> Tyrnauer, Matthew. "Empire by Martha." *Vanity Fair,* Sept. 2002, <u>pp. 364+</u>.

27. EDITORIAL OR LETTER TO THE EDITOR

Include the writer's name, if given, and the title, if any. Then end with the <u>label</u> *Editorial* or *Letter.*

> "California Dreaming." *The Nation,* 25 Feb. 2008, p. 4. <u>Editorial</u>.

> MacEwan, Valerie. *The Believer,* vol. 12, no. 1, Jan. 2014, p. 4. <u>Letter</u>.

28. REVIEW

> Nussbaum, Emily. "Change Agents: Review of *The Americans* and *Silicon*
>
> *Valley.*" *The New Yorker,* 31 Mar. 2014, p. 68.

> Schwarz, Benjamin. <u>Review of</u> *The Second World War: A Short History,* by
>
> R. A. C. Parker, *The Atlantic Monthly,* May 2002, pp. 110-11.

Digital written-word sources

Digital sources such as websites differ from print sources in the ease with which they can be changed, updated, or eliminated. The most commonly cited electronic sources are documents from websites and databases.

29. WORK FROM A DATABASE

For an article that is available in print but that you access in an online database such as Academic Search Premier, begin with the name(s) of the author(s), the title of the work, the <u>title of the periodical</u>, volume/issue, and date of the publication of the print version of the work. Give page numbers for the print version. Then give the name of the <u>online database</u> and the location — a DOI or other stable link. The source map on pp. 434–35 shows where to find information for a work from a database.

> Reich, Elizabeth. "The Power of Black Film Criticism." *Film Criticism,* vol. 40,
>
> no. 1, Jan. 2016, pp. 1-3. *Omnifile Full Text Select*, doi:10.3998/
>
> fc.13761232.0040.126.

30. ARTICLE FROM A JOURNAL ON THE WEB

Begin an entry for an online journal article as you would one for a print journal article (see model 23). End with the <u>online location</u> (permalink, DOI, or URL) and a period.

Clark, Msia Kibona. "Hip Hop as Social Commentary in Accra and Dar es

Salaam." *African Studies Quarterly,* vol. 13, no. 3, Summer 2012, <u>asq</u>

<u>.africa.ufl.edu/files/Clark-V131s3.pdf</u>.

Quick Help

Citing Works from Websites

When citing online sources, give as many of the following elements as you can find:

1. **Author.** Provide the author of the work, if you can find one. End with a period.

2. **Title.** Give the title of the work you are citing, ending with a period. If the work is part of a larger container (such as a video on YouTube), put the title in quotation marks.

3. **Website title.** If the title that you have identified is not the name of the website itself, list the website title, in italics, followed by a comma.

4. **Publisher or sponsor.** If the site's publisher or sponsor is different from the title of the site, identify the publisher or sponsor, followed by a comma. If the name is very similar to the site title, omit the publisher.

5. **Date of publication.** Give the date of publication or latest update, followed by a comma.

6. **Permalink or URL.** Give a permalink (if you can find one) or URL. End with a period. If you have to break a URL across lines, break it before a period or hyphen or before or after any other mark of punctuation.

7. **Date of access.** If the work does not include any date, add "Accessed" and the day, month (abbreviated, except for May, June, and July), and year you accessed the source. End with a period. If you provided a date before the URL, omit the access date.

Articles from Databases

Library subscriptions provide access to huge databases of articles, such as Academic Search Premier, ProQuest, and JSTOR.

① **Author.** List the last name first. End with a period. For variations, see models 2–5.

② **Article title.** Enclose the title and any subtitle in quotation marks. End with a period.

③ **Periodical title.** Italicize it. Follow it with a comma.

④ **Volume and issue.** For journal articles, list the volume and issue number, if any, separated by commas. Use the abbreviations *vol.* and *no.*

⑤ **Date of publication.** Include the day (if given), month or season, and year, in that order. Add a comma.

⑥ **Page numbers.** Give the inclusive page numbers from the print version, using the abbreviations *p.* or *pp.* End with a period.

⑦ **Database name.** Italicize the name of the database. End with a period.

⑧ **Location.** Give the DOI or other permalink. If neither is available, give the URL for the home page of the database, omitting the protocol *http://*.

A citation for the article on p. 435 would look like this:

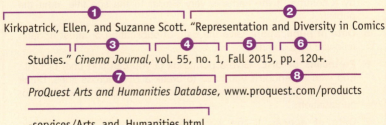

Kirkpatrick, Ellen, and Suzanne Scott. "Representation and Diversity in Comics Studies." *Cinema Journal*, vol. 55, no. 1, Fall 2015, pp. 120+. *ProQuest Arts and Humanities Database*, www.proquest.com/products -services/Arts_and_Humanities.html.

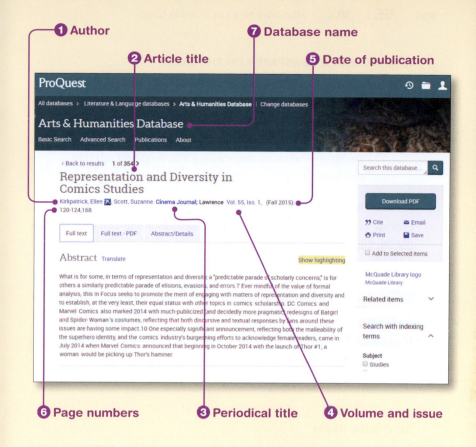

❶ Author

❼ Database name

❷ Article title

❺ Date of publication

ProQuest

All databases > Literature & Language databases > **Arts & Humanities Database** | Change databases

Arts & Humanities Database

Basic Search   Advanced Search   Publications   About

‹ Back to results   1 of 354 ›

Representation and Diversity in
Comics Studies

Kirkpatrick, Ellen 🖂. Scott, Suzanne. **Cinema Journal; Lawrence** Vol. 55, Iss. 1, (Fall 2015):
120-124,168.

| Full text | Full text - PDF | Abstract/Details |

Abstract Translate   Show highlighting

What is for some, in terms of representation and diversity, a "predictable parade of scholarly concerns," is for others a similarly predictable parade of elisions, evasions, and errors.7 Ever mindful of the value of formal analysis, this in Focus seeks to promote the merit of engaging with matters of representation and diversity and to establish, at the very least, their equal status with other topics in comics scholarship. DC Comics and Marvel Comics also marked 2014 with much-publicized (and decidedly more pragmatic) redesigns of Batgirl and Spider-Woman's costumes, reflecting that both discursive and textual responses by fans around these issues are having some impact.10 One especially significant announcement, reflecting both the malleability of the superhero identity, and the comics industry's burgeoning efforts to acknowledge female readers, came in July 2014 when Marvel Comics announced that beginning in October 2014 with the launch of Thor #1, a woman would be picking up Thor's hammer.

Search this database... 🔍

Download PDF

❞ Cite   ✉ Email
🖶 Print   💾 Save

☐ Add to Selected items

McQuade Library logo
McQuade Library

Related items   ⌄

Search with indexing
terms   ⌃

Subject
☐ Studies

❻ Page numbers   **❸ Periodical title**   **❹ Volume and issue**

31. ARTICLE IN A MAGAZINE ON THE WEB

List the author, the article title, and the name of the magazine. Then identify the date of publication, and provide a permalink or DOI, if one is available, or a URL.

Landhuis, Esther. "Is Dementia Risk Falling?" *Scientific American,* 25 Jan.

2016, www.scientificamerican.com/article/is-dementia-risk

-falling/.

32. ARTICLE IN A NEWSPAPER ON THE WEB

After the name of the newspaper, give the publication date and the perma-link (if you can find one) or URL.

> Hirsh, Marc. "Pop Perfection: What Makes a Song a Classic?" *Boston Globe,*
> 10 Nov. 2017, www.bostonglobe.com/arts/music/2017/11/09/pop
> -perfection-what-makes-song-classic/2SPDGw5PgQty1lPyeTKYRN/
> story.html.

33. DIGITAL BOOK

Provide information as for a print book (see models 6–22); then give the digital container title and any other relevant information, including the location.

> Euripides. *The Trojan Women.* Translated by Gilbert Murray, Oxford UP, 1915.
> *Internet Sacred Text Archive,* 2011, www.sacred-texts.com/cla/eurip/
> trok_w.htm.

If you read the book on an e-reader such as a Kindle or Nook, specify the type of reader file you used.

> Schaap, Rosie. *Drinking with Men: A Memoir.* Riverhead / Penguin, 2013.
> Kindle.

34. ONLINE POEM

Include the poet's name, the title of the poem, and the print publication information (if any) for the first container. For the second container, give the title, the date, and the DOI, permalink, or URL.

> Geisel, Theodor. "Too Many Daves." *The Sneetches and Other Stories,* Random
> House, 1961. *Poetry Foundation,* 2015, www.poetryfoundation.org/
> poem/171612.

35. ONLINE EDITORIAL OR LETTER TO THE EDITOR

Include the author's name (if given) and the title (if any). Follow the appropriate model for the type of source you are using. (Check the list on pp. 409–10.) End with the label *Editorial* or *Letter.*

> "Migrant Children Deserve a Voice in Court." *The New York Times,* 8 Mar. 2016,
> www.nytimes.com/2016/03/08/opinion/migrant-children-deserve-a
> -voice-in-court.html. Editorial.

> Starr, Evva. "Local Reporting Thrives in High Schools." *The Washington Post,*
> 4 Apr. 2014, wpo.st/7hmJ1. Letter.

36. ONLINE REVIEW

Cite an online review as you would a print review (see model 28). End with the name of the website, the date of publication, and the URL or permalink.

> O'Hehir, Andrew. "Aronofsky's Deranged Biblical Action Flick." *Salon,* 27 May
> 2014, www.salon.com/2014/03/27/noah_aronofskys_deranged_biblical
> _action_flick/.

37. ENTRY IN AN ONLINE REFERENCE WORK OR WIKI

Begin with the title unless the author is named. (A wiki, which is collectively edited, will not include an author.) Include the title of the entry; the name of the work, italicized; the sponsor or publisher; the date of the latest update; and the location (permalink or URL). Before using a wiki as a source, check with your instructor.

> Cartwright, Mark. "Apollo." *Ancient History Encyclopedia,* 18 May 2012, www
> .ancient.eu/apollo/.

> "Gunpowder Plot." *Wikipedia,* 4 Mar. 2016, en.wikipedia.org/wiki/Gunpowder
> _Plot.

38. SHORT WORK FROM A WEBSITE

To cite a work on a website that is not part of a regularly published journal, magazine, or newspaper, include all of the following elements that are available: the author, the title of the work, the title of the website, the publisher or sponsor, the date of publication or latest update, and the URL. If the site is undated, include "Accessed" and the date you visited the site.

> Bali, Karan. "Kishore Kumar." *Upperstall.com,* upperstall.com/profile/kishore
> -kumar/. Accessed 2 Mar. 2019.

> "Our Mission." *Trees for Life International,* 2011, www.treesforlife.org/our
> -work/our-mission.

39. ENTIRE WEBSITE

Follow the guidelines for a work from the web, beginning with the name of the author or editor (if any), followed by the title of the website, italicized; the name of the sponsor or publisher (if different from the name of the site); the date of publication or last update; and the location.

> Glazier, Loss Pequeño, director. *Electronic Poetry Center.* State U of New York
> Buffalo, 1994-2016, epc.buffalo.edu/.

> *Weather.com.* Weather Channel Interactive, 1995-2016, weather.com/.

Works from Websites

1 **Author.** List the last name first. End with a period. If no author is given, begin with the title. For variations, see models 2–5.

2 **Title of work.** Enclose the title and any subtitle of the work in quotation marks.

3 **Title of website.** Give the title of the entire website, italicized. Follow it with a comma.

4 **Publisher or sponsor.** Look for the sponsor's name at the bottom of the home page. If the sponsor's name is roughly the same as the site title, omit the sponsor. Follow it with a comma.

5 **Date of publication or latest update.** Give the most recent date, followed by a comma.

6 **Location.** Give the permalink, if you can find one, or the site's URL, followed by a period.

7 **Date of access.** If the site is undated, end with *Accessed* and the date you accessed the site.

A citation for the website on p. 439 would look like this:

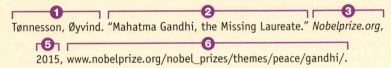

Tønnesson, Øyvind. "Mahatma Gandhi, the Missing Laureate." *Nobelprize.org*,

2015, www.nobelprize.org/nobel_prizes/themes/peace/gandhi/.

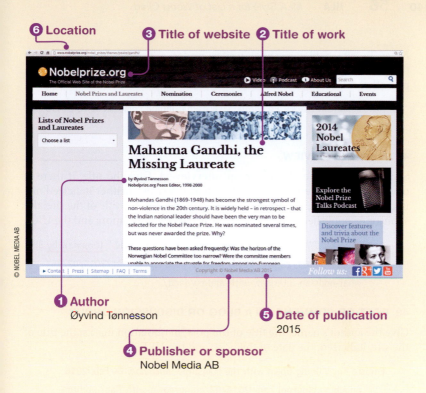

6 Location

3 Title of website **2 Title of work**

Nobelprize.org
The Official Web Site of the Nobel Prize

| Home | Nobel Prizes and Laureates | Nomination | Ceremonies | Alfred Nobel | Educational | Events |

Lists of Nobel Prizes
and Laureates

Choose a list

Mahatma Gandhi, the Missing Laureate

by Øyvind Tønnesson
Nobelprize.org Peace Editor, 1998-2000

Mohandas Gandhi (1869-1948) has become the strongest symbol of non-violence in the 20th century. It is widely held – in retrospect – that the Indian national leader should have been the very man to be selected for the Nobel Peace Prize. He was nominated several times, but was never awarded the prize. Why?

These questions have been asked frequently: Was the horizon of the Norwegian Nobel Committee too narrow? Were the committee members unable to appreciate the struggle for freedom among non-European

2014 Nobel Laureates

Explore the Nobel Prize Talks Podcast

Discover features and trivia about the Nobel Prize

► Contact | Press | Sitemap | FAQ | Terms   Copyright © Nobel Media AB 2015   Follow us:

1 Author
Øyvind Tønnesson

5 Date of publication
2015

4 Publisher or sponsor
Nobel Media AB

© NOBEL MEDIA AB

For a personal website, include the name of the person who created the site as you would with a site's author or editor. If the site is undated, end with your date of access.

> Enright, Mike. *Menright.com.* www.menright.com. Accessed 30 Mar. 2019.

40. BLOG

For an entire blog, give the author's name; the title of the blog, italicized; the date; and the URL. If the site is undated, end with your access date.

> Levy, Carla Miriam. *Filmi Geek.* 2006-2015, www.filmigeek.com.

> *Little Green Footballs.* littlegreenfootballs.com. Accessed 4 Mar. 2019.

Note: To cite a blogger who writes under a pseudonym, begin with the pseudonym and then put the writer's real name (if you know it) in parentheses.

> Atrios (Duncan Black). *Eschaton.* www.eschatonblog.com. Accessed 8 Mar.
> 2019.

41. ONLINE INTERVIEW

Start with the name of the person interviewed. Give the title, if there is one. If not, give a <u>descriptive label</u> such as *Interview*, neither italicized nor in quotation marks, and the interviewer, if relevant; the title of the site; the sponsor or publisher (if there is one); the date of publication; and the URL.

> Ladd, Andrew. "What Ends: An Interview with Andrew Ladd." <u>Interview by</u> Jill.
> *Looks & Books,* 25 Feb. 2014, www.looksandbooks.com/2014/02/25/
> what-ends-an-interview-with-andrew-ladd/.

42. POST OR COMMENT ON A BLOG OR DISCUSSION GROUP

Give the author's name; the title of the post, in quotation marks; the title of the site, italicized; the date of the post; and the URL.

> Edroso, Roy. "Going Down with the Flagship." *Alicublog,* 24 Feb. 2016,
> alicublog.blogspot.com/2016/02/going-down-with-flagship.html.

For a comment on an online post, give the writer's name or screen name; a <u>label</u> such as *Comment on*, not italicized; the title of the article commented on; and the label *by* and the article author's name. End with the citation information for the type of article.

> JennOfArk. <u>Comment on</u> "Going Down with the Flagship," by Roy Edroso.
> *Alicublog,* 24 Feb. 2016, alicublog.blogspot.com/2016/02/going-down
> -with-flagship.html#disqus_thread.

43. POSTING ON A SOCIAL NETWORKING SITE

To cite a posting on Facebook, Instagram, or another social networking site, include the writer's name; up to 140 characters of the posting, in quotation marks (or a description such as *Photograph*, not italicized and not in quotation marks, if there's no text); the name of the site, italicized; the date of the post; and the location of the post (URL).

> Cannon, Kevin. "Portrait of Norris Hall in #Savannah, GA — home (for a few
> months, anyway) of #SCAD's sequential art department." *Instagram,* Mar.
> 2014, www.instagram.com/p/lgmqk4i6DC/.

44. EMAIL OR MESSAGE

Include the writer's name; the subject line, in quotation marks, if one is provided, or a descriptive message such as *Text message*; *Received by* (not italicized or in quotation marks) followed by the recipient's name; and then the date of the message.

> Carbone, Nick. "Screen vs. Print Reading." Received by Karita dos Santos,
>
> 17 Apr. 2016.

45. TWEET

Begin with the writer's Twitter handle, and put the real name, if known, in parentheses. Include the entire tweet, in quotation marks. Give the site name in italics (*Twitter*), the date and time of the message, and the tweet's URL. When alphabetizing in the list of works cited, ignore the @ symbol and alphabetize using the first few letters.

> @LunsfordHandbks (Andrea A. Lunsford). "Technology & social media
>
> have changed the way we write. That doesn't mean literacy has
>
> declined https://community.macmillan.com/groups/macmillan-news/
>
> blog/2016/02/24/the-literacy-revolution... @MacmillanLearn."
>
> *Twitter*, 24 Feb. 2016, 10:17 a.m., twitter.com/LunsfordHandbks/
>
> status/702512638937460736.

Visual, audio, multimedia, and live sources

46. FILM (THEATRICAL, DVD, OR OTHER FORMAT)

If you cite a particular person's work, start with that name. If not, start with the title of the film; then name the director, distributor, and year of release. Other contributors, such as writers or performers, may follow the director. If you cite a feature from a disc, treat the film as the first container and the disc as the second container.

> Bale, Christian, performer. *Vice*. Directed by Adam McKay, Annapurna Pictures,
>
> 2018.

> Lasseter, John. Introduction. *Spirited Away*, directed by Hayao Miyazaki, 2001.
>
> Walt Disney Video, 2003, disc 1.

47. ONLINE VIDEO

Cite an online video as you would a short work from a website (see model 38).

> Nayar, Vineet. "Employees First, Customers Second." *YouTube*, 9 June 2015,
>
> www.youtube.com/watch?v=cCdu67s_C5E.

48. TELEVISION (BROADCAST OR ON THE WEB)

For a show broadcast on television, begin with the <u>title of the program</u>, italicized (for an entire series), or the title of the episode, in quotation marks. Then list important contributors (writer, director, actor); season and episode number (for a specific episode); the <u>network</u>; the local station and city, if the show appeared on a local channel; and the broadcast date(s). For a show accessed on a network website, include the URL after the date of posting.

> <u>*Breaking Bad*</u>. Created by Vince Gilligan, performances by Bryan Cranston,
> Aaron Paul, and Anna Gunn, <u>AMC</u>, 2008-2013.

> "Time Zones." <u>*Mad Men,*</u> written by Matthew Weiner, directed by Scott
> Hornbacher, season 7, episode 1, <u>AMC</u>, 13 Apr. 2014, www.amc.com/
> shows/mad-men/season-7/episode-01-time-zones.

49. RADIO (BROADCAST OR ON THE WEB)

If you are citing a <u>particular episode</u> or segment, cite a radio broadcast as you would a television episode.

> <u>"Tarred and Feathered."</u> *This American Life,* narrated by Ira Glass, WNYC,
> 11 Apr. 2013.

For a show or segment accessed on the web, follow the date of posting with the website title, a comma, the URL, and a period.

50. TELEVISION OR RADIO INTERVIEW

List <u>the person interviewed</u> and then the <u>title</u>, if any. If the interview has no title, use the <u>label</u> *Interview* and the name of the interviewer, if relevant. Then identify the source. End with information about the program and the interview date(s). (For an online interview, see model 41.)

> <u>Russell, David O.</u> <u>Interview by</u> Terry Gross. *Fresh Air,* WNYC, 20 Feb. 2014.

51. PERSONAL INTERVIEW

List the <u>person who was interviewed</u>; the <u>label</u> *Telephone interview, Personal interview,* or *Email interview*; and the date the interview took place.

> Freedman, Sasha. <u>Personal interview</u>. 10 Nov. 2015.

52. SOUND RECORDING

List the name of the <u>person or group you wish to emphasize</u> (such as the composer, conductor, or band); the title of the recording or composition;

the artist, if appropriate; the manufacturer; and the year of issue. If you are citing a particular song or selection, include its title, in quotation marks.

> Bach, Johann Sebastian. *Bach: Violin Concertos.* Performances by Itzhak
> Perlman and Pinchas Zukerman, English Chamber Orchestra, EMI, 2002.

> Rihanna. "Work." *Anti,* Roc Nation, 2016.

Note: If you are citing instrumental music that is identified only by form, number, and key, do not underline, italicize, or enclose it in quotation marks.

> Grieg, Edvard. Concerto in A minor, op. 16. Conducted by Eugene Ormandy,
> Philadelphia Orchestra, RCA, 1989.

53. MUSICAL COMPOSITION

When you are not citing a specific published version, first give the composer's name, followed by the title.

> Mozart, Wolfgang Amadeus. *Don Giovanni*, K527.

> Mozart, Wolfgang Amadeus. Symphony no. 41 in C major, K551.

Note: Cite a published score as you would a book. If you include the date that the composition was written, do so immediately after the title.

> Schoenberg, Arnold. *Chamber Symphony No. 1 for 15 Solo Instruments, Op. 9.*
> 1906. Dover, 2002.

54. VIDEO GAME

Start with the developer or author (if any). After the title, give the distributor and the date of publication.

> Harmonix. *Rock Band Blitz.* MTV Games, 2012.

55. LECTURE OR SPEECH

For a live lecture or speech, list the speaker; the title (if any), in quotation marks; the sponsoring institution or group; the place; and the date. Add the label *Lecture* or *Speech* after the date if readers will not otherwise be able to identify the work.

> Eugenides, Jeffrey. Portland Arts and Lectures. Arlene Schnitzer Concert Hall,
> Portland, OR, 30 Sept. 2003.

For a lecture or speech on the web, cite as you would a short work from a website (see model 38).

Burden, Amanda. "How Public Spaces Make Cities Work." *TED.com,* Mar. 2014,
www.ted.com/talks/amanda_burden_how_public_spaces_make_cities
_work.

56. LIVE PERFORMANCE

List the title, the appropriate names (such as the writer or performer), the
place, and the date.

The Sea Ranch Songs. By Aleksandra Vrebalov, performed by the Kronos
Quartet, White Barn, The Sea Ranch, CA, 23 May 2015.

57. PODCAST

Cite a podcast as you would a short work from a website (see model 38).

Fogarty, Mignon. "Begs the Question: Update." *QuickandDirtyTips.com,*
Macmillan, 6 Mar. 2014, www.quickanddirtytips.com/education/
grammar/begs-the-question-update.

58. WORK OF ART OR PHOTOGRAPH

List the artist's or photographer's name; the work's title, italicized; and the
date of composition. Then cite the name of the museum or other location
and the city. To cite a reproduction in a book, add the publication information. To cite online artwork, add the title of the database or website,
italicized, and the URL or permalink.

Bronzino, Agnolo. *Lodovico Capponi.* 1550-55, Frick Collection, New York.

General William Palmer in Old Age. 1810, National Army Museum, London.
White Mughals: Love and Betrayal in Eighteenth-Century India, by William
Dalrymple, Penguin Books, 2002, p. 270.

Hura, Sohrab. *Old Man Lighting a Fire.* 2015, *Magnum Photos,* pro
.magnumphotos.com/Asset/-2K1HRG6NSSEE.html.

59. MAP OR CHART

Cite a map or chart as you would a short work within a longer work. For
an online source, include the location. End with the label *Map* or *Chart* if
needed for clarity.

"Australia." *Perry-Castaneda Library Map Collection,* U of Texas, 1999, www.lib
.utexas.edu.maps.australia_pol99.jpg.

California. Rand McNally, 2002. Map.

60. CARTOON OR COMIC STRIP

List the artist's name; the title of the cartoon or comic strip, in quotation marks; and the publication information. You may end with a <u>label</u> (*Cartoon* or *Comic strip*) for clarity.

> Flake, Emily. *The New Yorker,* 13 Apr. 2015, p. 66. <u>Cartoon</u>.

> Munroe, Randall. "Heartbleed Explanation." *xkcd.com,* xkcd.com/1354/. <u>Comic strip</u>.

61. ADVERTISEMENT

Include the <u>label</u> *Advertisement* at the end of the entry.

> Ameritrade. *Wired,* Jan. 2014, p. 47. <u>Advertisement</u>.

> Lufthansa. *The New York Times,* 16 Apr. 2014, www.nytimes.com.
>
> <u>Advertisement</u>.

Other sources (including digital versions)

If an online version is not shown in this section, use the appropriate model for the source and then end with a DOI, permalink, or URL.

62. REPORT OR PAMPHLET

Follow the guidelines for a print book (models 6–22) or a digital book (model 33).

> Rainie, Lee, and Maeve Duggan. *Privacy and Information Sharing.* Pew
>
> Research Center, 14 Jan. 2016, www.pewinternet.org/files/2016/01/
>
> PI_2016.01.14_Privacy-and-Info-Sharing_FINAL.pdf.

63. GOVERNMENT PUBLICATION

Begin with the author, if identified. Otherwise, start with the name of the government, followed by the agency. For congressional documents, cite the number, session, and house of Congress; the type (*Report, Resolution, Document*); and the number. End with the publication information. For online versions, follow the models for a short work from a website (model 38) or an entire website (model 39).

> Gregg, Judd. *Report to Accompany the Genetic Information Act of 2003.* US
>
> 108th Congress, 1st session, Senate Report 108-22, Government Printing
>
> Office, 2003.

> United States, Department of Health and Human Services, National Institutes
>
> of Health. *Keep the Beat Recipes: Deliciously Healthy Dinners.* Oct. 2009,
>
> healthyeating.nhlbi.nih.gov/pdfs/Dinners_Cookbook_508-compliant.pdf.

64. PUBLISHED PROCEEDINGS OF A CONFERENCE

Cite the proceedings as you would a book.

> Cleary, John, and Gary Gurtler, editors. *Proceedings of the Boston Area*
> *Colloquium in Ancient Philosophy 2002.* Brill Academic Publishers, 2003.

65. DISSERTATION

Enclose the title in quotation marks. Add the label *Dissertation*, the school, and the year the work was accepted.

> Thompson, Brian. "I'm Better Than You and I Can Prove It: Games, Expertise,
> and the Culture of Competition." Dissertation, Stanford U, 2015.

Note: Cite a published dissertation as a book, adding the identification *Dissertation* and the university after the title.

66. DISSERTATION ABSTRACT

Cite the abstract as you would an unpublished dissertation, and add the label *Abstract* after the year. For an abstract that uses *Dissertation Abstracts International*, include the volume, year, and page number.

> Huang-Tiller, Gillian C. "The Power of the Meta-Genre: Cultural, Sexual, and
> Racial Politics of the American Modernist Sonnet." Dissertation, U of
> Notre Dame, 2000. Abstract. *Dissertation Abstracts International,* vol. 61,
> 2000, p. 1401.

> Moore, Courtney L. "Stress and Oppression: Identifying Possible Protective
> Factors for African American Men." Dissertation, Chicago School of
> Professional Psychology, 2016. Abstract. *ProQuest Dissertations and*
> *Theses,* search.proquest.com/docview/1707351557.

67. LETTER

Cite a published letter as a work in an anthology (see model 9). If the letter is unpublished, follow this form:

> Anzaldúa, Gloria. Letter to the author. 10 Sept. 2002.

68. MANUSCRIPT OR OTHER UNPUBLISHED WORK

List the author's name; the title (if any) or a description of the material; any identifying numbers; and the name of the library or research institution housing the material, if applicable.

> Woolf, Virginia. "The Searchlight." Papers of Virginia Woolf, 1902-1956, Series
> III, Box 4, Item 184, Smith College, Northampton.

69. LEGAL SOURCE

To cite a court case, give the names of the first plaintiff and defendant, the case number, the name of the court, and the date of the decision. To cite an act, give the name of the act followed by its Public Law (*Pub. L.*) number, its Statutes at Large (*Stat.*) cataloging number, and the date the act was enacted.

> Citizens United vs. FEC. 558 US 310. Supreme Court of the US. 2010. Legal
>
> Information Institute, Cornell U Law School, www.law.cornell.edu/supct/
>
> pdf/08-205P.ZS.

> Museum and Library Services Act of 2003. Pub. L. 108-81. Stat. 117.991. 25
>
> Sept. 2003.

Note: You do not need an entry on the list of works cited when you cite articles of the U.S. Constitution and laws in the U.S. Code.

57 A Student Research Essay, MLA Style

A research-based argument by Julia Sakowitz appears on the following pages. Julia followed the MLA guidelines described in Chapters 54–56.

Student Writing

Julia Sakowitz

COURTESY OF JULIA SAKOWITZ

Sakowitz 1

Name, instructor, course, and date aligned at left

Julia Sakowitz

Professor Yamboliev

PWR 1

21 May 2018

Title centered

"We're A Lot More Than Gospel Singing":

Tourism in Harlem

Connects her personal experience to the topic of the essay, establishing a narrative frame

    As a New York City resident of the new millennium, I grew up barely aware that Harlem had ever been a *no-go* zone and couldn't understand why people of the older generation, my parents included, were afraid to venture uptown. I knew nothing about the heroin and crack epidemics of the 1960s, 70s, and 80s and in general was accustomed to a New York City that was safer than it had been in years.

Provides background information on problems in Harlem and responses to them

    Harlem has changed rapidly over the past several decades. As problems with crime and drug abuse in the storied New York neighborhood decreased in the 1980s and 1990s, new government-sponsored and privately funded economic initiatives like the Upper Manhattan Empowerment Zone (UMEZ) pushed for outside investment and economic development (Hoffman 288; Zukin et al.). In a recent interview, Carolyn Johnson, owner of "Welcome to Harlem," a boutique tour company, recalled that "[Harlem] went from 0 to 100 in a short period of time," to the point that even Harlem residents themselves weren't aware of new businesses in their neighborhood. Tourism in Harlem clearly played a central role in this process, both responding to and creating social and economic change. By 2000, more than 800,000 people were visiting Harlem each year (Hoffman 288).

Introduces a key area of debate

    It's clear that Harlem's surge in tourism is good for the city. But an equally important and more complex question is whether tourism benefits Harlem residents or sells them short. Close examination of current policy and tour business in Harlem

Annotations indicate effective choices or **MLA-style formatting**.

Sakowitz 2

reveals problems that come with tourism, such as cultural commodification and commercial gentrification, which are made worse by an Empowerment Zone program that favors only the most socioeconomically advantaged residents and outsiders. Although there is no simple solution for tourism in Harlem, small minority- and resident-owned tour businesses have the potential to more directly and widely benefit the community while causing fewer social and economic problems.

Economic development policy, particularly the UMEZ, has played a major role in shaping tourism's growth. Founded in 1994, the organization operates programs targeting business investment, loans to small businesses, grants for arts and culture, and employment and business training for residents (UMEZ). But promoting tourism is one of its most important aims.

The UMEZ especially focuses on cultural initiatives as a means of drawing tourism, sponsoring a "Catalyst Fund" specifically to "build cultural tourism," funding marketing and publicity for "UMEZ-eligible cultural organizations" (UMEZ). This cultural marketing approach to Harlem tourism is not unique to the UMEZ. Recent scholarship on tourism in Harlem concludes that marketing black and Latino culture is Harlem's golden ticket to escape economic marginalization. Scholar Lily Hoffman identifies black culture as the driving force that increased tourism to Harlem, claiming that for visitors, Harlem is the embodiment of "Black America and its music and entertainment traditions" (288). In Hoffman's eyes, "capitalizing on ethnic culture" for tourism not only generates revenue but also promotes cultural flourishing and instills community pride (297). Other scholars echo these sentiments, emphasizing that "diversity" or minority culture is Harlem's major and perhaps only asset and that "cultural tourism" has the additional benefit of promoting tolerance and de-stigmatization (Fainstein and Powers; Huning and Novy). But

Writer's last name and page number appear on every page

Presents explicit thesis statement at the end of introductory paragraphs

Provides detailed discussion of the UMEZ organization and its effects in Harlem

When the author is mentioned in a signal phrase, only a page number is needed in the parenthetical citation for a source with page numbers

Uses a semicolon to separate information about two sources in one citation

Sakowitz 3

although it seems reasonable to assume that most tourists come to Harlem expecting to experience black culture, significant cultural complications still stand.

Cultural tourism comes with problems. The power dynamic between a tourist with means and mobility, and Harlem residents, who might lack both, is skewed. One of the most obvious dangers is that visitors will disrespect Harlem and the people who live there, participating in "negative sightseeing" or treating locals as if they're "put on exhibit" (Fainstein and Powers 14). In the popular Lonely Planet guide to New York City, there are hints of a clash between tourists and locals over cultural tourism: "Many locals are upset by visitors [to Harlem churches] who chat during sermons, leave in the middle of services or show up in skimpy attire," Lonely Planet warns. "Plus, for some, there's the uncomfortable sense that African American spirituality is something to be consumed like a Broadway show" (St. Louis and Bonnetto 254).

> Defines a key term ("gentrification") and shows how it relates to tourism and affects the community

Another, equally important issue stemming from tourism is commercial gentrification, the phenomenon of large chain stores and boutiques replacing stores that serve the poor (Zukin et al. 48). Such changes have long been viewed as positive. A low-income neighborhood often lacks necessary retail infrastructure, instead featuring businesses like used merchandise outlets, check cashing operations, liquor stores, or job training and family services (Hoffman 288). Tourism can encourage middle-class economic activity like supermarkets, commercial banks, and legal and accounting services, which are as much needed by low-income residents as wealthier ones (Hoffman 288). But boutique stores and

> Refers to visual in the text of the essay

chain stores, seen in fig. 1, can replace services that might still be needed by the poor, leaving low-income residents feeling unwelcome (Zukin et al. 48). Economic gain from new businesses also bypasses most Harlem residents: fewer than half of new retail

Sakowitz 4

COURTESY OF GRAY LINE CITYSIGHTSEEING NEW YORK

Fig. 1. This photo shows a typical tour bus passing Harlem's historic Apollo Theater, which now sits amid chain stores such as Banana Republic and GameStop (City Sightseeing New York).

Provides figure number, explanatory caption, and source information for a visual

entrepreneurs are residents, according to Zukin and others, and even those entrepreneurs who are residents overwhelmingly come from the newly arrived middle class (59).

Commercial gentrification can feed into residential gentrification as the neighborhood becomes attractive to new middle class residents. These might be any of a variety of races and nationalities, including African and African American, but tend to be better educated, have more money, and come from outside New York City (Zukin et al. 59). In fact, tourism itself can facilitate residential gentrification, sometimes overtly through real estate tours much like the Harlem "brownstone tours" that first occurred in the 1980s ("House Tours Galore"; Sandford 103). Today, this kind of "neighborhood-shopping" continues. Non-Harlemite New Yorkers, visitors, and even real estate moguls will often visit Harlem with Big Onion Walking Tours to ask pointed questions about whether Harlem is a friendly and safe place to live (Kamil).

Sakowitz 5

Both commercial and residential gentrification favor outsiders and newcomers. While it is possible for tourism to economically empower Harlem and its residents, in reality the greatest economic gains bypass low-income residents completely.

In this context, Carolyn Johnson, Harlem resident and founder of "Welcome to Harlem," a self-described "certified minority and women-owned visitor center and boutique-tour company," is a unique player ("About Us"). In the early 2000s, Johnson realized her neighborhood was changing rapidly and started the website "Welcome to Harlem" in 2004 as an informational tool for the community, so residents could learn about Harlem's new businesses and venues. In 2008, Johnson decided to branch out into tourism. Seeing outsiders coming to Harlem to give bus and walking tours, she decided to complete a short tour guide training program and start leading tours herself (Interview). "Welcome to Harlem" now features six different tours, including jazz tours, food-tasting tours, and historic tours, as well as "music programs and workshops" ("About Us").

Includes two personal interviews as field research

For Johnson, running her own business can be an economic challenge, but another, equally serious problem is developing a trustworthy reputation to attract clients. She says she struggled to get recognition outside the community, noting it was more common for hotels and tour agencies to recommend large non-Harlem-based tour companies, which might be able to pay a sizeable commission. Visibility is a common problem for Harlem-based tour companies. Almost half of the listed businesses resulting from a Google search for "Harlem tour" are not Harlem-based businesses, but larger outside companies, like "New York Visions," "Free Tours by Foot," and "Big Onion Walking Tours."

In the tour business, which aims to represent a neighborhood for outsiders, issues of cultural representation are important. For

Sakowitz 6

Harlem-based entrepreneurs, offering tours can be a means of self-representation. Johnson's own identity as a Harlem resident motivates her to create tours that disprove negative stereotypes. "Most people think that Harlem is just Sylvia's, the Apollo, and gospel on Sunday," Johnson says. She wants to show that Harlem is a self-contained community, "a lot more than just gospel singing" (Interview).

Demon- strates the benefits of having a Harlem resident represent the com- munity in all its richness

This point of "authenticity" is so important that Harlem- based companies compete with even more exclusive definitions. The "Welcome to Harlem" website states, "Our tours are led by true Harlemites (those who grew up here or live here) which allows for an authentic and personal experience." According to Seth Kamil, owner of "Big Onion Walking Tours," "authenticity" is not an asset at all. Kamil, who founded his business 25 years ago as a graduate student at Columbia University, believes that living in a certain place is no qualification for leading tours, and that the best tours are strongly academic, offering historical fact. Kamil employs mainly graduate students as guides, and his Harlem guides are neither African American nor necessarily Harlem locals. In a recent interview, Kamil questioned the motives of tourists seeking a minority or Harlemite guide and suggested that there is a "subtle racism" that drives tourists to request a minority guide in Harlem, but not in other economically challenged minority neighborhoods like Chinatown. He stated simply, "We don't play that game" (Kamil).

Presents an opposing point of view

But at the same time, much like "Welcome to Harlem" or Harlem Heritage Tours, Kamil is concerned about representing Harlem fairly and dispelling stereotypes. In addition to focusing on history, his tours aim to express the struggles of living in Harlem because of its continued lack of infrastructure that many middle-class New Yorkers take for granted. He notes that the biggest problem with Harlem tours are "perceptions that customers have" and he tries to avoid

Sakowitz 7

disrespecting the community, refusing to take part in "Gospel Tours," which he sees as violating Harlem's places of worship. He also cares about what Harlem residents think of his tours. In his opinion, Big Onion Walking Tours has "a unique relationship with the community," and he notes that many black residents will stop to listen to his white guides, to check that they're being respectful and accurate (Kamil).

Kamil seemed to view "cultural" tours as, at worst, empty and unethical, and, at best, self-commodifying. Could he be partially right? Is Harlem-based tour companies' heavy-handed advertising of "authenticity" based on minority status and Harlem residence demeaning for Harlem residents?

Introduces a third important voice in the debate

Coming at this same question of cultural commodification from a different perspective is Arlene Dávila, a scholar whose focus on Latino issues in East Harlem, or El Barrio, led her to surprising conclusions about the UMEZ policies. Commodifying minority culture is problematic, Dávila claims, because in the eyes of tourists, policymakers, and even scholars, not all culture is created equal. For example, Harlem is internationally famous as a "black Mecca," yet it is also more than half Latino and a center for "Nuyorican" identity, urban Latindad, and Latino dance and music (52). But what happens when visitors' needs and residents' reality just don't align? Dávila writes:

Block format for a quotation of more than four lines; quotation marks are not needed

By limiting East Harlem's funding eligibility to certain sections and imposing requirements that only institutionalized cultural industries could meet, EZ virtually guaranteed that cultural institutions in Central and West Harlem, which are the most established cultural institutions in Upper Manhattan, would be most prominently featured in EZ-sponsored tourist promotional materials and the ones eligible for the largest amounts of funding. (51)

Note that the parenthetical citation comes after the period that ends the sentence

Sakowitz 8

When Latino cultural initiatives have applied for UMEZ funding, the UMEZ board has questioned the appeal of Latino culture, in one instance rejecting a salsa museum's application because it doubted the international popularity of salsa and the museum's ability to create at least five jobs (Dávila 59). The results of such policy for El Barrio are dramatic: Dávila estimates that as little as 6% of the UMEZ cultural funding was given to Latino initiatives (51).

But Latino Harlemites aren't the only ones who suffer from the UMEZ policies. Even though the UMEZ funding of tourism and cultural initiatives is supposed to be an equalizing force that elevates those with few resources, its economic prerequisites favor those with money and education (Dávila 58). Harlem residents echo these sentiments. Deborah Faison, a Harlem resident, commented that the technical training the UMEZ provides is "by itself . . . not enough" and that it's necessary to be "in a strong position already to participate" in the program (qtd. in Maurrasse 164). Carolyn Johnson, who receives funding for "Welcome to Harlem" through the UMEZ, believes that UMEZ doesn't do enough for small business and the "people who have been here" (Interview). The ultimate result of the UMEZ's supposedly equal-access programs of economic empowerment through culture is that the "largest beneficiaries under the EZ were developers and outside visitors" (Dávila 61).

If tourism is going to be a means of economic empowerment for Harlem, there's an urgent need to revise UMEZ policy. For example, when allocating funding, the UMEZ should focus less on the revenue and jobs a cultural initiative will create and more on its cultural value to the community. Harlem's cultural life is as important as its economic life, *especially* from the perspective of tourism, because cultivating genuine culture that comes from and serves the community keeps Harlem authentically itself, which is what draws tourists in the first place. Doing otherwise sells the soul of the

Transition to final point

Includes "qtd. in" to indicate an indirect quotation (source quoted in another source)

Writer proposes a policy change and gives examples

Sakowitz 9

neighborhood, turning it into a hollow Disneyland version of itself. The UMEZ also needs to take civic participation and empowerment more seriously. Instead of providing sparse job training and business skills classes, it should take steps to organize community meetings and start more comprehensive programs that would create a genuine sense of resident involvement and power.

Finally, the UMEZ can't remain socioeconomically blind. Doing so benefits those who have economic or social advantage, enabling commercial gentrification rather than uplifting the community. The organization should develop a policy of need-based preference, giving special consideration to long-term residents, minorities, and economically disadvantaged entrepreneurs. Instead of selecting businesses based on how accomplished they seem already, the UMEZ should award grants based on their potential to grow.

Conclusion sums up writer's argument and reiterates thesis

With these changes to the UMEZ, Harlem entrepreneurs will be able to receive funding and compete on an even playing field with outside companies like Big Onion Walking Tours without having to sell their identity. Small business will be able to flourish, and Harlem will remain resilient and diverse, a wonderful place to live and a wonderful place to visit.

Sakowitz 10

Works Cited

Dávila, Arlene. "Empowered Culture? New York City's Empowerment Zone and the Selling of El Barrio." *The Annals of the American Academy of Political and Social Science,* vol. 594, no. 1, July 2004, pp. 49-64.

Fainstein, Susan, and John Powers. "Tourism and New York's Ethnic Diversity: An Underutilized Resource?" *Tourism, Ethnic Diversity, and the City,* edited by Jan Rath, Routledge, 2007, pp. 143-63.

Hoffman, Lily M. "The Marketing of Diversity in the Inner City: Tourism and Regulation in Harlem." *International Journal of Urban and Regional Research,* vol. 27, no. 2, June 2003, pp. 286-99. *Academic Search Premier,* doi:10.1111/1468-2427.00448.

"House Tours Galore: Where to Get a Look inside NYC's Most Fabulous Homes." *6sqft.* www.6sqft.com/house-tours-galore -where-to-get-a-look-inside-the-areas-most-fabulous-homes -and-gardens/. Accessed 23 Apr. 2018.

Huning, S., and J. Novy. "Tourism as an Engine of Neighborhood Regeneration?" *CMS Working Paper Series.* Center for Metropolitan Studies, 2006, citeseerx.ist.psu.edu/viewdoc/ download? doi:10.1.1.544.6506&rep=rep1&type=pdf.

Johnson, Carolyn. "About Us." *Welcome to Harlem,* welcometoharlem .com/page/aboutus/. Accessed 15 May 2018.

---. Interview. Conducted by Julia Sakowitz, 9 May 2018.

Kamil, Seth. Interview. Conducted by Julia Sakowitz, 11 May 2018.

Maurrasse, David. *Listening to Harlem: Gentrification, Community, and Business,* Routledge, 2006.

Sandford, Mariellen R. "Tourism in Harlem: Between Negative Sightseeing and Gentrification." *The Journal of American Culture,* vol. 10, no. 2, Summer 1987, pp. 99-105. *Wiley Online Library,* doi:10.1111/j.1542-734X.1987.1002_99.x.

Heading centered

Print journal article

Chapter in a book with an editor

Article found in a database

Information from a website

Online report

Personal interview

Print book

Second and subsequent lines of each entry are indented

Sakowitz 11

St. Louis, Regis, and Cristian Bonnetto. "Harlem and Upper
    Manhattan." *Lonely Planet New York City*. Lonely Planet, 2014.

Upper Manhattan Empowerment Zone (UMEZ). "Upper Manhattan
    Empowerment Zone: Who We Are." Upper Manhattan
    Empowerment Zone Development Corporation, 2016, umez.org.

Photograph   *Uptown Tour*. 2016. City Sightseeing New York, www
    .citysightseeingnewyork.com/nyc-bus-tours/uptown-treasures
    -harlem-tour-plus.html. Photograph.

Zukin, Sharon, et al. "New Retail Capital and Neighborhood
    Change: Boutiques and Gentrification in New York City." *City &
    Community,* vol. 8, no. 1, Mar. 2009, pp. 47-64.

▲ **For visual analysis** This illustration suggests the kinds of disciplines in which you might use APA style and some of the kinds of research you might do. What sources will you need to cite?

APA Documentation

Documentation styles in different disciplines vary according to what information is valued most highly. Thus in the social sciences, where timeliness of publication is crucial, the date of publication comes up front, right after the author's name.

— ANDREA A. LUNSFORD

List of Examples

In-text citations in APA style (Chapter 59)

References in APA style (Chapter 60)

Guidelines for author listings

Print books

Print periodicals

> **Source maps are visual guides to citing common sources.**

Digital written-word sources

58 The Basics of APA Style

Chapters 58–61 discuss the basic formats prescribed by the American Psychological Association (APA), guidelines that are widely used in the social sciences. For further reference, consult the *Publication Manual of the American Psychological Association*, Seventh Edition (2020).

58a Think about what readers need from you.

Why does academic work call for very careful citation practices when writing for the general public may not? The answer is that readers of your academic work expect source citations for a number of reasons:

- Source citations demonstrate that you've done your homework on your topic and that you are a part of the conversation surrounding it.
- Source citations show that you understand the need to give credit when you make use of someone else's intellectual property. (See Chapter 12 for details.)
- Source citations give explicit directions to guide readers who want to look for themselves at the works you're using.

The guidelines for APA style tell you exactly what information to include in your citation and how to format that information.

58b Identify the type of source you are using.

Before you can decide how to cite your source following APA guidelines, you need to determine what kind of source you're using.

Types of sources

Refer to the List of Examples on pp. 461–62 to locate guidelines on citing various types of sources — print books (or parts of print books), print periodicals (journals, magazines, and newspapers), and digital written-word sources (an online article or a book on an e-reader). A digital version of a source may include updates or corrections that the print version lacks, so it's important to provide the correct information for readers. For sources that consist mainly of material other than written words — such as a film, song, or artwork — consult the "other sources" section of the directory.

A note about articles from web and database sources

You need a subscription to look through most databases, so individual researchers almost always gain access to articles in databases through a library that pays to subscribe. The easiest way to tell whether a source comes from a database, then, is that its information is *not* generally available for free. Many databases are digital collections of articles that originally appeared in edited print periodicals, ensuring that an authority has vouched for the accuracy of the information. Such sources often have more credibility than free material available on the web.

58c Plan and connect your citations.

APA citations appear in two connected parts of your text — a brief in-text citation in the body of your written text and a full citation in the list of references, to which the in-text citation directs readers. The most straightforward in-text citations include the author's name, the publication year, and the page number, but many variations on this basic format are discussed in Chapter 59.

In the text of her research essay (see 15c), Tawnya Redding includes a paraphrase of material from an online journal that she accessed through the publisher's website. She cites the authors' names and the year of publication in a parenthetical reference, pointing readers to the entry for "Baker, F., & Bor, W. (2008)" in her references list, shown below.

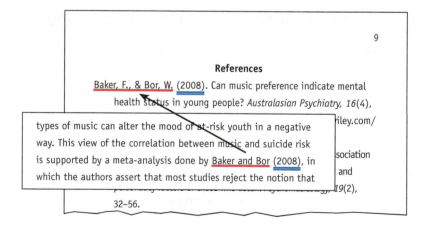

9

References

Baker, F., & Bor, W. (2008). Can music preference indicate mental
   health status in young people? *Australasian Psychiatry, 16*(4),
   [iley.com/]

types of music can alter the mood of at-risk youth in a negative
way. This view of the correlation between music and suicide risk
is supported by a meta-analysis done by Baker and Bor (2008), in
which the authors assert that most studies reject the notion that

[sociation]
[and]
19(2),

32–56.

58d   Include notes as needed.

APA style allows you to use content notes, either at the bottom of the page or on a separate page at the end of the text, to expand or supplement your text. Indicate such notes in the text by superscript numerals ([1]). Single-space all entries. Indent the first line of each note five spaces, but begin subsequent lines at the left margin.

SUPERSCRIPT NUMBER IN TEXT

The age of the children involved in the study was an important factor in the selection of items for the questionnaire.[1]

FOOTNOTE

[1] Marjorie Youngston Forman and William Cole of the Child Study Team provided great assistance in identifying appropriate items for the questionnaire.

 58e   Follow APA format.

The following formatting guidelines are adapted from the APA recommendations for student papers. However, you may want to check with your instructor before preparing your final draft.

For a sample student essay in APA style, see Chapter 61.

- *Title page.*   A few double-spaced lines from the top margin, center the title of the paper in bold font. After one blank double-spaced line, include the following details on separate lines: your name, the department and school in which the course is offered, the course number and name, the instructor's name, and the assignment due date.
- *Margins and spacing.*   Leave margins of at least one inch at the top and bottom and on both sides of the page. Do not justify the right margin. Double-space throughout the text, except for footnotes, which should be single-spaced. Indent one-half inch from the left margin for the first line of a paragraph and all lines of a quotation over forty words long.
- *Page numbers.*   Place the page number in the upper-right corner of each page, including the title page.

- *Long quotations.* For a quotation of forty or more words, indent it one-half inch from the left margin, and do not use quotation marks. Place the page reference in parentheses one space after the final punctuation.

- *Headings.* Headings are frequently used within the text of APA-style projects. In a text with only one or two levels of headings, center the main headings in bold font, and position any subheadings flush with the left margin in bold font. Capitalize all major words; however, do not capitalize any articles, short prepositions, or coordinating conjunctions unless they are the first word or follow a colon.

- *Visuals.* Tables should be labeled "Table" and numbered in bold font. All other visuals (such as charts, graphs, photographs, and drawings) should be labeled "Figure" and numbered in bold font. Both tables and figures should have a title in italics on the line below the label. Provide any source information in a note below the table or figure. Begin with the word "Note," italicized and followed by a period. Remember to refer to each visual in your text, stating how it contributes to the point(s) you are making. Tables and figures should generally appear after the paragraph in which it is called out.

APA also publishes guidelines for professional papers, which include elements such as an abstract, or overview of the work, and a running head, or shortened title at the top of each page. For most college papers, the student guidelines will be acceptable; if your instructor requires an abstract or running head, see an example on page 500.

59 APA Style for In-Text Citations

An in-text citation in APA style always indicates which source on the references page the writer is referring to, and it explains in what year the material was published; for quoted material, the in-text citation also indicates where in the source the quotation can be found.

Note that APA style generally calls for using the past tense or present perfect tense for signal verbs: "Baker (2018) showed" or "Baker (2018) has shown." Use the present tense only to discuss results ("the experiment demonstrates") or widely accepted information ("researchers agree").

We have used underlining in some examples only to draw your attention to important elements. Do not underline anything in your own citations.

1. BASIC FORMAT FOR A QUOTATION

Generally, use the author's name in a signal phrase to introduce the cited material, and place the date, in parentheses, immediately after the author's name. The page number, preceded by "p.," appears in parentheses after the quotation.

> Gitlin (2001) pointed out that "political critics, convinced that the media are rigged against them, are often blind to other substantial reasons why their causes are unpersuasive" (p. 141).

If the author is not named in a signal phrase, place the author's name, the year, and the page number in parentheses after the quotation: (Gitlin, 2001, p. 141). For a long, set-off quotation (more than forty words), place the page reference in parentheses one space after the final quotation.

For quotations from works without page numbers, include other information from the source, such as a section heading, a paragraph number, a figure number, or a time stamp, to help readers find the cited passage.

> Driver (2007) has noticed "an increasing focus on the role of land" in policy debates over the past decade (para. 1).

2. BASIC FORMAT FOR A PARAPHRASE OR SUMMARY

Include the author's last name and the year as in model 1. A page number is not required for a summary or a paraphrase, but include one if it would help readers find the material in a long work.

> Gitlin (2001) has argued that critics sometimes overestimate the influence of the media on modern life (p. 141).

3. TWO AUTHORS

Use both names in all citations. Use "and" in a signal phrase, but use an ampersand (&) in parentheses.

> Babcock and Laschever (2003) have suggested that many women do not negotiate their salaries and pay raises as vigorously as their male counterparts do.

> A recent study has suggested that many women do not negotiate their salaries and pay raises as vigorously as their male counterparts do (Babcock & Laschever, 2003).

4. THREE OR MORE AUTHORS

Use only the first author's name and "et al." in a signal phrase or in parentheses.

As Soleim et al. (2017) demonstrated, advertising holds the potential for manipulating "free-willed" consumers.

A recent study has demonstrated that advertising holds the potential for manipulating "free-willed" consumers (Soleim et al., 2017).

5. CORPORATE OR GROUP AUTHOR

If the name of the organization or corporation is long, spell it out the first time you use it, followed by an abbreviation in brackets. In later references, use the abbreviation only.

FIRST CITATION	The national conversation about bullying has changed recently to include the dangers of social media (Centers for Disease Control and Prevention [CDC], 2018).
LATER CITATIONS	Though bullying is defined by some as a form of "youth violence," current social media channels offer evidence that social bullying is not restricted to youth (CDC, 2018).

6. UNKNOWN AUTHOR

Use the title or its first few words in a signal phrase or in parentheses. A book's title is italicized, as in the following example; an article's title is placed in quotation marks.

The employment profiles for this time period substantiated this trend (*Federal Employment*, 2001).

7. TWO OR MORE AUTHORS WITH THE SAME LAST NAME

Include the authors' initials in each citation.

S. Bartolomeo (2000) conducted the groundbreaking study on teenage childbearing.

8. TWO OR MORE WORKS BY AN AUTHOR IN A SINGLE YEAR

Assign lowercase letters ("a," "b," and so on) alphabetically by title, and include the letters after the year.

Gordon (2017b) examined this trend in more detail.

9. TWO OR MORE SOURCES IN ONE PARENTHETICAL REFERENCE

List any sources by different authors in alphabetical order by the authors' last names, separated by semicolons: (Cardone, 2018; Lai, 2014). List works by the same author in chronological order, separated by commas: (Lai, 2014, 2017).

10. SOURCE REPORTED IN ANOTHER SOURCE

Use the phrase "as cited in" to indicate that you are reporting information from a secondary source. Name the original source in a signal phrase or in parentheses, and list the secondary source in parentheses and in your list of references.

Amartya Sen developed the influential concept that land reform was necessary for "promoting opportunity" among the poor (as cited in Driver, 2007, para. 2).

11. PERSONAL COMMUNICATION

Cite any personal letters, email messages, electronic postings, telephone conversations, or interviews as shown. Do not include personal communications in the reference list.

R. Tobin (personal communication, November 4, 2006) supported his claims about music therapy with new evidence.

12. ELECTRONIC SOURCE

Cite a web or electronic source as you would a print source, using the author's name and date.

Link and Phelan (2005) argued for broader interventions in public health that would be accessible to anyone, regardless of individual wealth.

The APA recommends the following for electronic sources without names, dates, or page numbers:

Author unknown Use a shortened form of the title in a signal phrase or in parentheses (see model 6). If an organization is the author, see model 5.

Date unknown Use the abbreviation "n.d." (for "no date") in place of the year: (Hopkins, n.d.).

No page numbers If a source lacks stable page numbers, include paragraph numbers, section headings, or both. If a source lacks numbered paragraphs or headings, count the paragraphs manually. If you shorten a long heading, place it in quotation marks: ("What Is It" section). When quoting audio or video sources, use a time stamp to indicate the start of the quotation. Do not include location numbers for sources in e-book format.

> Jacobs and Johnson (2007) have argued that "the South African media is still highly concentrated and not very diverse in terms of race and class" (South African Media after Apartheid section, para. 3).

13. TABLE OR FIGURE REPRODUCED IN THE TEXT

Number figures (graphs, charts, illustrations, and photographs) and tables separately.

For both tables and figures, place the label ("Table 1") and an informative heading ("Hartman's Key Personality Traits") above the table or figure; below, provide information about its source. Begin with the word "Note," italicized and followed by a period.

Table 1

Hartman's Key Personality Traits

Trait category	Color			
	Red	Blue	White	Yellow
Motive	Power	Intimacy	Peace	Fun
Strengths	Loyal to tasks	Loyal to people	Tolerant	Positive
Limitations	Arrogant	Self-righteous	Timid	Uncommitted

Note. Adapted from *The Hartman Personality Profile*, by N. Hayden (http://students.cs.byu.edu/~nhayden/Code/index.php).

If you do not cite the source of the table or figure elsewhere in your text, you do not need to include the source in your list of references.

60 APA Style for a List of References

The alphabetical list of the sources cited in your document is called "References." If your instructor asks that you list everything you have read — not just the sources you cite — call the list "Bibliography."

All the entries in this chapter of the book use hanging indent format, in which the first line aligns on the left and the subsequent lines indent one-half inch or five spaces. This is the customary APA format.

Guidelines for author listings

List authors' last names first, and use only initials for first and middle names. The in-text citations in your text point readers toward particular sources in your list of references (see Chapter 59).

NAME CITED IN SIGNAL PHRASE IN TEXT

Lapowsky (2017) has noted . . .

NAME IN PARENTHETICAL CITATION IN TEXT

. . . (Lapowsky, 2017).

BEGINNING OF ENTRY IN LIST OF REFERENCES

Lapowsky, I. (2017).

Models 1–5 explain how to arrange author names. The information that follows the name of the author depends on the type of work you are citing — a book (models 6–14), a print periodical (models 15–21), a digital written-word source (models 22–31), or another kind of source (models 32–46).

1. ONE AUTHOR

Give the last name, a comma, the initial(s), and the date in parentheses.

Zimbardo, P. G. (2009).

2. MULTIPLE AUTHORS

List up to twenty authors, last name first, with commas separating authors' names and an ampersand (&) before the last author's name.

Walsh, M. E., & Murphy, J. A. (2003).

Note: For a work with more than twenty authors, list the first nineteen, then an ellipsis (. . .), and then the final author's name.

Quick Help

Formatting a List of References

- Start your list on a new page after the text of your document but before appendices or notes. Continue consecutive page numbers.

- Center the heading "References" in bold one inch from the top of the page.

- Begin each entry flush with the left margin, but indent subsequent lines one-half inch or five spaces. Double-space the entire list.

- List sources alphabetically by author's last name. If no author is given, alphabetize the source by the first word of the title other than "A," "An," or "The." If the list includes two or more works by the same author, list them in chronological order.

- Italicize titles and subtitles of books and periodicals. Do not italicize titles of articles, and do not enclose them in quotation marks.

- For titles of books and articles, capitalize only the first word of the title and the subtitle and any proper nouns or proper adjectives.

- For titles of periodicals, capitalize all major words.

Quick Help

Combining Parts of Models

What should you do if your source doesn't match the model exactly? Suppose, for instance, that your source is a translation of a republished book with an editor.

- Identify a basic model to follow. If you decide that your source looks most like a republished book, for example, start with a citation that looks like model 13.

- Look for models that show additional elements in your source. For this example, you would need elements of model 9 (for the translation) and model 7 (for the editor).

- Add new elements from other models to your basic model in the order that makes the most sense to you.

- If you still aren't sure how to arrange the pieces to create a combination model, ask your instructor or a consultant in the writing center.

3. CORPORATE OR GROUP AUTHOR

Resources for Rehabilitation. (2016).

4. UNKNOWN AUTHOR

Begin with the work's title. Italicize the titles of works that are a stand-alone item, such as a novel, a movie, a one-time TV special (such as the 2020 Grammy Awards), or a podcast series. Do not italicize titles of works that are part of a larger whole, such as an article in a journal, a chapter in a book, or an episode of a TV or podcast series. Capitalize only the first word of the title and subtitle (if any) and proper nouns and proper adjectives.

Safe youth, safe schools. (2009).

5. TWO OR MORE WORKS BY THE SAME AUTHOR

List works by the same author in chronological order. Repeat the author's name in each entry.

Goodall, J. (2009).

Goodall, J. (2013).

If the works appeared in the same year, list them alphabetically by title, and assign lowercase letters ("a," "b," etc.) after the dates.

Shermer, M. (2002a). On estimating the lifetime of civilizations. *Scientific American, 287*(2), 33.

Shermer, M. (2002b). Readers who question evolution. *Scientific American, 287*(1), 37.

If the works appeared in the same year but use a more specific date that includes the month or month and day, list the works in chronological order.

Print books

6. BASIC FORMAT FOR A BOOK

Begin with the author name(s). (See models 1–5.) Then include the publication year, title and subtitle, and the publisher. The source map on pp. 474–75 shows where to find information in a typical book.

Kahneman, D. (2011). *Thinking fast and slow.* Farrar, Straus and Giroux.

Books

Take information from the book's title page and copyright page, not from the book's cover or a library catalog.

1 **Author.** List all authors' last names first, and use only initials for first and middle names. For more about citing authors, see models 1–5.

2 **Publication year.** Enclose the year of publication in parentheses.

3 **Title.** Italicize the title and any subtitle. Capitalize only the first word of the title and the subtitle and any proper nouns or proper adjectives.

4 **Publisher.** List the publisher's name, dropping any terms that indicate corporate structure, such as "Inc." or "Ltd."

A citation for the book on p. 475 would look like this:

Tsutsui, W. (2004). *Godzilla on my mind: Fifty years of the king of monsters.*

Palgrave Macmillan.

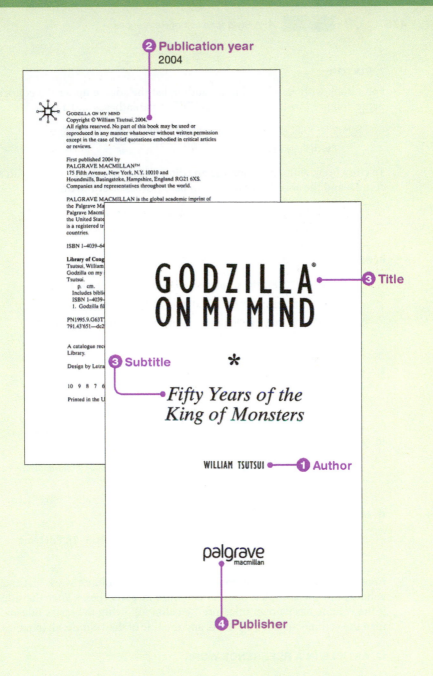

2 Publication year
2004

3 Title

3 Subtitle

1 Author

4 Publisher

GODZILLA® ON MY MIND

*

Fifty Years of the King of Monsters

WILLIAM TSUTSUI

palgrave
macmillan

7. EDITOR

For a book with an editor but no author, list the source under the editor's name, followed by the abbreviation "Ed." in parentheses and a period.

> Schwartz, R. G. (Ed.). (2009). *Handbook of child language disorders.*
> Psychology Press.

To cite a book with an author and an editor, place the editor's name, with a comma and the abbreviation "Ed.," in parentheses after the title.

> Austin, J. (1995). *The province of jurisprudence determined* (W. E. Rumble,
> Ed.). Cambridge University Press.

8. SELECTION IN A BOOK WITH AN EDITOR

> Pettigrew, D. (2018). The suppression of cultural memory and identity in
> Bosnia and Herzegovina. In J. Lindert & A. T. Marsoobian (Eds.),
> *Multidisciplinary perspectives on genocide and memory* (pp. 187–198).
> Springer.

9. TRANSLATION

> Calasso, R. (2019). *The unnamable present* (R. Dixon, Trans.). Farrar, Straus
> and Giroux. (Original work published 2017)

10. EDITION OTHER THAN THE FIRST

> Berger, K. S. (2018). *The developing person through childhood and adolescence*
> (11th ed.). Worth Publishers.

11. MULTIVOLUME WORK WITH AN EDITOR

> Barnes, J. (Ed.). (1995). *Complete works of Aristotle* (Vols. 1–2). Princeton
> University Press.

Note: If you are citing just one volume of a multivolume work, list that volume, not the complete span of volumes, in parentheses after the title. If the volume has its own title, insert a colon following the series title and then the volume number, a period, and the title of the volume, all in italics.

12. ARTICLE IN A REFERENCE WORK

> Dean, C. (1994). Jaws and teeth. In S. Jones, R. Martin, & D. Pilbeam (Eds.),
> *The Cambridge encyclopedia of human evolution* (pp. 56–59). Cambridge
> University Press.

If no author is listed, begin with the title.

13. REPUBLISHED BOOK

Fremlin, C. (2017). *The hours before dawn*. Dover Publications. (Original work published 1958)

14. BOOK WITH A TITLE WITHIN THE TITLE

Do not italicize or enclose in quotation marks a title within a book title.

Klarman, M. J. (2007). Brown v. Board of Education *and the civil rights movement*. Oxford University Press.

Print periodicals

Begin with the author name(s). (See models 1–5.) Then include the publication date, the article title, the title of the periodical, the volume and issue information, and the page numbers. The source map on pp. 478–79 shows where to find information in a sample periodical.

15. ARTICLE IN A JOURNAL

Include the issue number (in parentheses and not italicized) after the volume number (italicized).

Ganegoda, D. B., & Bordia, P. (2019). I can be happy for you, but not all the time: A contingency model of envy and positive empathy in the workplace. *Journal of Applied Psychology, 104*(6), 776–795.

16. ARTICLE IN A MAGAZINE

Include the month (and day, if given).

Solomon, A. (2014, March 17). The reckoning. *The New Yorker, 90*(4), 36–45.

17. ARTICLE IN A NEWSPAPER

Finucane, M. (2019, September 25). Americans still eating too many low-quality carbs. *The Boston Globe,* B2.

Articles from Print Periodicals

1 **Author.** List all authors' last names first, and use only initials for first and middle names. For more about citing authors, see models 1–5.

2 **Publication date.** Enclose the date in parentheses. For journals, use only the year. For magazines and newspapers, use the year, a comma, the month (spelled out), and the day, if given.

3 **Article title.** Do not italicize or enclose article titles in quotation marks. Capitalize only the first word of the article title and subtitle and any proper nouns or proper adjectives.

4 **Periodical title.** Italicize the periodical title (and subtitle, if any), and capitalize all major words. Follow the periodical title with a comma.

5 **Volume and issue numbers.** Give the volume number (italicized) and, without a space in between, the issue number (if given) in parentheses. Follow with a comma.

6 **Page numbers.** Give the inclusive page numbers of the article. End the citation with a period.

A citation for the article on p. 479 would look like this:

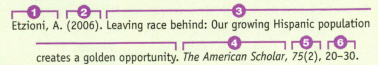

Etzioni, A. (2006). Leaving race behind: Our growing Hispanic population creates a golden opportunity. *The American Scholar, 75*(2), 20–30.

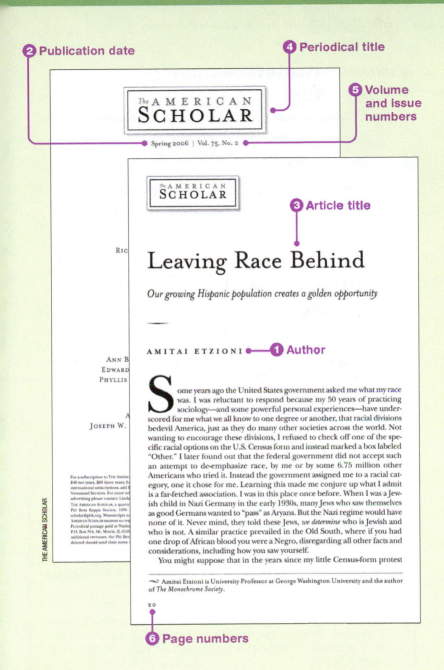

2 Publication date

4 Periodical title

The AMERICAN
SCHOLAR

5 Volume and issue numbers

Spring 2006 | Vol. 75, No. 2

The AMERICAN
SCHOLAR

3 Article title

RIC

Leaving Race Behind

Our growing Hispanic population creates a golden opportunity

AMITAI ETZIONI **1 Author**

ANN B
EDWARD
PHYLLIS

S ome years ago the United States government asked me what my race was. I was reluctant to respond because my 50 years of practicing sociology—and some powerful personal experiences—have underscored for me what we all know to one degree or another, that racial divisions bedevil America, just as they do many other societies across the world. Not wanting to encourage these divisions, I refused to check off one of the specific racial options on the U.S. Census form and instead marked a box labeled "Other." I later found out that the federal government did not accept such an attempt to de-emphasize race, by me or by some 6.75 million other Americans who tried it. Instead the government assigned me to a racial category, one it chose for me. Learning this made me conjure up what I admit is a far-fetched association. I was in this place once before. When I was a Jewish child in Nazi Germany in the early 1930s, many Jews who saw themselves as good Germans wanted to "pass" as Aryans. But the Nazi regime would have none of it. Never mind, they told these Jews, *we determine* who is Jewish and who is not. A similar practice prevailed in the Old South, where if you had one drop of African blood you were a Negro, disregarding all other facts and considerations, including how you saw yourself.

JOSEPH W.

You might suppose that in the years since my little Census-form protest

For a subscription to THE AMERIC
$48 two years, $69 three years; fo
international subscriptions, add $
Newsstand Services. For more in
advertising please contact: Linda
THE AMERICAN SCHOLAR, a quarte
Phi Beta Kappa Society, 1006
scholar@pbk.org. Manuscripts m
AMERICAN SCHOLAR assumes no res
Periodical postage paid at Washi
P.O. Box 354, Mt. Morris, IL 6105
additional revenues, the Phi Bet
deleted should send their name

THE AMERICAN SCHOLAR

⬸ Amitai Etzioni is University Professor at George Washington University and the author of *The Monochrome Society.*

6 Page numbers

18. EDITORIAL OR LETTER TO THE EDITOR

Add an identifying label.

> Doran, K. (2019, October 12). Homeless who look like grandma or grandpa
> [Letter to the editor]. *The New York Times,* A22.

19. UNSIGNED ARTICLE

> Annual meeting announcement. (2003, March). *Cognitive Psychology, 46,* 227.

20. REVIEW

Identify the work reviewed.

> Douthat, R. (2019, October 14). A hustle gone wrong [Review of the film
> *Hustlers*, by L. Scafaria, Dir.]. *National Review, 71*(18), 47.

21. PUBLISHED INTERVIEW

For an interview published in print, begin with the interviewer. If the interviewee is not named in the title of the work, as in this example, include the interviewee's name in a signal phrase.

> Tracy, A. (2019, December). The Super Speaker. *Vanity Fair,* (712), 96–103.

Digital written-word sources

> ## Quick Help
>
> ### Citing Digital Sources
>
> When citing sources accessed online, include as many of the following elements as you can find:
>
> - **Author.** Give the author's name, if available.
> - **Publication date.** Include the date of electronic publication or of the latest update, if available. When no publication date is available, use "n.d." ("no date").
> - **Title.** If the source is not from a larger work, italicize the title.
> - **Print publication information.** For articles from online journals, magazines, or reference databases, give the publication title and other publishing information as you would for a print periodical (see models 15–21).
> - **Retrieval information.** If a DOI (digital object identifier) is available, include it after the publication information with no period at the end. If there is no DOI, include a URL for the article except if the article is from a database. If a DOI or URL is long, you can include a shortened form by using a site like shortdoi.org or bitly.com.

> ## Quick Help
>
> ### Citing Sources without Models in APA Style
>
> You may need to cite a source for which you cannot find a model in APA style. If so, collect as much information as you can find about the creator, title, sponsor, date, and so on, with the goal of helping readers find the source for themselves. Then look at the models in this chapter to see which one most closely matches the type of source you are using.
>
> In an academic project, before citing an electronic source for which you have no model, ask your instructor's advice.

22. ARTICLE FROM AN ONLINE PERIODICAL

Give the author, date, title, and publication information as you would for a print document. Include both the volume and issue numbers for all journal articles. If the article has a digital object identifier (DOI), include it. If there is no DOI, include the URL for the article.

> Bruns, A. (2017). Consequences of partner incarceration for women's employment. *Journal of Marriage and Family, 79*(5), 1331–1352. https://doi.org/10.1111/jomf.12412
>
> Srinivasan, D. (2019, June 4). How digital advertising markets really work. *The American Prospect.* https://prospect.org/article/how-digital-advertising-markets-really-work

23. ARTICLE FROM A DATABASE

For an article that is available in print but that you access in an online database, provide the author(s), date, title of the work, the title of the periodical, and volume/issue information. Give page numbers for the print version. Then give the DOI. If there is no DOI, do not include a URL. The source map on pp. 482–83 shows where to find information for a typical article from a database.

> Hazleden, R. (2003). Love yourself: The relationship of the self with itself in popular self-help texts. *Journal of Sociology, 39*(4), 413–428. https://doi.org/10.1177/0004869003394006

Articles from Databases

1 Author. Include the author's name as you would for a print source. List all authors' last names first, and use initials for first and middle names. For more about citing authors, see models 1–5.

2 Publication date. Enclose the date in parentheses. For journals, use only the year. For magazines and newspapers, use the year, a comma, the month, and the day if given.

3 Article title. Capitalize only the first word of the article title and the subtitle and any proper nouns or proper adjectives.

4 Periodical title. Italicize the periodical title.

5 Volume and issue numbers. For journals and magazines, give the volume number (italicized) and the issue number (in parentheses).

6 Page numbers. Give inclusive page numbers.

7 Retrieval information. If the article has a DOI (digital object identifier), include it after the publication information; do not include the name of the database. If there is no DOI, do not include a URL. Do not add a period after the DOI.

A citation for the article on p. 483 would look like this:

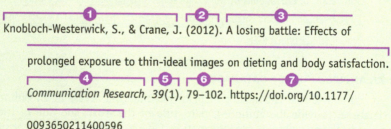

Knobloch-Westerwick, S., & Crane, J. (2012). A losing battle: Effects of

prolonged exposure to thin-ideal images on dieting and body satisfaction.

Communication Research, 39(1), 79–102. https://doi.org/10.1177/

0093650211400596

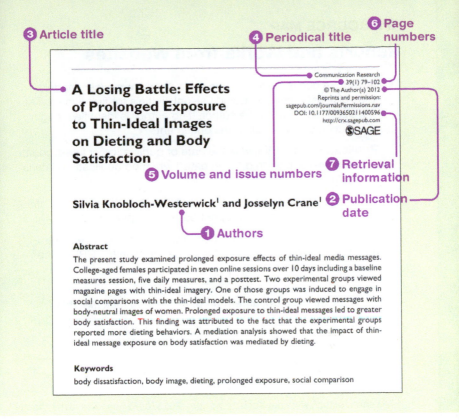

③ Article title

⑥ Page numbers

④ Periodical title

Communication Research
39(1) 79–102
© The Author(s) 2012
Reprints and permission:
sagepub.com/journalsPermissions.nav
DOI: 10.1177/0093650211400596
http://crx.sagepub.com
SAGE

A Losing Battle: Effects of Prolonged Exposure to Thin-Ideal Images on Dieting and Body Satisfaction

⑦ Retrieval information

⑤ Volume and issue numbers

② Publication date

Silvia Knobloch-Westerwick[1] and Josselyn Crane[1]

① Authors

Abstract

The present study examined prolonged exposure effects of thin-ideal media messages. College-aged females participated in seven online sessions over 10 days including a baseline measures session, five daily measures, and a posttest. Two experimental groups viewed magazine pages with thin-ideal imagery. One of those groups was induced to engage in social comparisons with the thin-ideal models. The control group viewed messages with body-neutral images of women. Prolonged exposure to thin-ideal messages led to greater body satisfaction. This finding was attributed to the fact that the experimental groups reported more dieting behaviors. A mediation analysis showed that the impact of thin-ideal message exposure on body satisfaction was mediated by dieting.

Keywords

body dissatisfaction, body image, dieting, prolonged exposure, social comparison

24. ABSTRACT FOR AN ONLINE ARTICLE

Include a label.

Gudjonsson, G. H., & Young, S. (2010). Does confabulation in memory predict suggestibility beyond IQ and memory? [Abstract]. *Personality & Individual Differences, 49*(1), 65–67. https://doi.org/10.1016/j.paid.2010.03.014

25. COMMENT ON AN ONLINE ARTICLE

Give the writer's real name (if known) or screen name. Use up to the first twenty words of the comment in the title position. Add the label "Comment on the article" and then the title of the article in quotation marks. Provide a URL to the comment (if available) or to the article.

lollyl2. (2019, September 25). My husband works in IT in a major city down South. He is a permanent employee now, but for years [Comment on the article "The Google workers who voted to unionize in Pittsburgh are part of tech's huge contractor workforce"]. *Slate.* https://fyre.it/0RT8HmeL.4

Reports and Works from Websites

1 Author. If one is given, include the author's name (see models 1–5). List last names first, and use only initials for first names. The site's sponsor may be the author. If no author is identified, begin the citation with the title of the document.

2 Publication date. Enclose the date of publication or latest update in parentheses. Use "n.d." ("no date") when no publication date is available.

3 Title of work. Italicize the title. Capitalize only the first word of the title and subtitle and any proper nouns or proper adjectives.

4 Retrieval information. Include the website name unless the author and website name are the same. Provide the URL to the work.

A citation for the web document on p. 485 would look like this:

Parker, K., & Wang, W. (2013, March 14). *Modern parenthood: Roles of moms and dads converge as they balance work and family.* Pew Research Center. http://www.pewsocialtrends.org/2013/03/14/modern-parenthood-roles-of-moms-and-dads-converge-as-they-balance-work-and-family/

② Publication date
March 14, 2013

④ Retrieval information

Released: March 14, 2013

Modern Parenthood
Roles of Moms and Dads Converge as They Balance Work and Family

by *Kim Parker* and *Wendy Wang*

OVERVIEW

The way mothers and fathers spend their time has changed dramatically in the past half century. Dads are doing more housework and child care; moms more paid work outside the home. Neither has overtaken the other in their "traditional" realms, but their roles are converging, according to a new Pew Research Center analysis of long-term data on time use.

At the same time, roughly equal shares of working mothers and fathers report in a new Pew Research Center survey feeling stressed about juggling work and family life: 56% of working moms and 50% of working dads say they find it very or somewhat difficult to balance these responsibilities.

Still, there are important gender role differences. While a nearly equal share of mothers and fathers say they wish they

Moms and Dads, 1965-2011: Roles Converge, but Gaps Remain
Average number of hours per week spent on ...

REPORT MATERIALS
- Complete Report
- Topline Questionnaire

Quiz: Which Parent Does More in Your Home?

Slideshow: Key Findings from the Survey

Data Trends: Parental Time Use Since 1965

TABLE OF CONTENTS

① Authors
Kim Parker and Wendy Wang

③ Title of work

---

26. REPORT OR DOCUMENT FROM A WEBSITE

Include all of the following information that you can find: the author, the publication date or "n.d." if no date is given, the title of the work, the name of the website if different from the author, and the URL.

> Tahseen, M., Ahmed, S., & Ahmed, S. (2018). *Bullying of Muslim youth: A review of research and recommendations.* The Family and Youth Institute. http://www.thefyi.org/wp-content/uploads/2018/10/FYI-Bullying-Report.pdf

27. ONLINE BOOK

Give the original print publication date, if different.

> Russell, B. (2008). *The analysis of mind.* Project Gutenberg. http://
> www.gutenberg.org/files/2529/2529-h/2529-h.htm (Original work
> published 1921)

28. EMAIL OR PRIVATE MESSAGE

Do not include entries for email messages or any postings that are private and cannot be retrieved by readers. Instead, cite these sources in your text as forms of personal communication (see p. 469).

29. POSTING ON PUBLIC SOCIAL MEDIA

List an online posting in the references list only if it is retrievable by readers. Provide the author's name, if given, followed by the screen name in brackets. If only the screen name is known, provide it without brackets. Include the date of posting and up to the first twenty words of the post. List any attachments, such as images, videos, or links, and include a descriptive label, such as "[Tweet]" or "[Status update]," in separate brackets. Provide the website or app name and the URL for the post.

> National Science Foundation [@NSF]. (2019, October 13). *Understanding
> how forest structure drives carbon sequestration is important for
> ecologists, climate modelers and forest managers, who are working on*
> [Thumbnail with link attached] [Tweet]. Twitter. https://twitter.com/
> NSF/status/1183388649263652864

30. BLOG POST

Include the title of the blog post and the name of the blog.

> Fister, B. (2019, February 14). Information literacy's third wave. *Library
> Babel Fish.* https://www.insidehighered.com/blogs/library-babel-fish/
> information-literacy%E2%80%99s-third-wave

31. ONLINE REFERENCE WORK OR WIKI ENTRY

Use the date of posting, or "n.d." ("no date") if there is none. Include the retrieval date and URL. If the wiki has archived versions, like Wikipedia, instead use the date of posting and URL of the archived version you read.

> Merriam-Webster. (n.d.). Adscititious. In *Merriam-Webster.com dictionary.*
> Retrieved November 5, 2019, from https://www.merriam-webster.com/
> dictionary/adscititious

Other sources (including online versions)

32. GOVERNMENT PUBLICATION

Berchick, E. R., Barnett, J. C., & Upton, R. D. (2019, September 10). *Health
  insurance coverage in the United States: 2018* (Report No. P60–267).
  U.S. Census Bureau. https://www.census.gov/library/publications/2019/
  demo/p60-267.html

If no author is listed, begin with the department that produced the
document. Any broader organization the department belongs to can be
included as the publisher.

National Park Service. (2019, April 11). *Travel where women made history:
  Ordinary and extraordinary places of American women.* U.S. Department of
  the Interior. https://www.nps.gov/subjects/travelwomenshistory/index.htm

33. DATA SET

Reid, L. (2019). *Smarter homes: Experiences of living in low carbon homes 2013–
  2018* [Data set]. UK Data Service. https://doi.org/10.5255/UKDA-SN-853485

34. DISSERTATION

If you retrieved the dissertation from a database, include the granting university in brackets after the title. Do not include a URL.

Bacaksizlar, N. G. (2019). *Understanding social movements through simulations
  of anger contagion in social media* (Publication No. 13805848) [Doctoral
  dissertation, University of North Carolina at Charlotte]. ProQuest
  Dissertations & Theses.

If you retrieve a dissertation from a website, provide the URL.

Degli-Esposti, M. (2019). *Child maltreatment and antisocial behaviour in
  the United Kingdom: Changing risks over time* [Doctoral dissertation,
  University of Oxford]. Oxford University Research Archive. https://ora.
  ox.ac.uk/objects/uuid:6d5a8e55-bd19-41a1-8ef5-ef485642af89

35. TECHNICAL OR RESEARCH REPORT

Give the report number, if available, in parentheses after the title.

McCool, R., Fikes, R., & McGuinness, D. (2003). *Semantic web tools for
  enhanced authoring* (Report No. KSL-03-07). Knowledge Systems, AI
  Laboratory. http://www.ksl.stanford.edu/KSL_Abstracts/KSL-03-07.html

36. CONFERENCE PROCEEDINGS

Robertson, S. P., Vatrapu, R. K., & Medina, R. (2009). YouTube and Facebook: Online video "friends" social networking. In *Conference proceedings: YouTube and the 2008 election cycle* (pp. 159–176). ScholarWorks@UMass Amherst. http://scholarworks.umass.edu/jitpc2009

37. PAPER PRESENTED AT A MEETING OR SYMPOSIUM, UNPUBLISHED

Include the dates of the entire meeting or symposium even if the paper presentation occurred on a specfic day.

Vasylets, O. (2019, April 10–13). *Memory accuracy in bilinguals depends on the valence of the emotional event* [Paper presentation]. XIV International Symposium of Psycholinguistics, Tarragona, Spain. https://psico.fcep. urv.cat/projectes/gip/files/isp2019.pdf

38. POSTER SESSION

Wood, M. (2019, January 3–6). *The effects of an adult development course on students' perceptions of aging* [Poster session]. Forty-First Annual National Institute on the Teaching of Psychology, St. Pete Beach, FL, United States. https://nitop.org/resources/Documents/2019%20Poster%20Session%20II.pdf

39. PRESENTATION SLIDES

Mader, S. (2007, March 27). *The Zen aesthetic* [Presentation slides]. SlideShare. http://www.slideshare.net/slmader/the-zen-aesthetic

40. FILM

Begin with the director and include the production company after the title.

Peele, J. (Director). (2017). *Get out* [Film]. Universal Pictures.

Separate multiple production companies with semicolons. If the film is a special version, like an extended cut, include that information in brackets after the title. Always include the original release year.

Hitchcock, A. (Director). (1959). *The essentials collection: North by northwest* [Film; five-disc special ed. on DVD]. Metro-Goldwyn-Mayer; Universal Pictures Home Entertainment.

41. ONLINE VIDEO

The New York Times. (2018, January 9). *Taking a knee and taking down a monument* [Video]. YouTube. https://www.youtube.com/watch?v=qY34DQCdUvQ

Wray, B. (2019, May). *How climate change affects your mental health* [Video]. TED Conferences. https://www.ted.com/talks/britt_wray_how_climate_change_affects_your_mental_health

42. TELEVISION PROGRAM, SINGLE EPISODE

Imperioli, M. (Writer), & Buscemi, S. (Director). (2002, October 20). Everybody hurts (Season 4, Episode 6) [TV series episode]. In D. Chase (Executive Producer), *The Sopranos*. Chase Films; Brad Grey Television; HBO.

43. TELEVISION SERIES

Waller-Bridge, P., Williams, H., & Williams, J. (Executive Producers). (2016–2019). *Fleabag* [TV series]. Two Brothers Pictures; BBC.

44. PODCAST EPISODE

West, S. (Host). (2018, July 27). Logical positivism (No. 120) [Audio podcast episode]. In *Philosophize this!* https://philosophizethis.org/logical-positivists/

45. PODCAST SERIES

Abumrad, J., & Krulwich, R. (Hosts). (2002–present). *Radiolab* [Audio podcast]. WNYC Studios. https://www.wnycstudios.org/podcasts/radiolab/podcasts

46. RECORDING

Carlile, B. (2018). The mother [Song]. On *By the way, I forgive you*. Low Country Sound; Elektra.

61 A Student Research Essay, APA Style

On the following pages is a paper by Martha Bell that conforms to the APA guidelines described in this chapter.

Student Writer

Martha Bell

Page number appears flush right on first line of every page

Title (bold-face), writer's name, department and school, course number and title, professor, and date centered and double-spaced

The Mystery of Post-Lyme Disease Syndrome

Martha Bell

Department of Language and Literature, Eastern

Mennonite University

College Writing 130C

Professor Eads

October 29, 2014

Annotations indicate effective choices or **APA-style formatting**.

2

The Mystery of Post-Lyme Disease Syndrome

The Centers for Disease Control and Prevention (CDC) estimates a total of 300,000 cases of Lyme disease annually. Many medical professionals believe Lyme disease can be cured in a matter of weeks with a simple antibiotic treatment. In some cases, however, patients develop post-Lyme disease syndrome, sometimes called "chronic Lyme disease," exhibiting persistent symptoms of Lyme after initial treatment is completed. The scientific community, divided over the causes of post-Lyme disease syndrome, cannot agree on the best treatment for the syndrome. Although Lyme disease is preventable, people are still vulnerable to infection; consequently, there is a need for more research and collaboration with a focus on developing the technology to perform replicable studies, which may subsequently lead to an effective treatment algorithm for post-Lyme disease syndrome.

Prevention

Ixodes ticks, also known as blacklegged and deer ticks, are infected with the bacterium *Borrelia burgdorferi*, responsible for Lyme disease (Hawker et al., 2012). Since being bitten by an infected tick is the only known way of contracting Lyme disease, evading Ixodes ticks is an effective measure. According to M'ikanatha et al. (2013), "Lyme disease is acquired peridomestically and the risk is highest in residential settings abutting areas with forests, meadows, and high prevalence of deer" (p. 168). While adult ticks are more active in the cooler months, developing Ixodes ticks, called nymphs, feed the most during the spring and summer months (Centers for Disease Control and Prevention [CDC], 2014d). Therefore, avoiding areas such as meadows and grasslands in the spring and summer seasons aids in preventing Lyme disease.

Full title boldface and centered

Introduction provides background information

Boldface centered headings help organize review

Reference to work with more than two authors uses "et al."

First reference to organization gives abbreviation for later references

3

Using permethrin repellent on clothes and 20 to 30 percent DEET insect repellent on the skin also keeps ticks away (Brody, 2013). Other measures include wearing light-colored clothing to make ticks more visible, wearing long sleeves and long pants, tucking shirts into pants and pants into socks, and taping closed open areas of clothing when spending time outdoors in areas where ticks are prevalent (Hawker et al., 2012). Additionally, individuals should keep yards and houses clean to avert mammals, such as deer and rodents, that carry Ixodes ticks, and should check pets for ticks.

Though all of these measures greatly reduce the chance of receiving a tick bite, they are not foolproof. The bacterium *B. burgdorferi* takes approximately 36 to 48 hours to become infectious after the tick has bitten an individual (Hawker et al., 2012). A bull's-eye rash called erythema migrans is the only unique symptom of Lyme disease. It appears 3 to 32 days after infection (Hawker et al., 2012). According to one study, only 70 to 80 percent of Lyme disease victims develop erythema migrans; therefore, other symptoms must be assessed (Steere & Sikand, 2003, p. 2472). Other characteristics of Lyme disease include fevers, headaches, stiff neck, swollen lymph nodes, body aches, fatigue, facial palsy, polyarthritis, aseptic meningitis, peripheral root lesions, radiculopathy, and myocarditis (CDC, 2014c; Hawker et al., 2012).

Multiple citations in parentheses listed alphabetically and separated by semicolon

On average, it takes a few weeks for infected individuals to produce antibodies against *B. burgdorferi* (CDC, 2014a). Consequently, most cases of Lyme disease have better outcomes and recovery rates when antibiotics are administered quickly (CDC, 2014e). Administered in the beginning stages of Lyme disease, antibiotics help speed recovery and prevent more serious symptoms, such as heart and nervous system problems, from developing (Lantos, 2011, Introduction section).

4

Erythema migrans is not always present, and other symptoms of Lyme disease are similar to those of other illnesses. Therefore, Lyme disease may be misdiagnosed and untreated. Stricker (2007) explained that "in the absence of typical features of Lyme disease, patients may go on to develop a syndrome with multiple nonspecific symptoms that affect various organ systems, including the joints, muscles, nerves, brain, and heart" (p. 149). Conversely, even when patients receive proper antibiotic treatment for two to four weeks, they can continue to experience symptoms.

Parenthetical citation for quotation includes page number

Post-Lyme Disease Syndrome

The majority of Lyme disease patients are cured after multiple weeks of antibiotics; however, 10 to 15 percent of patients acquire relapsing nonspecific symptoms such as fatigue, arthritis, and short-term memory problems that can persist for months or even years (Brody, 2013). When there is no other possible origin of the nonspecific symptoms, and the individual has had proper treatment for Lyme disease, the patient is classified as having post-Lyme disease syndrome (Lantos, 2011). Marques (2008) explained, "The appearance of post-Lyme disease symptoms seems to correlate with disseminated diseases, a greater severity of illness at presentation, and delayed antibiotic therapy, but not with the duration of the initial antibiotic therapy" (p. 343). The medical community is unsure of how to treat the nonspecific symptoms or what causes them (Lantos, 2011, "A Clinical Approach" section).

Possible Sources of Post-Lyme Disease Syndrome

Scientists are unable to identify the exact source of post-Lyme disease syndrome for several reasons. Identifying patients is difficult because of the general nature of the symptoms. Several surveys demonstrate that a relatively high percentage of the overall population reports nonspecific symptoms, such as fatigue, chronic

5

pain, or cognitive dysfunction after a tick bite (Lantos, 2011, Post-Lyme Disease Syndromes section). In addition, researchers struggle to find participants for their studies (Marques, 2008, p. 342). Study participants must have previous documentation of contracting Lyme disease, which significantly diminishes the testing population (Lantos, 2011).

Scientists and physicians suspect the source of post-Lyme disease syndrome to be multifactorial. Plausible causes of reoccurring nonspecific symptoms include "persistent infection of *B. burgdorferi*, other tick-borne infections, part of the expected resolution of symptoms after treatment, postinfective fatigue syndrome, autoimmune mechanisms, and intercurrent conditions" (Marques, 2008, p. 343). Nevertheless, only a few ideas have been thoroughly explored thus far by the scientific community. The majority of scientists believe remaining damage to tissue and the immune system from the infection causes post-Lyme disease syndrome; however, some believe persistent infection of the bacteria is the source (CDC, 2014b).

Despite complications, a majority of the medical community considers persistent symptoms to be a result of residual damage to the tissues and the immune system that occurred during the infection. These "auto-immune" reactions, which the body uses against foreign elements, occur in infections similar to Lyme disease such as campylobacter, chlamydia, and strep throat (CDC, 2014b). Patients report their nonspecific symptoms improving over time after the typical antibiotic treatment (Marques, 2008, p. 342). Physicians who followed their patients with post-Lyme disease syndrome for extended times also see nonspecific symptoms resolve without further antibiotic treatment (Marques, 2008, p. 347). Consequently, post-Lyme disease syndrome may be a natural evolution of the body healing after an intense infection.

A smaller portion of the medical community considers persistent infection of the microorganism *B. burgdorferi* as the

6

cause of post-Lyme disease syndrome. Recently published studies performed on animals show signs of ongoing infection of the bacterium. One scientific study infected mice with *B. burgdorferi* and gave them intense treatment of antibiotics that should have wiped out the bacterium (Bockenstedt et al., 2012). Bockenstedt et al. (2012) observed the mice over a period of time and found "that infectious spirochetes are rapidly eliminated after institution of antibiotics, but inflammatory *B. burgdorferi* antigens persist adjacent to cartilage and in the enthuses" (p. 2652). This is one of the first studies to show continuous effects of the harmful microorganism in post-Lyme disease syndrome. (Embers et al., 2012, Discussion section). Another scientific study was conducted on nonhuman primates, rhesus macaques. Once again the scientists infected the animals with *B. burgdorferi* and then four to six months later administered an antibiotic treatment to half of the monkeys (Embers et al., 2012). Their results also confirmed that *B. burgdorferi* could withstand antibiotic treatment in rhesus macaques and proceed to cause post-Lyme disease syndrome (Embers et al., 2012, Discussion section). Nonetheless, these results showing perpetual infection as the cause of post-Lyme disease syndrome have yet to be replicated in humans.

In contrast, many studies over the years contradict the theory of ongoing infection, though these studies have not been confirmed true in humans. Lantos (2011) clarified that "no adequately controlled, hypothesis-driven study using a repeatable method has demonstrated that viable *B. burgdorferi* is found in patients with persistent post-Lyme symptoms any more frequently than in those with favorable outcomes" (Biological Plausibility section). Most scientific studies trying to prove persistent infection of *B. burgdorferi* have not been replicated because their procedures and techniques are at fault. The problem derives from the technology that detects the microorganism (Lantos, 2011, Biological Plausibility section).

7

PCR and *B. burgdorferi* culture are commonly used to find evidence of the bacteria in the body; however, both have "low sensitivity in most body fluids from patients with Lyme disease" (Marques, 2008, p. 353). Even though other methods, such as finding antibodies in immune complexes, changes in C6 antibody levels, and PCR in urine samples, have been tried, none prove helpful (Marques, 2008, p. 353). Therefore, the persistent infection of *B. burgdorferi* has not yet successfully been proven as the cause of post-Lyme disease syndrome.

Post-Lyme Disease Syndrome Treatment

Since the cause of post-Lyme disease syndrome is controversial, treatment for the infection varies from patient to patient and physician to physician. Treatment is still in the experimental stages, meaning no set treatment algorithm currently exists. Numerous patients rely on long-term antibiotic medication, despite the overwhelming defying scientific evidence against this treatment (CDC, 2014b). The research studies that focus on prolonged antibiotic treatment observe no dramatic difference in benefits or recoveries of those who had the treatment and those who did not (Marques, 2008, p. 353). On the contrary, many long-term antibiotic research studies found that post-Lyme disease syndrome patients develop harmful side effects. These adverse health effects include "catheter-associated venous thromboembolism, catheter-associated septicemia, allergic reactions and ceftriaxone-induced gallbladder toxicity" (Lantos, 2011, "Extended Antibiotics" section). Therefore, most of the scientific community considers long-term antibiotic treatment for chronic Lyme disease a harmful, risky, and unbeneficial plan.

Most of the scientific community advises against the use of long-term antibiotics because of potential adverse effects. Nevertheless, a small minority of physicians have observed improvements with long-term antibiotics. Because numerous studies

Shortened section heading in quotation marks

8

show a lack of benefit to long-term antibiotics, these hopeful patients may be experiencing a placebo effect, which occurs when patients improve because they believe they are receiving an effective treatment (Marques, 2008, p. 356).

Solving the Mystery

Individuals can take various simple preventive measures to avoid contracting Lyme disease. If the infection is contracted, those who seek prompt treatment increase the chance of full recovery and decrease the chance of developing post-Lyme disease syndrome. However, these steps do not guarantee complete avoidance of post-Lyme disease syndrome. Finding the source of post-Lyme disease syndrome will lead to a specific treatment plan that effectively heals patients. Many scientists deem the source of post-Lyme disease syndrome to be a natural autoimmune reaction; conversely, a few other scientists consider persistent infection as the cause. Both theories, however, need better technology to prove their accuracy. Since scientists disagree about the source of post-Lyme disease syndrome, a variety of experimental treatments have arisen. Replicable studies are needed so that an effective treatment for post-Lyme disease syndrome can be found.

Conclusion indicates need for further research

9

References begin on a new page; heading is centered and boldface

References

Bockenstedt, L., Gonzalez, D., Haberman, A., & Belperron, A. (2012). Spirochete antigens persist near cartilage after murine Lyme borreliosis therapy. *The Journal of Clinical Investigation, 122*(7), 2652–2660. https://doi.org/10.1172/JCI58813

Article from an online newspaper

Brody, J. (2013, July 8). When Lyme disease lasts and lasts. *The New York Times.* https://well.blogs.nytimes.com/2013/07/08/when-lyme-disease-lasts-and-lasts

Two or more works by the same author in the same year arranged alphabetically by title; letters added after year

Centers for Disease Control and Prevention. (2014a). *Diagnosis and testing.* https://www.cdc.gov/lyme/diagnosistesting/index.html

Centers for Disease Control and Prevention. (2014b). *Post-treatment Lyme disease syndrome.* https://www.cdc.gov/lyme/postlds/index.html

Centers for Disease Control and Prevention. (2014c). *Signs and symptoms of untreated Lyme disease.* https://www.cdc.gov/lyme/signs_symptoms/index.html

Centers for Disease Control and Prevention. (2014d). *Transmission.* https://www.cdc.gov/lyme/transmission/index.html

Centers for Disease Control and Prevention. (2014e). *Treatment.* https://www.cdc.gov/lyme/treatment/index.html

All authors up to twenty listed

Embers, M. E., Barthold, S. W., Borda, J. T., Bowers, L., Doyle, L., Hodzic, E., Jacobs, M. B., Hasenkampf, N. R., Martin, D. S., Narasimhan, S., Phillippi-Falkenstein, K. M., Purcell, J. E., Ratterree, M. S., & Philipp, M. T. (2012). Persistence of *Borrelia burgdorferi* in rhesus macaques following antibiotic treatment of disseminated infection. *PLoS ONE, 7*(1). https://doi.org/10.1371/journal.pone.0029914

Hawker, J., Begg, N., Blair, L., Reintjes, R., Weinberg, J., & Ekdahl, K. (2012). *Communicable disease control and health protection handbook* (3rd ed.). John Wiley & Sons.

10

Lantos, P. (2011). Chronic Lyme disease: The controversies and the science. *Expert Review of Anti-Infective Therapy, 9*(7), 787–797. https://doi.org/10.1586/eri.11.63

Marques, A. (2008). Chronic Lyme disease: A review. *Infectious Disease Clinics of North America, 22*(2), 341–360. https://doi.org/10.1016/j.idc.2007.12.011

M'ikanatha, N. M., Lynfield, R., Van Beneden, C. A., & de Valk, H. (2013). *Infectious disease surveillance* (2nd ed.). John Wiley & Sons.

Steere, A., & Sikand, V. (2003). The presenting manifestations of Lyme disease and the outcomes of treatment [Letter to the editor]. *The New England Journal of Medicine, 348*(24), 2472–2474. https://doi.org/10.1056/NEJM200306123482423

Stricker, R. (2007). Counterpoint: Long-term antibiotic therapy improves persistent symptoms associated with Lyme disease. *Clinical Infectious Diseases, 45*(2), 147–157. https://doi.org/10.1086/518853

Journal article with DOI

Letter to the editor

ABSTRACT AND RUNNING HEAD (FOR PROFESSIONAL PAPERS)

Running head (title shortened to 50 characters or fewer) in all capital letters on every page; heading centered and boldface

Abstract

Lyme disease, prevalent in parts of the United States, is a preventable illness spread by tick bites. Lyme disease is considered treatable with a course of antibiotics in the early stages of infection. In some cases, however, symptoms of Lyme disease persist in individuals who have completed antibiotic treatment. The causes of post-Lyme disease syndrome, sometimes called "chronic Lyme disease," are unknown, and treatment of those suffering post-Lyme disease syndrome is controversial, with some physicians arguing for long-term antibiotic treatment and others convinced that such treatments are harmful to patients. There is a need for more research with a focus on developing the technology to perform replicable studies and eventually an effective treatment algorithm for post-Lyme disease syndrome.

Keywords: Lyme disease, ticks, post-Lyme treatment, erythema migrans

Abstract required for professional papers submitted for publication

Keywords help readers find article online or in a database

▲ **For visual analysis** This illustration, which depicts the 120-year-old bronze lions flanking the Art Institute of Chicago, suggests the history of *Chicago* style and its usefulness in researched writing in many disciplines. What sources will you need to cite?

Chicago Documentation

Chicago style is based on the *Chicago Manual of Style*, first published in 1906 but regularly updated to keep up with changes in publishing practices and technologies. It has long been used not only in the humanities but across disciplines, and it is a trusted resource used by many popular, academic, and scholarly publishers—including the publisher of this book.

— ANDREA A. LUNSFORD

Chicago Documentation 501 – 526

List of Examples

Notes and bibliographic entries in *Chicago* style (Chapter 63)

Source maps are visual guides to citing common sources.

62 The Basics of *Chicago* Style

The style guide of the University of Chicago Press has long been used in history as well as in other areas of the arts and humanities. The Seventeenth Edition of *The Chicago Manual of Style* (2017) provides a complete guide to *Chicago* style, including two systems for citing sources. This chapter presents the notes and bibliography system. For easy reference, examples of notes and bibliographic entries are shown together in Chapter 63.

62a Think about what readers need from you.

Why does academic work call for very careful citation practices when writing for the general public may not? The answer is that readers of academic work expect source citations for several reasons:

- Source citations demonstrate that you've done your homework on your topic and that you are a part of the rich conversation surrounding it.

- Source citations show that you understand the need to give credit when you make use of someone else's intellectual property. (See Chapter 12 for more details.)

- Source citations give explicit directions to guide readers who want to look for themselves at the works you're using.

Guidelines from *The Chicago Manual of Style* will tell you exactly what information to include in your citation and how to format that information.

Types of sources

Refer to the List of Examples on p. 503 to locate guidelines for citing sources in *Chicago* style. You will need to be careful to tell your readers whether you read a print version or a digital version of a source. Digital magazine and newspaper articles may include updates or corrections that the print version lacks; digital books may not number pages or screens the same way the print book does. If you are citing a source with media elements — such as a film, song, or artwork — consult the "other sources" section of the examples. And if you can't find a model exactly like the source you've selected, see the box on p. 508.

ARTICLES FROM WEB AND DATABASE SOURCES

You need a subscription to look through most databases, so individual researchers almost always gain access to articles in databases through a school or public library that pays to subscribe. The easiest way to tell whether a source comes from a database, then, is that its information is *not* generally available free to anyone with an Internet connection. Many databases are digital collections of articles that originally appeared in edited print periodicals, ensuring that an authority has vouched for the accuracy of the information. Such sources may have more credibility than free material available on the web.

62b Plan and connect your citations.

Citations in *Chicago* style will appear in three places in your text — a note number in the text marks the material from the source, a footnote or an endnote includes information to identify the source (or information about supplemental material), and the bibliography provides the full citation.

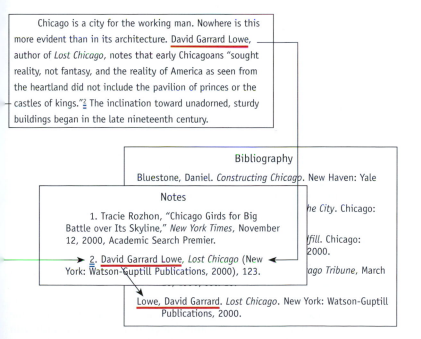

Chicago is a city for the working man. Nowhere is this more evident than in its architecture. David Garrard Lowe, author of *Lost Chicago*, notes that early Chicagoans "sought reality, not fantasy, and the reality of America as seen from the heartland did not include the pavilion of princes or the castles of kings."² The inclination toward unadorned, sturdy buildings began in the late nineteenth century.

Bibliography

Bluestone, Daniel. *Constructing Chicago*. New Haven: Yale

...he City. Chicago:

...fill. Chicago:
2000.

...ago Tribune, March

Notes

1. Tracie Rozhon, "Chicago Girds for Big Battle over Its Skyline," *New York Times*, November 12, 2000, Academic Search Premier.

2. David Garrard Lowe, *Lost Chicago* (New York: Watson-Guptill Publications, 2000), 123.

Lowe, David Garrard. *Lost Chicago*. New York: Watson-Guptill Publications, 2000.

62c Follow *Chicago* format.

The *Chicago Manual of Style* recommends the following format for the manuscript of a research paper. However, check with your instructor before preparing your final draft.

For a sample student essay in *Chicago* style, see Chapter 64.

- *Title page.* About halfway down the title page, center the full title of your project and your name. Unless otherwise instructed, at the bottom of the page also list the course name, the instructor's name, and the date submitted. Do not type a number on this page.

- *Margins and spacing.* Leave one-inch margins at the top, bottom, and sides of your pages. Double-space the entire text, including block quotations and between entries in the notes and bibliography.

- *Page numbers.* Number all pages (except the title page) in the upper right-hand corner. Also use a short title or your name before page numbers. Check to see if your instructor has a preference on whether to count the title page as part of the text (if so, the first text page will be page 2) or as part of the front matter (if so, the first text page will be page 1).

- *Long quotations.* For a long quotation, indent one-half inch (or five spaces) from the left margin and do not use quotation marks. *Chicago* defines a long quotation as one hundred words or eight lines, though you may set off shorter quotes for emphasis (48b).

- *Headings.* *Chicago* style allows, but does not require, headings. Many students and instructors find them helpful.

- *Visuals.* Visuals (photographs, drawings, charts, graphs, and tables) should be placed as near as possible to the relevant text. (See 12c for guidelines on incorporating visuals into your text.) Tables should be labeled *Table,* numbered, and captioned. All other visuals should be labeled *Figure* (abbreviated *Fig.*), numbered, and captioned. Remember to refer to each visual in your text, pointing out how it contributes to the point(s) you are making.

Notes

Notes can be footnotes (each one appearing at the bottom of the page on which its citation appears) or endnotes (in a list on a separate page at the end of the text). (Check your instructor's preference.) Indent the first line of each note one-half inch and begin with a number, a period, and one space before the first word. All remaining lines of the entry are flush with the left margin. Single-space footnotes and endnotes, with a double space between each entry.

Use superscript numbers (^{1}) to mark citations in the text. Place the superscript number for each note just after the relevant quotation, sentence, clause, or phrase. Type the number after any punctuation mark except the dash, and do not leave a space before the superscript. Number citations sequentially throughout the text. When you use signal phrases to introduce source material, note that *Chicago* style requires you to use the present tense (*citing Bebout's studies, Meier argues . . .*).

IN THE TEXT

Thompson points out that African American and Puerto Rican prisoners at Attica were more likely than white prisoners to have their mail censored and family visits restricted.[19]

IN THE FIRST NOTE REFERRING TO THE SOURCE

19. Heather Ann Thompson, *Blood in the Water: The Attica Prison Uprising of 1971 and Its Legacy* (New York: Pantheon Books, 2016), 13.

After giving complete information the first time you cite a work, shorten additional references to that work: list only the author's last name, a shortened version of the title, and the page number. If the second reference to the work immediately follows the first reference, list only the author's name and the page number.

IN FIRST AND SUBSEQUENT NOTES

19. Heather Ann Thompson, *Blood in the Water: The Attica Prison Uprising of 1971 and Its Legacy* (New York: Pantheon Books, 2016), 13.

20. Thompson, 82.

21. Julia Sweig, *Inside the Cuban Revolution* (Cambridge, MA: Harvard University Press, 2002), 21.

22. Thompson, *Blood in the Water,* 304.

Bibliography

Begin the list of sources on a separate page after the main text and any endnotes. Continue numbering the pages consecutively. Center the title *Bibliography* (without underlining, italics, or quotation marks) one inch below the top of the page. Double-space, and then begin each entry at the left margin. Indent the second and subsequent lines of each entry one-half inch, or five spaces.

List sources alphabetically by authors' last names or by the first major word in the title if the author is unknown. See Chapter 63 for an example of a *Chicago*-style bibliography.

In the bibliographic entry, include the same information as in the first note for that source, but omit the page reference. Give the first author's last name first, followed by a comma and the first name; separate the main elements of the entry with periods rather than commas; and do not enclose the publication information for books in parentheses.

IN THE BIBLIOGRAPHY

Thompson, Heather Ann. *Blood in the Water: The Attica Prison Uprising of 1971 and Its Legacy*. New York: Pantheon Books, 2016.

63   *Chicago* Style for Notes and Bibliographic Entries

The following examples demonstrate how to format both notes and bibliographic entries according to *Chicago* style. The note, which is numbered, appears first; the bibliographic entry, which is not numbered, appears below the note. We have used underlining in some examples only to draw your attention to important elements. Do not underline anything in your own citations.

Print and digital books

The note for a book typically includes five elements: author's name, title and subtitle, city of publication and publisher, year, and page number(s) or electronic locator information for the information in the note. The bibliographic entry usually includes all these elements but the page number (and does include a URL or other locator if the book is digitally published), but it is styled differently: commas separate major elements of a note, but a bibliographic entry uses periods. The author's name is first name first in the note but last name first in the bibliography. For multiple authors, invert just the first author's name in the bibliography.

Quick Help

Citing Sources without Models in *Chicago* Style

To cite a source for which you cannot find a model, collect as much information as you can find — about the creator, title, date of creation or update, and location of the source — with the goal of helping your readers find the source for themselves, if possible. Then look at the models in this chapter to see which one most closely matches the type of source you are using.

In an academic writing project, before citing an electronic source for which you have no model, also be sure to ask your instructor's advice.

1. ONE AUTHOR

1. Nell Irvin Painter, *The History of White People* (New York: W. W. Norton, 2010), 119.

Painter, Nell Irvin. *The History of White People*. New York: W. W. Norton, 2010.

2. MULTIPLE AUTHORS

2. Mark Littman and Fred Espenak, *Totality: The Great American Eclipses of 2017 and 2024* (New York: Oxford University Press, 2017), 35.

Littman, Mark, and Fred Espenak. *Totality: The Great American Eclipses of 2017 and 2024*. New York: Oxford University Press, 2017.

With four or more authors, you may give the first-listed author followed by *et al.* in the note. In the bibliography, list all the authors' names.

2. Stephen J. Blank et al., *Conflict, Culture, and History: Regional Dimensions* (Miami: University Press of the Pacific, 2002), 276.

Blank, Stephen J., Lawrence E. Grinter, Karl P. Magyar, Lewis B. Ware, and Bynum E. Weathers. *Conflict, Culture, and History: Regional Dimensions*. Miami: University Press of the Pacific, 2002.

3. ORGANIZATION AS AUTHOR

3. World Intellectual Property Organization, *Intellectual Property Profile of the Least Developed Countries* (Geneva: World Intellectual Property Organization, 2002), 43.

World Intellectual Property Organization. *Intellectual Property Profile of the Least Developed Countries*. Geneva: World Intellectual Property Organization, 2002.

4. UNKNOWN AUTHOR

4. *Broad Stripes and Bright Stars* (Kansas City, MO: Andrews McMeel, 2002), 10.

Broad Stripes and Bright Stars. Kansas City, MO: Andrews McMeel, 2002.

5. ONLINE BOOK

5. Dorothy Richardson, *Long Day: The Story of a New York Working Girl, as Told by Herself* (New York: Century, 1906; UMDL Texts, 2010), 159, http://quod.lib.umich.edu/cgi/t/text/text-idx?c=moa;idno=AFS7156 .0001.001.

Richardson, Dorothy. *Long Day: The Story of a New York Working Girl, as Told by Herself*. New York: Century, 1906. UMDL Texts, 2010. http://quod.lib .umich.edu/cgi/t/text/text-idx?c=moa;idno=AFS7156.0001.001.

6. ELECTRONIC BOOK (E-BOOK)

6. Atul Gawande, *Being Mortal: Medicine and What Matters in the End* (New York: Metropolitan, 2014), chap. 3, Nook.

Gawande, Atul. *Being Mortal: Medicine and What Matters in the End*. New York: Metropolitan, 2014. Nook.

7. BOOK WITH AN EDITOR

7. Leopold von Ranke, *The Theory and Practice of History,* ed. Georg G. Iggers (New York: Routledge, 2010), 135.

von Ranke, Leopold. *The Theory and Practice of History*. Edited by Georg G. Iggers. New York: Routledge, 2010.

If an edited book has no author, put the editor's name first.

7. James H. Fetzer, ed., *The Great Zapruder Film Hoax: Deceit and Deception in the Death of JFK* (Chicago: Open Court, 2003), 56.

Fetzer, James H., ed. *The Great Zapruder Film Hoax: Deceit and Deception in the Death of JFK*. Chicago: Open Court, 2003.

8. SELECTION IN AN ANTHOLOGY OR CHAPTER IN A BOOK WITH AN EDITOR

8. Denise Little, "Born in Blood," in *Alternate Gettysburgs,* ed. Brian Thomsen and Martin H. Greenberg (New York: Berkley Publishing Group, 2002), 245.

Give the inclusive page numbers of the selection or chapter in the bibliographic entry.

Little, Denise. "Born in Blood." In *Alternate Gettysburgs*. Edited by Brian Thomsen and Martin H. Greenberg, 242–55. New York: Berkley Publishing Group, 2002.

9. INTRODUCTION, PREFACE, FOREWORD, OR AFTERWORD

9. Ta-Nehisi Coates, foreword to *The Origin of Others,* by Toni Morrison (Cambridge, MA: Harvard University Press, 2017), xi.

Give the inclusive page number of the section cited in the bibliographic entry.

Coates, Ta-Nehisi. Foreword to *The Origin of Others,* by Toni Morrison, vii–xvii. Cambridge, MA: Harvard University Press, 2017.

10. TRANSLATION

10. Suetonius, *The Twelve Caesars,* trans. Robert Graves (London: Penguin Classics, 1989), 202.

Suetonius. *The Twelve Caesars.* Translated by Robert Graves. London: Penguin Classics, 1989.

11. EDITION OTHER THAN THE FIRST

11. Dee Brown, *Bury My Heart at Wounded Knee: An Indian History of the American West,* 4th ed. (New York: Owl Books, 2007), 12.

Brown, Dee. *Bury My Heart at Wounded Knee: An Indian History of the American West,* 4th ed. New York: Owl Books, 2007.

12. MULTIVOLUME WORK

12. John Watson, *Annals of Philadelphia and Pennsylvania in the Olden Time,* vol. 2 (Washington, DC: Ross & Perry, 2003), 514.

Watson, John. *Annals of Philadelphia and Pennsylvania in the Olden Time.* Vol. 2. Washington, DC: Ross & Perry, 2003.

13. WORK WITH A TITLE WITHIN THE TITLE

Use quotation marks around any title within a book title.

13. John A. Alford, *A Companion to "Piers Plowman"* (Berkeley: University of California Press, 1988), 195.

Alford, John A. *A Companion to "Piers Plowman."* Berkeley: University of California Press, 1988.

14. SACRED TEXT

Include sacred texts in notes but not the bibliography.

14. Luke 18:24–25 (New International Version).

14. Qur'an 7:40–41.

15. SOURCE QUOTED IN ANOTHER SOURCE

Identify both the original and the secondary source.

15. Frank D. Millet, "The Filipino Leaders," *Harper's Weekly,* March 11, 1899, quoted in Richard Slotkin, *Gunfighter Nation: The Myth of the Frontier in Twentieth-Century America* (New York: HarperCollins, 1992), 110.

Millet, Frank D. "The Filipino Leaders." *Harper's Weekly,* March 11, 1899. Quoted in Richard Slotkin, *Gunfighter Nation: The Myth of the Frontier in Twentieth-Century America* (New York: HarperCollins, 1992), 110.

Print and digital periodicals

The note for an article in a periodical typically includes the author's name, the article title, and the periodical title. The format for other information, including the volume and issue numbers (if any) and the date of publication, as well as the page number(s) to which the note refers, varies according to the type of periodical and whether you consulted it in print, on the web, or in a database. In a bibliographic entry for a journal or magazine article from a database or a print periodical, also give the inclusive page numbers.

16. ARTICLE IN A PRINT JOURNAL

16. Catherine Bishop and Angela Woollacott, "Business and Politics as Women's Work: The Australian Colonies and the Mid-Nineteenth-Century Women's Movement," *Journal of Women's History* 28, no. 1 (2016): 87.

Bishop, Catherine, and Angela Woollacott. "Business and Politics as Women's Work: The Australian Colonies and the Mid-Nineteenth-Century Women's Movement." *Journal of Women's History* 28, no. 1 (2016): 84–106.

17. ARTICLE IN AN ONLINE JOURNAL

Give the DOI, preceded by *https://doi.org/*. If there is no DOI, include the article URL. If page numbers are provided, include them as well.

17. Jeffrey J. Schott, "America, Europe, and the New Trade Order," *Business and Politics* 11, no. 3 (2009), https://doi.org/10.2202/1469 -3569.1263.

Schott, Jeffrey J. "America, Europe, and the New Trade Order." *Business and Politics* 11, no. 3 (2009). https://doi.org/10.2202/1469-3569.1263.

18. ARTICLE FROM A DATABASE

Give the name of the author followed by the article title and title of the periodical. After volume and issue information and date, list the page(s). For the note, give the page where the information is found; in the bibliographic entry, give the entire page range. End with retrieval information. The source map and additional examples on pp. 514–15 show where to find information for a typical article from a database.

18. Elizabeth Tucker, "Changing Concepts of Childhood: Children's Folklore Scholarship since the Late Nineteenth Century," *Journal of American Folklore* 125, no. 498 (2012): 399, https://doi.org/10.5406 /jamerfolk.125.498.0389.

Tucker Elizabeth. "Changing Concepts of Childhood: Children's Folklore Scholarship since the Late Nineteenth Century." *Journal of American Folklore* 125, no. 498 (2012): 389–410. https://doi.org/10.5406 /jamerfolk.125.498.0389.

19. ARTICLE IN A PRINT MAGAZINE

19. Terry McDermott, "The Mastermind: Khalid Sheikh Mohammed and the Making of 9/11," *New Yorker,* September 13, 2010, 42.

McDermott, Terry. "The Mastermind: Khalid Sheikh Mohammed and the Making of 9/11." *New Yorker,* September 13, 2010, 38–51.

20. ARTICLE IN AN ONLINE MAGAZINE

20. Tracy Clark-Flory, "Educating Women Saves Kids' Lives," *Salon,* September 17, 2010, http://www.salon.com/life/broadsheet/2010/09/17/education_women/index.html.

Clark-Flory, Tracy. "Educating Women Saves Kids' Lives." *Salon,* September 17, 2010. http://www.salon.com/life/broadsheet/2010/09/17/education_women/index.html.

21. MAGAZINE ARTICLE FROM A DATABASE

21. Sami Yousafzai and Ron Moreau, "Twisting Arms in Afghanistan," *Newsweek,* November 9, 2009, 8, Academic Search Premier.

Yousafzai, Sami, and Ron Moreau. "Twisting Arms in Afghanistan." *Newsweek,* November 9, 2009. 8. Academic Search Premier.

22. ARTICLE IN A NEWSPAPER

Do not include page numbers for a newspaper article, but you may include the section, if any.

22. Caroline E. Mayer, "Wireless Industry to Adopt Voluntary Standards," *Washington Post,* September 9, 2003, sec. E.

Chicago recommends that newspaper articles appear in the notes section only, not in the bibliography. Check your instructor's preference. A bibliography entry would look like this:

Mayer, Caroline E. "Wireless Industry to Adopt Voluntary Standards." *Washington Post,* September 9, 2003, sec. E.

23. ARTICLE IN AN ONLINE NEWSPAPER

23. Somini Sengupta, "How a Seed Bank, Almost Lost in Syria's War, Could Help Feed a Warming Planet," *New York Times,* October 13, 2017, https://www.nytimes.com/2017/10/13/climate/syria-seed-bank.html.

Sengupta, Somini. "How a Seed Bank, Almost Lost in Syria's War, Could Help Feed a Warming Planet." *New York Times,* October 13, 2017. https://www.nytimes.com/2017/10/13/climate/syria-seed-bank.html.

Articles from Databases

1 **Author.** In a note, list the author(s) first name first. In the bibliographic entry, list the first author last name first, comma, first name; list other authors first name first.

2 **Article title.** Enclose the title and subtitle (if any) in quotation marks, and capitalize major words. In the notes section, put a comma before and after the title. In the bibliography, put a period before and after.

3 **Periodical title.** Italicize the title and subtitle, and capitalize all major words. For a magazine or newspaper, follow with a comma.

4 **Volume and issue numbers (for journals) and date.** For journals, follow the title with the volume number, a comma, the abbreviation *no.,* and the issue number; enclose the publication year in parentheses and follow with a colon. For other periodicals, give the month and year or month, day, and year, not in parentheses, followed by a colon.

5 **Page numbers.** In a note, give the page where the information is found. In the bibliographic entry, give the page range.

6 **Retrieval information.** Provide the article's DOI, if one is given, the name of the database, or a stable URL for the article. Because you provide stable retrieval information, you do not need to identify the electronic format of the work (e.g., PDF). End with a period.

Citations for the article on p. 515 would look like this:

ENDNOTE

1. Deborah R. Coen, "Big Is a Thing of the Past: Climate Change and Methodology in the History of Ideas," *Journal of the History of Ideas* 77, no. 2, April 2016: 310, OmniFile Full Text Select.

BIBLIOGRAPHIC ENTRY

Coen, Deborah R. "Big Is a Thing of the Past: Climate Change and Methodology in the History of Ideas." *Journal of the History of Ideas* 77, no. 2, April 2016: 305–21. OmniFile Full Text Select.

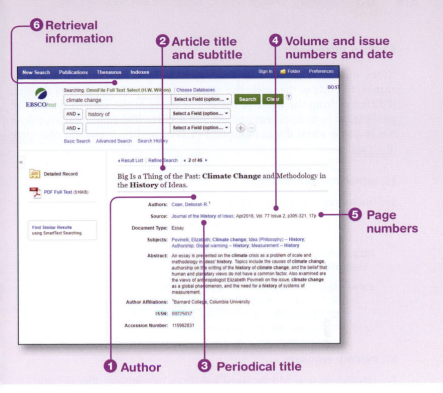

⑥ Retrieval information

② Article title and subtitle

④ Volume and issue numbers and date

⑤ Page numbers

① Author

③ Periodical title

24. NEWSPAPER ARTICLE FROM A DATABASE

24. Demetria Irwin, "A Hatchet, Not a Scalpel, for NYC Budget Cuts," *New York Amsterdam News,* November 13, 2008, Academic Search Premier.

Irwin, Demetria. "A Hatchet, Not a Scalpel, for NYC Budget Cuts." *New York Amsterdam News,* November 13, 2008. Academic Search Premier.

25. BOOK REVIEW

Give the name of the reviewer and title of the review, if any, followed by information about the book. End with publication information for the source.

25. Roderick MacFarquhar, "China's Astounding Religious Revival," review of *The Souls of China: The Return of Religion after Mao,* by Ian Johnson, *New York Review of Books,* June 8, 2017, http://www.nybooks.com /articles/2017/06/08/chinas-astounding-religious-revival/.

MacFarquhar, Roderick. "China's Astounding Religious Revival." Review of *The Souls of China: The Return of Religion after Mao,* by Ian Johnson. *New York Review of Books,* June 8, 2017. http://www.nybooks.com /articles/2017/06/08/chinas-astounding-religious-revival/.

Online sources

Notes and bibliographic entries for online sources typically include the author; the title of the work; the name of the site; the sponsor of the site, if different from the name of the site or name of the author; the date of publication or most recent update; and a URL. If the online source does not indicate when it was published or last modified, include your date of access.

26. WORK FROM A WEBSITE

See the source map on pp. 518–19.

> 26. Rose Cohen, "My First Job," Remembering the 1911 Triangle Factory Fire, Cornell University ILR School, accessed October 13, 2017, http://trianglefire.ilr.cornell.edu/primary/testimonials/ootss _RoseCohen.html?sto_sec=sweatshops.

> Cohen, Rose. "My First Job." Remembering the 1911 Triangle Factory Fire. Cornell University ILR School. Accessed October 13, 2017. http://trianglefire.ilr.cornell.edu/primary/testimonials/ootss _RoseCohen.html?sto_sec=sweatshops.

27. ENTIRE WEBSITE

For clarity, you may add the word *website* in parentheses after the title.

> 27. Rutgers School of Arts and Sciences, Rutgers Oral History Archive (website), 2017, http://oralhistory.rutgers.edu/.

> Rutgers School of Arts and Sciences. Rutgers Oral History Archive (website). 2017. http://oralhistory.rutgers.edu/.

28. ONLINE REFERENCE WORK

In a note, give the title of the work and the heading of the section in which the information appears. Use *s.v.* (*sub verbo* is Latin for "under the word") before the heading. Include the date the entry was posted, last modified, or accessed. Do not list reference works such as encyclopedias or dictionaries in your bibliography.

> 28. *Encyclopedia Britannica,* s.v. "Monroe Doctrine," accessed October 12, 2017, https://www.britannica.com/event/Monroe-Doctrine.

29. BLOG POST

Treat a blog post as a short work from a website (see model 26).

> 29. Jai Arjun Singh, "On the Road in the USSR," *Jabberwock* (blog), November 29, 2007, http://jaiarjun.blogspot.com/2007/11/on-road-in -ussr.html.

Chicago recommends that blog posts appear in the notes section only, not in the bibliography. Check your instructor's preference. A bibliography reference would look like this:

> Singh, Jai Arjun. "On the Road in the USSR." *Jabberwock* (blog). November 29, 2007. http://jaiarjun.blogspot.com/2007/11/on-road-in-ussr.html.

30. EMAIL, SOCIAL MEDIA MESSAGES, AND OTHER PERSONAL COMMUNICATIONS

Cite email messages, social media messages, personal interviews, and other personal communications, such as letters and telephone calls, in the text or in a note only; do not cite them in the bibliography.

> 30. Kareem Adas, Facebook private message to author, February 11, 2018.

31. SOCIAL MEDIA POST

In place of a title, include the text of the post, up to the first 160 characters.

> 31. NASA (@nasa), "This galaxy is a whirl of color," Instagram photo, September 23, 2017, https://www.instagram.com/p/BZY8adnnZQJ/.

> NASA. "This galaxy is a whirl of color." Instagram photo, September 23, 2017. https://www.instagram.com/p/BZY8adnnZQJ/.

32. PODCAST

Treat a podcast as a short work from a website (see model 26). Include the type of podcast or file format (if downloadable), the time stamp, and the URL.

> 32. Toyin Falola, "Creativity and Decolonization: Nigerian Cultures and African Epistemologies," Episode 96, November 17, 2015, in *Africa Past and Present,* African Online Digital Library, podcast, MP3 audio, 43:44, http://afripod.aodl.org/2015/11/afripod-96/.

> Falola, Toyin. "Creativity and Decolonization: Nigerian Cultures and African Epistemologies." Episode 96, November 17, 2015. *Africa Past and Present*. African Online Digital Library. Podcast, MP3 audio, 43:44. http://afripod.aodl.org/2015/11/afripod-96/.

33. ONLINE AUDIO OR VIDEO

Treat an online audio or video source as a short work from a website (see model 26). If the source is downloadable, give the medium or file format before the URL.

> 33. Alyssa Katz, "Did the Mortgage Crisis Kill the American Dream?" YouTube video, 4:32, posted by NYCRadio, June 24, 2009, http://www .youtube.com/watch?v=uivtwjwd_Qw.

> Katz, Alyssa. "Did the Mortgage Crisis Kill the American Dream?" YouTube video, 4:32. Posted by NYCRadio. June 24, 2009. http://www.youtube .com/watch?v=uivtwjwd_Qw.

Works from Websites

① **Author.** In a note, list the author(s) first name first. In a bibliographic entry, list the first author last name first, comma, first name; list additional authors first name first.

② **Document title.** Enclose the title in quotation marks, and capitalize all major words. In a note, put a comma before and after the title. In the bibliography, put a period before and after the title.

③ **Title of website.** Capitalize all major words. Italicize the website title only if it is an online book or periodical. In the notes section, put a comma after the title. In the bibliography, put a period after the title.

④ **Sponsor of site.** If the sponsor is the same as the author or site title, you may omit it. End with a comma (in the note) or a period (in the bibliography).

⑤ **Date of publication or last modification.** If a time stamp is given, include it. If no date is available, include your date of access. End with a comma (in the note) or a period (in the bibliography).

⑥ **Retrieval information.** Give the URL for the work and end with a period.

Citations for the website on p. 519 would look like this:

ENDNOTE

1. Evan Haefeli, "Liberty, Diversity, and Slavery: The Beginnings of American Freedom," Preserving American Freedom: The Evolution of American Liberties in Fifty Documents, Historical Society of Pennsylvania, accessed October 13, 2017, https://digitalhistory.hsp.org/pafrm/essay/liberty-diversity-and-slavery-beginnings-american-freedom.

BIBLIOGRAPHIC ENTRY

Haefeli, Evan. "Liberty, Diversity, and Slavery: The Beginnings of American Freedom." Preserving American Freedom: The Evolution of American Liberties in Fifty Documents. Historical Society of Pennsylvania. Accessed October 13, 2017. https://digitalhistory.hsp.org/pafrm/essay/liberty-diversity-and-slavery-beginnings-american-freedom.

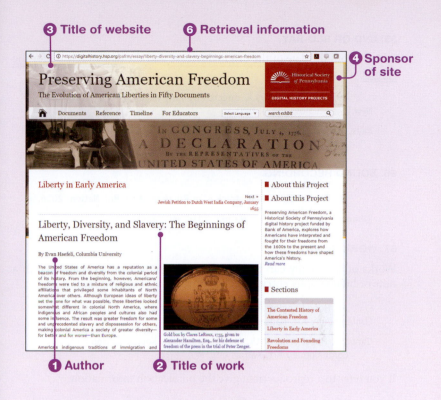

❸ Title of website　**❻ Retrieval information**

❹ Sponsor of site

❶ Author　❷ Title of work

Other sources

34. PUBLISHED OR BROADCAST INTERVIEW

34. David O. Russell, <u>interview by</u> Terry Gross, *Fresh Air*, WNYC, February 20, 2014.

Russell, David O. <u>Interview by</u> Terry Gross. *Fresh Air*. WNYC, February 20, 2014.

Interviews you conduct are considered personal communications (see model 30).

35. DVD OR BLU-RAY

Include both the date of the original release and the date of release for the format you are citing.

35. *American History X,* directed by Tony Kaye (1998; Los Angeles: New Line Studios, 2002), DVD.

Kaye, Tony, dir. *American History X.* 1998; Los Angeles: New Line Studios, 2002. DVD.

36. SOUND RECORDING

36. "Work," MP3 audio, track 4 on Rihanna, *Anti,* Roc Nation, 2016.

Rihanna. "Work." *Anti.* Roc Nation, 2016, MP3 audio.

37. WORK OF ART

Works of art usually can be mentioned in the text rather than cited in a note or bibliography entry. Check your instructor's preference.

37. Hope Gangloff, *Vera,* 2015, acrylic on canvas, Kemper Museum of Contemporary Art, Kansas City, MO.

Gangloff, Hope. *Vera.* 2015. Acrylic on canvas. Kemper Museum of Contemporary Art, Kansas City, MO.

If you refer to a reproduction, give the publication information.

37. Mary Cassatt, *The Child's Bath,* 1893, oil on canvas, *Art Access,* The Art Institute of Chicago, accessed October 13, 2017, http://www.artic.edu /aic/collections/exhibitions/Impressionism/Cassatt.

Cassatt, Mary. *The Child's Bath.* 1893. Oil on canvas. *Art Access.* The Art Institute of Chicago. Accessed October 13, 2017. http://www.artic.edu /aic/collections/exhibitions/Impressionism/Cassatt.

38. PAMPHLET, REPORT, OR BROCHURE

Information about the author or publisher may not be readily available, but give enough information to identify your source.

38. International Monetary Fund, *Western Hemisphere: Tale of Two Adjustments,* World Economic and Financial Surveys (Washington, DC: International Monetary Fund, 2017), 29.

International Monetary Fund. *Western Hemisphere: Tale of Two Adjustments.* World Economic and Financial Surveys. Washington, DC: International Monetary Fund, 2017.

39. GOVERNMENT DOCUMENT

39. U.S. House Committee on Ways and Means, *Report on Trade Mission to Sub-Saharan Africa*, 108th Cong., 1st sess. (Washington, DC: Government Printing Office, 2003), 28.

U.S. House Committee on Ways and Means. *Report on Trade Mission to Sub-Saharan Africa*. 108th Cong., 1st sess. Washington, DC: Government Printing Office, 2003.

64   An Excerpt from a Student Research Essay, *Chicago* Style

On the following pages is an excerpt from an essay by Amanda Rinder that conforms to the *Chicago* guidelines described in this chapter.

Student Writer

Amanda Rinder

Student Writing
Chicago

Title announces topic clearly and succinctly

Sweet Home Chicago: Preserving the Past,
Protecting the Future of the Windy City

Title and writer's name centered

Amanda Rinder

Course title, instructor's name, and date centered at bottom of title page

Twentieth-Century U.S. History
Professor Goldberg
November 27, 2006

Annotations indicate effective choices or ***Chicago*-style formatting**.

Rinder 2

Only one city has the "Big Shoulders" described by Carl Sandburg: Chicago (fig. 1). So renowned are its skyscrapers and celebrated building style that an entire school of architecture is named for Chicago. Presently, however, the place that Frank Sinatra called "my kind of town" is beginning to lose sight of exactly what kind of town it is. Many of the buildings that give Chicago its distinctive character are being torn down in order to make room for new growth. Both preserving the classics and encouraging new creation are important; the combination of these elements gives Chicago architecture its unique flavor. Witold Rybczynski, a professor of urbanism, told Tracie Rozhon of the *New York Times,* "Of all the cities we can think of . . . we associate Chicago with new things, with building new. Combining that with preservation is a difficult task, a tricky thing. It's hard to find the middle ground in Chicago."[1] Yet finding a middle ground is essential if the city is to retain the original character that sets it apart from the rest. In order to

Sidebar notes:
First page of body text is p. 2

Paper refers to each figure by number

Thesis introduced

Double-spaced text

Source cited using superscript numeral

Fig. 1. Chicago skyline, circa 1940s. (Postcard courtesy of Minnie Dangburg.)

Figure caption includes number, short title, and source

Rinder 3

Opening paragraph concludes with formal thesis statement

maintain Chicago's distinctive identity and its delicate balance between the old and the new, the city government must provide a comprehensive urban plan that not only directs growth, but calls for the preservation of landmarks and historic districts as well.

Chicago is a city for the working man. Nowhere is this more evident than in its architecture. David Garrard Lowe, author of *Lost Chicago,* notes that early Chicagoans "sought reality, not fantasy, and the reality of America as seen from the heartland did not include the pavilions of princes or the castles of kings."[2] The inclination toward unadorned, sturdy buildings began in the late nineteenth century with the aptly named Chicago School, a movement led by Louis Sullivan, John Wellborn Root, and Daniel

Second paragraph provides background

Burnham and based on Sullivan's adage, "Form follows function."[3] The early skyscraper, the very symbol of the Chicago style, represents the triumph of function and utility over sentiment, America over Europe, and perhaps, as Daniel Bluestone argues, even the frontier over the civilization of the East Coast.[4] These ideals of the original Chicago School were expanded upon by architects of the Second Chicago School. Frank Lloyd Wright's legendary organic style and the famed glass and steel constructions of Mies van der Rohe are often the first images that spring to mind when one thinks of Chicago.

Clear transition from previous paragraph

Yet the architecture that is the city's defining attribute is being threatened by the increasing tendency toward development. The root of Chicago's preservation problem lies in the enormous drive toward economic expansion and the potential in Chicago for such growth. The highly competitive market for land in the city means that properties sell for the highest price if the buildings on them can be obliterated to make room for newer, larger developments. Because of this preference on the part of potential buyers, the label "landmark" has become a stigma for property owners. "In other cities, landmark . . .

Rinder 9

Notes

1. Tracie Rozhon, "Chicago Girds for Big Battle over Its Skyline," *New York Times,* November 12, 2000, Academic Search Premier.

Newspaper article in database

2. David Garrard Lowe, *Lost Chicago* (New York: Watson-Guptill, 2000), 123.

Print book

3. *Columbia Encyclopedia,* 6th ed. (2000), s.v. "Louis Sullivan."

4. Daniel Bluestone, *Constructing Chicago* (New Haven: Yale University Press, 1991), 105.

5. Alan J. Shannon, "When Will It End?" *Chicago Tribune,* September 11, 1987, quoted in Karen J. Dilibert, *From Landmark to Landfill* (Chicago: Chicago Architectural Foundation, 2000), 11.

Indirect source

6. Steve Kerch, "Landmark Decisions," *Chicago Tribune,* March 18, 1990, sec. 16.

7. John W. Stamper, *Chicago's North Michigan Avenue* (Chicago: University of Chicago Press, 1991), 215.

8. Alf Siewers, "Success Spoiling the Magnificent Mile?" *Chicago Sun-Times,* April 9, 1995.

9. Paul Gapp, "McCarthy Building Puts Landmark Law on a Collision Course with Developers," *Chicago Tribune,* April 20, 1986, quoted in Karen J. Dilibert, *From Landmark to Landfill* (Chicago: Chicago Architectural Foundation, 2000), 4.

10. Gapp, 4.

Reference to preceding source

11. Rozhon, "Chicago Girds for Big Battle."

12. Kerch, "Landmark Decisions."

Second reference to source

13. Robert Bruegmann, *The Architects and the City* (Chicago: University of Chicago Press, 1997), 443.

Rinder 10

Bibliography starts on new page

Print book

Pamphlet

Newspaper article

Article from database

Bibliography entries use hanging indent and are not numbered

Bibliography

Bluestone, Daniel. *Constructing Chicago*. New Haven: Yale University Press, 1991.

Bruegmann, Robert. *The Architects and the City*. Chicago: University of Chicago Press, 1997.

Dilibert, Karen J. *From Landmark to Landfill*. Chicago: Chicago Architectural Foundation, 2000.

Kerch, Steve. "Landmark Decisions." *Chicago Tribune,* March 18, 1990, sec. 16.

Lowe, David Garrard. *Lost Chicago*. New York: Watson-Guptill, 2000.

Rozhon, Tracie. "Chicago Girds for Big Battle over Its Skyline." *New York Times,* November 12, 2000. Academic Search Premier.

Siewers, Alf. "Success Spoiling the Magnificent Mile?" *Chicago Sun-Times,* April 9, 1995.

Stamper, John W. *Chicago's North Michigan Avenue*. Chicago: University of Chicago Press, 1991.

Glossaries
and Index

There is nothing like looking, if you want to find something.

— J. R. R. TOLKIEN

Glossary of Usage

Conventions of usage might be called the "good manners" of discourse. And just as manners vary from culture to culture and time to time, so do conventions of usage. Matters of usage, like other language choices you must make, depend on what your purpose is and on what is appropriate for a particular audience at a particular time.

a, an   Use *a* with a word that begins with a consonant (*a book*), a consonant sound such as "y" or "w" (*a euphoric moment, a one-sided match*), or a sounded *h* (*a hemisphere*). Use *an* with a word that begins with a vowel (*an umbrella*), a vowel sound (*an X-ray*), or a silent *h* (*an honor*).

accept, except   The verb *accept* means "receive" or "agree to." *Except* is usually a preposition that means "aside from" or "excluding." *All the plaintiffs except Mr. Kim decided to accept the settlement.*

advice, advise   The noun *advice* means "opinion" or "suggestion"; the verb *advise* means "offer advice." *Doctors advise everyone not to smoke, but many people ignore the advice.*

affect, effect   As a verb, *affect* means "influence" or "move the emotions of"; as a noun, it means "emotions" or "feelings." *Effect* is a noun meaning "result"; less commonly, it is a verb meaning "bring about." *The storm affected a large area. Its effects included widespread power failures. The drug effected a major change in the patient's affect.*

all ready, already   *All ready* means "fully prepared." *Already* means "previously." *We were all ready for Lucy's party when we learned that she had already left.*

all right, alright   Avoid the spelling *alright*.

all together, altogether   *All together* means "all in a group" or "gathered in one place." *Altogether* means "completely" or "everything considered." *When the board members were all together, their mutual distrust was altogether obvious.*

allude, elude   *Allude* means "refer indirectly." *Elude* means "avoid" or "escape from." *The candidate did not even allude to her opponent. The suspect eluded the police for several days.*

allusion, illusion   An *allusion* is an indirect reference. An *illusion* is a false or misleading appearance. *The speaker's allusion to the Bible created an illusion of piety.*

a lot   Avoid the spelling *alot*.

already   See *all ready, already*.

alright   See *all right, alright*.

altogether   See *all together, altogether*.

among, between   In referring to two things or people, use *between*. In referring to three or more, use *among*. *The relationship between the twins is different from that among the other three children.*

amount, number   Use *amount* with quantities you cannot count; use *number* for quantities you can count. *A small number of volunteers cleared a large amount of debris.*

an   See *a, an.*

and/or   Avoid this term except in business or legal writing. Instead of *fat and/or protein*, write *fat, protein,* or *both.*

any body, anybody, any one, anyone   *Anybody* and *anyone* are pronouns meaning "any person." *Anyone* [or *anybody*] *would enjoy this film. Any body* is an adjective modifying a noun. *Any body of water has its own ecology. Any one* is two adjectives or a pronoun modified by an adjective. *Customers could buy only two sale items at any one time. The winner could choose any one of the prizes.*

anyplace   In academic and professional discourse, use *anywhere* instead.

anyway, anyways   In writing, use *anyway*, not *anyways.*

as   Avoid sentences in which it is not clear whether *as* means "when" or "because." For example, does *Carl left town as his father was arriving* mean "at the same time as his father was arriving" or "because his father was arriving"?

as, as if, like   In academic and professional writing, use *as* or *as if* instead of *like* to introduce a clause. *The dog howled as if* [not *like*] *it were in pain. She did as* [not *like*] *I suggested.*

assure, ensure, insure   *Assure* means "convince" or "promise"; its direct object is usually a person or persons. *She assured voters she would not raise taxes. Ensure* and *insure* both mean "make certain," but *insure* usually refers specifically to protection against financial loss. *When the city rationed water to ensure that the supply would last, the Browns could no longer afford to insure their car-wash business.*

as to   Do not use *as to* as a substitute for *about. Karen was unsure about* [not *as to*] *accepting the job offer.*

at, where   See *where.*

awhile, a while   Always use *a while* after a preposition such as *for, in,* or *after. We drove awhile and then stopped for a while.*

bad, badly   Use *bad* after a linking verb such as *be, feel,* or *seem.* Use *badly* to modify an action verb, an adjective, or another verb. *The hostess felt bad because the dinner was badly prepared.*

because of, due to   Use *due to* when the effect, stated as a noun, appears before the verb *be. His illness was due to malnutrition.* (*Illness*, a noun, is the effect.) Use *because of* when the effect is stated as a clause. *He was sick because of malnutrition.* (*He was sick*, a clause, is the effect.)

beside, besides   *Beside* is a preposition meaning "next to." *Besides* can be a preposition meaning "other than" or an adverb meaning "in addition." *No one besides Francesca would sit beside him.*

between   See *among, between.*

can, may   *Can* refers to ability and *may* to possibility or permission. *Since I can ski the slalom well, I may win the race.*

compare to, compare with   *Compare to* means "regard as similar." *Jamie compared the loss to a kick in the head. Compare with* means "examine to find differences or similarities." *Compare Tim Burton's films with David Lynch's.*

complement, compliment   *Complement* means "go well with." *Compliment* means "praise." *Guests complimented her on how her earrings complemented her gown.*

comprise, compose   *Comprise* means "contain." *Compose* means "make up." *The class comprises twenty students. Twenty students compose the class.*

conscience, conscious   *Conscience* means "a sense of right and wrong." *Conscious* means "awake" or "aware." *Lisa was conscious of a guilty conscience.*

consequently, subsequently   *Consequently* means "as a result"; *subsequently* means "then." *He quit, and subsequently his wife lost her job; consequently, they had to sell their house.*

continual, continuous   *Continual* means "repeated at regular or frequent intervals." *Continuous* means "continuing or connected without a break." *The damage done by continuous erosion was increased by the continual storms.*

could of   *Have,* not *of,* should follow *could, would, should,* or *might. We could have* [not *of*] *invited them.*

criteria, criterion   *Criterion* means "standard of judgment" or "necessary qualification." *Criteria* is the plural form. *Image is the wrong criterion for choosing a president.*

data   *Data* is the plural form of the Latin word *datum,* meaning "fact." Although *data* is used informally as either singular or plural, in academic or professional writing, treat *data* as plural. *These data indicate that fewer people are smoking.*

different from, different than   *Different from* is generally preferred in academic and professional writing, although both phrases are widely used. *Her lab results were no different from* [not *than*] *his.*

disinterested, uninterested   *Disinterested* means "unbiased." *Uninterested* means "indifferent." *Finding disinterested jurors was difficult. She was uninterested in the verdict.*

distinct, distinctive   *Distinct* means "separate" or "well defined." *Distinctive* means "characteristic." *Germany includes many distinct regions, each with a distinctive accent.*

doesn't, don't   *Doesn't* is the contraction for *does not.* Use it with *he, she, it,* and singular nouns. *Don't* stands for *do not;* use it with *I, you, we, they,* and plural nouns.

due to   See *because of, due to.*

each other, one another   Use *each other* in sentences involving two subjects and *one another* in sentences involving more than two. *Sarang and Mina gave each other a gift for Valentine's Day. The children in Mr. Yee's class gave one another handmade cards.*

effect   See *affect, effect.*

elude   See *allude, elude.*

emigrate from, immigrate to   *Emigrate from* means "move away from one's country." *Immigrate to* means "move to another country." *We emigrated from Norway in 1999. We immigrated to the United States.*

ensure   See *assure, ensure, insure.*

every day, everyday   *Everyday* is an adjective meaning "ordinary." *Every day* is an adjective and a noun, meaning "each day." *I wore everyday clothes almost every day.*

every one, everyone   *Everyone* is a pronoun. *Every one* is an adjective and a pronoun, referring to each member of a group. *Because he began after everyone else, David could not finish every one of the problems.*

except   See *accept, except.*

explicit, implicit   *Explicit* means "directly or openly expressed." *Implicit* means "indirectly expressed or implied." *The explicit message of the ad urged consumers to buy the product, while the implicit message promised popularity if they did so.*

farther, further   *Farther* refers to physical distance. *How much farther is it to Munich? Further* refers to time or degree. *I want to avoid further delays.*

fewer, less   Use *fewer* with nouns that can be counted. Use *less* with general amounts that you cannot count. *The world needs fewer bombs and less hostility.*

firstly, secondly, etc.   *First, second,* etc., are more common in U.S. English.

former, latter   *Former* refers to the first and *latter* to the second of two things previously mentioned. *Kathy and Anna are athletes; the former plays tennis, and the latter runs.*

further   See *farther, further.*

good, well   *Good* is an adjective and should not be used as a substitute for the adverb *well. Gabriel is a good host who cooks well.*

good and   *Good and* is colloquial for "very"; avoid it in academic and professional writing.

hanged, hung   *Hanged* refers to executions; *hung* is used for all other meanings.

herself, himself, myself, yourself   Do not use these reflexive pronouns as subjects or as objects unless they are necessary. *Jane and I* [not *myself*] *agree. They invited John and me* [not *myself*].

himself   See *herself, himself, myself, yourself.*

hisself   Use *himself* instead in academic and professional writing.

hopefully   *Hopefully* is often used informally to mean "it is hoped," but its formal meaning is "with hope." *Sam watched the roulette wheel hopefully* [not *Hopefully, Sam will win*].

hung   See *hanged, hung.*

illusion   See *allusion, illusion.*

immigrate to   See *emigrate from, immigrate to.*

impact   Some readers object to the colloquial use of *impact* or *impact on* as a verb meaning "affect." *Population control may reduce* [not *impact*] *world hunger.*

implicit   See *explicit, implicit.*

imply, infer   To *imply* is to suggest indirectly. To *infer* is to guess or conclude on the basis of an indirect suggestion. *The note implied they were planning a small wedding; we inferred we would not be invited.*

inside of, outside of   Use *inside* and *outside* instead. *The class regularly met outside* [not *outside of*] *the building.*

insure   See *assure, ensure, insure.*

interact, interface   *Interact* is a vague word meaning "do something that somehow involves another person." *Interface* is computer jargon; when used as a verb, it means "discuss" or "communicate." Avoid both verbs in academic and professional writing.

irregardless, regardless   *Irregardless* is a double negative. Use *regardless.*

is when, is where   These vague expressions are often incorrectly used in definitions. *Schizophrenia is a psychotic condition in which* [not *is when* or *is where*] *a person withdraws from reality.*

its, it's   *Its* is the possessive form of *it. It's* is a contraction for *it is* or *it has. It's important to observe the rat before it eats its meal.*

know, no   Use *know* to mean "understand." *No* is the opposite of *yes.*

later, latter   *Later* means "after some time." *Latter* refers to the second of two items named. *Juan and Chad won all their early matches, but the latter was injured later in the season.*

latter   See *former, latter* and *later, latter.*

lay, lie   *Lay* means "place" or "put." Its main forms are *lay, laid, laid*. It generally has a direct object, specifying what has been placed. *She laid her books on the desk. Lie* means "recline" or "be positioned" and does not take a direct object. Its main forms are *lie, lay, lain. She lay awake until two.*

leave, let   *Leave* means "go away." *Let* means "allow." *Leave alone* and *let alone* are interchangeable. *Let me leave now, and leave* [or *let*] *me alone from now on!*

less   See *fewer, less*.

let   See *leave, let*.

lie   See *lay, lie*.

like   See *as, as if, like*.

literally   *Literally* means "actually" or "exactly as stated." Use it to stress the truth of a statement that might otherwise be understood as figurative. Do not use *literally* as an intensifier in a figurative statement. *Mirna was literally at the edge of her seat* may be accurate, but *Mirna is so hungry that she could literally eat a horse* is not.

loose, lose   *Lose* is a verb meaning "misplace." *Loose* is an adjective that means "not securely attached." *Sew on that loose button before you lose it.*

lots, lots of   Avoid these informal expressions meaning "much" or "many" in academic and professional discourse.

man, mankind   Replace these terms with *people, humans, humankind, men and women,* or similar wording.

may   See *can, may*.

may be, maybe   *May be* is a verb phrase. *Maybe* is an adverb that means "perhaps." *He may be the head of the organization, but maybe someone else would handle a crisis better.*

media   *Media* is the plural form of the noun *medium* and takes a plural verb. *The media are* [not *is*] *obsessed with scandals.*

might of   See *could of*.

moral, morale   A *moral* is a succinct lesson. *The moral of the story is that generosity is rewarded. Morale* means "spirit" or "mood." *Office morale was low.*

myself   See *herself, himself, myself, yourself*.

no   See *know, no*.

number   See *amount, number*.

off, off of   Use *off* without *of. The spaghetti slipped off* [not *off of*] *the plate.*

one another   See *each other, one another*.

outside of   See *inside of, outside of*.

passed, past   Use *passed* to mean "went by" or "received a passing grade": *The marching band passed the reviewing stand.* Use *past* to refer to a time before the present: *Historians study the past.*

per   Use the Latin *per* only in standard technical phrases such as *miles per hour.* Otherwise, find English equivalents. *As mentioned in* [not *As per*] *the latest report, the country's average food consumption each day* [not *per day*] *is only 2,000 calories.*

percent, percentage   Use *percent* with a specific number; use *percentage* with an adjective such as *large* or *small. Last year, 80 percent of the members were female. A large percentage of the members are women.*

precede, proceed   *Precede* means "come before"; *proceed* means "go forward." *Despite the storm that preceded the ceremony, the wedding proceeded on schedule.*

principal, principle   When used as a noun, *principal* refers to a head official or an amount of money; when used as an adjective, it means "most significant." *Principle* means "fundamental law or belief." *Albert went to the principal and defended himself with the principle of free speech.*

proceed   See *precede, proceed.*

quotation, quote   *Quote* is a verb, and *quotation* is a noun. *He quoted the president, and the quotation* [not *quote*] *was preserved in history books.*

raise, rise   *Raise* means "lift" or "move upward." (Referring to children, it means "bring up.") It takes a direct object; someone raises something. *The guests raised their glasses to toast. Rise* means "go upward." It does not take a direct object; something rises by itself. *She saw the steam rise from the pan.*

real, really   *Real* is an adjective, and *really* is an adverb. Do not substitute *real* for *really.* In academic and professional writing, do not use *real* or *really* to mean "very." *The old man walked very* [not *real* or *really*] *slowly.*

reason is because   Use either *the reason is that* or *because* — not both. *The reason the copier stopped is that* [not *is because*] *the paper jammed.*

reason why   This expression is redundant. *The reason* [not *reason why*] *this book is short is market demand.*

regardless   See *irregardless, regardless.*

respectfully, respectively   *Respectfully* means "with respect." *Respectively* means "in the order given." *The children treated their grandparents respectfully. Karen and David are, respectively, a juggler and an acrobat.*

rise   See *raise, rise.*

set, sit   *Set* usually means "put" or "place" and takes a direct object. *Sit* refers to taking a seat and does not take an object. *Set your cup on the table, and sit down.*

should of   See *could of.*

since   Be careful not to use *since* ambiguously. In *Since I broke my leg, I've stayed home*, the word *since* might be understood to mean either "because" or "ever since."

sit   See *set, sit.*

so   In academic and professional writing, avoid using *so* alone to mean "very." Instead, follow *so* with *that* to show how the intensified condition leads to a result. *Aaron was so tired that he fell asleep at the wheel.*

someplace   Use *somewhere* instead in academic and professional writing.

some time, sometime, sometimes   *Some time* refers to a length of time. *Please leave me some time to dress. Sometime* means "at some indefinite later time." *Sometime I will take you to London. Sometimes* means "occasionally." *Sometimes I eat sushi.*

subsequently   See *consequently, subsequently.*

supposed to, used to   Be careful to include the final *-d* in these expressions. *He is supposed to attend.*

sure, surely   Avoid using *sure* as an intensifier. Instead, use *certainly. I was certainly glad to see you.*

than, then   Use *than* in comparative statements. *The cat was bigger than the dog.* Use *then* when referring to a sequence of events. *I won, and then I cried.*

that, which   A clause beginning with *that* singles out the item being described. *The book that is on the table is a good one* specifies the book on the table as opposed to some other book. A clause beginning with *which* may or may not single out the item, although some writers use *which* clauses only to add more information about an item being described. *The book, which is on the table, is a good one* contains a *which* clause between the commas. The clause simply adds extra, nonessential information about the book; it does not specify which book.

theirselves   Use *themselves* instead in academic and professional writing.

then   See *than, then.*

thorough, threw, through   *Thorough* means "complete": *After a thorough inspection, the restaurant reopened. Threw* is the past tense of *throw*, and *through* means "in one side and out the other": *He threw the ball through a window.*

to, too, two   *To* generally shows direction. *Too* means "also." *Two* is the number. *We, too, are going to the meeting in two hours.* Avoid using *to* after *where. Where are you flying* [not *flying to*]?

two   See *to, too, two.*

uninterested   See *disinterested, uninterested.*

unique   Some people argue that unique means "one and only" and object to usage that suggests it means merely "unusual." In formal writing, avoid constructions such as *quite unique*.

used to   See *supposed to, used to*.

very   Avoid using *very* to intensify a weak adjective or adverb; instead, replace the adjective or adverb with a stronger, more precise, or more colorful word. Instead of *very nice*, for example, use *kind, warm, sensitive, endearing*, or *friendly*.

well   See *good, well*.

where   Use *where* alone, not with words such as *at* and *to. Where are you going* [not *going to*]?

which   See *that, which*.

who, whom   Use *who* if the word is the subject of the clause and *whom* if the word is the object of the clause. *Monica, who smokes incessantly, is my godmother.* (*Who* is the subject of the clause; the verb is *smokes*.) *Monica, whom I saw last winter, lives in Tucson.* (*Whom* is the object of the verb *saw*.)

who's, whose   *Who's* is a contraction for *who is* or *who has. Who's on the patio? Whose* is a possessive form. *Whose sculpture is in the garden? Whose is on the patio?*

would of   See *could of*.

your, you're   *Your* shows possession. *Bring your sleeping bag along. You're* is the contraction for *you are. You're in the wrong sleeping bag.*

yourself   See *herself, himself, myself, yourself*.

Index

Words in **blue** are followed by a definition. **Boldface** terms in definitions are themselves defined elsewhere in this index.

A

a, an (articles)
  as adjectives, 290
  capitalization of, in titles, 397
  as determiners for nouns, 324
  for multilingual writers, 324–27
  with nouns, 288, 324–27
abbreviations, 398–401
  acronyms, punctuation with, 379
  in APA references, 467, 468, 470, 474, 476, 478
  in *Chicago* notes and bibliography, 514, 516
  in informal writing, 9
  in MLA works cited, 416, 417, 420, 424, 426, 430, 434
  and numbers, 401
  online communication, 241
  periods with, 379–80, 399
  of state names, 379
  texting and, 248
absolute concepts, 347
absolute phrases, 303
abstract
  conventional format, 183
  in the natural and applied sciences, 183
  sample student writing, 179
  in the social sciences, 175–76
abstract words, 249
academic institutions, capitalization for, 396
academic writing
  assignments for, 12–13
  audience for, 10–11
  authority in, 5–6
  collaborating on, 19
  conventions of writing, 6
  directness and clarity in, 6, 238
  in the disciplines, 161–62
  ethics and integrity, 165–66
  expectations for, 5, 162, 238–41
  genres of, 15–16
  media for, 15–16
  plagiarism, avoiding, 143–58

portfolios of, 56–57
purpose for, 12–13
Quick Help, 26
reading and, 7–8
research for, 8–9
rhetorical situation for, 10–17
social writing versus, 11
stance in, 12–13
"standard" English for, 5
style for, 16–17
Talking the Talk, 6
topic and message, 11–12
visuals and multimedia, 26
accept, except, 529
accuracy, of sources, 64–65
acknowledgments, 151–52
acronyms, 379
actio (speaker's delivery), 195
active listening, 7–8
active reading, 7–8. *See also* critical thinking and reading

active voice The form of a **verb** when the **subject** performs the action: *Lata sang the chorus.*

  conciseness, 271
  shifts to passive, 252, 267, 320
AD, A.D., 379
addresses. *See also* URL, citing
  commas in, 374, 403
  numbers in, 403
  slashes in, 393
ad hominem fallacy, 87

adjective, 290, 342–50 A word that modifies, quantifies, identifies, or describes a **noun** or words acting as a noun.

  absolute concepts, 347
  adverb versus, 342
  capitalization of, 290, 395–96
  comparative, 345–47
  compound, 283
  ending in *-ed* and *-ing,* 347–48
  hyphen with, 283
  in informal writing, 350
  Language, Culture, and Context, 345
  after linking verb, 290
  for multilingual writers, 345, 348
  object complement as, 299

F

Acknowledgments

Annie Dillard. "Solar Eclipse." From *The Abundance: Narrative Essays Old and New*. Copyright © 2016 by Annie Dillard. Published by arrangement with Ecco, an imprint of HarperCollins Publishers.

Joy Harjo. Excerpt from "Suspended." From *Joy Harjo's Poetic Adventures in the Last World Blog*, Mekko Productions, Inc., September 3, 2006. Used by permission of the author.

Langston Hughes. "Harlem [2]—A Dream Deferred." From *The Collected Poems of Langston Hughes*, edited by Arnold Rampersad with David Roessel, Associate Editor. Copyright © 1994 by the Estate of Langston Hughes. Used by permission of Alfred A. Knopf, a division of Random House, Inc., and Harold Ober Associates, Ltd.

James Hunter. "Outlaw Classics: The Albums That Kept Nashville Real in the Sixties and Seventies." From *Rolling Stone*, March 9, 2006, p. 95. Copyright © 2006 Rolling Stone LLC. All rights reserved. Used by permission.

Problem Statement and Objective from Proposal "Wildland Firefighter Smoke Exposure." SJ & Jessie E. Quinney College of Natural Resources, Utah State University. Copyright © Utah State University. Used with permission.

Naomi Wadler. Excerpt from speech at "March for Our Lives, Washington, DC." Used with permission.

Lists for Reference

Student Writing

PRESENTING AND SPEAKING

COMPOSING DIGITAL PROJECTS

EMBRACING TRANSLINGUAL APPROACHES

Quick Help

Source Maps

Talking the Talk

Considering Disabilities

Advice for Multilingual Writers

Multilingual   Look for the "Multilingual" icon to find advice of special interest to international students and others whose home language is not English. The numbers refer to a chapter number or a section of a chapter.

Revision Symbols

Some instructors use these symbols as a kind of shorthand to guide you in revision. The numbers refer to a chapter number or a section of a chapter.

abb	abbreviation **51a–g**		//	faulty parallelism **4d, 29**
ad	adjective/adverb **39**		para	paraphrase **12a–b**
agr	agreement **37, 38f**		pass	inappropriate passive **30c, 35g**
awk	awkward		ref	unclear pronoun reference **38g**
cap	capitalization **50**			
case	case **38a–d**		run-on	run-on (fused) sentence **42**
cliché	cliché **5e, 26a**			
co	coordination **27a**		sexist	sexist language **25b, 38f**
coh	coherence **4d**			
com	incomplete comparison **28e**		shift	shift **30**
			slang	slang **26a**
concl	weak conclusion **4e, 12h**		sub	subordination **27b**
			sum	summarize **12a–b, 14b**
cs	comma splice **32, 42**			
d	diction (word choice) **26**		t	tone **5e, 11c, 26**
def	define **4c**		trans	transition **4d**
dm	dangling modifier **40c**		u	unity **4a**
doc	documentation **54–64**		vague	vague statement, **26, 32**
emph	emphasis unclear **27**			
ex	example needed **4b–c**		verb	verb form **35a–d**
frag	sentence fragment **32, 43**		vt	verb tense **35e–h**
			wv	weak verb **35**
fs	fused sentence **32, 42**		wrdy	wordy **31**
hyph	hyphen **53**		ww	wrong word **5e, 26, 32**
inc	incomplete construction **28**		,	comma **44**
intro	weak introduction **4e, 12h**		;	semicolon **45**
			. ? !	period, question mark, exclamation point **46**
it	italics **52**			
jarg	jargon **26a**		'	apostrophe **47**
lc	lowercase letter **50**		" "	quotation marks **48**
lv	language variety **23**		( ) [ ] —	parentheses, brackets, dash **49a–c**
mix	mixed construction **28a**			
mm	misplaced modifier **40a**		: / ...	colon, slash, ellipsis **49d–f**
ms	manuscript format **54e, 58e, 62c**		^	insert
no ,	no comma **44j**		~	transpose
num	number **51h–j**		⌒	close up
¶	paragraph **4**		X	obvious error

581

Contents